Data Processing and
Management Information Systems

GW00703512

DATA PROCESSING
AND MANAGEMENT INFORMATION SYSTEMS

Society of Company and Commercial Accountants
Annual Textbook Award
1974

THE M & E HANDBOOK SERIES

Data Processing
and Management
Information Systems

R G Anderson
FCMA, M Inst AM(Dip), FMS

FIFTH EDITION

Pitman Publishing Ltd
128 Long Acre, London WC2E 9AN
A Longman Group Company

First published 1974
Reprinted 1975 (twice), 1976
Second edition 1978
Third edition 1979
Reprinted 1981, 1982
Fourth edition 1983
Reprinted 1983
Fifth edition 1984
Reprinted 1986

© Pitman Publishing Ltd 1984

British Library Cataloguing in Publication Data

Anderson, R. G.
   Data processing and management information
   systems.—5th ed.—(The M & E HANDBOOK series,
   ISSN 0265-8828)
   1. Management—Data processing
   I. Title
   658'.05   HD30.2

   ISBN 0-7121-0187-X

Typeset, printed and bound in Great Britain

PREFACE TO THE FIFTH EDITION

The fifth edition of this HANDBOOK was commenced at the time the fourth edition was published, such is the velocity of technological development in the field of data processing, information technology and computers.

This edition has two main aims, the first being to present information to the reader in an easily assimilated form in pursuit of success in the examinations of the various examining bodies for whom this book is specially written. The second is to bring to the attention of the reader not only the principles and concepts relating to data processing, computing and management information systems but to highlight the current developments in the relevant technology.

This edition has been restructured and rebalanced to accord to current needs of the student, the administrator, systems staff and the general reader. Details relating to punched cards and paper tape have been largely eliminated as these media are not used now to any great extent. Expert systems are also included.

Electronic desktop systems using icons are included as are Local Area Networks (LANs). Chapters relating to data capture and computer input methods have been enlarged and their coverage expanded as have the section on computer storage methods including electronic document storage and retrieval systems. The chapter on computer output includes details of the latest electronic printing systems and printer/plotters as used on small computers.

Greater emphasis has been placed on the software for micros and small business computers which exists in such profusion. This includes utilities, disassemblers, electronic diaries and electronic spreadsheets for business planning, database systems, systems to convert micros into word processors, accounting packages and packages for insurance brokers and for tax computations. The information given on programming concepts has been increased as has that relating to public databases, such as Prestel, and private databases, such as ICL's Bulletin, as well as those databases developed for the microcomputer.

As the graphical presentation of information is gaining momen-

tum computer graphics relating to pixel, sprite and turtle graphics
has been included. Current computer architecture and VLSI (Very
Large Scale Integration) technology embracing an outline of mainframe computers and details relating to the IBM PC, ACT Apricot,
NCR's Decision Mate V and their new Tower computer system
have also been included.

Concepts regarding computer logic based on Boolean algebra
have been provided greater prominence as have details relating to
computer literacy in modern society. A new chapter has been
included covering checks and controls in computerised systems.

This edition also includes details of systems analysis and design,
processing techniques including batch, on-line processing encom-
passing transaction, real-time and time sharing, as well as data
entry systems and random enquiries, centralised and distributed
processing and multiprogramming.

Cybernetic concepts are also included as well as system concepts
relating to systems in general and management information systems
and data bases in particular. Considerations of privacy and confidentiality of information are also outlined.

This HANDBOOK is designed to provide a comprehensive
course of study, and to act as a work of reference, concerning the
field of data processing, general systems concepts and management
information systems. Its contents should prove invaluable for
administrative managers, accountants, and anyone requiring a
basic knowledge of data processing methods, concepts and principles
together with an appreciation of the importance of management
information in the everyday running of a business.

In particular, the HANDBOOK should be invaluable for
students preparing for professional examinations where a
knowledge of data processing, systems concepts, types of systems,
systems behaviour and systems analysis and design is required. The
syllabuses of the following bodies have been catered for:

Chartered Institute of Finance and Accountancy (CIFA).
City and Guilds of London Institute (Data Processing for Com-
    puter Users) (C & G).
Institute of Data Processing Management (IDPM).
The Institute of Cost and Management Accountants (ICMA).
Institute of Administrative Accountants (IAA).
The Institute of Administrative Management (IAM).
The Institute of Management Services (IMS).
The Association of Certified Accountants (ACA).
Association of International Accountants (AIA).

The Institute of Chartered Secretaries and Administrators (ICSA).
The Institute of Chartered Accountants (ICA).
The Society of Company and Commercial Accountants (SCCA).
The Association of Accounting Technicians (AAT).
The HANDBOOK is also suitable for the requirements of the Business and Technician Education Council (BTEC).

Attributed examination questions for these bodies have been included in the progress tests at the end of each chapter. In most cases it will be possible to ascertain the answers to these questions by reference to the text of the relevant chapter.

The reader is recommended to refer to the author's *A Dictionary of Data Processing and Computer Terms* for a concise Glossary of Terms.

Acknowledgments. I gratefully acknowledge permission to quote from the past examination papers of The Institute of Cost and Management Accountants, The Association of Certified Accountants, the City and Guilds of London Institute and the Institute of Data Processing Management. The cooperation and assistance of the following organisations and persons, without whose help this book would not have been possible, are also gratefully acknowledged.

ACT (UK) Limited: provision of details and photographs relating to the Apricot computer.

Apple Computer (UK) Limited: for details relating to Lisa.

Mr J. K. Atkin (author of Basic Computer Science): provision of information relating to bubble and holographic memory.

British Telecom: provision of information relating to Datel services, Prestel viewdata system, packet switching, electronic mail and Teletex.

Cadbury Limited: provision of details relating to the EAN bar code.

Compsoft Limited: details relating to their Data Management System.

Major R.S. Conder AIDPM RAPC: suggestions for improving various flowcharts illustrated in this book.

Data Card (UK) Limited: provision of details and photographs relating to Data Key.

Datastream International Limited: provision of details relating to their on-line financial information service.

DVW Microelectronics Limited: provision of details and photograph of the Husky microcomputer.

Electronic Business Systems Ltd: provision of details and

photograph relating to the Facit D12E electronic accounting machine (office computer).

IBM United Kingdom Limited: provision of information and various pamphlets and photographs relating to magnetic tape code, tape drives, 3081 computer, IBM3290 Information Panel and the IBM Personal Computer.

ICL: details, diagrams and photographs relating to Bulletin viewdata system, the DRS20 workstation, networks, DNX-2000 digital PABX exchange and various other items.

Integer Computer Systems: details of TAXCOMP packages.

Intelligence (UK)PLC: details and diagram of Micromodeller and Microbroker package.

Jones Sewing Machine Company Limited: Details and photograph of the Brother EP22 printer.

Keen Computers Limited: details and diagram relating to the Corvus Omninet local area network.

Litton Business Systems Ltd: examples of Kimball tags.

MicroProducts Software Limited: details relating to accounting packages-BOS (Business Operating Software).

Midlands Electricity Board: supply of optical mark meter reading sheets and procedure chart.

NCR Limited: details and photographs relating to minicomputer configuration, NCR 9300, NCR Tower 1632, NCR Decision Mate V, diagram of processor module and details of Integrated General ledger package.

Office Technology Ltd: details and photograph of the Information Management Processor,

Philips Data Systems: details and photograph of optical disc.

Quest Micropad Limited: details and photograph of Micropad.

Rank Xerox (UK) Limited: details and photographs of the Xerox 2700 distributed electronic printer, Xerox 9700 electronic printing system, diagram of mouse, details and diagram of Xerox 8000 Ethernet network system and the Star Information System together with diagrams of icons.

J. Sainsbury Ltd: details of supermarket ordering system.

Sharp Electronics (UK) Ltd: details of MZ-80K display code and the MZ-3541 Business computer.

Sinclair Research Ltd, details and photographs of ZX Microdrive.

Telford Management Services Ltd: details and photograph of TEL-time terminal system.

Contents

Preface to the Fifth Edition   v
Acknowledgments   vi

PART ONE: PROFILE OF DATA PROCESSING
AND COMPUTING

  I   *Data Processing and Computing Concepts*   1
Data processing—a specialist activity; Nature of
data processing and computer systems; The need
for computer literacy in modern society; Conversing with computers; Spectrum of computers;
Criteria for assessing the economic viability of a
computer; Current developments in the use of computers; General aspects of computers; Social
aspects of computers

  II *The Electronic Computer and its Development*   25
Definition and mode of operation of a computer;
ASCII and EBCDIC; The development of computer technology; Mainframe computer configurations; Current status of mainframe technology:
NCR 9300; The central processing unit; The control
unit; The arithmetic/logic unit; Computer logic;
Internal storage; Advantages and disadvantages of
a computer

  III *Microcomputers in Business*   52
General outline of microcomputers; The
microprocessor; General considerations; Interface
and bus; Keyboards; Sound generation; Clock;
Character set; Display code and display screen;
Fourth generation microcomputers: The ACT
Apricot; NCR Tower 1632 computer; IBM PC;
NCR Decision Mate V personal computer

  IV *Organisation of a Data Processing Department
and a Management Services Department*   77

Organisation of a data processing department: by function or activity; Organisation of a data processing department: by purpose; Organisation of a management services department

PART TWO: COMPUTER INPUT, OUTPUT, INFORMATION STORAGE AND RETRIEVAL, DATABASES AND BACKING STORAGE AND MEDIA

V   *Computer Input*   86
Computer input media and data capture methods and techniques; Punched input cards, tags and paper tape; Magnetic input; Magnetic ink characters; Optical characters; Optical marks; Terminals; Data collection systems; Portable computers and handprint data entry terminal; Workstations; Speech synthesis and analog input

VI   *Computer Output*   121·
Printed; Punched and magnetically encoded; Visual display unit and graph plotter; Computer output on microfilm (COM); Computer graphics; Pixel and high resolution graphics; Block and sprite graphics; Turtle graphics; User defined graphic characters and computer aided design (CAD)

VII   *Information Storage and Retrieval: Basic Concepts*   138
Master files; Relationship between master files, transaction files and reference files; File organisation; Virtual storage; File organisation-magnetic tape; File access methods; Other storage aspects; Structured master files; Electronic document storage and retrieval

VIII   *Databases*   165
Database defined; Structure and problems of setting up a database; Structural data relationships; Database and data management systems; Expert systems; Logical and physical files in a database; The database administrator; Public database: Prestel; Private database: Travicom and Bulletin; Datastream

IX   *Backing Storage Devices and Media*   183
The nature of backing storage; Magnetic tape (reels); Parity checking of magnetic tape

characters; Advantages and disadvantages of magnetic tape; Cassette tape; Hard discs; Soft discs; Personality module, silicon disc and optical disc; Integrated discs and microdrive; Advantages and disadvantages of direct access storage

PART THREE: CHECKS, CONTROLS AND PROCESSING TECHNIQUES

X   *Checks and Controls in Computerised Systems*   200
Spectrum of control; Procedural and operational controls; File security; Batch control; Auditing and the computer; Software (program) checks; Datakey: the key with a memory; Systems development controls; Data processing standards

XI   *Processing Techniques (1) – Batch Processing*   221
General outline of technique; Stages of processing a factory payroll; Problems of dealing with random enquiries in batch processing environments;

XII   *Processing Techniques (2) – On-line, Real-time, Multiprogramming and Time Sharing*   229
On-line processing; Dialogue design; Real-time processing; Multiprogramming; Time sharing

XIII   *Processing Techniques (3) – Interactive Processing Applications*   245
Basic considerations; Interactive general ledger system

XIV   *Processing Techniques (4) – Centralised and Distributed Processing*   256
Concepts of centralised processing; Concepts of distributed processing; Distributed office systems: ICL DRS 20

XV   *Computer Bureaux and Computing Services*   265
Computer bureaux; Data processing by computer bureau; Computing services

PART FOUR: DEVELOPMENT OF COMPUTER SYSTEMS

XVI   *Implementing a Computer*   273
Initial considerations for successful implementation of a mainframe computer; Feasibility study; Systems analysis; Collecting facts; Recording

techniques used in systems analysis; Systems design; Systems specification; Diagrams, charts and flowcharts; Input, output and file specifications; Systems implementation, monitoring and maintenance; Benchmark tests; Coding systems

XVII *Flowcharting Computer Applications* 304
Runs, routines and symbols; Applications; ICMA Question one solutions

XVIII *Computer Programming:* 330
Principles and Concepts
Program specification, documentation and standards; Nature of computer programming; Development of programming languages; High level languages; Monolithic, modular and structured programming; Approach to program design; Program dumps and restart procedures; Compile time and execution time errors; Closed and open shop programming; Closed and open subroutines

XIX *Flowcharting Computing Problems* 349
Program flowcharts; Program flowcharting exercises

XX *Decision Tables* 358
General considerations for the construction and use of decision tables; Decision tables and program flowcharts

XXI *Software Profile* 369
The nature of software; Operating systems; Job control language (JCL); Utility programs; Application packages; Outline of accounting packages; Taxcomp: specialist tax sofware for practising accountants; Microbroker: specialist software for insurance brokers; Electronic card index and electronic diary; Arguments for and against the use of packages; Assembler; Compiler; Interpreter; Telesoftware and cable games; Modelling packages and spreadsheets; Micromodeller modelling package

PART FIVE: PROFILE OF ELECTRONIC TECHNOLOGY

XXII *The Nature of Electronic Technology* 397
Office technology; Electronic mail; Word processing; Digital PABX telephone exchange

XXIII   *Local Area Networks and Electronic Desktop*   406
        display systems
        Local area networks; Electronic desktop display
        systems

XXIV   *Data Transmission*   416
        Basic   concepts;   Communication   equipment;
        Telecom Datel services; Other Telecom services;
        Terms used in data transmission

PART SIX: GENERAL SYSTEMS CONCEPTS AND
MANAGEMENT INFORMATION SYSTEMS

XXV   *General Systems Theory and its Relationship*   425
        to Long-Term Planning, Policy Making and
        the Principles of Management
        General Systems Theory (GST); Characteristics of
        systems; System relationships; Classification of
        systems

XXVI   *Goals and Objectives of Systems*   434
        Overall objectives, unity of direction and corporate
        objectives; System and sub-system objectives;
        Motivational influences and conflict of system goals

XXVII   *Control systems theory*   441
        Basic elements of control; Cybernetic control;
        Feedback and feedforward; Open-loop system;
        Closed-loop system; Delay factor; Communication
        theory

XXVIII *Concepts of Management Information Systems*   460
        Basic requirements of management information
        systems (MIS); Retrieval and privacy of informa-
        tion; Data relating to business operations; Informa-
        tion relating to business operations; Planning
        information; Control information

XXIX   *Development of Management Information*   473
        Systems
        Establishing the information needs of manage-
        ment; The approach to the development of MIS;
        Corporate information adviser; Information and
        the level of management; Information related to
        the type of business

XXX *Use of Computers In Management*   481
      Information Systems
      Management planning and decisions; Business
      models and simulation

      Appendix   487
      Examination Technique

PART ONE

PROFILE OF DATA PROCESSING AND COMPUTING

CHAPTER 1

Data Processing and Computing Concepts

DATA PROCESSING—A SPECIALIST ACTIVITY

1. Data processing defined. Data processing is a specialist activity performed by the administrative organisation for the business as a whole and is concerned with the systematic recording, arranging, filing, processing and dissemination of facts relating to the physical events occurring in the business.

Before production can be commenced in the factory, raw materials and parts have to be procured, which involves the data processing system in the preparation of purchase orders. When supplies are received they have to be recorded on appropriate stock or job records, which again involves data processing. The accounts of suppliers have to be updated to show the value of the goods purchased from them and the remittances made to them.

When production is due to commence, materials and parts have to be issued to the production centres and suitability recorded on issue notes which are subsequently recorded on stock and job records. The issues are often priced and extended, which are also data processing operations.

Factory operatives are remunerated either for their attendance time, piecework or bonus earnings, and here the data processing system is concerned with wages calculation, preparation of payslips and payrolls and the collection and summarisation of data with regard to production orders or jobs.

On completion of production, the goods are despatched to customers, which involves the data processing system in the preparation of despatch documentation, invoices, sales ledger updating and the preparation of statements of account. Eventually, remittances are received from customers, which involves further

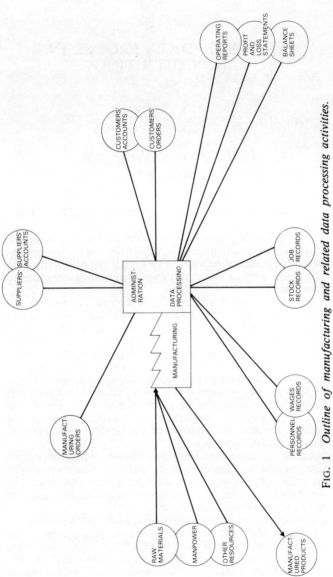

FIG. 1 *Outline of manufacturing and related data processing activities.*

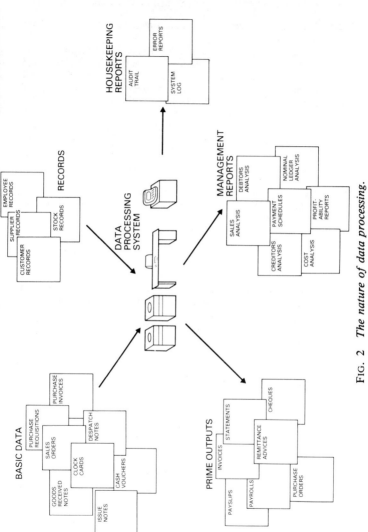

FIG. 2 *The nature of data processing.*

data processing in respect of adjustments to the balances on customers' accounts.

The results of business operations for specific operation periods are summarised and presented to management in the form of operating reports, profit and loss statements and balance sheets. All of this, and more, is the province of data processing which, if effectively performed, may be classified as the information service of the business (*see* Figs. 1 and 2).

From this, it can be seen that data processing systems provide information and information provides the basis for managerial control of business operations to achieve corporate objectives as effectively as possible, which means making the most suitable decisions based on the information provided.

A management information system therefore embraces the data processing systems, control systems (using information provided by the data processing system) and decision-making based on the facts indicated by the control systems.

2. Processing operations. In order to put data processing into its correct perspective, it is important to appreciate that although data processing activities are largely computerised there is very little actual "computing" performed in most business applications. No doubt this is why the activity is called "data processing"(*see* **1**) and not "computing". Computing is a term restricted to performing "number crunching", i.e. arithmetical calculations including adding, multiplying, subtracting and dividing as well as exponentiation (raising numbers to specified powers) etc. The primary operations for processing business data are summarised below.

(*a*) Capture and record data.

(*b*) Collect/transmit data.

(*c*) Control data throughout all stages of processing-prepare control totals.

(*d*) Prepare data in machine sensible form when relevant.

(*e*) Verify accuracy of data preparation.

(*f*) Input data to the computer.

(*g*) Validate data and generate control totals.

(*h*) Sort data to master file sequence.

(*i*) Compute value of variables.

(*j*) Update master files.

(*k*) Print list of transactions and control totals for accounting and audit trail purposes.

(*l*) Print schedules.

(*m*) Reinput data.

(*n*) Re-sort data for analysis purposes.

(*o*) Produce analyses and statistical reports.
(*See* Fig. 89.)

TABLE I   COMPUTING EXAMPLES

Application	*Computations*	
Invoicing	Gross value	= Quantity sold × Price
	Discount	= Gross value × Discount rate
	Net value	= Gross value − Discount
	VAT	= Net value × VAT rate
	Invoice value	= Net value + VAT
Wages	Gross wages	= Standard hours × standard rate
		+
		Hours @ time and half × premium rate
		+
		Hours @ double time × premium rate
		or:
		Number of units produced × piece rate
		+
		Piecework supplement
	Net wages	= Gross wages − (income tax + standard deductions, etc.)
Stock control	New quantity in stock	= Old quantity in stock
		+
		Receipts
		+
		Returns to store
		−
		Issues
		−
		Returns to supplier
Electricity bill	Amount due	= Standing charge + Unit charge
	Unit charge	= (Present reading − Previous reading) × unit rate
Telephone bill	Total payable	= Rental and other standing charges
		+
		Unit charge
		+
		Value added tax at 15.00%
	Unit charge	= (Present reading − Previous reading) × unit rate

Examples of computing operations performed by a computer for a number of business applications include those shown in Table I on p. 5.

It is the phenomenal speed of computers that makes them particularly well suited to pursuing activities that require instant solutions to complex dynamic problems. They are thus extensively used in the control and monitoring of space vehicles; where they can respond to situations as they are occurring and in a fraction of a second make the corrections necessary to keep the vehicles on course. In addition, computers are ideal for high volume computing tasks such as the computation and analysis of statistical and mathematical data as well as scientific and engineering calculations.

NATURE OF DATA PROCESSING AND COMPUTER SYSTEMS

3. Elements of a data processing system. A data processing system in its simplest form consists of three primary elements, i.e. input, processing and output. These elements apply whether the system is manual, mechanical or electronic. Data relating to business transactions such as items sold to customers, issues to production from the stores and hours worked by employees is input for processing. The data is subjected to processing operations in order to convert it into a more meaningful form prior to being output. The output, referred to as information, consists of documents such as invoices and payslips; schedules such as payrolls and sales summaries; and reports relating to customer credit standing and stock availability.

4. Characteristics of a data processing system. The characteristics of a data processing system may be contrasted with those of a factory manufacturing system; they are very similar although one processes raw facts and the other raw materials. The input to the factory system consists of raw materials for conversion into finished or partly finished products, whereas the finished product of a data processing system is information.

Two secondary, but nevertheless important, elements may be added to the primary elements of a data processing system. These are storage and control. Storage is concerned with filing documents and records relating to business transactions so that the state of affairs of specific business situations is readily available; e.g. amounts owing to customers, amounts owed by suppliers and the quantity of items in stock. Control relates to the monitoring by a supervisor to ensure that activities are conducted in the prescribed manner (*see* Fig. 3).

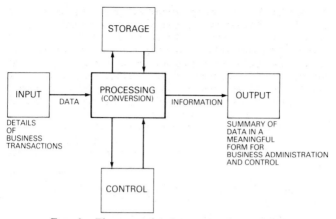

FIG. 3 *Elements of a data processing system.*

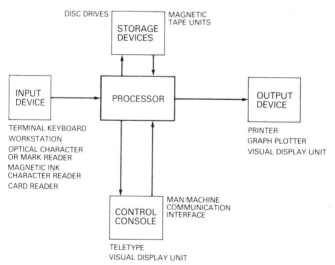

FIG. 4 *Elements of a computer system.*

5. Elements of a computer system. A computer system also consists of the same five elements, viz. input, processing, output, storage and control. Special devices are used for input, such as terminal keyboards, card readers and bar code scanners. Processing is performed by the processor known as the central processing unit or CPU. After processing the data in the form indicated by the stored program, the results are output to a specific type of output device which may be a line printer, video screen or plotter, or to backing storage—tape or disc (*see* Fig. 4).

Records are stored in master files consisting of tape or disc storage media. Control is effected by an internally stored program containing all the processing steps, known as instructions, which are executed to accomplish a specific task. A computer operator also controls processing activities by means of a console unit, which is an interface between the human element and the machine element, i.e. the computer system.

The processor consists of three elements (*see* II, **16**), i.e. the internal memory, the arithmetic/logic unit, usually abbreviated to ALU or AU, and the control unit. It may be said, therefore, that a computer consists of six elements, assuming the console to be an extension of the control element. These are input, internal storage, AU, control unit, output and backing storage.

6. Application processing. All applications, whether processed on a computer or performed manually, consist of primary activities such as those outlined in Table II below.

TABLE II   RELATIONSHIP OF INPUT AND OUTPUT

Application	Input	Processing	Output
Payroll	Clock cards including hours worked and rates of pay	Computing gross to net wages, tax and standard deductions, updating payroll file	Payslips, payrolls, tax and deduction summaries
Stock control	Source documents indicating issues from store and receipts into store	Computing value of transactions, updating stock file	Stock list, reorder list
Sales	Sales orders indicating items required by customers	Computing value of items inc. VAT, updating customer file	Invoices, sales summaries, statements of account

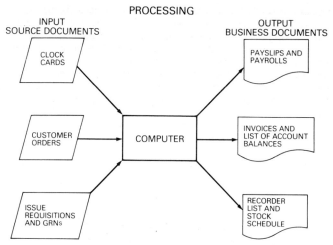

FIG. 5 *Relationship of input and output.*

(See Fig. 5)

7. Purpose of computers. It is important to be aware of the purpose of computers, particularly microcomputers, in this modern technological age. They are primarily used in business for the processing of business data, as indicated above, to maintain control of business operations and for the provision of information in a meaningful form for this purpose (*see* 1 and 2).

Microcomputers are used in an information processing role, but may also be used for data processing activities in the smaller business. Many users employ them in a computing role for performing mathematical computations and statistical analysis. Many microcomputer installations are interconnected by a network, known as a Local Area Network (LAN), for the purpose of sharing resources such as high-speed storage, including a disc resident database and high speed printers.

Mainframe computers are used for large volume data processing commitments as they are capable of operating automatically at high speed. They print out invoices, payslips, payrolls, purchase orders, cheques and remittance advice slips in great volumes in a very short space of time according to the needs of individual systems.

Whichever type of computer is used for business data processing it is essential for information stored by the system to be as up to date as is necessary for effective control of business activities. This may require the implementation of real-time systems to control events as they happen. Information files must be updated as events occur so that they always represent the true status of the real life system. In other instances, pseudo real-time systems may be used as a matter of convenience rather than operational necessity. On-line systems enable direct enquiries to be made about such matters as stock availability and the credit status of customers. Instant responses are obtained from such enquiries and this improves administrative efficiency and customer relationships in many instances. On-line systems use direct entry keyboards for the input of data for processing, making the computer system more flexible and convenient to operate.

THE NEED FOR COMPUTER LITERACY IN MODERN SOCIETY

8. Underlying philosophy. Almost everyone will need to become familiar with data processing and computing (particularly microcomputing) to a greater or lesser extent, whether in the home, office, school, college or factory. The microcomputer is now widely accepted as a very efficient device for performing many types of operation, such as the display of business and other information from a Prestel database; for performing computations of varying types at high speed including professional, scientific, engineering and accounting calculations, as well as mathematical calculations for the classroom and word processing in typing and secretarial departments.

In business, the computer, whether a mainframe, mini or micro, is recognised as a means of increasing administrative efficiency in payroll processing, sales invoicing, order processing, stock control and production planning. Insurance renewal notices and gas and electricity bills for example are usually printed by computer. This means that almost everyone will need to become what may be termed "literate" in the computer context.

The nature of clerical work whether in the wages office, the order office, the accounting section, the stock control office or the person-nel department is changing as jobs are restructured to take advan-tage of the new technology (*see* XXII). Many clerks are being provided with workstations, instead of pens and pads of forms, for dealing with customer orders being phoned in, so that the order details can be directly input to the computer for processing. This is known as an on-line order entry system (*see* Fig. 118). These new roles not only provide increased administrative efficiency but also increase the level of job enrichment as clerks become more interested and feel part of the new technology. Clerks do not need to become involved with the programming of computers as this is the prerogative of the systems staff. Package programs may be used for the various applications in most instances.

It is very interesting to obtain an understanding of how a computer functions and how it can be made to do what is required. It is a challenge to one's mental ability and imagination to determine the nature of a problem and write a program to solve it. Computer literacy requires some familiarisation with data processing and computer terminology, and students in particular are advised to consult a reference work such as the author's *A Dictionary of Data Processing and Computer Terms*, published by Macdonald & Evans Ltd. In addition, it is advisable and interesting to understand the nature of computer hardware, i.e. the machines and devices which make up a computer system and the nature of software, i.e. the programs without which a computer is inanimate.

9. Computing concepts. Not only is it useful to be aware of the nature of hardware and software but it is advisable to obtain an appreciation of other computing concepts, such as the way in which characters are generated and stored in a computer. This knowledge is more for interest than operational necessity but does provide a greater understanding of computers. The stored program concept is fundamental and of primary concern to the functioning of a computer.

The old story says that the driver of a car does not need to know what goes on under the bonnet to get from A to B. The new story says that you do not need to know what goes on in a computer system before you can use it. Quite true, it is necessary to know the controls in both instances but a knowledge of the inner workings and the conceptual aspects of any subject creates a greater interest and understanding and often leads to more efficient use of the system.

CONVERSING WITH COMPUTERS

10. Computerspeak: the language of the computer. This term relates to the various languages which exist for communicating with a computer. It is necessary for the user to understand the language of the computer in order to "speak" to it. Sometimes this may be the specific language of a particular computer, i.e. machine code, or it may be assembly code, i.e. a mnemonic code which has to be "assembled" into machine code by software known as an assembler. It is more usual for business use to employ a high-level language for writing programs such as BASIC, COBOL, Fortran or

Algol, Forth or Pascal depending upon the type of computer in use and the nature of the applications to be processed. High-level languages are "compiled" by software known as a compiler which converts instructions in high-level language into machine code.

11. Operation and programming of a computer. Microcomputers can be programmed and operated by non-specialists with a little extensive study of the language BASIC and the computer operating manual. It is still necessary, however, for mainframes and minicomputers to be programmed and operated by specialists due to their added complexity in comparison with microcomputers.

Since the advent of the silicon chip, which has had the effect of reducing the size of computers, it seems that the skill required to operate a small computer has become more prevalent. The reduction in the size of computers has had an inverse effect upon the ease with which they can be used.

Microcomputers are now within the financial reach of many more people and businesses and their use for educational purposes in schools and colleges is also increasing. In the business environment accountants, amongst others, are becoming conversant with, and capable of writing the less complex type of program for such applications as those relating to costing and wages computations and perhaps those of a more complex nature relating to discounted cash flow, break-even analysis and projected profit and loss accounts, etc.

12. Use of dialogue. When conversing with mainframes, computer operators use commands which form part of a job control language which enables them to communicate with the operating system for controlling the processing of the various jobs (*see* XXI, **8**). A similar facility is required for accountants and other users of microcomputers in order to communicate in conversational mode, as it is called, for interactive processing. Programs can be written in such a way that they ask the user questions at appropriate stages of processing, e.g. to input the value of a variable required by the program. In other instances, the computer may display a message on the screen indicating a syntax error in the program. This interchange of messages is known as conversational mode processing or interactive processing achieved by means of a dialogue.

SPECTRUM OF COMPUTERS

13. Difficulty of classifying computers. It is very difficult to classify computers into specific types as there is a tendency for their operating characteristics to overlap, particularly in respect of storage capacity and speed of operation. It is useful, however, to be able to categorise them into mainframes, minis and micros for discussion and comparison purposes. It is often necessary to compare different models to assess their relative advantages and disadvantages in relation to their suitability for specific applications in a particular business.

14. Mainframe computer. Initially when computers came on the scene, the term mainframe referred to the main structure or framework of a central processing unit on which the arithmetic unit, main memory and control unit were mounted. The term now tends to be used in a number of ways, mainly to distinguish a large batch-processing/real-time computer from the smaller mini and microcomputers. The modern mainframe often supports a database accessible by distributed mini or micro computers.

A mainframe is the largest type of computer used for business and accounting applications in various environments including central and local government and other institutional bodies, such as professional organisations, universities and polytechnics. As stated previously, mainframes are used as powerful "number crunchers" satisfying the requirement of high volume processing, including holiday confirmations and invoices, insurance premium reminders, banking and building society operations and hotel management systems.

(Courtesy IBM UK Limited)

FIG. 6   *IBM 3081 computer.*

Mainframes are available with the features of powerful minis at one end of the range and at the other there are installations filling large rooms with hardware including banks of magnetic tape drives, printers, disc drives and communication equipment consisting of banks of modems in racks, device controllers, multiplexors, front-end processors for handling terminal operations and dispersed workstations connected to the processor by communication lines (*see* Fig. 6 and II, **9, 13–15**).

15. Minicomputer. This type of computer performs data processing activities in the same way as a mainframe but on a smaller scale. The cost of minis is lower and generally suits the needs of the medium size business. Data is usually input by means of a keyboard. As the name implies, a minicomputer is small compared with a mainframe and may be called a scaled-down mainframe as the processor and peripherals are physically smaller. Minis have a memory capacity in the region of 128K bytes whereas the larger mainframe has a capacity in the region of two to eight Megabytes. In contrast, micros have a memory capacity in the region of 48–64K bytes (*see* Fig. 7). A typical mini consists of the following.

(*a*) Processor 128–512K bytes.
(*b*) Video screen (display terminal—up to 24 in some instances).
(*c*) Integrated disc unit (often incorporated in processor cabinet). Capacity in the region of 80 to 320 Megabytes.
(*d*) Cassette unit (often incorporated in processor cabinet).
(*e*) Printers with a speed in the region of 900 lpm.
(*f*) Tape drives.

Originally, minicomputers were developed for process control and system monitoring, etc. They were complicated to program and had minimal input/output capabilities as they were mainly concerned with "number crunching" rather than handling large amounts of data relating to business transactions. However, they are now fully developed, powerful computers with a wide range of peripherals to perform a wide range of data processing and computing activities.

Minis operate faster than micros and tend to have sixteen-bit words whereas micros have tended to have eight-bit words. This is changing to some extent, however, as micros now have sixteen-bit words and thirty-two-bit machines will be becoming available.

16. Microcomputers. This type of computer is important in business and society generally and it is proposed to devote a chapter solely to microcomputers, outlining their characteristics and other important aspects (*see* III). A micro is a small computer consisting

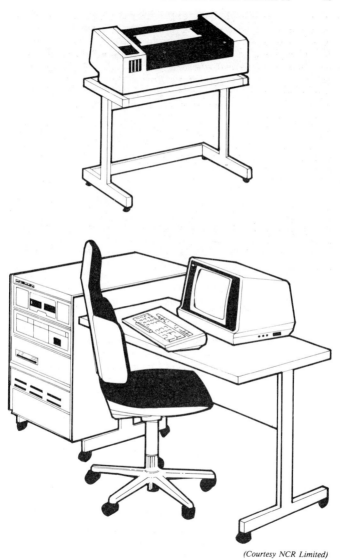

(Courtesy NCR Limited)

FIG. 7   *Minicomputer configuration.*

(Courtesy IBM UK Limited)

FIG. 8   *IBM Personal Computer.*

of a processor on a single silicon chip mounted on a circuit board together with memory chips, ROMs and RAM chips, etc. It has a keyboard for the entry of data and instructions and a screen for display purposes. It has interfaces for connecting peripherals such as plotters, cassette units, disc drives, light pens, a mouse, paddles and joysticks.

Micros are used within the smaller business for normal data processing applications such as stock control, invoicing and payroll for which packages are available. Micros are widely used in schools for educational purposes and on a personal basis for playing computer games for which there are hundreds of packages available (*see* Fig. 8).

17. Benefits of using a computer in business. At one time, mainframes cost a fantastic amount of money and it was only the larger company that could justify their use both financially and from an administrative point of view, as it was necessary to have a computer due to the increasing volume of paperwork that had to be processed and the increasing cost of administrative staff. It was thought that a computer would decrease costs, which no doubt they did in some instances, but in general other types of benefits were achieved. These are outlined below. Due to the high cost of mainframes it was often necessary to operate them round the clock as it were, that is on a multi-shift basis in order to achieve an acceptable pay-back period. No doubt this factor still applies in many instances. The cost of a microcomputer is very low, however, even for a complete business system, and its use quickly recoups its cost even when used only on an intermittent basis. The benefits obtained depend upon the type of computer and the use made of it. Prospective benefits depending upon individual circumstances may include some of those listed below:

(*a*) Improved customer relations due to fewer computational errors, more timely invoices and statements and speedier response to enquiries regarding the status of accounts and the availability of products.

(*b*) Improved cash flows due to improved sales accounting systems particularly those relating to credit control, invoicing and statement preparation.

(*c*) More effective control procedures including production control, sales control, cost control, budgetary control and credit control.

(*d*) Improved flow of information and information retrieval by means of on-line direct access enquiry systems.

(*e*) Greater control of raw material and other stocks allowing the investment in stock to be optimised and stock-out occasions to be minimised.

(*f*) Greater degree of systems integration on the basis that the output of one part of a system (sub-system) provides the input to a related sub-system which has the effect of eliminating duplication and delay.

(*g*) Simplification of problem solving by the use of problem solving software.

Similar benefits to those outlined above may also be achieved by using a microcomputer in the business environment, but the benefits of using a personal micro are more likely to be from the enjoyment obtained from its use and from achieving skill in developing programs of various types.

CRITERIA FOR ASSESSING THE ECONOMIC VIABILITY OF A COMPUTER

18. Cost effectiveness. It is often considered that cost savings are essential for ensuring the economic viability of a computer. It goes without saying that cost savings should always be striven for and the usual way in which this factor is assessed is to compare the annual operating costs of the new or proposed computer system with those of the current system. If the comparison proves unfavourable then an erroneous decision may be made not to proceed with the new system proposal because all relevant factors have not been considered. An important factor, that has not been taken into account, is the benefits which the new system is capable of achieving compared with those of the current system. The golden rule to apply is "if the value of benefits exceeds the cost of obtaining them—then it is a viable proposition".

In such cases it is possible to increase annual operating costs to those currently incurred without being concerned, especially if the cost of the present system is lower than it should be. This may occur in some instances because of outmoded systems which fail to achieve current requirements in respect of work volumes or providing output at the right time—in such instances the systems may be said to be inefficient. As an example, invoices and statements of account may be running several weeks late resulting in an inadequate cash flow which is a critical factor in the efficient running of a business.

When operating cost reductions are considered feasible, they may not materialise immediately owing to the necessity of operating both the old and new systems concurrently, that is in parallel, until the results obtained from computer operations are proved to be satisfactory.

Initially, costs may increase due to the need to employ additional staff to run both systems side-by-side, afterwards cost reductions may be achieved when the old system has been dispensed with.

19. Speed and volume factors. Due to the phenomenal speed with which a computer can process data, a much higher volume can be processed in a specified time than is possible by other methods. In such cases, even though the annual operating costs of a computer application may exceed those of the previous system, the cost of processing each unit of data is likely to be lower.

The speed of processing is particularly important if the previous system was overloaded, as additional staff would be required to cope with increasing volumes and the use of a computer obviates the need for this course of action. Even with additional staff, however, it is doubtful, in many instances, it the work could be accomplished in a suitable time scale. Once again this is where the speed of the computer comes to the fore as management information is often required speedily, without unnecessary delay, for control purposes.

20. Accuracy of information. Management not only require timely information but also reliable information and this is facilitated by a computer as error detection routines are incorporated in computer programs. Such routines are referred to as validation checks. Information produced by a computer is generally more reliable than that produced by clerical systems as human fallibility is eliminated to a great extent. Once a program has been written incorporating appropriate checks than errors are disclosed automatically. A clerk may be distracted by environmental conditions such as the need to answer the telephone or the need to discuss work problems with a colleague. In such circumstances concentration is lost and errors often get overlooked and remain undetected. This is not to say, however, that clerical systems do not incorporate checks and controls, indeed they do, but the automatic checking facilities provided by computer programs may be said to be superior.

Undetected errors in data not only affect internal operations but external operations also which can have economic consequences on the business. Inaccurate control data, for instance, can cause management to make incorrect decisions because the real situation is not disclosed in the data. Similarly, it is possible to order ten times the quantity of materials required by the erroneous insertion of an additional nought in the order quantity on the purchase order form.

CURRENT DEVELOPMENTS IN THE USE OF COMPUTERS

21. Mainframes *v* mini and microcomputers. The development of mini and microcomputers for business use will tend to reduce the demand for mainframes as the smaller computer will, in many cases, be adequate for a business's data processing commitment. This means that with the wider range of computers available it is possible to select the size most relevant to the needs of the business, thus avoiding excessive capital expenditure (or higher rental costs) on a computer with excess capacity to current or foreseeable future needs. In fact, some companies may "swap" their mainframe for a number of minis which can be dispersed throughout the organisation on the basis of allocating computer power where it is most needed—the philosophy of distributed processing.

22. Small computer *v* computer bureaux. Small computers may also affect the business of computer bureaux because many small businesses which previously employed a bureau may now find it feasible to implement a small computer into the organisation on a do-it-yourself (DIY) basis. This creates advantages to the business because it can regulate the turnround time of reports from the data processing system, since it is more controllable than it was when the work was done by the bureau. This allows information to become available sooner. Also, confidentiality of information is more easily achieved as data does not leave the organisation's environment. Processing costs should also be reduced and a greater degree of job interest created because of the hands-on experience being obtained. Package programs are available for most business applications and these guide the user through successive processing stages on an interactive basis without undue complexity.

The disadvantages of this course of action revolve around the need to purchase or rent equipment but the cost of some computers is so low as not to be of any great concern—certainly not a deterrent. Cost was a critical factor when only mainframes were available, as they cost many thousands of pounds and so were beyond the financial resources of the business at prices which were not compatible with system needs. There is also the problem of gaining experience in the use of a small computer, but this is not so complex as with mainframes, which require specialised staff for their operation.

Compromise solutions are likely to be developed on an increasing scale whereby companies with their own small computer can have a communication link to a computer bureau for large-volume, month-end requirements—the best of both worlds as it were. The small computer could be used for preparing the payroll, invoicing and stock control, etc. and the bureau to print out month-end statements and management reports together with year-end accounting and tax schedules and stock lists, for instance.

23. Electronic ledger card accounting machine. It is therefore surprising to know that electronic ledger card accounting machines are still marketed. An example of this type of machine is the Facit D12E (*see* Fig. 9), classed as an office computer. It is not much larger than a typewriter and stores data on a micro-cassette. The micro-cassette stores programs and accounting information such as customer names and addresses, credit limits, account balances and an analysis of the amount outstanding. The cassette is inserted into the machine and transferred into the internal memory where it is available for rapid retrieval. Ledger cards are inserted into the machine and the machine then produces invoices, updates sales accounts, stock files and month-end statements automatically.

It has a normal typewriter style keyboard and a ten-key numeric pad. Other features include facilities for duplication of documents;

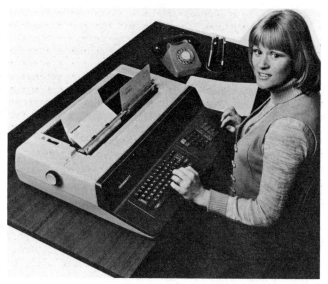

(Courtesy Facit and Electronic Business Systems Limited)

FIG. 9   *Facit D12E Office Computer (Electronic ledger card accounting machine).*

advanced document handling with a capability of dealing with several documents simultaneously, a multiple split platen; and an optional screen display.

GENERAL ASPECTS OF COMPUTERS

24. Selection of a computer. It is essential for a business to select the type of computer most suitable for its needs. A mainframe operates faster than a mini or micro and is capable of storing much more information in backing storage due to higher capacity hard discs as opposed to floppy discs or integrated discs.

It is of course essential to consider the processing commitment of the business as the volumes of data to be processed provide an indicator to the size of computer required. The limitations of a particular computer system will depend upon the amount of information to be stored, accessed and updated. The larger the files required for specific applications such as large customer, supplier or stock files, the larger the computer system needed to handle them. Whereas an application with one to three thousand records could be processed on a mini or micro. The basic factors to consider include speed of processing, storage capacity, volume of records on files, the amount of details in the records and the file activity ("hit" rate).

Visible record computers (VRCs) have largely been superseded by microcomputers using floppy discs. This manifestation has occurred mainly because of the acceptance of business records on other than ledger cards, particularly in the smaller business. The larger business has for a long time been used to the absence of ledger cards because its records have been stored on tapes or discs for processing by mainframe computer and such computers never did provide ledger card facilities (*see* **23**).

25. The Computer Users' Year Book. A reference manual for the data processing professional from Computing Publications Limited, Evelyn House, 62 Oxford Street, London, W1A 2HG. The Year Book contains information on special recruitment consultants and training courses for staff; advice on the suitability of a programming language for particular applications; equipment suppliers by product and manufacturer; classified guide to accessories; details of over ten thousand installations in the United Kingdom.

It also includes an annual review of computer technology, including details of data communications and networks: financial services including details of insurance companies, brokers and specialist work. A salary analysis is also included.

SOCIAL ASPECTS OF COMPUTERS

26. Primary problem. The primary problem stemming from the increasing use of computers in industry and commerce is the increasing level of unemployment as computer controlled manufacturing and administrative activities supersede the older technologies and working methods.

High unemployment causes many social problems and, as world demand for goods and services has declined, even fewer people are required to satisfy this demand, creating further redundancy in addition to that attributable directly to the implementation of computers.

High unemployment places an additional burden on the working population, as they are required to pay higher levels of taxation than would otherwise be required for the purpose of providing funds for the provision of unemployment pay and other social security payments.

Possibly the only remedy is a reduction in the world's population, reducing it to the level which is required to satisfy the world demand for goods and services and which the international economy can effectively cope with to provide a minimum standard of living for everyone.

How to overcome these problems is of paramount importance to the governments of the world. One remedy is the retraining of personnel in the new technologies: in the areas of computer-aided design, design of computers, design of systems and of programming techniques. This would reduce the level of unemployment due to the technological factor.

Higher levels of productivity attained by automated processes and the use of robotics should reduce the cost of production. If such decreases are reflected in selling prices then demand, in theory, should increase thereby reducing the level of unemployment.

The retirement age could be lowered allowing the employed people to vacate their jobs earlier, thereby providing vacancies for the unemployed. This policy creates a financial burden on the government and the working population, as funds with which to finance early retirement pensions may create additional taxation unless monies for this purpose are redeployed from some other source.

27. Leisure time. The increasing amount of leisure time available to the population, owing to increasing unemployment and the shorter hours worked by the employed because of the introduction of new technology, has created a demand for more leisure facilities (at least for those who can afford them) thus providing some additional employment to offset the unemployment caused by the increasing use of computers (discussed in **26**).

28. Changing technology. Many people, particularly the older generation, cannot and do not want to change their ways of life, although changing technology tends to enforce this on the population. We are now approaching the era of supermarket shopping direct from the home by the use of home computers linked to Viewdata television sets; financial transactions occur between accounts filed electronically rather than between people, creating a cashless society. Even the cheque, which itself replaced cash in many transactions, is on the way out. The transfer of documents by mail services is also on the wane as teletex services and electronic mail systems take over. Holidays may be booked and hotel accommodation and airline seats reserved directly by computer from the home.

29. Social unrest. Computerisation should lead to a more efficient society, on the other hand, it may also lead to social unrest as many people suffer from a lack of financial resources due to being made redundant. This can only be remedied in the long term by an enlightened world populace realising that technology marches on, the same as "tide and time", and it is an irresistible force which must be accepted. Change must be seen as a challenge, not viewed apathetically, which must be taken up in the quest for a new and more interesting life style.

PROGRESS TEST 1

1. Specify the nature of data processing activities. **(1)**

2. List the primary operations relevant to processing business data. **(2)**

3. Specify the elements comprising a data processing system. **(3, 4)**

4. Specify the elements of a computer system. **(5)**

5. What purposes do computers serve? **(7)**

6. Indicate your views on the need for computer literacy in modern society. **(8, 9)**

7. How is it possible to converse with computers? **(10–12)**

8. How would you attempt to classify the various types of computers? **(13–16)**

9. What benefits would you expect a business to achieve from using a computer? **(17)**

10. What criteria would you apply for assessing the economic viability of a computer? **(18–20)**

11. Indicate some of the current developments in the use of computers. **(21–3)**

12. What factors would you take into account when selecting a computer for business use? **(24)**

13. Write an essay about the problems caused by increasing computerisation, suggesting how they might be solved. **(26–9)** (*C & G*)

CHAPTER II

The Electronic Computer and its Development

DEFINITION AND MODE OF OPERATION OF A COMPUTER

1. Definition of a computer. A computer consists of not one machine but a series of related machines. Normally, however, the generic term "computer" is widely used to describe the central processing unit and the peripheral devices used for electronic data processing. The term will be used in this sense throughout the book.

A computer may be defined as a machine which accepts data from an input device, performs arithmetical and logical operations in accordance with a predefined program and finally transfers the processed data to an output device either for further processing or in final printed form, such as business documents, schedules and management control reports.

2. Mode of operation of a computer. Before computer processing can commence, the data must first be prepared in machine-sensible form. Data may be represented by magnetised spots (bits) on magnetic tape or disc. In addition, data may be input in the form of optical or magnetic characters.

Whichever mode of representing data is selected, it is necessary to have a special input device for the purpose of sensing the data and transferring it into the computer's internal memory for processing. The device may be a tape deck or disc drive, optical character reader or magnetic ink character reader, etc., depending upon the mode of input selected.

It is necessary to represent data for processing in a computer by binary coded characters which create pulse sequences (electrical flows) to allow data to flow through electronic circuits for processing. As the pulse sequences are represented by "on" and "off" electrical states this forms the basis of representing data in binary code. Binary is a two-state number system which is compatible with electrical flows which are also two-state, "on" and "off". The two numbers of the binary number system are "1" and "0" and these are represented by an electrical "pulse" and "no pulse" signal respectively. Combinations of pulses, that is sequences of "on" and "off" states, are the basis of forming binary coded characters. Each character is formed by a series of binary digits referred to as "bits", which is a contraction using the first and last letters of "binary digits".

It is important to appreciate that descriptive data elements such as customer, supplier and employee names and addresses, etc. are processed in binary coded characters but data to be used in calculations, i.e. quantities and prices, must be processed in pure binary form (*see* **3** and **4**).

The data is processed at electronic speed under the control of the computer's control unit and the internally stored program. All operations are performed automatically and the output is usually produced by an output device known as a line printer.

Master files are usually stored magnetically in the form of magnetic tapes or magnetic discs. Programs are stored on either magnetic tape or magnetic disc.

It is normal practice to have the input, output and storage devices attached to the central processing unit which controls their use. In this case, the devices are said to be "on-line".

A computer may be used for an infinite variety of tasks, including the preparation of payrolls, payslips, invoices, statements and purchase orders as well as updating master files containing historical records relating to employees, stocks, suppliers' accounts, customers' accounts, costs and production. They are also used for planning, problem-solving and presenting information to management on which to base decisions.

ASCII AND EBCDIC

3. ASCII. ASCII is an abbreviation for *A*MERICAN *S*TANDARD *C*ODE for *I*NFORMATION *I*NTERCHANGE, a character code adopted as standard by the American National Standards Institute in 1963. It has also been adopted in Europe.

ASCII is one of the two principal character codes. Some manufacturers, such as SHARP, with their MZ-80K models of microcomputer have their own DISPLAY code as well as ASCII. ASCII is widely accepted for use on microcomputers and it provides a basis for the transfer of data between devices such as a processor and printer or terminal (VDU).

To display an ASCII character it is necessary to use CHR$ which substitutes the ASCII character for the defined code number, e.g.

in respect of the SHARP MZ-80K the statement PRINT CHR$ (70) displays the character F on the screen. The statement PRINT/P CHR$ (70) prints the character on the printer. To find the code number of an ASCII character the required statement is PRINT ASC ("F") which, in this instance, displays 70. Examples of characters in ASCII numbers and binary code are shown in Table III.

TABLE III ASCII

Character	Code no.	Binary code
A	65	0100 0001
B	66	0100 0010
C	67	0100 0011
X	88	0101 1000
Y	89	0101 1001
Z	90	0101 1010
1	49	0011 0001
2	50	0011 0010
3	51	0011 0011
8	56	0011 1000
9	57	0011 1001

The code provides for 256 different characters including control and graphics symbols as well as those for punctuation requirements and other special characters (*see* Fig. 10).

4. EBCDIC. EBCDIC is an acronym for *E*xtended *B*inary *C*oded *D*ecimal *I*nterchange *C*ode. The code uses eight binary positions for each character format and forms the basis of the eight-bit byte. This enables a character repertoire of 256 characters to be used, including upper and lower case alphabetic characters and an extended range of special and control characters. The code is mostly used on IBM mainframe computers.

An EBCDIC oriented IBM terminal cannot communicate with an ASCII-oriented system as the codes are incompatible. The structure of the EBCDIC is shown in Table IV below on the following basis:

Check bit	Zone bits	Numeric bits
as appropriate	0123	4567

Examples of code combinations are shown in Table IV.

The following are the ASCII codes for characters:

Code	Symbol	Code	Symbol	Code	Symbol	Code	Symbol	Code	Symbol	Code	Symbol	Code	Symbol
32	SP	64	@	96		128	SP	160	q	192	SP	224	
33	!	65	A	97	H	129		161	a	193		225	
34	"	66	B	98	I	130		162	z	194		226	
35	#	67	C	99	大	131		163	w	195		227	
36	$	68	D	100		132		164	s	196		228	
37	%	69	E	101		133		165	u	197		229	
38	&	70	F	102	¥	134		166	i	198		230	
39	'	71	G	103		135		167		199		231	
40	(	72	H	104		136		168	Ö	200		232	
41	)	73	I	105		137		169	k	201		233	
42	*	74	J	106		138		170	f	202		234	
43	+	75	K	107		139		171	v	203		235	
44	,	76	L	108	K	140		172	III	204		236	
45	-	77	M	109	K	141		173	ü	205		237	
46	.	78	N	110		142		174	β	206		238	
47	/	79	O	111		143		175	j	207		239	
48	0	80	P	112		144		176	n	208		240	
49	1	81	Q	113		145		177		209		241	
50	2	82	R	114		146	e	178	Ü	210		242	
51	3	83	S	115		147		179	m	211		243	
52	4	84	T	116		148		180		212		244	
53	5	85	U	117		149		181		213		245	
54	6	86	V	118		150	t	182		214		246	
55	7	87	W	119		151	g	183	o	215		247	
56	8	88	X	120		152	h	184	l	216		248	
57	9	89	Y	121		153		185	Ä	217		249	
58	:	90	Z	122		154	b	186	ö	218		250	
59	;	91	[	123	o	155	x	187	ä	219		251	
60	<	92	\	124		156	d	188		220		252	
61	=	93	]	125		157	r	189	y	221		253	
62	>	94	↑	126		158	p	190		222		254	
63	?	95	←	127		159	c	191		223		255	

Note: The code is based on the decimal system. SP represents a space.

FIG. 10   *ASCII Code Table.*

TABLE IV EBCDIC

Character	Zone bits	Numeric bits
A	1100	0001
B	1100	0010
C	1100	0011
X	1110	0111
a	1000	0001
b	1000	0010
c	1000	0011

THE DEVELOPMENT OF COMPUTER TECHNOLOGY

Electronic computers were first used for commercial processing during the early 1950s, and they were based on a technology now referred to as the First Generation. Technological developments occurred at a very fast rate and in the late 1950s the technology applied to the design of computers became known as the Second Generation. Eventually, in the early 1960s technological developments were such that a Third Generation of computers became available. Fourth Generation computers came into existence in 1974.

The technical characteristics of computers may be classified according to the "generation" to which they belong.

5. First generation computers. The first generation of computers were in operation during the years 1954–59, and their technological basis was circuitry consisting of wires and thermionic valves. The valves, being hollow in construction, were non-solid state as electrical pulses had to flow through the space (vacuum) in the valve, much as in the pre-transistorised type of radio. Computers belonging to this generation had the following characteristics:

(*a*) comparatively *large* in size compared with present-day computers;

(*b*) generated a *lot of heat,* which was not consistent with reliability as the valves tended to fail frequently;

(*c*) *low capacity internal storage*;

(*d*) *individual* non-related models;

(*e*) processors operated in the *millisecond speed range* (one-thousandth of a second);

(*f*) internal storage consisted of a *magnetic drum* and *delay lines.*

6. Second generation computers. This generation was in operation during the years 1959–64. The advance of technological knowledge enabled the wires and thermionic valves of the first generation to be replaced with printed circuits, diodes and transistors. These components were based on "solid state" technology, as electricity did not have to flow through space as in the thermionic valve. "Solid state" is the technology applied to the design of modern domestic tape recorders and transistor radios.

Computers of this generation had the following characteristics:

(*a*) *smaller* in size compared to the first generation computers;

(*b*) generated a *lower level of heat,* as the components were much smaller;

(*c*) *greater* degree of *reliability,* as transistors and solid state components generally are not subject to such a high failure rate as thermionic valves;

(*d*) *higher capacity internal storage*;

(*e*) use of *core storage* instead of magnetic drum and delay lines;

(*f*) related series of processors—the *family concept*;

(*g*) processors operated in the *microsecond speed range* (one-millionth of a second);

(*h*) high cost *direct access storage*.

7. Third generation computers. Third generation computers came into existence in 1964 and are in current use. The technology forming the basis of their design is microminiaturisation, consisting of micro-integrated circuits very similar to the solid state technology of the second generation but much more compact. The circuits are built of a number of integrated components rather than individual components which require to be soldered together. Integrated circuits, based on silicon technology (*see* III, 6), are much smaller than their predecessors, which enables higher processing speeds to be achieved, because with smaller circuits data pulses can flow from point A to point B much more quickly than is possible with larger circuits. The reason for this is that electricity flows at a constant speed (the speed of light) and the only way in which data pulses can be speeded up is by reducing the distance they have to travel.

Computers of this generation have the following characteristics:

(*a*) *smaller* in size compared with the second generation computers;

(*b*) *higher capacity internal storage*;

(*c*) remote *communication* facilities;

(*d*) *multi-programming* facilities;

(*e*) *reduced cost of direct access storage*;

(*f*) processors which operate in the *nanosecond speed range* (one-thousandth of a microsecond—American billionth of a second);

(*g*) ranges of computers with a common architecture whereby the models in a range are upward compatible; i.e. a program written for one model can be run without any significant change on a larger and more powerful computer in the range;

(*h*) use of high-level languages such as COBOL;

(*i*) wide range of optional peripherals.

8. Fourth generation computers. The introduction of systems network architecture in 1974 may be considered to be the inception of the fourth generation. A standard architecture was derived which provided for upgrading networks of computers without alteration of application programming. This compares with the upward compatibility of computers in a range which was a feature of the third generation (*see* 7). This generation also included the introduction of microtechnology and the advent of microcomputers, retail terminal systems, databases and extremely large internal and external storage capacity, office information systems, word processing and electronic mail and local area networks.

MAINFRAME COMPUTER CONFIGURATIONS

9. Definition of configuration. A computer configuration is the collection of machines (hardware) which form a complete computer system; consisting of a central processor and its peripheral devices. Peripheral devices consist of input, backing storage and output devices which are normally connected to, and controlled by, the processor. Modern computer technology is such that a wide range of peripheral devices and processors are available from which to build the computer configuration most suitable for the processing needs of a particular business. The choice of the most suitable configuration is established during the feasibility study.

A computer configuration is selected initially to suit both the current and the foreseeable future needs of the business with regard to the volume and type of data to be processed.

Eventually, it may be necessary to increase the processing power of the computer installation to contend with increasing volumes of data and the need for more management information. At one time, under these circumstances, it was necessary to change the existing computer for a more powerful model, but this is now unnecessary. Computer installations may now be enhanced on site on a modular basis, as required, for example by:

(*a*) increasing the *capacity of storage* by the addition of storage modules;

(*b*) the installation of *additional exchangeable disc storage devices* for increasing the volume of data which is immediately accessible during processing or to obtain direct access to programs;

(*c*) increasing the speed of output by exchanging a slow line printer for a faster model or by substituting computer output by microfilm (*see* VI, **13–15**);

(*d*) exchanging the processor for a more powerful model;

(*e*) addition of workstations for on-line processing.

10. Virtual machines. A virtual machine is one which supports an interpreter for emulating another machine, in the sense that it is capable of running software originally compiled for other machines. In other words, one machine acts as if it is another. This is transparent to the user as he may be running a CP/M operating system on a non CP/M machine in emulation mode. System performance may be enhanced in some instances if the host computer is using high-speed hard disc backing storage instead of floppy discs.

The author has a Sharp MZ-80K which can emulate a Sharp MZ-80A by loading the relevant version of BASIC. The "Z" then acts as if it is the "A".

11. Batch processing configuration. The older type of third generation computer configuration typically consists of the following (*see* Figs. 11 and 12).

(*a*) *Input devices.*

(*i*) A card reader with a reading speed of 300 or 600 cards a minute. This device would only be used for transferring transaction data into the computer's working store.

(*ii*) A paper tape reader may be used (as an alternative, or in addition, to a card reader) capable of transferring 1 000 characters a second into the computer's working store.

Data may be captured in paper tape as a by-product of other accounting machine operations by means of a tape punching attachment.

(*b*) *Output device.* A line printer with a printing speed of 300 or 600 lines a minute.

(*c*) *Processing.* A central processing unit with 32,000 units or more (words, bytes or characters) of core store capacity.

(*d*) *Backing storage devices.*

(*i*) Four tape decks would usually be required to facilitate sorting and file updating.

(*ii*) Two or three disc drives are usually required for storing master files, data to be used in multiprogramming operations

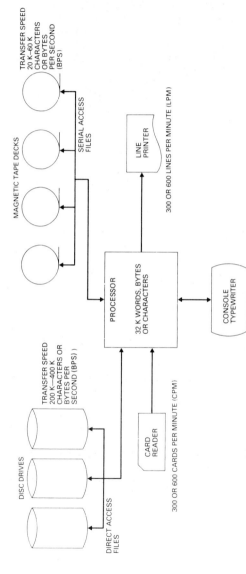

FIG. 11 *Older type of batch processing mainframe computer configuration.*

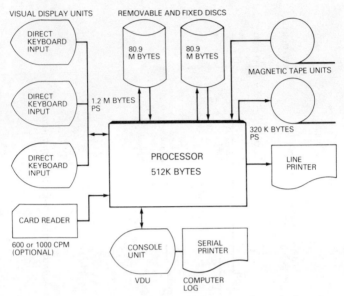

FIG. 12 *Diagram outlining the main features of a typical modern mainframe computer.*

required on demand, segments of operating systems and application programs.

12. Real-time processing configuration. The cost of a computer capable of handling real-time processing need not be great as the current range of medium scale mainframes and some minis are designed to perform this type of processing as they have telecommunication facilities for controlling on-line terminals. The particular configuration depends entirely on the type of operation to be controlled, be it an airline reservation system or steel mill for real-time control of steel production to optimise the level of scrap from slab lengths in relation to order requirements. A typical real-time configuration may consist of:

(*a*) a powerful processor supported by high capacity disc storage;

(*b*) communication lines for connecting dispersed terminals to the processor, which should be located at strategic points in the organisation;

(c) modems and multiplexors and/or communications processors;

(d) terminal controllers;

(e) back-up facilities, such as two processors in tandem, one operating on batch processing, for instance, until switched over to real-time processing in the event of failure of the normal real-time processor.

CURRENT STATUS OF MAINFRAME TECHNOLOGY: THE NCR 9300

13. General characteristics. This machine is chosen as an example of the current "state of the art" technology relating to the larger computer. It is completely modular, incorporating independent subsystems and is suitable for use as a stand-alone computer system for the small business and for driving a large network of terminals. It is externally micro-programmable which allows the 9300 architecture to support systems which were originally designed to run on another computer; the 9040 in this instance. One emulates the other by means of micro-program chip sets. The 9300 is in fact a 32-bit processor whereas the 9040 is a 16-bit processor (*see* **10**).

Its telecommunications, distributed data processing and Systems Network Architecture (SNA) capabilities make it suitable for use in large DP networks. The electronics are based on 32-bit VLSI (Very Large Scale Integration) which enables the circuits previously contained in ten printed circuit boards to be on a single chip the size of a five pence piece. Its logic circuitry uses the semiconductor NMOS silicide process.

The NCR 9300 functions under the control of the Interactive Transaction Executive (ITX), which is an operating system with multiprogramming facilities, allowing the interfacing of multiple CRTs (VDUs), industrial terminals, retail terminals and financial terminals both locally and remotely (*see* Figs. 13 and 14).

14. Processor subsystem. The processor box measures only two cubic feet and weighs fifty pounds. It can be located on a desk or set on a portable floor stand module. The circuit board consists of four processor chips, i.e. Central Processor Chip (CPC) containing more than 40 000 transistors; an Address Translation Chip (ATC); and two System Interface Chips (SIC). In addition the board consists of an Instruction Storage Unit, processor memory bus, a memory interface, a set of memory array chips, Input/Output Sub-System (IOSS) and Link Level Communications Subsystem interfaces, etc.

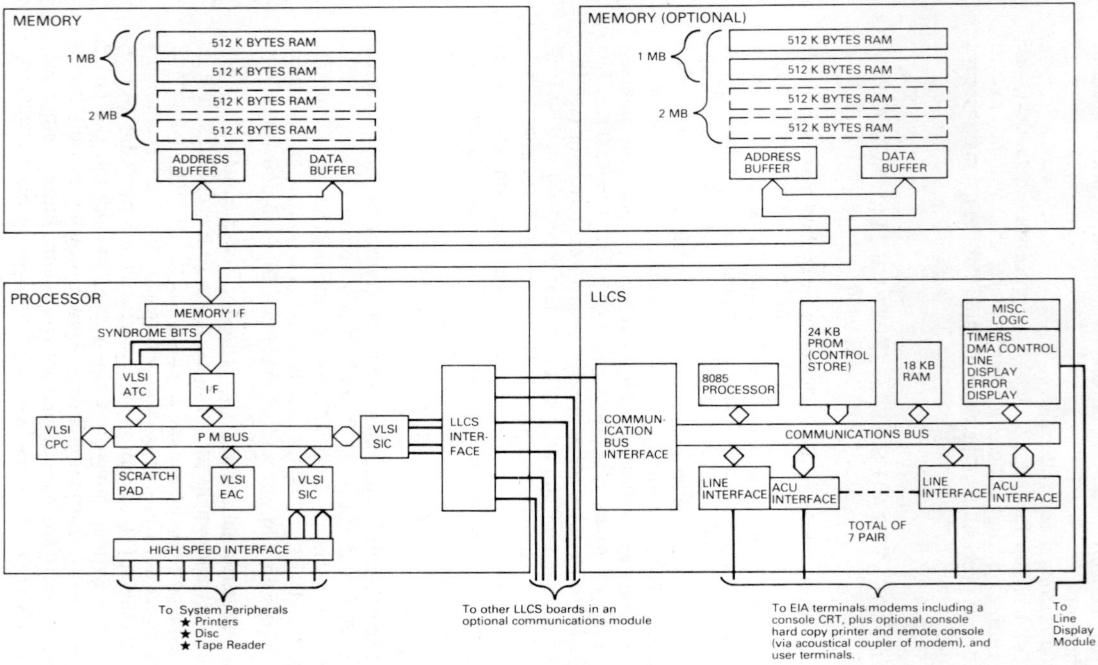

Fig. 13 NCR 9300 Processor Module.

(Courtesy NCR Limited)

(Courtesy NCR Limited)

FIG. 14   *NCR 9300 Computer.*

The memory has one million bytes (one megabyte) of RAM expandable up to four megabytes in one megabyte segments (*see* Fig. 13). The memory interface provides the logical connection between memory array chips and the address translation chip. It is capable of addressing up to 128 megabytes of main storage. Data is transferred as four-byte words.

An advantage of VLSI technology is that signals in the circuits only travel short distances resulting in improved internal performance, provides greater reliability, has a lower power consumption, is smaller in size and costs less.

The address translation chip provides the interface between the central processor and the main storage unit. It features a 128 million bytes main storage unit address capability and provides internal and virtual memory operations.

The system interface chips operate under the control of the central processor chip. They provide support for the Input/Output SubSystem and have direct access to the main storage unit through the processor memory bus. The communications subsystem (LLCS) is a microprocessor based controller that appears to the host software as a communications multiplexor with asynchronous and synchronous adapters. Additional LLCS boards can be connected. The Input/Output SubSystem interfaces the peripherals.

15. Configuration overview. The 9300 computer system consists of the following peripherals and software support:

(*a*) fixed and removable discs—storage capacity 135 MB + ;
(*b*) magnetic tape units—high speed transfers;
(*c*) video display units;
(*d*) various models of printer up to 2 000 lpm;
(*e*) COBOL or BASIC programming language;
(*f*) database management;
(*g*) report program generator;
(*h*) on-line program development;
(*i*) general business applications relating to accounting and information processing.

THE CENTRAL PROCESSING UNIT

16. General characteristics and compatibility of processors. The central processing unit or processor (often abbreviated to CPU) is the main unit within a computer system, and consists of three components: arithmetic/logic unit, control unit and internal working memory (*see* Fig. 15).

The processor accepts data for processing from an input device, carries out instructions specified by the program and outputs the results by means of an output device. Modern computers are often designed as a related family or series, whereby each processor in the series is compatible with each other. Compatibility is a design

CENTRAL PROCESSING UNIT (CPU)		
ARITHMETIC/LOGIC UNIT	INTERNAL WORKING STORAGE	CONTROL UNIT
ARITHMETIC: – ADDITION	ACCUMULATORS	INSTRUCTION REGISTER
– SUBTRACTION	SUPERVISOR PROGRAM	INSTRUCTION REGISTER
– DIVISION	APPLICATION PROGRAM	OPERATION DECODER
MULTIPLICATION	INPUT DATA	OPERATION DECODER
LOGIC: – COMPARING	WORKING STORAGE	ADDRESS REGISTER
– MATCHING	OUTPUT INFORMATION	ADDRESS REGISTER
– SORTING	CONSTANTS	INSTRUCTION COUNTER
DECISIONS	TABLES	INSTRUCTION COUNTER

FIG. 15 *Major elements of a central processing unit.*

technique which enables any peripheral device to be connected to any processor in the series. The more powerful processors operate more efficiently, however, with the peripherals which are most suitable with regard to speed of operation. Program portability (transferability) is also a feature of computers within a series.

17. The power of processors. The power of processors increases progressively throughout the series, and may be distinguished by the following attributes:

   (*a*) store cycle time;
   (*b*) storage capacity;
   (*c*) number of data transfer channels;
   (*d*) number of programs which may be interleaved for multiprogramming operations;
   (*e*) real-time processing capability;
   (*f*) number of work stations which can be on-line for multi-user needs.

THE CONTROL UNIT

18. Purpose and characteristics of a control unit. The overall control of a computer system is accomplished by the control unit, which is an integral part of the central processing unit.

The control unit coordinates the various parts of the computer system—the arithmetic/logic unit, internal working store and the peripheral units—to form a composite, integrated data processing system. In addition, the control unit also controls the transfer of data to, from and within the working store, as required by the program. The control unit also acts as a switching device to enable data pulses to flow along the appropriate channels.

A control unit, in respect of a single-address type of computer, consists of the following components:

   (*a*) instruction register;
   (*b*) decoder;
   (*c*) address register;
   (*d*) instruction counter.

The instruction register receives instructions from the internal working store in the sequence required for processing. The function or operation part of the instruction is then transferred to a decoder for translation of the operation to be executed, which causes the appropriate circuits to be connected for carrying out the operation in the arithmetic/logic unit.

The address register makes the required circuit connections to enable the data contained in a store location to be transferred to a specified accumulator via a register.

An instruction counter is used for recording the number of instructions executed, and is incremented by 1 after completing each instruction.

19. Cycle of operations. As both instructions and data are in binary form, there must be some means of enabling the computer to distinguish between them to avoid processing instructions as data. This is achieved by two distinct operation cycles known as "instruction" and "execution" cycles. The instruction cycle is concerned with connecting store locations to the adder to allow the transfer of data for processing. The execution cycle carries out the requirements of the instruction.

THE ARITHMETIC/LOGIC UNIT

The arithmetic/logic unit performs arithmetic operations, data handling operations and logical functions. The unit consists of a "mill" (adder/subtractor), electronic circuits, one or more "working registers" to which operands may be transferred whilst being operated on and, in some computers, accumulators for storing the results of calculations.

20. Arithmetic operations. Although a computer performs all types of arithmetic operations—addition, subtraction, multiplication and division—it is important to appreciate that subtraction is performed by the addition of the "complement" of the number to be subtracted to the other number involved in the calculation.

Multiplication is performed by combinations of "shifts" to the left and addition. Division is performed by combinations of "shifts" to the right and subtraction.

21. Logic operations and automatic decision making. Logic operations, as distinct from arithmetic operations, are concerned with comparing, selecting, matching, sorting and merging of data. When comparing data factors, the logical ability of the arithmetic/logic unit differentiates between positive and negative differences between the data factors and, in accordance with the results of the comparison, the alternative sequence of instructions to be executed is determined automatically. This is known as a "conditional" transfer, and it provides the means for processing data on the "exception" basis—that is, data requiring special processing according to the circumstances disclosed by the data.

Conditional transfers of this type are appropriate when it is necessary to compare the credit limit of each customer with their account balance for the purpose of indicating by means of a special print-out, those customers whose balances exceed the credit limit for credit control. This is referred to as "exception reporting". In a stock control application the program may provide for the comparison of stock balances with reorder levels to indicate those items which require replenishment. This may be done either by printing out a reorder list or a purchase order directly. This may be referred to as "automatic decision-making".

Similarly, within a budgetary control application actual costs may be compared with budgeted costs and variance reports printed out, again on the basis of exception reporting. It is this important attribute of computers that makes them so useful as a tool of management.

COMPUTER LOGIC

22. Boolean algebra. The name is derived from the mathematician, George Boole. The relevance of Boolean algebra to the logic of computers is based on two possible "truth values" of a statement, i.e. true and false. These values are represented by the binary values 1 and 0 respectively, thus enabling Boolean principles to be applied to the logical circuitry of a computer. As a computer operates on the basis of electrical states, on or off, representing binary digits 1 and 0, circuits can be designed to facilitate Boolean operations by means of logic circuits (or gates).

23. Logic gate/logic circuit. These are synonymous terms for describing the logic circuits which have several inputs and one or two outputs depending upon the nature of the logic gate. Gates provide the foundations of all logic circuits which are etched on the surface of a silicon chip. Logic gates include: AND, NAND (Not AND), NOT, Inclusive OR, Exclusive OR and NOR. These are illustrated in Figure 16. Each logic gate has a truth table outlining its mode of operation which is based on Boolean algebra as indicated above.

24. Truth table. A truth table shows the outputs obtained from a logic circuit or gate as a consequence of specific inputs. Due to this relationship both truth tables and logic gates will be discussed together (*see* Fig. 16).

(*a*) *AND*. AND gates are sometimes referred to as "coincidence gates" for reasons to be indicated. An AND gate gives an output

LOGIC GATE

TRUTH TABLE

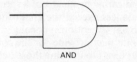

AND

INPUT	OUTPUT
0 0	0
0 1	0
1 0	0
1 1	1

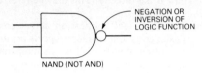

NEGATION OR
INVERSION OF
LOGIC FUNCTION

NAND (NOT AND)

INPUT	OUTPUT
0 0	1
0 1	1
1 0	1
1 1	0

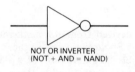

NOT OR INVERTER
(NOT + AND = NAND)

INPUT	OUTPUT
0	1
1	0

OR (INCLUSIVE OR)
NOT + OR = NOR)

INPUT	OUTPUT
0 0	0
0 1	1
1 0	1
1 1	1

X – OR (EXCLUSIVE OR)
ALSO KNOWN AS NON-EQUIVALENCE GATE (NEQ)

INPUT	OUTPUT
0 0	0
0 1	1
1 0	1
1 1	0

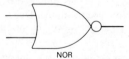

NOR

INPUT	OUTPUT
0 0	1
0 1	0
1 0	0
1 1	0

FIG. 16 *Logic gates and truth tables.*

of logical value 1 only when all of its inputs are logical value 1 (*see* Fig. 16). This facility could be used to find the carry digit when two binary digits are added together, as there is a carry of 1 only when the two digits to be added are both 1. Assume the content of an accumulator is 0001 1110 and the value of the operand to be added to the contents of the accumulator is 0100 1101. The result would be as follows.

contents of accumulator	0001 1110
value of operand	0100 1101
contents of accumulator after AND	0000 1100

(*b*) *NAND (Not AND).* This gate produces an output of logical value 1 when any or all of its inputs do *not* contain a logical 1 (*see* Fig. 16). By joining the two inputs together on a NAND gate it becomes a NOT gate or an "inverter" (*see* (*c*)). A NAND gate has the same effect as an AND gate connected to a NOT gate (inverter). Refer to relevant truth tables in Fig. 16 for AND and NAND. It will be seen that the outputs are the complete opposite of each other.

(*c*) *NOT or INVERTER.* The logical value of the output of this gate is always the opposite to that of the input, as shown on the truth table in Fig. 16. When combined with an AND gate it inverts the output to that of a NAND gate. When combined with an OR gate it inverts the output to that of a NOR gate.

(*d*) *OR (inclusive OR).* The output of this gate is a logical 1 when *any* or all of its inputs are logical 1, as the truth table indicates.

(*e*) *X-OR (exclusive OR).* This gate is sometimes referred to as an anticoincidence gate or digital comparator. It is also known as a "non-equivalence" gate. If the inputs of this gate are different then a logical 1 is output and a 0 is output if they are the same. It follows the rule of "either" but not "both". The gate can be used to determine whether two binary digits are the same or different. It can also be used for adding two binary digits ignoring the carry digit and is sometimes referred to as a "half adder" for this reason.

(*f*) *NOR.* This has the same function as NOT OR. Its output has a value of logical 1 only when *all* its inputs have a value of 0 otherwise its output is 0.

25. Application of logic concepts. A number of business orientated examples will perhaps clarify the way in which truth tables are used in conjunction with the three principle logic elements, AND, OR and NOT.

(a) AND   *input output*

    (i) It is true that a customer has placed an order **(1)**
AND
It is true that the credit limit is not exceeded **(1)**
It is true that the order is acceptable **(1)**

   (ii) It is true that a customer has placed an order **(1)**
AND
It is not true that the credit limit is not exceeded **(0)**
It is not true that the order is accepted **(0)**

(b) OR

    (i) It is true that the level of stock has reached the reorder level (equal to) **(1)**
OR
It is true that the level of stock is below the reorder level (less than) **(1)**
It is true that stock should be reordered **(1)**

   (ii) It is true that the value of the order is less than £50 **(1)**
OR
It is not true that the delivery distance is greater than 20 miles **(0)**
It is true that delivery is to be charged **(1)**

  (iii) It is true that the value of the order is greater than £50 **(1)**
OR
It is not true that the delivery distance is less than 20 miles **(0)**
It is true that delivery is not to be charged **(1)**

  (iv) It is not true that the value of the order is less than £50 **(0)**
OR
It is not true that the delivery distance is greater than 20 miles **(0)**
It is not true that delivery is to be charged **(0)**

(c) NOT

    (i) It is true we have excess stock **(1)**
It is not true that a purchase order is required **(0)**

   (ii) It is not true that we have excess stock **(0)**
It is true that a purchase order is required **(1)**

INTERNAL STORAGE

26. General outline. Developments in electronic and related technology have affected the type of internal storage used in computers. Early computers had internal memories consisting of nickel delay lines or magnetic drums. More recent computers have core storage but this has tended to be replaced by semiconductor (MOS) memory in later computers.

27. Summary of types of internal memory. The most usual types of memory in current use are:

    (*a*) core storage;
    (*b*) semiconductor memory (MOS).
        (*i*) RAM;
       (*ii*) ROM;
      (*iii*) PROM;
      (*iv*) EPROM;
    (*c*) bubble memory;
    (*d*) holographic (optical) memory;
    (*e*) cache memory.

28. Purpose of internal memory. The internal memory of a computer is an integral element of the processing unit and may be referred to as the computer's working memory. It is used for storing software in the form of operating systems, application programs and utility routines, etc. In addition, the data input for processing is stored in the memory, as are the results of processing until they are output either to backing storage or to an output device such as a printer or VDU.

Data stored in the memory, as well as instructions, can be addressed and accessed very quickly and for this reason internal memory is often referred to as "immediate access storage" (IAS). This attribute is ideal for having all programs and master files (consisting of business records and reference files) stored internally for immediate access when required. Unfortunately, however, internal storage, particularly core storage, has tended to be expensive and it has been necessary to use slower and less expensive types of storage for such purposes. Internal storage has to be complemented therefore by external storage, that is storage external to the processor, which is referred to as "backing storage". This is used for mass storage needs whereas internal storage is used for immediate access requirements.

Backing storage is less expensive, and has a higher storage capacity but a slower access time than internal storage. Programs, master files and reference files are stored in backing storage until required for processing, when they are transferred to the internal memory. All programs and data must be resident in the internal memory before processing is possible (*see* IX).

29. Units of storage. The units of storage in a computer system are usually expressed in bytes and/or words, which indicates the number of binary digits (bits) in a unit of storage. At one time computers had units of storage expressed in terms of characters consisting of six bits but these have tended to be replaced by the byte which consists of eight bits. Mainframes tend to have thirty-two-bit words equivalent to four bytes. The modern small computer tends to have a unit of storage in the form of a sixteen-bit word but an exception to this is the Radio Shack TRS-80 microcomputer which consists of an eight-bit processor.

30. Capacity of storage. Until recently medium scale mainframe computers had internal storage capacities, typically in the region of 32 to 48Kbytes, but even the small mini or micro now has a capacity which greatly exceeds this. Typical storage capacities may be summarised as follows:

(*a*) micros 4K to 64Kbytes +;
(*b*) minis 48K to 128Kbytes +;
(*c*) modern mainframes 128K to 512K; $\frac{3}{4}$ to 2 million bytes +.

The abbreviation "K" is used to denote 1 000 units of storage but it is actually 1 024 units of storage, i.e. 2^{10} which is an expansion of base 2, the base of the binary number system "K" should not be confused with kilo (k) which stands for 1 000, i.e. 10^3 which is an expansion of base 10, the base of the decimal number system.

31. Core storage. This type of storage consists of small rings (cores) of ferromagnetic material which are threaded on wires by hand which makes this type of storage very expensive to produce. Core storage consists of a number of adjacent core planes for storing bytes, one plane for each bit position in the byte.

The cores are magnetised to represent binary numbers—a zero is represented by negative polarity and a one by positive polarity. By means of combinations of negative and positive states in adjacent core planes it is possible to represent numeric, alphabetic and special characters each of which have their individual binary code.

32. Semiconductor memory. This type of memory has tended to supersede core storage in most computers, i.e. micros, minis and mainframes. The reason for this is attributable to four factors, viz.

it is smaller, has a higher capacity, is less costly and is faster with regard to access time.

Semiconductor memory is produced from silicon chips and is based on *m*etal *o*xide *s*emiconductor (MOS) technology. It is also referred to as "*m*etal *o*xide *s*emiconductor *f*ield *e*ffect *t*ransistor technology", i.e. MOSFET. Field *e*ffect *t*ransistor technology is abbreviated to FET.

There are two types of semiconductor memory:

(*a*) random access memory (RAM);
(*b*) read-only memory (ROM).

33. Random access memory (RAM). This type of memory is used for working storage requirements when running application programs. Its capacity can usually be increased on-site on many computers (large and small) by adding RAM chips to the circuit boards. This type of memory can be directly addressed in the same way as core storage to access specific data or instructions.

RAM is either "static" or "dynamic". Static RAM remains unchanged until an electrical pulse is generated to change it. Dynamic RAM is volatile as it requires continual refreshing by electrical pulses. When the processor is switched off the contents are destroyed and the memory must be reloaded with the same program to restart the job. The same considerations apply for processing a job again at a later date—it is necessary to reload the program. To overcome the consequences of a power failure some computers have a memory support system using batteries to energise the memory when necessary to avoid loss of data.

34. Read only memory (ROM). The contents of ROM are physically fixed and cannot be accessed to alter them as can be done with RAM. The reason for this is that the writing circuit is disconnected during manufacture. Small computers use this type of internal memory for storing a BASIC interpreter which converts program statements in BASIC programming language into machine code. This is done during the running of a program. The contents of ROM are not destroyed when the computer is switched off as ROM is non-volatile because its contents have been burnt in during manufacture. Microprograms for input/output operations are stored on ROM chips.

35. PROM. There are variations of ROM, e.g. PROM which stands for "Programmable Read-Only Memory". Whereas ordinary ROM is preprogrammed at the factory, PROM can be programmed by the user. A special device is required for putting the "bit" pattern into a PROM chip; this is called a PROM programmer.

36. EPROM. This is a further variation of ROM, which stands for "Erasable Programmable Read-Only Memory". When data is recorded on this type of memory it is in effect the same as ordinary ROM in its behaviour but if the user requires to change the content of the chip an ultraviolet light is used to revert all the cells to "1s". New data or programs can then be written on the chip.

37. Bubble memory. Bubbles may be described as cylindrical magnets which are formed from magnetic regions called "domains" after the application of a critical bias value magnetic field. The bubbles are created on memory chips with capacities of typically 64K and 256K bytes. Rockwell has a bubble memory system with a megabyte of storage and a module with a capacity of one megabit.

Developments are taking place to reduce the size of the bubble or magnetic domain to less than two microns to enable one megabyte of memory to be stored on to a chip not greater than about half a cubic inch (approximately $8\,000$ mm^3) in over-all size. Strings of bubbles allow streams of bits carried by the bubbles to become a series of electrical pulses providing output from the bubble memory.

The Sharp PC5000 has 128K bytes of bubble memory RAM, expandable in two steps of 64K to 256K bytes. All the memory is housed in the machine. The ICL DNX − 2000 digital PABX system also uses bubble memory so it seems that this type of memory is likely to be widely used in future.

38. Holographic (optical) memory. This is a ROM optical memory system whereby a pattern is recorded on a photosensitive plate by mixing laser light from a reference beam and laser light scattered from the object bearing the information to be recorded. The data in the hologram is effectively "smeared" over the whole of the plate. A degree of redundancy is built into the system so that dust and scratches on the emulsion have little effect on the recorded information.

Data in the reconstructed image are arranged as an array of dots—one dot for each "bit". Information may be read out by directing a laser beam on to the hologram so that the reconstructed image falls onto a photodiode array on a silicon chip. At present the main limitation is that information on a holographic store is generally fixed and is presently of value for storing large amounts of fixed information such as machine instructions.

39. Cache memory. A highspeed memory capable of keeping up with the CPU. It acts as a buffer between the CPU and the slower main memory. As the CPU is not delayed by memory accesses the overall speed of processing is increased. Segments of program and data are transferred from disc backing storage into the cache buffer by the operating system. This type of memory is mainly applicable to the larger computer.

ADVANTAGES AND DISADVANTAGES
OF A COMPUTER

40. Advantages. These are summarised as follows:

(*a*) *Speed of operation.* The central processor of a computer system operates at electronic speed, that is at the speed of light, which means that data pulses flow through the system at 2.997 925 $\times 10^8$ m/s (186 000 miles per second).

(*b*) *Automatic operation.* Once data has been input to the processor all data processing is automatic under the control of the internally stored program.

(*c*) *Flexibility.* The modern general purpose computer may be used for a variety of purposes, i.e. concurrent batch and on-line processing, multi-programming, real-time processing and data collection, etc.

(*d*) *Reliability.* As the main unit in a computer system, the central processor, is constructed from electronic components it is not so prone to malfunctions from wear and tear in use as are machines of a mechanical nature.

(*e*) *Choice of configuration.* A wide range of optional peripherals are available for many computer systems which allow a business to implement those which most suit its processing requirements, i.e. an optical character reader may be used instead of a terminal keyboard.

(*f*) *Management information.* Due to the characteristics of a computer it is possible to increase the level of useful information supplied to management for control and decision making.

(*g*) *Accuracy.* Due to program checks and controls applied to data before and during processing, invalid data is detected and corrected. This factor ensures that the ultimate output from a computer has a high degree of accuracy and is, therefore, more reliable.

41. Disadvantages. Considering all of the advantages listed above, it would not appear that there could be any disadvantages, but unfortunately there are. They may be enumerated as follows.

(*a*) Unless the *feasibility study* is carried out satisfactorily, the resulting decision may be to go ahead and install a computer when in fact it should not be, or not to install a computer when in fact it should be. Either result will have repercussions on the business.

(*b*) Analysing and designing computer systems is a skilled task and the ultimate results will *reflect the skill and care* applied to this activity.

(*c*) Similary the care and skill applied in *writing* the computer programs will affect the ultimate results.

(*d*) The whole of the business administration requires to be *investigated,* and changes effected, to obtain the best results, and this may cause drastic upheavals for both systems and staff. Of course, changes must take place to keep up to date with changing circumstances, but this is a problem that has to be overcome.

(*e*) Several man-years of investigation and preparation may have elapsed before a computer system becomes *operational.*

(*f*) It is extremely difficult to obtain *skilled systems analysts and programmers* because of the increasing demand for them.

(*g*) The *initial cost* of a large installation can be very high, but this may be offset by the rental terms and tax allowances which are available. Minis and micros cost much less than mainframes, however.

(*h*) Because of the speedy development of new technology in the field of electronics, and electronic computers in particular, a computer may be *technologically obsolete* before it is installed. However, unless the decision to go ahead is given to install the latest model of computer available, stagnation may follow, or, at the least, competitors will gain advantages.

(*i*) The need to obtain *standby facilities* in the event of break-down of any part of the computer system.

PROGRESS TEST 2

1. Define the term computer. **(1)**
2. Specify the way in which a computer functions. **(2)**
3. What do ASCII and EBCDIC stand for and in what context are they used? **(3, 4 and Tables III and IV)** (*C & G*)
4. The technology of computers is classified according to the generation to which they belong. Discuss. **(5–8)**
5. Define the term configuration. **(9)**
6. What is meant by the term virtual machine? **(10)**
7. Outline the make-up of a typical third generation batch processing computer. **(11)**

8. What are the essential requirements for a dispersed real-time configuration?   **(12)**

9. Define the characteristics of current mainframe technology. **(13–15)**

10. What are the general characteristics and functions of a processor?   **(16, 17)**

11. Describe briefly the functions of the control unit of a computer system.   **(18, 19)** (*C & G*)

12. What are the functions of the arithmetic/logic unit?   **(20, 21)**

13. Define the features of Boolean algebra on which computer logic is based.   **(22)**

14. What is a logic gate or logic circuit?   **(23)**

15. What is a truth table?   **(24)**

16. State the features and types of internal storage.   **(26–39)**

17. What is meant by the following terms: (*a*) ROM; (*b*) RAM;(*c*) bubble memory; (*d*) optical memory; and (*e*) cache memory? **(33–9)**

18. Define the terms PROM and EPROM.   **(35, 36)**

19. List the advantages and disadvantages of a computer. **(40, 41)**

CHAPTER III

Microcomputers in Business

GENERAL OUTLINE OF MICROCOMPUTERS

1. Definition. A microcomputer is a small computer consisting of a processor on a single silicon chip, which is mounted on a circuit board with other chips containing the computer's internal memory in the form of read only memory (ROM) and random access memory (RAM). It has a keyboard for the entry of data and instructions and a screen for display purposes. It has interfaces for the connection of peripherals in the form of plotters, printers, cassette units, disc drives, light pens, a mouse, paddles and joysticks, etc. It is interesting to note that the first computer cost in the region of one million pounds. Today, it is possible to obtain a microcomputer with greater reliability,thirty thousand times smaller with greater capacity and higher performance for around two hundred and fifty pounds.

2. Configurations. Microcomputers are manufactured in a number of different configurations according to the design requirements of a particular computer manufacturer. Basic configurations can be enhanced by add-on units such as printers and disc drives, as indicated above. Some are fully integrated units with a processor and memory, visual display unit (VDU), a keyboard, built-in cassette units and/or disc drives.

A microcomputer for business use would require backing storage devices and a printer, but it is possible to purchase only the basic unit for personal computing, for playing computer games or for mathematical, statistical and financial calculations, thereby saving the expense of purchasing discs and a printer. It may be impractical however, even for personal computing, to load programs, especially lengthy ones, through the keyboard each time they are to be run, in which case it would be advantageous to have at least a cassette unit (*see* Figs. 17–21).

3. Elemental structure of a microcomputer. A microcomputer including optional peripherals and other add-on units may consist

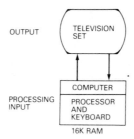

FIG. 17 *Basic personal microcomputer.*

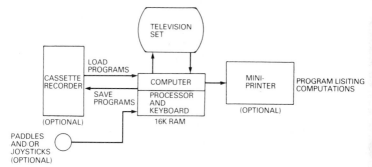

FIG. 18 *Basic personal microcomputer with optional add-on units.*

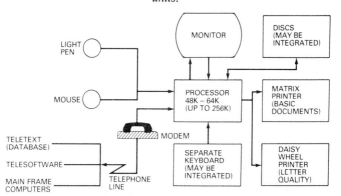

FIG. 19 *Microcomputer for business use facilitating data and word processing including graphics and communications.*

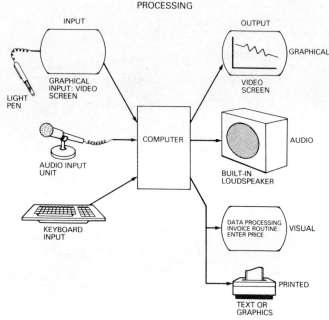

FIG. 20 *Relationship of input and output devices.*

of the elements listed below (*see* Figs. 20 and 21):

(*a*) 8,16 or 32-bit processor;

(*b*) internal memory 4K – 64K +;

(*c*) backing storage—cassette, floppy disc, microfloppy discs, microdrive, silicon disc or hard disc;

(*d*) keyboard and screen (input and output);

(*e*) interface (for the connection of peripherals);

(*f*) bus (communication and control channels) (*see* **14**);

(*g*) printer and/or plotter (multicolour text and graphics);

(*h*) pulse generator (clock);

(*i*) light pens, mouse, paddles/joysticks (graphics and games);

(*j*) software (programs).

Some small personal micros such as the Sinclair ZX81 have interfacing facilities which allow them to use a domestic television set as a video display screen instead of using a monitor or built-in VDU. For this purpose it is necessary to tune the television to the

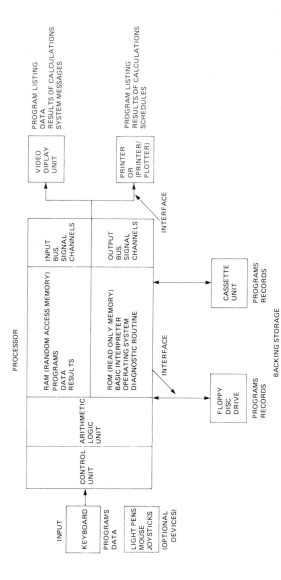

FIG. 21 *Microcomputer configuration for business applications.*

frequency of the computer by using a channel not used for domestic viewing. Audio cassette units, i.e. those used for playing music in the hi-fi can be used for backing storage requirements to store programs, etc. This type of computer may have a memory capacity of 1K or 4K which is smaller than that required for business use, as business programs tend to be rather lengthy compared with some games programs, but then, there are also lengthy games programs. Some of the very small micros are more suitable for the hobbyist as they are only capable of being programmed in machine code as opposed to BASIC, Forth or Pascal—the high-level languages used on microcomputers.

4. Microcomputer business applications. In general, business orientated microcomputers are used for similar applications in the smaller business as mini and mainframe computers are used for in the larger business. The typical business applications include payroll processing, stock control, purchase accounting, invoicing and sales ledger and general ledger.

Ambitious accountants keen to get "to grips" with the ramifications of programming may "try their hand" at accounting type problems. In general, it is economically justifiable to install a micro wherever it may be usefully employed in the business without having to go to the lengths of capital investment approvals.

The various ways in which a microcomputer will be utilised in an organisation will vary according to the nature of the business, its organisation, management style, geographical dispersion of operating units and the incidence of data processing and computing in the business. The list which follows is an indication of the various ways in which micros may be used:

(*a*) predominantly as a means of processing business data;

(*b*) for solving statistical, mathematical and engineering problems and for data analysis in a "computing" rather than a "data processing" role;

(*c*) as an aid to business and accounting problem solving in such areas as simulation, discounted cash flow, investment appraisal, linear programming and other financial modelling areas such as projected profit and loss accounts and break-even models perhaps using spreadsheet programs;

(*d*) stand alone machines distributed throughout the organisation;

(*e*) dedicated machines for specific tasks;

(*f*) microcomputer networks both in the classroom and business office for intercommunication and sharing common resources such as Winchester discs and high speed printers;

(*g*) portable microcomputers can be used by travelling representatives and engineers for performing computing whilst in a hotel room, for instance.

THE MICROPROCESSOR

5. Microprocessor defined. The microprocessor is that part of a microcomputer which contains the circuitry for performing arithmetic and logic operations, usually contained on a single silicon chip. It also interprets and executes instructions. It is the equivalent of the central processing unit of a mainframe computer.

6. Silicon chip. A small piece of silicon containing a completely unpackaged semiconductor device, i.e. a transistor, diode or integrated circuit (IC). Due to technological developments it is now possible to have many thousands of transistors and diodes on a single chip of silicon with dimensions of not more than five mm square. This is largely due to the development of photolithographic techniques capable of forming transistors and their interconnecting circuits on a very small scale generating VLSI (Very Large Scale Integration). A silicon chip is produced by creating microscopic layers of metal and component material on a silicon wafer using successive photolithographic masks to obtain the required electronic components and the relevant microcircuits. A chip is encapsulated in a ceramic cover which has a number of connector pins for mounting on a printed circuit board (*see* Fig. 22). Chips are produced from a wafer which is a circular slice of semiconductor material cut from a single crystal of silicon. The slice is exposed to steam to form an oxide film on its surface. The slice is then treated

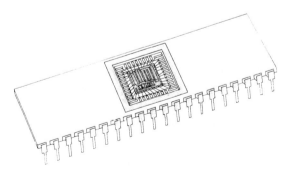

FIG. 22 *Microprocessor chip.*

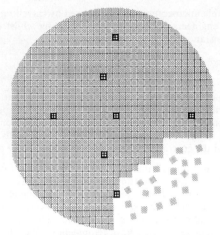

FIG. 23 *Wafer.*

by a photoengraving/diffusion/oxidisation process to form the circuits of the processor. The slice is then cut into many individual chips (*see* Fig. 23).

7. Microprocessor applications. Microprocessors are not unique to microcomputers as they have many and varied potential and actual applications including:

(*a*) monitoring laboratory experiments;

(*b*) controlling continuous processes such as chemicals and petrol refining;

(*c*) the heart of a word processor used for text processing in the office;

(*d*) banking terminals;

(*e*) point-of-sale terminals;

(*f*) controlling petrol consumption in a motor car;

(*g*) control of a fully automatic electric cooker;

(*h*) basic unit in pocket calculators and digital watches.

8. 8, 16 and 32-bit processors. Two microprocessor chips predominate; these are the MOS Technology 6502 and the Zilog Z80. The 6502 is widely used in personal computers such as the PET, Apple and Atari. CP/M is not available on the 6502 but CP/M adaptors are available, i.e. Softbox for the PET and Soft-card for the Apple. The Zilog Z80 is used on Tandy and Sinclair micros and the Sharp MZ-80 as well as many others. It incorporates the instruction set of Intel's 8080 and provides a faster processor.

Whereas an 8-bit processor can process an 8 digit binary number at one time, a 16-bit processor can handle numbers of 16 digits in length. This increases the power of the 16-bit machine compared with that of the 8-bit computer. This appears as if a 16-bit machine is in the region of being twice as fast but this is not so due to the variation in the speed of the pulse generator, known as the clock. An 8-bit processor runs at 2 MHz or 4MHz whereas the IBM personal computer operates at 5 MHz. This implies that a 16-bit, 5 MHz processor has the edge over an 8-bit, 2 MHz processor to the extent of being five times faster, i.e. two and a half times as fast due to the speed of the pulse generator and being twice as fast in the handling of numbers, therefore $2\frac{1}{2} \times 2 = 5$. This is influenced by the number of channels on the data bus; some chips have eight channels others have sixteen. If the bus has eight channels it can only handle 16-bit numbers in two stages but a 16-channel data bus can deal with a 16-bit number in its entirety at the same time, i.e. as a single unit of data.

The address bus of most 8-bit processors is sixteen channels or bits wide which implies that it addresses each memory location with a sixteen digit binary number up to 65 536 which is the highest number possible from the combinations of sixteen bits, i.e. $2^{16} = 65 536$ or 64K bytes which signifies the maximum memory capacity possible from an address bus of sixteen channels.

A 16-bit processor such as the 8088 has a 20-bit address bus which determines its memory capacity. In this instance, the maximum memory capacity is established from the various combinations of 20 bits which are possible, this is $2^{20} = 1 048 576$ or one megabyte. A 16-bit processor chip is constrained however, as it has to slow down its speed of operation to contend with the slower speed of input and output transfers via its connector pins.

Zilog is developing a chip, the Z800, which is a very fast 8-bit processor which means that computers based on this chip will be faster than those using the current Z80 chip. This may mean that some users will have ample power for their needs without upgrading to a 16-bit micro.

At the other end of the scale 32-bit machines will be becoming available which means that this new breed will be as powerful as earlier mainframes such as the IBM 360 series which have a 32-bit unit of storage. The main difference will no doubt be a reduction in physical size compared to that of the mainframe, but not in the level of power which will be phenomenal.

In conclusion it would seem that the main benefits to be obtained from the 16- and 32-bit processors lie in their ability to process bigger numbers, to perform computing at a higher speed, a greater internal memory capacity and faster output.

9. Chip and bit slice microprocessors. In respect of chip slice microprocessor the functions of a microprocessor chip can be implemented on several chip slices for improving performance by overcoming the limitations of a single microprocessor. A bit slice microprocessor is a semiconductor component which is effectively a high-speed, limited-function microprocessor. Some control systems are too complex for a single microprocessor and to overcome this a bit slice microprocessor system is used whereby the codes on the data bus are broken into slices each having the same number of bits, i.e. 16 bits into 4 slices of 4 bits. Each of the slices is then processed in separate processors.

GENERAL CONSIDERATIONS

10. Internal memory. The internal memory of all computers is based on the same technology but the capacity and speed of operation vary according to the type of computer. The main types of memory used on microcomputers are ROM, RAM and Bubble memory (*see* II, **27**).

11. Backing storage. This topic has been dealt with in detail in IX. However, for clarity Table V may assist the reader in identifying the type of backing storage used on microcomputers:

TABLE V. MICROCOMPUTER BACKING STORAGE

Type	*Form/usage*
Disc drive	8″ (200 mm) floppy disc
	5¼″ (133 mm) mini-floppy disc
	(*see* Fig. 24)
Micro-floppy disc drive	3½″ (88,67 mm) micro-floppy disc
Microdrive (Sony)	3½″ (88.67 mm) micro-floppy disc
Microdrive (Sinclair)	Tape cartridge
Hard discs	Winchester
RAM card-silicon disc	Use of a RAM card as if it were a disc
Disc drive and personality module	Avoids changing disc drives when changing to a different computer
Cassette recorder	Cassette tape (*see* Fig. 25)

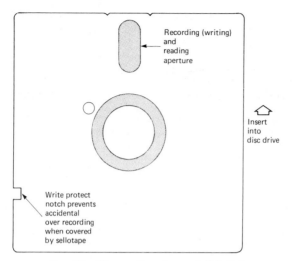

FIG. 24 *Floppy disc storage (diskette).*

FIG. 25 *Cassette storage.*

12. Software. Software is used on all computers but the nature of the software varies according to the type of computer. Whether it is a micro, mini or mainframe also has a bearing on the internal memory capacity and reflects on the complexity of the software used. The larger the memory then the more complex the software which can be used. The higher the resolution of a computer the more powerful the graphics which may be applied to a specific machine. In general, software is available for micros in the following categories: games, education, business applications, statistics, graphics, databases, electronic diary, electronic spreadsheet for business planning, disassemblers, word processing and toolkits, etc. This topic has been dealt with at length in XXI.

INTERFACE AND BUS

13. Interface. An interface is the interconnecting device between various elements of a system. The most usual type of interface in a computing system is a plug, socket and cable. The interface between a processor and its peripheral devices, i.e. the cassette recorder, disc unit and printer, is the cable which connects them together. The cable enables information to be transmitted from one to the other. Special types of connector are used for connecting peripherals.

14. Bus. A bus is used as a means of interconnecting all the circuit boards of a computer system to provide communication channels for handling input and output transfers to and from memory and other peripheral devices. The channels consist of a control bus, data bus, address bus and peripheral bus. A typical microprocessor has eight data lines, sixteen address lines and several control lines.

The address channels are connected to the internal memory, the data channels to memory and input/output ports. When it is necessary to transfer data in the processor the CPU sets up the address of the memory location where the data is stored on the address channels. A WRITE command on a control channel generates the data on a data channel. The data may then be output to a peripheral device by a peripheral channel.

KEYBOARDS

15. General outline. Some micros have an ASCII, i.e. QWERTY type standard typewriter keyboard with a full range of characters. Others have a flat-type keyboard with non-moving keys such as those on the Sinclair ZX81 which has touch-sensitive keys. The number of keys varies on some computers which is a measure of the versatility of particular machines, as the greater the number of keys the greater the flexibility of operation. With a limited number of keys, such as the ZX81, a single key has to perform more functions, in combination with SHIFT keys, which can become confusing. When there are more keys on the keyboard they need only perform one or two functions which leads to less complexity in use.

The keyboard is sometimes integrated with the computer but

some computers have separate keyboards which have to be interfaced. Some micros have keyboards with separate numeric keypads which facilitates the high speed entry of numeric data. Some keyboards have graphic keys which can be accessed with a SHIFT key which allows graphic characters to be displayed on the screen or built into a computer program direct from the keyboard. Some keyboards have automatic repeat on all keys.

16. Function keys. These keys allow the user to perform specific tasks such as BREAKing the running of a program, or CONTinuing the running of a program, after it has been interrupted for some reason. Cursor control keys have arrows on them, in some cases, for moving the cursor to specific positions on the screen for editing, to INSERT/DELETE characters in a statement, for instance. Other keyboards do not have arrow keys so cursor control has to be accomplished by the use of other keys in combination with ESCape keys as on the Apple II.

17. Single key keyword keyboards. This type of keyboard has facilities for inputting BASIC commands such as PRINT, POKE, INPUT, RETURN, CLS, NEW and SAVE by a single key depression rather than typing out the word in full, character by character. This is a feature of the ZX81 and Spectrum.

18. Shift keys. These enable particular keys to be used for different characters in accordance with the characters and functions which have been assigned to them. This extends the flexibility of a keyboard without having to increase the number of keys unnecessarily.

19. Add-on keyboards. Add-on keyboards are available from suppliers of computer equipment which are aimed at improving the keyboards of those micros which do not have a full typewriter keyboard; the ZX81, for instance.

20. User definable keys. Some computers, such as the VIC-20, have keys which are not defined for any specific use when the computer is switched on, but the user may assign any BASIC command or instruction to them under program control. If the keys are SHIFTed it doubles the number of user definable keys, say from four to eight (*see* Fig. 26).

SOUND GENERATION

21. Sound effects. Some computers, the ORIC-I and Atmos, the VIC-20 and the Sinclair Spectrum, amongst others, have sound

(Courtesy ACT (UK) Limited)

FIG. 26   *Keyboard of Apricot computer.*

effects for making games more realistic and for representing music so that it is possible to compose passages of music on very inexpensive computers. The sounds available on the ORIC-I, for instance, include SHOOT, EXPLODE, PING and ZAP. The Spectrum has a sound-BEEP command with variable pitch and duration.

22. Loudspeaker and sound synthesiser. Computers are equipped with loudspeakers and sound synthesising circuits for producing sound effects some of which produce sound over six octaves.

23. Envelope. This is a term associated with the sound generating facilities of a microcomputer. An envelope command is used to construct different sounds by varying pitch and amplitude envelopes. The variations are determined by parameters. The way in which sound starts, continues and stops is referred to as the envelope. Different musical instruments have their own characteristics and for their sound to be simulated by the computer it is necessary to define appropriate envelopes.

24. White noise. This is a "hissing" noise produced by a microcomputer's sound generator which is derived by mixing a note of every pitch. This may be compared with the composition of white light which consists of a mixture of light of every colour.

CLOCK

25. Pulse generator. A processor has an electronic pulse generator, known as a clock, which transmits synchronised streams of pulses to specific parts of the computer for the interpretation and execution of instructions according to requirements. Everything that happens in a computer is under strict control of the clock.

26. Different speeds. The various computers have clocks which operate at different speeds which is one of the features which must be established when selecting a computer for a given task. A faster clock achieves faster processing, e.g. a 2 MHz (megahertz) computer will operate at twice the speed of a 1 MHz machine.

CHARACTER SET

27. Range of characters. The term character set is used to define the range of characters which can be displayed by a computer. The type of characters include alphabetic, i.e. letters, numeric, i.e. numbers which are usually referred to as digits, punctuation symbols, i.e. special characters, and graphical characters for generating pictures, etc.

Some computers have both upper case, i.e. capital letters, and lower case, i.e. small letters, whereas others have only upper case. The shape of some characters can be altered by the user which allows different typefaces to be used.

The ORIC-I computer, for instance, provides a choice of a full ASCII keyboard or Teletext (Ceefax/Oracle) Alpha Mosaic graphics and the ability for the user to create up to eighty characters. It can also produce double height characters and cause characters to flash on and off approximately twice per second.

28. Character generator. Characters are generated in a computer system by hardware or software facilities which convert binary code into alphabetic, numeric and graphical symbols on the screen and printer (*see* **29-34**). Some computers allow the user to define his own characters, for example, when the ORIC computer is switched on both the standard and alternate character sets are loaded into RAM. It is possible to redefine standard characters, particularly those used infrequently, into those required for a particular purpose. To access the contents of a memory location a PEEK command is used. The contents can be changed by a series of POKE commands, POKEing specific binary codes into specific RAM locations. When the standard key is pressed on the keyboard it will be displayed as the redefined character.

DISPLAY CODE AND DISPLAY SCREEN

29. Character set. All computers have a character set known as a display code which is specific to that particular micro as all micros

Code	Symbol	Code	Symbol	Code	Symbol	Code	Symbol	Code	Symbol	Code	Symbol	Code	Symbol	Code	Symbol
0	SP	32	0	64	SP	96	▨	128	SP	160	▨	192	▨	224	▨
1	A	33	1	65	▨	97	▨	129	a	161	▨	193	▨	225	▨
2	B	34	2	66	▨	98	▨	130	b	162	▨	194	▨	226	▨
3	C	35	3	67	▨	99	▨	131	c	163	▨	195	▨	227	▨
4	D	36	4	68	▨	100	S	132	d	164	▨	196	▨	228	▨
5	E	37	5	69	▨	101	%	133	e	165	▨	197	▨	229	▨
6	F	38	6	70	▨	102	&	134	f	166	▨	198	▨	230	▨
7	G	39	7	71	▨	103	▨	135	g	167	▨	199	▨	231	▨
8	H	40	8	72	▨	104	(	136	h	168	▨	200	▨	232	▨
9	I	41	9	73	?	105	)	137	i	169	▨	201	▨	233	▨
10	J	42	▨	74	▨	106	+	138	j	170	β	202	▨	234	▨
11	K	43	▨	75	▨	107	✳	139	k	171	ü	203	▨	235	▨
12	L	44	▨	76	▨	108	▨	140	l	172	ö	204	▨	236	▨
13	M	45	/	77	▨	109	X	141	m	173	Ü	205	¥	237	▨
14	N	46	▨	78	▨	110	▨	142	n	174	Ä	206	▨	238	▨
15	O	47	▨	79	▨	111	▨	143	o	175	Ö	207	▨	239	▨
16	P	48	▨	80	↑	112	▨	144	p	176	▨	208	▨	240	SP
17	Q	49	▨	81	◀	113	▨	145	q	177	▨	209	▨	241	▨
18	R	50	▨	82	▨	114	▨	146	r	178	▨	210	▨	242	▨
19	S	51	▨	83	♥	115	▨	147	s	179	▨	211	▨	243	▨
20	T	52	▨	84	▨	116	▨	148	t	180	▨	212	▨	244	▨
21	U	53	▨	85	@	117	▨	149	u	181	▨	213	▨	245	▨
22	V	54	▨	86	▨	118	▨	150	v	182	▨	214	▨	246	▨
23	W	55	▨	87	▶	119	▨	151	w	183	▨	215	▨	247	▨
24	X	56	▨	88	↓	120	▨	152	x	184	▨	216	▨	248	▨
25	Y	57	▨	89	▨	121	▨	153	y	185	▨	217	▨	249	▨
26	Z	58	▨	90	→	122	▨	154	z	186	▨	218	▨	250	▨
27	▨	59	▨	91	▨	123	▨	155	ä	187	▨	219	▨	251	▨
28	▨	60	▨	92	▨	124	▨	156	▨	188	▨	220	▨	252	▨
29	▨	61	▨	93	▨	125	▨	157	▨	189	▨	221	▨	253	▨
30	▨	62	▨	94	▨	126	▨	158	▨	190	▨	222	▨	254	▨
31	▨	63	▨	95	▨	127	▨	159	▨	191	○	223	▨	255	▨

Note: SP represents a space or blank.

(Courtesy Sharp Electronics)

FIG. 27 *MZ-80K display code table. The code is based on the decimal system.*

```
10 PRINT " C "
20 FOR J = 0 TO 255
30 FOR I = 53248 TO 54247
40 POKE I,J
50 NEXT I
60 NEXT J
```

FIG. 28 *Program for displaying Sharp MZ-80K display code.*

do not have the same character set—alphabetic characters and numeric characters are very similar but they will no doubt have different display codes. The graphical characters are likely to differ on the various computers available as well as the display codes. The manual of the particular machine is therefore essential. It is possible to access the display code of a particular computer by a simple program containing the video RAM visible locations.

Microcomputers usually have 256 characters in their repertoire, i.e. display codes 0-255. The characters are coded in various combinations of BINARY DIGITS, i.e. BITS on the basis of the BINARY CODE. The binary code is based on the eight bits of a BYTE, which is another name for character, from which 256 bit combinations are possible, i.e. 2^8. The display code can be accessed on an individual character basis by POKEing the appropriate display code, or the whole of the display code can be displayed for interest. How this is accomplished will now be demonstrated for various microcomputers. Some computers use ASCII. *see* II, **3** (*see* Figs. 27 and 28).

30. General outline of display screen. Some microcomputers have a built-in screen, many of which typically display twenty-five lines of forty characters. Others have a built-in line display using LEDs (Light Emitting Diodes) or LCDs (Liquid Crystal Displays) instead of a built-in screen. This is a feature of some portable micros such as the Newbrain and Apricot.

Some micros have connected a monitor (screen) of the user's choice. A monitor is similar to a TV set without a modulator and has a direct video entry connection. Other micros can be connected to the aerial socket of an ordinary television set. It is possible to purchase secondhand colour TV sets for about £40 which can save considerable expense, assuming of course that it is reliable. Other micros have tinted, monochrome (black and white) or colour displays according to the particular computer. The screen displays program statements, data, commands, syntax errors and other system messages.

31. Use of the cursor. A cursor is a moving spot on a video screen which indicates the next position for entering characters. Sometimes a winking cursor is used which is useful for drawing attention to a specific element of data or part of the screen in use. The cursor can be programmed on some micros and is very useful for editing purposes.

32. Highlighting. It is sometimes possible and useful to HIGHLIGHT details on the screen by making them more prominent by making them flash or reversing them (reverse video) so that they become for example white on black instead of black on white. Colour computers allow displays to be in the colours the machine is designed to generate. The Commodore VIC-20 for instance, allows the user to change the colours of the characters entered by the keyboard by pressing the CTRL key and one of the eight colour/number keys. The colours are black, white, red, cyan, purple, green, blue and yellow. The colours can be set and changed within or outside a computer program.

33. Windows. The screen can be sectionalised so that different segments of the screen become in effect several separate small screens which are known as windows. In some data management systems windows are used for the displays of documents for editing and entry purposes.

34. Visual video RAM. The visual segment of the video RAM area of the internal memory, i.e. random access memory (RAM) allows display codes to be POKEd into the memory which are automatically displayed on the screen, Graphical displays on the screen for storage location outside the visible part of video RAM can be obtained by a PRINT PEEK command. Graphic characters in the form of space invaders can be made to move on the screen by appropriate statements.

FOURTH GENERATION MICROCOMPUTERS: THE ACT APRICOT

Microcomputer architecture has advanced from the early 8-bit second generation, through the 16-bit third generation, to the current fourth generation technology. The ACT Apricot (*see* Fig. 29) will here be used as an example to demonstrate the characteristics and features of a fourth generation microcomputer. It is illustrative of the technology of the more sophisticated computers available for use as small business systems.

(Courtesy ACT (UK) Limited)

FIG. 29 *Apricot computer.*

35. Characteristics and features.

(*a*) A "mouse" (See VI, **20**) can be used as a pointing device and for cursor control (thus eliminating the need to use a keyboard).

(*b*) Microscreen feature (*see* **37**).

(*c*) Multiprocessor architecture: Intel 8086 CPU; Intel 8089 input/output processor to handle disc drives and communications; and optional Intel 8087 mathematics processor.

(*d*) Built-in electronic desk top functions using icons (*see* XXIII, **8–12**).

(*e*) Built-in digital calendar and clock displayed on the microscreen (*see* **37**).

(*f*) Built-in auto dial/auto answer modem option for connection to electronic mail services and access to public databases.

(*g*) $3\frac{1}{2}$ inch disc technology: one or two $3\frac{1}{2}$ inch (88.67mm) Sony microdrives of 315K bytes capacity per drive. (Double sided $3\frac{1}{2}$ inch (88.67mm) microfloppy drives of 720K bytes storage capacity per drive are due for release in 1984.)

(*h*) Ergonomically designed.

(*i*) Portability—the computer can be as mobile as any executive.

(*j*) Multi-function keyboard (*see* **36**).

(*k*) 256K bytes RAM as standard—expandable to 768K bytes.

(*l*) RS232 serial port for synchronous and asynchronous communications.

(*m*) Standard Centronics parallel bi-directional port.

(*n*) Expansion slots.

(*o*) Monitor tilts, swivels and slides to suit the requirements of the individual.

(*p*) Can operate as a workstation on a local area network.

(*q*) Display uses a 9 inch green phosphor screen with anti-glare optical filter which can display 80 characters × 25 lines or 132 characters × 50 lines, or high resolution graphics of 800 × 400 pixels.

(*r*) Future developments will include integrated telephone, voice recognition and internal Winchester drives.

36. General features of keyboard. The keyboard of the Apricot has ninety keys. An electronic keyclick is produced by a built-in sound generator each time a key is pressed. There are eight fixed-function keys corresponding to the major functions inherent in all applications software including HELP, PRINT and MENU. There is also a full suite of text editing keys and a numeric key pad which includes standard calculator key instructions. The keyboard also has a built-in "mouse trap", a fast serial port designed to connect a cursor control mouse device for making selections on the screen. The keyboard is detachable, has a low profile and an alphanumeric layout to international standards (*see* Fig. 26).

37. Microscreen. On the ACT Apricot this is a two-line Liquid Crystal Display (LCD) and six touch-sensitive keys. It displays the day, date and time as soon as the system is powered up. Pressing the calculator key converts it into a powerful calculator without the need to load a disc. It provides dynamic labelling of the touch-sensitive keys within an application and an entry line for information, ensuring that the user is not constantly switching vision from screen to keyboard and back again. It acts as a window on the screen, displaying a line at a time, allowing the system to be used without a full monitor (thus enhancing its portability).The Sharp PC5000 uses a "flip-up" eighty column LCD screen, and the NEC

8201 and Tandy model 100 have built-in forty column LCD screens above their keyboards. The Newbrain is another machine which has an LCD display.

38. Software and programming languages. A three dimensional advanced management software suite integrates calculation facilities, text processing and a relational database. Three operating systems are included as standard, these are MS-DOS 2.0, CP/M-86 and concurrent CP/M. (BOS system and UCSD p system are also available.)

Over one thousand packages, i.e. application programs, are designed to run on Apricot which is also Sirius and IBM compatible. Full utilities include character font generator, disc copy routines, graphics applications and a communications package. The Apricot runs on MicroSoft BASIC and Digital Research Personal BASIC. The leading compiled languages are also available including C, Pascal, BASIC, Fortran and COBOL.

NCR TOWER 1632 COMPUTER

39. General characteristics. A 16-bit computer with the power and performance of a minicomputer based on the Motorola 68000 processor chip. The operating system is derived from UNIX of Bell Laboratories for maximisation of software portability and compatibility. Supports COBOL, BASIC, Fortran, C and Pascal.

The Tower (*see* Fig. 30) is very compact and fits alongside an office desk and needs no special power supply or air conditioning. It functions in multi-user, multi-task environments. The processor supports up to sixteen users each performing multiple functions. In addition to data processing it has facilities for communications and electronic mail. Future developments are to include colour graphics and word processing.

40. Configuration. The NCR Tower 1632 configuration is as outlined below:

(*a*) Processor (*see* **39**).

(*b*) Memory capacity: 512K bytes up to 2 million bytes of main memory in increments of 256K

(*c*) Detached keyboard.

(*d*) Display screen.

(*e*) Disc: $5\frac{1}{4}$ inch (133mm) floppy with a capacity of 1MB and up to 60 million bytes of $5\frac{1}{4}$ inch (133mm) Winchester disc storage in the main unit. An expansion cabinet can contain additional 84 MB drives and a streaming tape drive for back-up.

(*f*) Printer.

(Courtesy NCR Limited)

FIG. 30   *NCR Tower 1632 computer system.*

IBM PC

41. General characteristics. A personal computer system for producing charts, graphs, text, designs and processing data. It has a 16-bit 8088 processor and functions under the control of CP/M and MS-DOS operating systems. It has a built-in BASIC interpreter and supports other languages such as COBOL, C, Pascal and Fortran. It has networking capability.

42. Configuration. The IBM PC (*see* Fig. 8) configuration is as outlined below:

(*a*) Processor (*see* **41**).

(*b*) Memory capacity 64KB standard expandable to 576KB.

(*c*) Detached keyboard.

(*d*) Twelve inch display screen with a capacity of 25 rows of 80 characters; green screen but colour optional; resolution of graphics 640 × 200 pixels.

(*e*) Disc: $5\frac{1}{4}$ inch (133mm) floppy with a capacity of 160KB per side up to 640KB with two optional double-sided discs; hard disc options 5,10 or 20KB capacity.

(*f*) Bi-directional dot matrix graphics printer up to 132 characters per line.

(*g*) Provision for cassette unit.

43. Software. IBM has brought out its own general accounting package for the PC which can accommodate up to one thousand accounts. It prints cheques, generates balance sheets, profit and loss accounts and VAT returns.

The Lotus 1-2-3 spreadsheet modelling package seems to be highly favoured. It comes with a number of diskettes (floppy discs) to go on the IBM PC with 320KB of memory and a special circuit board to facilitate the colour graphics. The advantages of the 1-2-3 are that it is flexible, provides explanations on the screen, the training and learning curve is reduced and it has more features than exisiting packages.

NCR DECISION MATE V PERSONAL COMPUTER

44. General characteristics. A single station, personal computer system for the business professional, spanning the processing spectrum from an 8-bit single processor to a dual 8/16-bit processor. The 8-bit processor is a Z-80A and operates under the control of the CP/M80 operating system. The 16-bit processor is an 8088 chip which functions under various operating systems, i.e. CP/M80, CP/M86 or the MS-DOS. These industry standard operating systems support BASIC, COBOL and Pascal. Capable of supporting up to sixty four devices and remote batch communications to a mainframe. Software includes colour business graphics, financial planning, data processing and electronic mail. It also has networking capabilities.

45. Configuration. The Decision Mate V configuration (*see* Figs. 31 and 32) is as outlined below:

(*a*) Processor (*see* **44**).

(*b*) Memory capacity 64KB up to 512KB.

(*c*) Detached keyboard.

(*d*) Twelve inch, high-resolution monochrome or colour video display for colour graphics—screen capacity 25 rows of 80 characters with a resolution of 640 × 400 Pixels.

(*e*) Dual $5\frac{1}{4}$ inch (133mm) floppy discs of 500KB capacity each (unformatted) or 320KB each (formatted) (*see* VII, **26**).

(*f*) 10MB Winchester disc can be substituted for one floppy disc; capacity up to 96MB of Winchester disc.

(*g*) Printer.

PROGRESS TEST 3

1. What is a microcomputer? Describe an application of a microcomputer in a small business environment. Indicate the configuration necessary to perform this application. (**1–4, 35–45**) (*C & G*)

2. Describe in detail the hardware characteristics of a typical

(Courtesy NCR Limited)

FIG. 31 *NCR Decision Mate V Personal Computer system.*

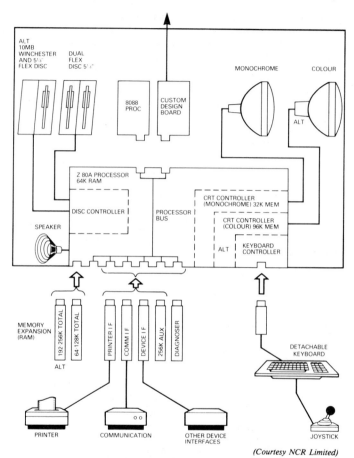

FIG. 32 *NCR Decision Mate V.*

(Courtesy NCR Limited)

microcomputer system for use in small businesses. (**1, 2, 35–45**) (*ACA*)

3. Distinguish between a microprocessor and a microcomputer giving an example of the use of EACH. (**1, 4–7**) (*C & G*)

4. Outline the ways in which a microcomputer may be used in business. (**4**)

5. Specify the characteristics of a silicon chip. (**6**)

6. Describe applications for which a microprocessor is used. **(7)**

7. Discuss the characteristics of 8-, 16- and 32-bit processors. **(8)**

8. What are chip and bit slice microprocessors? **(9)**

9. Specify the nature of internal memory and backing storage used on microcomputers. **(10, 11)**

10. What types of software are available for microcomputers? **(12)**

11. What is an interface and bus? **(13, 14)**

12. Describe the characteristics of microcomputer keyboards. **(15–20)**

13. Define the term sound generation. **(21–24)**

14. What is a clock in the context of computers? **(25, 26)**

15. Define the terms: (*a*) character set; (*b*) character generator; and (*c*) display code and display screen. **(27–34)**

CHAPTER IV

Organisation of a Data Processing Department and a Management Services Department

ORGANISATION OF A DATA PROCESSING DEPARTMENT: BY FUNCTION OR ACTIVITY

1. Main sections and types of staff. The sectional organisation of a batch processing installation is shown in Fig. 33 and may be summarised as follows.

(*a*) Head of department—data processing manager:

(*i*) responsible to: director of adminstration, managing director or company secretary according to specific requirements;

(*ii*) immediate subordinates: chief systems analyst, chief programmer and operations manager.

(*b*) Chief systems analyst responsible for activities of systems analysts.

(*c*) Chief programmer responsible for activities of programmers.

(*d*) Operations manager responsible for activities of chief computer operator and all operators, data preparation supervisor, tape and disc librarian and data control supervisor.

2. Principal duties of data processing manager. The duties of a data processsing manager may be summarised in the following manner:

(*a*) interpretation and execution of data processing policy as defined by the data processing steering committee or Board of directors;

(*b*) controlling immediate subordinates in the attainment of project objectives;

(*c*) participation in policy formulation;

(*d*) liaison with user departments to ensure their interests are fully provided for;

(*e*) ensuring that company policy is adhered to;

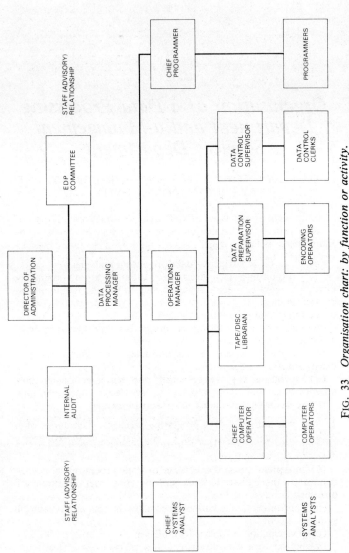

FIG. 33 *Organisation chart: by function or activity.*

(*f*) ensuring that computer operating instructions are updated when the need arises;

(*g*) assessing the effectiveness of the file maintenance procedures;

(*h*) assessing the suitability of file security procedures;

(*i*) ensuring that program modifications are applied effectively;

(*j*) monitoring test runs;

(*k*) post implementation evaluation;

(*l*) ensuring that staff attend suitable training courses for their development;

(*m*) assessing performance of staff for salary awards and promotion;

(*n*) coordinating the whole of the data processing operations and ensuring that work flows smoothly;

(*o*) resolving conflict between subordinates;

(*p*) providing guidance on data processing problems;

(*q*) development and implementation of data processing standards (*see* X, **33**).

3. Principal duties of chief systems analyst. The duties may be summarised as follows:

(*a*) liaison with user departments to ensure their requirements and problems are fully discussed before systems design and implementation;

(*b*) interpreting terms of reference before embarking upon systems investigations in order to establish the problem, areas of investigation and limits to the assignment;

(*c*) comparing the cost and performance of alternative processing methods and techniques;

(*d*) organising and coordinating the activities of systems analysts;

(*e*) reviewing performance of systems analysts;

(*f*) organising and reviewing systems documentation to ensure it complies with data processing standards;

(*g*) reviewing the progress of projects and reporting status to the data processing manager;

(*h*) presenting recommendations to data processing and user department management with regard to possible courses of action or design philosophy to achieve defined objectives;

(*i*) coordinating the implementation of new or modified systems.

(*j*) reviewing performance of implemented systems and assessing the need for amendments or additional training of staff;

(*k*) discussion of proposals with chief programmer.

4. Principal duties of chief programmer. These are summarised below:

(*a*) liasion with chief systems analyst to determine philosophy of proposed systems and establish the type of programming language to use—high level or assembly code (low level);

(*b*) review of systems specification to establish the details of systems requirements before discussing these with assigned programmers;

(*c*) defining test data requirements and monitoring test runs;

(*d*) reviewing programmers' performance;

(*e*) reporting status of program development to data processing manager.

5. Principal duties of operations manager. These are summarised as follows:

(*a*) control of all sections for which he is responsible, i.e. computer operations, data preparation and data control;

(*b*) development of operating schedules for all jobs to be run on the computer;

(*c*) ensuring that data is received on time from user departments;

(*d*) maintaining records on equipment utilisation;

(*e*) implementing standard procedures when appropriate to improve efficiency;

(*f*) controlling stocks of data processing supplies, tapes, stationery and discs, etc;

(*g*) maintaining a log of computer operations;

(*h*) report to data processing manager of situations such as hardware malfunctions, staffing problems and other operational matters.

ORGANISATION OF A DATA PROCESSING DEPARTMENT: BY PURPOSE

6. Structure of activities. It is sometimes found that a computer department is organised by "purpose" (*see* Fig. 34) rather than by "function" or "activity" as shown on Fig.33. In this type of structure the various activities are grouped together to achieve a defined purpose. In the case of a computer department the "purpose" may be multifold, i.e. to develop several systems for computerisation concurrently, in which case programmers and analysts would be combined into a project team for each project undertaken reporting to team leaders.

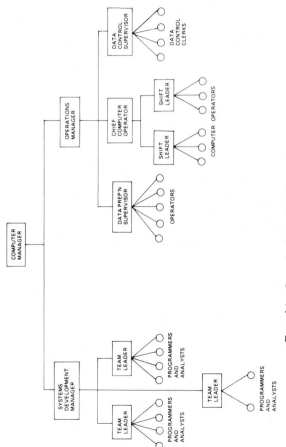

FIG. 34 *Organisation chart: by purpose.*

7. Examination question. The following question relating to this topic was set in an ACA paper.

ABC Ltd's computer department contains 35 members of staff, including the computer manager. Analysts and programmers work together in project teams under team leaders.
Required:

(*a*) Draft what in your opinion would be a typical organisation chart for this computer department. The distribution of staff should be clearly shown.

(*b*) Identify the principal responsibilities of the operations manager in a computer department.

The solution to part (*a*) is shown in Fig. 34 and the solution to part (*b*) is outlined above (*see* **5**).

ORGANISATION OF A MANAGEMENT SERVICES DEPARTMENT

8. General background. Some organisations, especially the larger ones, may structure management services (*see* Fig. 35) as a separate department or division incorporating operations research, data processing, work study and organisation and methods. Each of these disciplines would be under the control of a specialist manager reporting to a common superior, the manager of management services, or, in a very large combine, the director of group management services.

This form of structure recognises the importance of coordinating the interdisciplinary services at a high level in the organisation in order to gain the maximum benefit, for the corporate entity as a whole, by a planned use of skilled resources to optimise their use.

Requests for specific services from the different functions of the business would be channelled through a projects committee, in some instances, or directly through the management services manager in others.

9. Job specification—management services manager.

(*a*) Responsible to: managing director or director of group management services;

(*b*) Subordinates:
    (*i*) work study manager;
   (*ii*) operations research manager;
  (*iii*) data processing manager;
  (*iv*) organisation and methods manager.

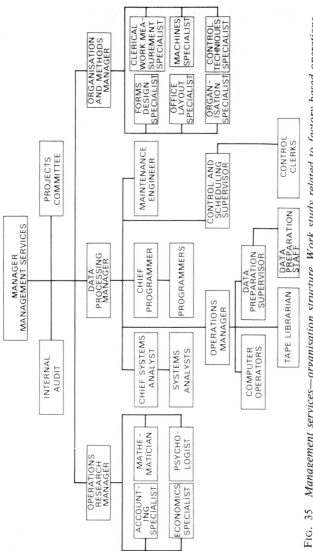

FIG. 35 *Management services—organisation structure. Work study related to factory-based operations may also be incorporated.*

(*c*) Functional relationships: all departmental managers.

(*d*) Responsible for:

    (*i*) coordinating all management services activities;

    (*ii*) recruiting and training staff;

    (*iii*) assessing performance of staff;

    (*iv*) ensuring staff keep up to date with management and problem solving techniques;

    (*v*) investigating problems throughout the organisation in respect of operations, computing, data processing and systems;

    (*vi*) allocating assignments to relevant subordinates;

    (*vii*) controlling the use of resources and time spent on projects;

    (*viii*) resolving conflicts between staff and functional departments;

    (*ix*) optimising use of equipment i.e. portable computers for capturing data relating to work study and operations research projects;

    (*x*) making recommendations to the board and advising functional departments of relevant courses of action in prescribed circumstances;

    (*xi*) monitoring performance of systems after new systems, methods or techniques have been implemented to ensure expected results are being achieved;

    (*xii*) authorising further study as necessary to remedy adverse situations.

(*e*) Limitations on authority: no direct authority over functional department staff unless specially delegated for a defined purpose. Direct authority only over management services personnel; otherwise advisory only.

PROGRESS TEST 4

1. Outline the main sections of a data processing department organised by function or activity. (**1**, Fig. 33)

2. (*a*) Draft the organisation chart of a computer department of forty staff. Your chart should show clearly how the staff are distributed in the department and any assumptions made must be stated. (*b*) Give a concise outline of the principal duties of a systems analyst during the life of a systems project.   (**1–5** and Fig. 33 provide guidance for part (*a*) of this question and XVI, **15** provides guidance for part (*b*)) (*ACA*)

3. Specify the principal duties of (*a*) a data processing manager;

(*b*) a chief system analyst; (*c*) a chief programmer; and (*d*) an operations manager. **(2,3,4,5)**

4. What are the responsibilities of the person in charge of a computer room? **(5)** (*C & G*)

5. State how you would organise a computer department by purpose. **(6, 7** and Fig. 34)

6. Outline the nature of a management services department. **(8)**

7. Your company has an organisation and methods section with five staff and a computer department with a total of thirty five staff (six systems analysts, eight programmers, fifteen staff engaged in data preparation and control and six operators). It has been decided to create a single management services department and to appoint a new manager. You are required to draft a job specification for the post of management services manager. **(9,** Fig. 35) (*ICMA*)

PART TWO

COMPUTER INPUT, OUTPUT, INFORMATION STORAGE AND RETRIEVAL, DATABASES AND BACKING STORAGE AND MEDIA

CHAPTER V

Computer Input

COMPUTER INPUT MEDIA AND DATA CAPTURE METHODS AND TECHNIQUES

1. General considerations. There exist many different ways in which data can be collected or captured for processing by computer. The specific method or media chosen for input depends on the type of computer configuration installed, which to some extent is dependent upon the nature of business operations. Some businesses require real-time systems for their effective operation, in which case data is input to the computer by on-line terminal. Other businesses, with less critical information requirements, have batch processing configurations using the long standing punched card or floppy disc for input, in order to optimise the speed of inputting batches of data, for processing the payroll or for producing invoices, etc. In this instance, direct entry by means of the keyboard of a terminal device or workstation may not be suitable—being too slow for the volume of data to be processed. Large computers in the past tended to use either punched card or paper tape input but this is being phased out for more specific methods in relation to the type of processing to be undertaken. The type of input selected also depends on the environment to which the data relates, which is why the "shop floor" in the factory sometimes has factory terminals installed at strategic locations or portable computers, for the collection of data relating to factory orders and other requirements (*see* **27, 31** and **32**). Supermarket check-out points need some speedy method of capturing data relating to the items sold as customers come to the check-out point to pay for the goods. Bar code scanning is widely used in this situation for speeding up the flow of customers and minimising the length of queue particularly at peak times.

It is unthinkable for banks to record every cheque transaction on a punched card with the many thousands of transactions which occur each day. Data would be punched into cards long after transactions had occurred and input bottlenecks would occur at an ever increasing velocity. For this reason, banks issue cheque books to customers with the cheques already encoded in magnetic ink characters.

2. Direct and indirect input. Input can broadly, but not precisely, be categorised, into two divisions: direct and indirect. The term "direct" should be interpreted to mean that data is in a form suitable for processing without the need for data conversion. Some systems have what may be called direct input media, such as optical marks on source documents but convert them into magnetic tape media prior to input to the computer. A typical example is the way in which meter readings are processed by electricity boards. Consumers' electricity usage is captured by having the meter read and by recording the reading in optical marks on a meter reading sheet. These sheets are read by an optical mark reader which transfers the data to a tape deck for recording the meter readings on magnetic tape. The details on the tape are then input for processing (*see* **20**). In this instance, the optical method is "indirect". It would be "direct" if the data was input into the computer without conversion. The same considerations apply to the use of Kimball tags as they are prepunched ready for input to the computer when transactions occur but the data they contain is usually converted to cassette tape prior to being input for processing. Such conversions are performed electronically and automatically and do not involve time consuming and costly puching and verifying operations, as is necesary for punched cards and paper tape. It is for this reason that punched cards and paper tape are being phased out in favour of more cost effective and efficient media methods.

Microcomputers often have input direct from the keyboard for transaction data but this depends upon the nature and size of the micro, as some are equipped with devices for graphical input such as light pens, a mouse or paddles/joysticks. A "mouse" is a small electronic device with one or two buttons on top and a ball bearing underneath which rolls on top of a desk. When the mouse is moved the cursor on the screen follows the direction of movement. This device allows the cursor to be moved to point at the required "icon". A click of a button selects this icon. This is a feature of electronic desktop display systems which will be discussed later (*see* XXIII, **8–12**).

Table VI summarises the various methods of input to a computer:

TABLE VI METHODS OF COLLECTING AND CAPTURING
DATA FOR COMPUTER INPUT

Method/mode	Media	Data preparation/ data capture device	Input device
Punched	Punched card	Card punch/ verifier	Card reader
	Prepunched card	Card punch/ verifier	Card reader
	Paper tape	Paper tape punch/verifier	Paper tape reader
	Prepunched tags (Kimball tags)	Tag punch	Tag reader
Magnetic	Magnetic tape (reel)	Encoder	Tape deck
	Magnetic tape (cassette) (Key-to-cassette)	Data entry terminal/ encoder	Cassette handler
	Floppy disc (key-to- diskette)	Encoding data station	Disc unit
	Exchangeable disc pack— exchangeable disc storage (EDS) (key-to- disc)	Key stations: VDU with keyboard	Magnetic disc data transferred to magnetic tape in some systems and input to computer is via a tape deck

Table Continued

TABLE VI Continued

Method/mode	Media	Data preparation/ data capture device	Input device
	Data transferred from punched cards to magnetic disc	Card reader/ disc drive Conversion by utility program Applicable for multi-programming operations	Disc drive
	Magnetically encoded characters: magnetic ink character recognition (MICR)	Characters printed when cheques are printed	Magnetic ink character reader/sorter
Handwritten, typed or printed optical characters	Documents prepared with optical characters: optical character recognition (OCR)	Hand, typewriter, line printer, cash register	Optical character reader
Handwritten optical marks	Documents prepared with optical marks: optical mark recognition (OMR)	Hand	Optical mark reader or Optical page reader
Handwritten normal characters	Pressure sensitive writing surface	Handprint data entry terminal	Handprint data entry terminal
Electronic sensing	Plastic card/ keyboard	Bank cash point terminal	Bank cash point terminal

Table Continued

TABLE VI *Continued*

Method/mode	Media	Data preparation/ data capture device	Input device
	Plastic badge— fixed data Prepunched card—fixed data Keyboard— variable data	Factory terminal	Factory terminal
	Graphical presentation of images on video screen	Light pen	Light pen/ computer
	Graphical input of images	Graphics tablet and stylus	Stylus/computer
Electronic scanning	Bar code/ optical characters printed on label	Retail terminal equipped with low-intensity laser scanner, light pens or slot scanners	Retail terminal or cassette handler
	Bar code labels	Portable computer equipped with bar code reading wand and keyboard	Portable computer
Audio	Human voice	Audio input unit	Audio input unit
Analogue	Electronic signals	Sensor	Digitiser
Digital	Electronic signals	Terminal keyboard	Terminal
	Electronic signals	Terminal keyboard	Intelligent terminal
	Electronic signals	Terminal keyboard	Workstation

Table Continued

TABLE VI *Continued*

Method/mode	Media	Data preparation/ data capture device	Input device
	Electronic signals	Paddles/ joysticks	Paddles/ joysticks/ computer
Electronic selection of icons	Electronic signals	Mouse	Mouse/ computer

PUNCHED INPUT: CARDS, TAGS AND PAPER TAPE

3. The 80-column punched card. The 80-column punched card is produced from a stiff, high-quality paper to avoid jamming in card reading equipment. Data is recorded on punched cards by means of holes forming the basis of a punched card code. This is sensed by a reading station in a card reader which converts the data to binary code when data is being transferred to the internal memory of a computer. However, as punched card input has been largely superseded by magnetic media (floppy discs and the like) it is not proposed to discuss this type of input further (*see* Figs. 36–8).

4. Prepunched cards. Prepunched cards are used to advantage in retail shoe shops as they can be prepunched with transaction data in advance of the transaction taking place. The data is immediately available for processing when the sale of shoes occurs. The cards are stored in shoe boxes containing the shoes to which the data on

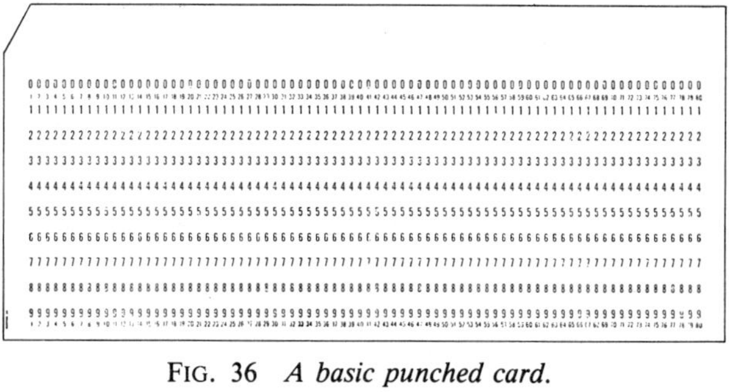

FIG. 36 *A basic punched card.*

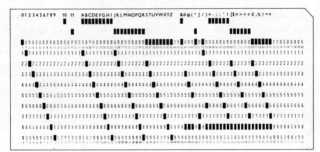

(Courtesy International Computers Limited)

FIG. 37   *A punched card showing ICL 64-character code.*

T	DATE			ORDER NUMBER	CUSTOMER NUMBER	COMMODITY CODE	TYPE CODE	QNTY
	DAY	MTH	YR					

| NUMBER OF DIGITS | 1 | 6 | | | 6 | 6 | 5 | 4 | 4 |

FIG. 38   *Sales order card.*

the card relates. When the shoes are sold the card is removed from the box and is subsequently processed for updating the stock status on the information file.

Prepunched cards are also used in the factory environment in conjunction with factory terminals. The cards contain fixed data relating to specific orders passing through the factory including the works order number, operation number and description, and machine to be used and the quantity to be produced. The cards are inserted in the terminal's card reader to transfer the details of operations completed to the computer (*see* **27**).

5. Kimball tags. Kimball tags are special types of price tag used in retailing which contain printed and punched or magnetically encoded information (*see* Fig. 39).

Tags are used to improve the control of merchandising by means of automated tag systems which provide automatic facilities for printing and punching information into tags. The tags are then attached to the appropriate merchandise ready for sale. When the merchandise is sold, the tags are removed and the information they contain is converted into paper tape for processing by electronic computer.

A system is also available for recording information contained in tags to magnetic tape in cassettes. The information is then transmitted from remote locations by telephone line to a data centre where the information is received and converted into punched tape or magnetic tape for computer input. This method eliminates mailing delays and provides management reports much more quickly.

Machines are available which encode both printed and magnetic language on tags and labels. The magnetic language is easily and accurately read by means of a hand-held magnetic scanning device such as the Datapen reader. By means of the reader information can be automatically captured at the point of the transaction from the magnetically-encoded documents. The encoded documents stay on the merchandise and can be read more than once to record transfers, returns and other inventory data. Such documents have

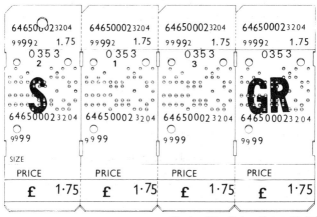

(Courtesy Litton Business Systems Limited)

FIG. 39 *Kimball tags.*

a large capacity for their size, and cannot easily be counterfeited or altered.

Such systems are aimed at capturing and processing data as economically and speedily as possible, in order to provide essential management information for forecasting and control of business operations.

6. Paper tape. At one time paper tape was widely used as an alternative form of input to punched cards but is now used very little, mainly because of its inflexibility. It is not a simple matter to add or delete records as a splicing operation is necessary. It also has a slow data transfer speed compared with magnetic media such as magnetic tape or disc.

Data is recorded on tape as a series of holes across the width of the tape. Each hole position is recorded on a track on the basis of paper tape code, whereby a hole represents a binary 1 and no hole represents a binary 0. The combination of holes across the width of the tape comprises a frame which stores one character.

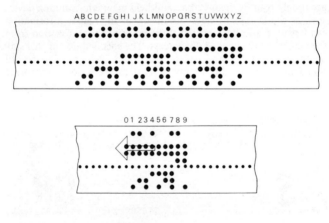

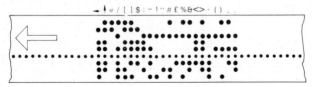

(Courtesy International Computers Limited)

FIG. 40   *The ICL eight-track paper tape code.*

Sprocket holes along the length of tape are used for clocking purposes during tape reading operations. Paper tape can either be five, six, seven or eight track, the latter being mostly used in data processing (*see* Fig. 40).

MAGNETIC INPUT

7. Keyboard encoding direct to magnetic tape (including verification). A keyboard very similar to that of a standard typewriter is used by the operator, who, reading from source documents depresses appropriate keys on the keyboard, causing the characters to be recorded on seven- or nine-track magnetic tape. For verification, the encoder compares the recorded data when it is keyed in a second time. This system is now being replaced by key-to-disc systems.

8. Keyboard encoding CRT display (including verification). This method is more sophisticated than the basic one indicated in **7**, even though a keyboard is used in a similar manner. The special features of this method are as follows.

(*a*) As the operator keys data from source documents, *it is displayed on a CRT*, thereby enabling her to check her work visually. In this case, data preparation also includes verification.

(*b*) To enable keyboard errors to be reduced, *magnetic tape cassettes* can be supplied which have a special format for display on the CRT as a visual replica of the source document. The operator then keys in the information as if completing a form on a typewriter. As the data being keyed is displayed in the appropriate data boxes it enables the operator visually to check and correct the data as appropriate before depressing the "send" key, which causes the data to be recorded on to magnetic tape.

(*c*) *Pooling is possible*, whereby a maximum of twelve operators can key into up to four tape drives.

9. Key-to-disc. Key-to-disc systems include a number of key stations (in the region of twelve to thirty-two) which enables that number of operators at one time to read data from source documents and encode the data onto magnetic disc. This is a more efficient method than punching data into cards and is more effective than the alternative method of encoding data to magnetic tape. This type of system is more than a data preparation system because in addition to encoding and verifying data, the system also provides for the validation of data fields, the generation or validation of check digits and the creation of batch totals, all under the control of a read-only program in the memory of the miniprocessor. Some systems are communications-oriented and transmit batches of data to a mainframe computer which may be located at a great distance away, such as another town.

After data has been encoded on disc, verified and validated, etc., records are written to magnetic tape ready for processing by a mainframe computer. The mainframe is then able to process the data which is free of errors and fully validated without having to carry out validation checks which saves valuable processing time.

Key stations may be located up to 300 metres from the processor, which enables them to be strategically sited near to data origination points in factory departments, stores or warehouses, etc.

The essential elements of a key-to-disc system include the key stations, miniprocessor, magnetic disc drive, magnetic tape deck and a supervisor's console for monitoring the status of the system.

When an operator keys in data, by means of a keyboard similar to that of a typewriter, it is automatically checked and invalid data generates a signal from the processor to the key station which causes the keyboard to lock, together with an audible or displayed warning. Error correction is facilitated by a VDU or panel display, which indicates the erroneous data by means of a cursor on the VDU or a light on the panel display.

Data is keyed into an entry buffer and when this is full the data is transferred to a defined area of the disc. When a key station is set to verify the appropriate record is retrieved from the disc and inserted into the key station's entry buffer so that it can be compared with the same record when keyed in for verification. Differences are displayed on the VDU for correction, either to the original record or the keyed in character by the verifier operator. Records are then moved to an output buffer on disc before being transferred to magnetic tape.

As with all magnetic file media, which can be accidentally erased or overwritten, security measures are necessary and in this instance data is retained on the disc until it has been processed successfully by the mainframe computer. Data is then erased from the disc to provide storage areas for the new batches of data (*see* Fig. 41).

10. Key-to-diskette. A data station is used for recording data on diskettes. As data is entered it is stored in a buffer on the data station and displayed on a screen for the purpose of correcting errors before being recorded on diskette. When data is received it can be recorded to diskette and stored until a further batch of similar data is received. Data is entered by means of a keyboard similar to an electric typewriter. The data station can be set to

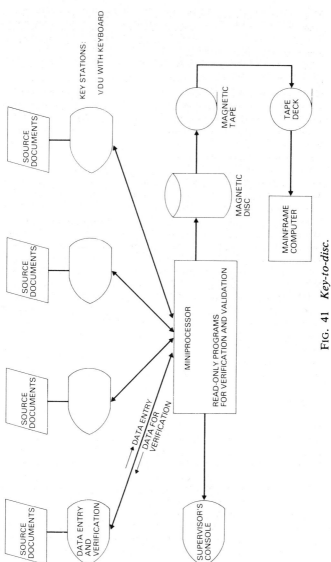

FIG. 41 *Key-to-disc.*

verify mode so that a second operator can re-enter the data from source documents to detect any errors before the data is input for processing. Input to a computer is accomplished by means of an integrated flexible disc unit built into a processor's cabinet or by a freestanding flexible disc unit depending upon the type of computer and the manufacturer.

11. Key-to-cassette. A key-to-cassette data entry terminal provides an efficient means of encoding data directly from source documents to magnetic tape stored in a cassette. Data is entered by a keyboard on the terminal and is displayed on a CRT screen. The lower portion of the screen is reserved for operator guidance messages, error warnings and system status displays.

When an error is detected the screen image begins pulsing to attract the operator's attention. When this occurs, the operator presses the keyboard release function key and a message describing the nature of the error is displayed.

Data may be entered and verified according to multi-level formats that are programmed to individual user needs. Within a level, fields are defined by number, name, length and field and data type. The terminal also provides facilities for check-digit generation and verification. During verification, source data is re-keyed for comparison with the original entry. If an error is discovered in the original data the operator has the option of correcting one character or of re-keying the entire field. Data recorded on cassette can be transmitted to another terminal or to a central processor over communication lines.

MAGNETIC INK CHARACTERS

Magnetic ink is required for printing the characters, so that they may be interpreted for processing. The characters, in addition to being printed with an ink containing a ferromagnetic substance, are also designed in a special type font. As with OCR characters, they may be interpreted both by humans and by machines. Magnetic ink character recognition is accomplished by an input device known as a magnetic ink character reader/sorter. The technique of MICR is mainly used in banking to cope with the enormous task of sorting cheques and updating customers' accounts. It is a more effective method of input than punching a card for each cheque transaction.

There are two MICR fonts:

E13B;
CMC7.

12. E13B. This font was developed in the United States for the American Banks Association, and has been adopted by British banks.

Each character is made as unique as possible, in order to avoid misinterpretation.

Magnetic ink characters can be overwritten with ordinary ink without affecting their legibility for interpretation by the reader/sorter.

If any attempt is made to alter a magnetic ink character the subsequent mutilation is detected when the character is being interpreted by the reader/sorter.

The E13B repertoire consists of ten numeric characters, 0–9, and four symbols to signify the meaning of fields (*see* Fig. 42).

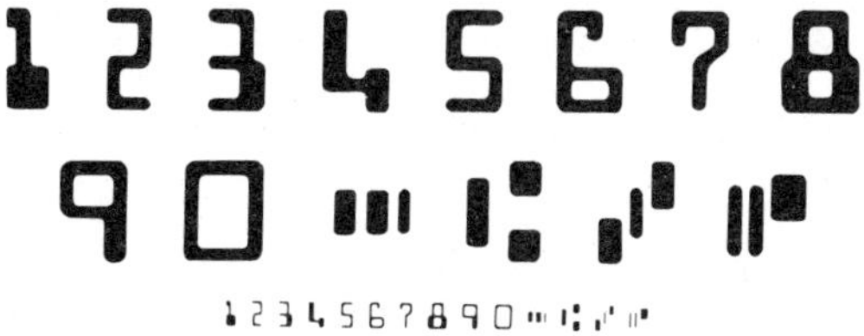

(Courtesy International Computers Limited)

FIG. 42 *MICR characters, E13B font.*

13. CMC7 (Caractère Magnétique Code). This font is the continental standard, and although the characters are encoded in magnetic ink their structure is altogether different to E13B. The characters are formed from a "gapped font" code, consisting of seven vertical bars.

Each character is identified by the format of the bars, which create a six-bit code. Each bar is separated by a gap; a wide gap equals 1 and a narrow gap equals 0. The MICR reader recognises each character by the variable distance between the vertical bars.

The CMC7 repertoire consists of ten numeric characters, 0–9, twenty-six alphabetic characters and five special symbols (*see* Fig. 43).

14. Magnetic ink character encoding. In respect of cheques magnetic ink characters may be encoded when the cheque is printed. The data pre-encoded would include:

(*a*) serial number of the cheque;
(*b*) bank branch number;
(*c*) customer's account number.

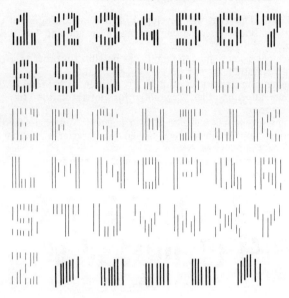

(Courtesy International Computers Limited)

FIG. 43 *MICR characters, CMC7 font.*

When a cheque is presented to a bank by a customer, the bank encodes the amount of the cheque. The encoding is carried out by a machine known as a MICR cheque encoder which has a manually operated keyboard. Alternatively, this may be performed by an encoding machine connected to a keyboard listing machine. When cheque details are recorded on a summary sheet the data is simultaneously encoded on the cheque by the encoder.

OPTICAL CHARACTERS

15. Special type font. Optical characters are designed in a special type font capable of being interpreted both by humans and by machine.

There are two basic OCR fonts in use, both of which are

approved by the International Standards Organisation;

OCR—A;
OCR—B.

Special ink is not required for printing OCR characters.

Optical characters are sensed by an input device, an optical character reader, which transfers data to the processor.

16. OCR—A. This font was developed, and is widely used, in the United States. It comprises sixty-six different characters—alphabetical characters, numbers and symbols—and four standard character sizes (*see* Fig. 44).

17. OCR—B. This font is the result of the work carried out by the European Computer Manufacturers' Association (ECMA), and is widely used in Europe. It comprises 113 different characters and four standard character sizes (*see* Fig. 45).

18. OCR character encoding. The printing of characters on documents for optical reading is not so complex as printing magnetic ink characters, mainly because the font is not so intricate and the use of special ink is unnecessary. It is still necessary, however, to print the characters with a high degree of precision.

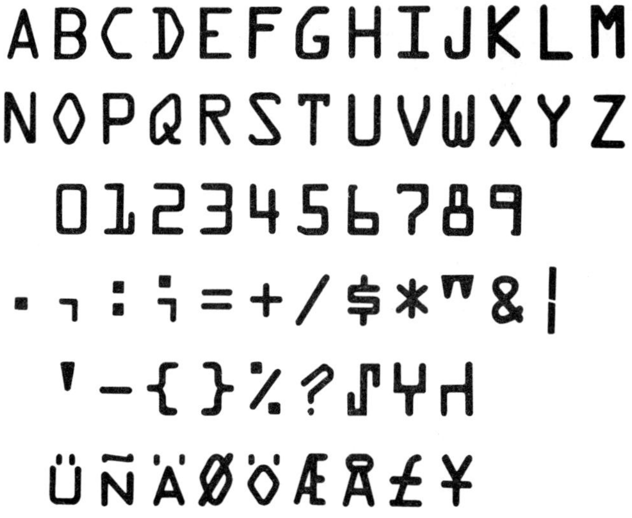

FIG. 44 *Optical characters, OCR-A.*

ABCDEFGH abcdefgh
IJKLMNOP ijklmnop
QRSTUVWX qrstuvwx
YZ*+,-./ yz m åøæ
01234567 £$:;<%>?
89   [@!#&,]
    (=)   "´`^ ~ ˇ
ÄÖÅÑÜÆØ ↑≤≥×÷º¤

FIG. 45 *Optical characters, OCR-B*

Encoding of characters may be performed in the following ways:

(*a*) *hand printing*, in accordance with specified rules for the formation of characters.

(*b*) by *typewriter* equipped with OCR font characters;

(*c*) *automatically*, by a line printer fitted with a print barrel embossed with OCR font characters;

(*d*) by cash registers, adding and accounting machines *equipped with OCR font characters*.

OPTICAL MARKS

19. Nature of optical marks. This method of collecting data utilises pre-printed source documents such as employee clock cards, confectionery order sheets and meter reading sheets as used by gas and electricity boards. It is a very speedy method of collecting data but care must be taken to ensure that marks are recorded, usually by hand, in the correct column otherwise invalid data will be processed causing error correction problems at a later date.

The documents are designed with predesignated column values and a mark is recorded in the appropriate column to indicate the number of hours worked on a specific job by an employee, etc. or to record the units consumed as indicated on a gas or electricity meter (*see* Figs. 46 and 47).

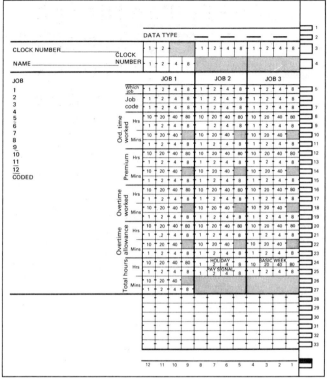

FIG. 46 *Employee clock-card.*

20. Example of OMR combined with OCR, demonstrating the use of turnaround documents. The Midlands Electricity Board produces meter reading sheets by computer which contain details printed in optical characters. The meter sheets are used by meter readers who record meter readings (electricity consumed by customers) by marks in pre-designated meter reading columns. The details are then transferred to magnetic tape by optical mark and optical character reading.

The magnetic tape file is then used to produce consumer bills with stubs. These are sent to the consumer who detaches the stub and returns it with the remittance. The stub is then read by an optical character reader and transferred to magnetic tape to pro-

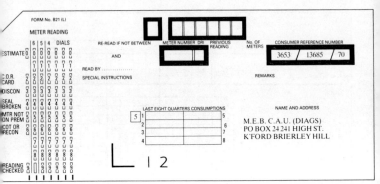

(Courtesy Midlands Electricity Board)

FIG. 47   *Meter reading sheet: OMR and OCR: offpeak supply.*

vide a file of cash receipts. The cash receipts are then recorded against the consumer record to provide an updated file of consumer details on magnetic tape. Both the meter sheet and the bill stub are turnaround documents as they are initially produced by the computer as an output and subsequently become the basis of input to the computer for further processing. The computer has actually produced its own input data at an earlier output stage (*see* Fig. 48).

TERMINALS

21. Nature of terminals. First and foremost, terminals are devices for transmitting and/or receiving data over a communication channel. They are connected to a computer which controls the transmission of data over telephone lines. Clusters of terminals are controlled by a cluster controller, which attends to the requirements of individual terminals on a shared line basis, facilitating economy in the use of telephone lines especially if they are leased private lines. For further details relating to data transmission the reader is recommended to refer to XXIV.

Terminals may either be special purpose or general purpose, depending upon the operating environment, because some types of business require terminals specially designed for the nature of their activities. They may then be defined as dedicated terminals, i.e. dedicated to performing a specific task which applies to retail, bank and factory terminals. (These will be outlined later in this chapter). Terminals operate in a conversational or interactive mode unless they are one-way terminals designed only for transmitting large

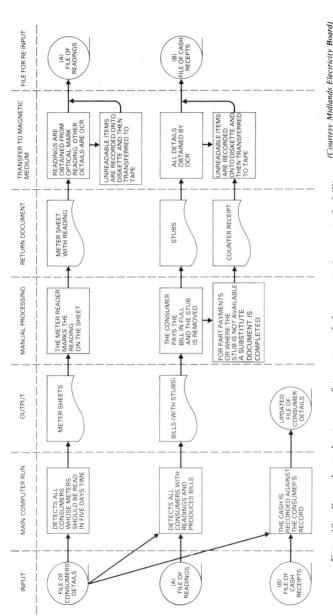

FIG. 48 *Procedure chart: use of turnaround documents in quarterly billing.* *(Courtesy Midlands Electricity Board)*

volumes of data from a remote location to a centralised computing facility; this is referred to as remote job entry, which enables a factory to transmit payroll data to the central computer for computing payslips and payrolls. Conversational or interactive processing means that the user and the computer communicate with each other by means of specific dialogue (*see* I, **12** and XII, **8**).

Terminals are used in many and varied environments, e.g. a portable terminal can be used in the home or hotel room, or anywhere there is a telephone extension for connecting the terminal to a computer, for such purposes as: time sharing or teleshopping via the videotex system such as the Prestel Viewdata facility; for airline seat reservations, booking hotel accommodation or theatre tickets; for the booking of holidays by tour operators; and for gas and electricity board consumer enquiry systems.

22. Summary of types of terminal. There exist many different types of terminal and the following summary will serve to identify them:

(*a*) teletype;
(*b*) visual display unit (VDU);
(*c*) intelligent terminal;
(*d*) factory terminal;
(*e*) bank cash point terminal;
(*f*) retail terminal;
(*g*) bulk transmission/remote batch terminal;
(*h*) handprint data entry terminal;
(*i*) workstations;
(*j*) branch terminal.

23. Purpose of terminals. It has already been indicated that the primary purpose of a terminal is the transmitting and/or receiving of data but a brief summary, prior to further study, of the different forms this may take should be beneficial.

(*a*) Transmission of data from one location to another or between computers in a local area network environment for text, data or electronic mail processing purposes.
(*b*) Access to a computer for time sharing facilities either for program development, problem solving or file processing.
(*c*) Random enquiry facilities for credit status enquiries, product availability, account status or hotel or airline seat availability.
(*d*) Real-time control of manufacturing processes and airline seat reservations.
(*e*) Point of sale data capture in supermarkets.

(*f*) Access to cash outside banking hours by means of cashpoint terminals.

(*g*) Processing business operations such as:

    (*i*) on-line order entry;
    (*ii*) on-line stock control;
    (*iii*) on-line payroll processing.

(*h*) Collection of data relating to works orders.

(*i*) Transmission of handwritten data and signatures by hand-print data entry terminal.

(*j*) Console unit for controlling computer operations.

24. Teletype. This type of terminal is actually a teleprinter or telex machine as used in the telex system of British Telecom. It is now used for other data communication purposes due to the growth in data communications between computers. It is probably the best known keyboard/printer terminal which transmits data via a telephone line by depressing keys on the keyboard. In a telex system data is transmitted along a telegraph line. Each telex machine is connected through the telex network to other telex machines. However, we are interested in the use of the teletype as a terminal device for transmitting and receiving data in time sharing systems and as a control console for man/machine communications in the older mainframe installations.

A modem or acoustic coupler is required for connecting the terminal to the telephone line, as it is necessary to convert the digital signals transmitted by the terminal into analog signals required by the voice grade telephone lines. When the signals are received at the computer end of the line they are converted back into digital signals from analog signals prior to processing (*see* XXIV, 5). This may change in the future with the advent of the Digital PABX telephone system which facilitates the digital transmission of both data and voice communications. Provision is made for prepunching paper tape for subsequent transmission of data at a faster speed than is possible by keyboard entry of data for direct transmission. Data can also be received on paper tape as well as being printed on the printing unit.

25. Visual display unit(VDU). The VDU (*see* Fig. 49), which is often referred to as a video unit or video terminal, is a general purpose terminal which can be used for a wide range of business applications including those itemised in **23** (*a*), (*b*), (*c*), (*d*), (*g*) (*see also* XII, **1** and **2**). It is more modern than the teletype and much quieter in operation, which is why the VDU is tending to replace it in most environments. In appearance a VDU is like a television set with a keyboard or even like a microcomputer. In fact a micro can function as an intelligent VDU. The screen is a cathode ray tube (CRT) which displays images such as graphs, diagrams, sprites and text. This is in contrast with the teletype which prints text and graphs on paper by means of the printing unit. If a copy is required of the screen image then this can be accomplished by copying the screen display to a printer connected to the VDU. A light pen may be used in conjunction with the VDU for graphical applications (*see* Fig. 50).

Data is displayed on the screen from incoming signals or direct from the keyboard as everything that is keyed in is displayed. The screen can be cleared by a function key without destroying the contents of the memory. Data can be corrected (edited) on the screen before transmitting it to another terminal or computer. Windows or split screens are available for displaying several different elements simultaneously; different document images for instance.

A cursor, a moving bright spot on the surface of the screen, indicates the next position for entering characters. Sometimes, a winking cursor is used as a prompt for drawing attention to a specific section of the screen. Data is usually buffered allowing it

(Courtesy IBM United Kingdom Limited)

FIG. 49   *IBM 3290 Information Panel.*

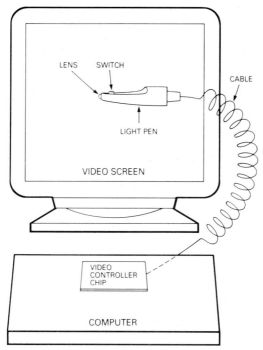

FIG. 50 *Video screen and light pen.*

to be transmitted in blocks of characters, instead of individual characters; this effectively increases the speed of transmission.

Other features which VDUs possess include character sets switchable to other languages such as Spanish, German, French and English. Some models have screens which can be tilted and swivelled to suit the ergonomic needs of individuals. In addition they have switchable emulation facilities which allows one model to act as a different model. Various character resolutions are also available including characters made up of a number of bits in a matrix, among which are 8×10, 7×10 and 14×10.

Figure 49 illustrates the IBM 3290 Information Panel used for database/data communications applications and other similar tasks.

26. Intelligent terminals. Terminals with inbuilt processing capabilities are referred to as being intelligent, as they can perform tasks such as validating data before it is transmitted to a main computer. This is very useful because it relieves the main computer from this task allowing it to concentrate on high speed "number crunching" activities. This of course generates a higher level of processing productivity. Intelligent terminals can be programmed to perform computing tasks which means that they are in effect computers which can be used on a stand-alone basis or can be part of a distributed network of terminals. Unintelligent terminals do not have built-in computing logic, only data transmission facilities.

DATA COLLECTION SYSTEMS

A data collection system is used for recording and transmitting data from remote locations to either a central point or directly to a computer. In general, data collection systems are applied where it is necessary speedily to collect data from dispersed locations within an organisation with a minimum of recording and in a form suitable for processing to obtain the desired information for the control of operations.

Applications include the recording of sales transactions at the point of sale and the recording of production data in respect of factory departments.

27. Factory terminal. The details which follow apply to the ICL Model 9603 factory terminal. It is a microprocessor-based terminal which allows data to be input via a keyboard, 10-column badge and 80-column punched card. It has a large, clear display for input instructions, error messages and replies to enquiries.

The prime types of data recorded include the completion of specific tasks, the movement of materials and components and attendance of personnel. Authorised personnel can retrieve up-to-date file information via the display. Typical enquiries include job status, next job details, component location or stock availability.

Variable information is entered via a 12-key numeric keyboard or a 42-key alpha-numeric keyboard. The keyboards are pressure sensitive. To simplify data entry, fixed information such as personnel or part numbers can be read in via a plastic badge.

The terminal has a card reader to accept standard or plastic 80-column punched cards. The terminal can hold up to 10 basic transaction programs which, together with guidance instructions, can be easily specified and amended by the user's own staff.

Initial program loading is directly from the 9600 System Controller, or via the card reader. A user identity check can be included

(Courtesy International Computers Limited)

FIG. 51   *ICL 9603 factory terminal.*

in any program. The terminals can be located up to 7.6 wire km (4.7 miles) from the processor but this can be extended by a modem booster. The transmission speed is up to 4800 baud (bits per second) (*see* Fig. 51).

28. Article numbering and checkout scanning. Article numbering and checkout scanning is one of the most dynamic developments in retailing since self-service was introduced. It is being adopted by many supermarkets. The article numbering takes the form of an EAN (European Article Number) bar code (*see* Fig. 52) which is a series of bars and spaces of varying width to a predetermined structure and standard. A bar code is the machine-sensible version of a product's article number which is unique to each size, colour and pack of every item. Checkout scanning involves the scanning of the bar code on items sold by a low-intensity laser scanner and other electronic scanning devices such as light pens or slot scanners. The advantage to shoppers is more efficient checkout service, itemised till receipts identifying each item and its price, fewer items

(Courtesy Cadbury Limited)

FIG. 52   *Example of bar-code.*

out of stock and possibly lower prices as a result of more efficient management of the supermarket.

29. Auto teller terminals. These terminals are for automating payments to bank customers and data collection. Many bank branches have facilities for providing customers with a cash withdrawal service outside normal banking hours. The availability of the service is determined by each bank. Each customer is provided with a plastic card which is placed in a special cash dispensing and recording machine (the auto teller terminal) installed through the wall of the bank. The customer keys in the personal number previously provided on the numeric keyboard of the terminal and enters the amount of money required on the same keyboard. The data is entered by the depression of a data entry key. The cash required is dispensed automatically (auto teller). The customer then removes the cash and the card from the terminal.

The transactions are recorded on the customer's statement, indicating which facility was used. A weekly withdrawal limit is given to each customer. The personal number ensures security because this is used in conjunction with the card. In the eventuality of the card being lost no one can use it without the personal number.

30. Remote batch terminals (distributed processing). Some remote batch terminals are designed as data communication systems for direct communication with a computer or as part of a comprehensive communications network forming a distributed processing system. Such terminals, at various remote locations, communicate with each other for the purpose of transmitting source data and printing documents from the transmitted data. They may also print documents from data prepared locally.

PORTABLE COMPUTERS AND HANDPRINT DATA ENTRY TERMINAL

31. Portable computer for data capture. One particular model of computer, different from the normal microcomputer in appearance, is the HUSKY marketed by DVW Microelectronics Limited (*see* Fig. 53). It can be used for portable data capture or normal computer applications. It is used for the collection of routine data by non-computer personnel in such environments as the stores for the capture of part numbers, quantities and other data by means of a bar code reading wand, which reads bar coded labels on the bins containing the various stored items.

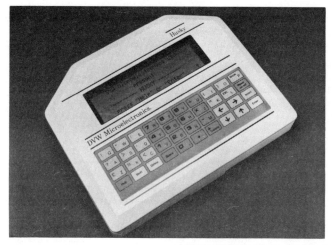

(Courtesy DVW Microelectronics Limited)

FIG. 53 *Husky microcomputer.*

The machine can be interfaced for printing reports on most types of printer. Data can be transmitted to a central database for compilation if required or the data can be retained in the internal memory until the next period. It can also be used for elecronic work study as its built-in calendar clock facilitates accurate timing of individual operations.

The features of the computer include a 40-key tactile keyboard; synchronous or asynchronous communication facilities; user programmability; a 128-character, 4-line LCD screen; a BASIC interpreter and a memory capacity of either 32K, 48K, 64K or 144K bytes.

32. TEL-time data collection terminal. TEL-time (*see* Fig. 54) is a system for the collection and analysis of work measurement data. The system uses portable data capture terminals which are programmable. They validate and store data entered by the observer ready for transfer to a microcomputer for analysis. The TEL-time is a flexible tool for use in work study and industrial engineering applications. It operates with the ACT Sirius and the IBM PC computers. The terminal is used to time each element and apply a performance rating. It is connected to a microcomputer and the study data is transferred to disc storage. The terminal and observer are then free to continue with the next study. The

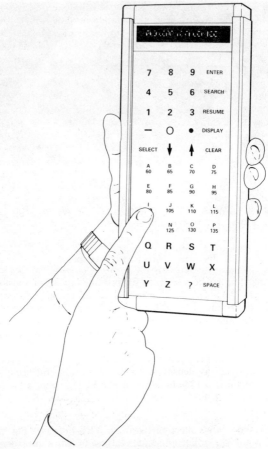

(Courtesy Telford Management Services Limited)

FIG. 54 *Tel-time terminal.*

computer analyses the data and prints the standard reports
included in the TEL-time package. The terminals can be either
hand-held or used with a study board. Data can be communicated
to the computer direct or by telephone line for remote operations.
The terminal has a built-in display and may be used for any data
capture/analysis applications.

33. Handprint data entry terminal. One such system is marketed by Quest CIL and is called Micropad Handprint data entry terminal (*see* Fig. 55). It is a local or remote terminal which enables handprinted data to be captured at the time of writing and the data is validated simultaneously. The device converts the handprinted alphanumeric characters into ASCII code and transmits this code to any host computer via a standard interface.

It comprises a pressure sensitive writing surface, an inbuilt microprocessor and an integral 40-character line display. Data and signatures are written using an ordinary ballpoint pen or pencil on documents designed by the user to suit their specific applications. This method of data capture may be used for entering customer order details, retail point of sale recording, payroll and file amendments, etc.

Available options allow the data to be transmitted immediately it is written or stored within Micropad and transmitted as a block of up to 512 characters, or validated locally within Micropad. Additional features include the ability to output alpha characters as upper or lower case and ASCII special and control characters. The Q-Sign option allows Micropad to function as a dynamic

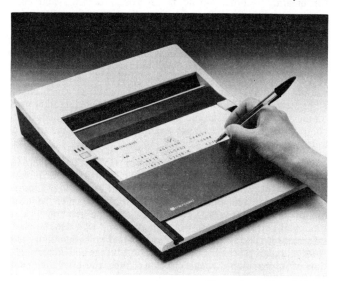

(Courtesy Quest Micropad Limited)

FIG. 55   *Handprint data entry terminal.*

signature verification terminal by comparing the user's signature as it is written with the reference signature. This provides immediate authorisation for transactions.

Data is validated character by character and field by field before being transmitted. Standard validation checks include:

(*a*) alpha/numeric/special characters;
(*b*) left/right/full field justification;
(*c*) mandatory/optional field;
(*d*) logical data checks;
(*e*) maximum data field length: 32 characters;
(*f*) maximum number of fields per document: 50.

Special European character sets are available including Swedish/Finnish, Danish/Norwegian, and Spanish/Portuguese.

WORKSTATIONS

34. General characteristics. Workstations provide the means of improving office productivity by using technologically based tools for creating records, amending records, processing and communicating information, inter-company transactions, electronic mail, electronic filing and word processing, etc.

The workstation consists of a video display unit (VDU), a keyboard, a microprocessor for text and image processing and also contains an internal memory. Workstations usually share printing and central storage resources when part of a network. Workstations may also have voice handling capabilities which enable voice messages to be stored and electronically mailed to other users on the network. Workstations may also be connected to mainframe computers for gaining access to a corporate database and to act as a data collection terminal.

35. Information Management Processor (IMP). This is an integrated office automation system available from Office Technology Limited (OTL)(which is part of Information Technology Limited (ITL)). It is a system aimed at improving the management of information in work groups, i.e. secretary-manager relationships or groups of personnel whose work interacts and who need to share information. The system integrates text and voice handling, and word and data processing in the creation, storage and communication of information through electronic filing and electronic mail. The system provides each user with an integrated multi-functional personal workstation capable of handling all forms of information across a wide range of needs (*see* Fig. 56).

(Courtesy Office Technology Limited)

FIG. 56 *OTL Information Management Processor.*

The system also aims at improving the productivity of office professionals and managers who originate and use information. The system's voice processing facilities enable these office principals, as they may be called, to create voice documents (or messages or annotation on existing documents) by speaking into the workstation's integrated handset and then SEND or FILE them just like text. The voice facility allows a "casual" user to add easily and effectively annotations and commentaries to drafts and other documents. The office principal can also receive quickly comments on a document from a number of people. Voice messages can be registered in the "IN-TRAY" facility, which enables a desk to be kept tidy and messages kept easily accessible, not buried under a mass of "debris".

An office system controller provides shared information storage and distribution resources for the whole system. The system has two modes of workstation, one of which has facilities for handling text, data and graphics and the principal workstation, which, in addition to these, also has voice input and output facilities. Each workstation maintains its processing independence with its own 16-bit microprocessor and 256K bytes of memory. A daisy wheel printer is used with a range of typestyles and a printing speed of 40 cps.

The system is designed to meet the physical and psychological needs of the personnel using the facilities. Accordingly the display screen is designed to provide maximum visual comfort in order to minimise eyestrain and fatigue. It can be tilted and swivelled, independently of the keyboard, to the most comfortable position for the user. Documents are displayed on the screen in paper-like black-on-white and scroll smoothly up and down and side to side, where necessary, for extra-wide pages. The user is guided through the operation of the system with clearly marked keys, helpful menus and prompts; HELP facilities are also available.

The system's document processing package facilitates record processing applications such as directories, personnel records, inventories and customer and supplier lists. These records can be selected against a range of criteria, sorted or rearranged for a particular purpose. Powerful letter or list processing facilities are also provided on the system to produce personalised letters by merging variable information from customer lists into standard letters. The system can also handle pre-printed or user-defined forms.

The system provides an "electronic" filing system on a high capacity, fast access filestore within the controller. The structure of the filing system is under the control of the user and can mimic the existing manual filing system in the way files are named, indexed, classified and accessed. Common information can be held in general files which are accessible to all members of a department. Personal files can be accessed only with knowledge of the individual user name and "key" or password, thus upholding privacy and confidentiality. When a document is no longer required for current use it can be relegated to a "wastebin" which is an extension of the electronic filing system. It can be retrieved in an "uncrumpled state" when reference to it is necessary.

SPEECH SYNTHESIS AND ANALOG INPUT

36. Speech synthesis. The recognition of speech is achieved using allophones, the basic speech sounds, by storing a digitised pattern in the form of a reference matrix. This is a pattern of signals unique for each vocabulary word; any English word can be constructed and spoken by this means. Words are recognised by a matching technique and the speech pattern of several speakers can be stored simultaneously. Having obtained a matrix pattern of the words the computer performs a search routine for the nearest match. When this is located it compares the bit count relationship with the memory pattern. The chosen word is then displayed. If a satisfactory match is not achieved it is necessary to repeat the word spoken.

It is possible to incorporate speech in BASIC programs to be run on microcomputers so that spoken words can be integrated in the normal program to be generated as output for games and other applications. Speech synthesisers have a built-in amplifier, volume control and speaker.

37. Analog (digital) input. This type of input is applicable to process and machine control, data logging, patient monitoring systems and laboratory projects, etc. A sensor collects details relating to the status of the system being controlled in the form of analog signals which are converted to digital signals by a digitiser. Analog data is represented in a continuous form as contrasted with digital data which is in discrete form, i.e. finite values. Analog data is represented by physical variables such as voltage, resistance, temperature, pressure and rate of flow. As variations in these variables take place they are input to the digitiser which is continously scanned by the computer.

PROGRESS TEST 5

1. Write short notes relating to computer input and data capture. (**1,2**)

2. Specify the nature of punched cards, tags and paper tape. (**3–6**)

3. Specify methods of preparing magnetic media for computer input. (**7–11**)

4. (*a*) Describe, with the aid of a block diagram, a computer controlled keying system (key-to-disc or key-to-tape). (*b*) What are the advantages of such a system over older methods of keypunching? List any disadvantages. (**7,9** and Fig. 41) (*C & G*)

5. Write brief notes on FOUR of the following techniques. Describe a situation in which EACH technique would be used: (*a*) optical character recognition (OCR); (*b*) magnetic ink character recognition (MICR); (*c*) bar codes; (*d*) key-to-disc systems; (*e*) optical mark readers (OMR). (**7, 9, 12–19, 28**) (*C & G*)

6. List the types of terminal which may be used for computer input. (**22**)

7. What purpose do terminals serve? (**23**)

8. VDUs and keyboard printer units are widely used as terminals to multi-access systems. Give for each device ONE example where it is preferable to the use of the other. Give reasons for your choice. (**24, 25**) (*C & G*)

9. What are intelligent terminals?   **(26)**

10. Write short notes on each of the following data collection systems: (*a*) factory terminal; (*b*) article numbering and checkout scanning; (*c*) auto teller terminals; (*d*) remote batch terminals.   **(27–30)**

11. Define the nature of the following methods of capturing data: (*a*) portable computer; (*b*) handprint data entry terminal.   **(31–3)**

12. Workstations provide the means for improving office productivity. Discuss.   **(34, 35)**

13. Computer input may be achieved by speech synthesis and analog signals. Indicate the nature and use of these methods.   **(36, 37)**

CHAPTER VI

Computer Output

PRINTED

1. Types of computer output. The various types of output from a computer system may be chosen from the following list according to specific requirements:

(*a*) printed;
(*b*) visual display;
(*c*) COM (Computer Output on Microfilm);
(*d*) graphical;
(*e*) punched;
(*f*) magnetically encoded.

2. Printed output. Most systems require printed output in the form of payrolls and invoices and management information, etc. and according to the type of computer in use a large range of printers and printing systems are available. These include:

(*a*) line printers;
(*b*) matrix printers;
(*c*) band printers;
(*d*) visual record printers;
(*e*) laser printers;
(*f*) teletype;
(*g*) page printing system;
(*h*) portable printer/printing terminal;
(*i*) distributed electronic printer;
(*j*) electronic printing system.

Line printers and matrix printers are referred to as impact printers which print characters by impact onto paper usually by means of a ribbon and print wires or print hammers. Line printers operate at various speeds according to the model, i.e. 200, 300, 600, 720, 1500 and 3000 lines per minute. Documentation Incorporated market an impact printer capable of 3000 lpm; the high speed capability is largely due to the machine having an integrated microprocessor controller and lightweight durable alloy hammers; it also has an interchangeable print band.

A laser printer available from Itel International prints on continuous form paper at a speed of 325 lines per second, which is ten times faster than some impact printers.

Teletypes are used as terminals in on-line systems as an alternative to VDUs for transmitting and receiving data. Transmitted data is recorded on rolls of paper and the responses, i.e. the messages from the computer, are also printed.

Honeywell market a system for large volume computer output which is referred to as a Page Printing System capable of printing at 8000, 12000 or even 18000 lines per minute. The system also performs perforating, punching, cutting, collating, stacking and addressing. The system is controlled by a minicomputer.

3. Hard copy. A printer is very useful, in fact imperative, in a business computer system for obtaining printed documents in the form of cheques, invoices and labels, etc. For normal computing purposes it is very useful to have a record of programs and these can be printed out from memory when required. Similarly, when a program is run, especially for complicated tabulations, it is useful to have the results printed out. This is in distinction to displaying results of calculations on the screen in a transitory manner which is adequate for some types of calculations.

4. Features of a printer. Two widely used types of printer used with microcomputers are the dot matrix and daisy wheel printer. The dot matrix printer has a higher speed than the daisy wheel but has lower print quality. Typical features of this type of printer include: printing speed of 150 cps, bi-directional printing, programmable line spacing, character font 5×8 matrix, 256 character set, cartridge ribbon, selectable tractor or friction feed. It is considered generally suitable for internal office printing requirements and for invoices, general business forms, mailing lists, cheques and program printouts, etc. It is capable of producing three copies. The daisy wheel printer has a speed in the region of 40 cps but a much higher print quality than the dot matrix printer and is more suitable for documentation of an external nature, such as personal letters and important correspondence as it creates a better image of the company. The general features of this type of printer include: plastic/metal daisy wheel, so called because the print head has print elements round its circumference with characters on the end of stalks radiating from a central hub, forming the appearance of a daisy. Other features include programmable line spacing, character size selected in accordance with the type of daisy wheel in use which also has optional character sets for several languages, paper feed friction with the option of tractor feed mechanism. It is capable of producing three copies. The type of paper may be single letterhead or continuous stationery. This type of printer also has a cartridge ribbon.

5. Printer/plotter. Printers or printer/plotters are now available for many microcomputers, one example being the MCP-40 which is used on the ORIC-1 computer. It is capable of printing and plotting in four colours and can print variable character sizes. A ROM chip contains software which provides a range of print/plotting features. It prints forty characters on each line.

6. Portable printer/printing terminal. An example of this type of machine is the Brother EP22 (*see* Fig. 57). It is a portable printer, typewriter and calculator. It can be used for typing on ordinary paper or can print on thermal paper by removing the ribbon cassette. It is completely silent which allows it to be used in a classroom, business meeting or even on an aircraft without disturbing anyone.

The machine incorporates a 2K text memory which permits the storage of a full page of text. Rough typing can be done for later adjustment either to delete or add sections of text. The text can be printed out as many times as required. It prints at seventeen cps and at three, four or six lines per inch. The printer incorporates a built-

(Courtesy Jones Sewing Machine Company Limited)

FIG. 57 *Brother EP22 printer.*

in RS-232C type serial interface for connection to compatible home computers, thus converting the machine to a terminal or output printer. It can print out the results of a program or list the program. In addition, the machine can be used as a calculator, and computations can be incorporated into the text to be printed out. It is battery powered.

7. Distributed electronic printer. An example of this type of machine is the Rank Xerox 2700 printer (*see* Fig. 58) which is

(Courtesy Rank Xerox (UK) Limited)

FIG. 58   *The Xerox 2700 distributed electronic printer.*

designed to operate anywhere; in the office, data centre or at a remote location. It is a small, quiet, multi-font laser printer designed for distributed printing in a general purpose data processing environment or as a printer on a small business computer. It can also be used in a network environment. It accepts digital input through communication lines or directly through parallel interfaces (either the standard Centronics or Dataproducts).

The machine produces high quality output on standard cut-sheet bond paper and provides the full International ISO 6937 character set, which encompasses the Teletex character set. A high-resolution laser prints 90000 spots per square inch. It can handle text applications such as letters and memos in addition to standard data processing outputs. It incorporates facilities to change font cartridges, and additional typefaces can be received from the host computer. An organisation's logos and executive signatures can be digitised and stored for use as required.

Typefaces can be changed within a single line to enable individual words or phrases to be emphasised. Simple forms or bar charts can be created through character substitution or by drawing rules. It can print up to twelve pages per minute. The heart of the system is a microprocessor and image generator.

8. Electronic printing system. The Xerox 9700 printing system (*see* Figs. 59 and 60) combines computer, laser and xerographic technologies. The system consists of a number of subsystems which are outlined below.

(*a*) *Input subsystem.* This provides data for the system via 9-track magnetic tape either 1 600 or 6250 bits (bytes, in effect) per

(Courtesy Rank Xerox (UK) Limited)

FIG. 59 *The Xerox 9700 electronic printing system.*

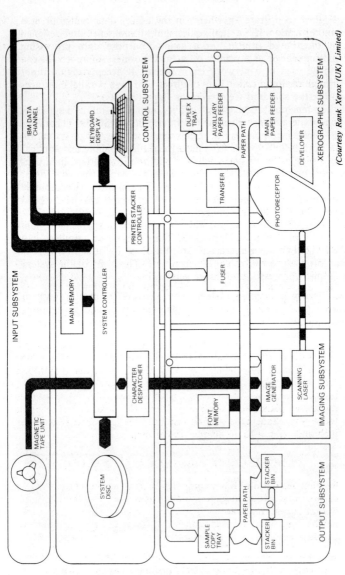

FIG.60   *Outline of Xerox 9700 electronic printing system.*

(*Courtesy Rank Xerox (UK) Limited*)

inch for off-line operation via a tape drive. An on-line interface allows the system to be directly connected to a host computer, or input can be obtained from an 850/860 word processor.

(*b*) *Control subsystem.* The system controller contains a 50 megabyte disc for input buffering and user file storage. The controller performs all the data handling, formatting and input buffering tasks. Operator control of the system is facilitated by means of a keyboard/display console which is used for initiating and monitoring jobs. It consists of a minicomputer and control electronics.

(*c*) *Imaging subsystem.* The image generator provides electronic control for the blue laser beam. It accesses the font memory in the controller to create character images and forms. It accepts the formatted page of data including forms and logos; and utilises a scanning laser beam to generate lines of modulated light for the continuously moving photoreceptor of the Xerographic subsystem.

(*d*) *Xerographic subsystem.* This incorporates all the normal functions of a xerographic printer including paper handling and development of the latent image on the output page.

(*e*) *Output subsystem.* A two bin output stacker provides the capability for paper stacking, report collating and sample prints in the sample print tray. Reports are separated by offsetting each copy set approximately 12mm from the previous one. When the active bin has been filled, if the second bin is full, the system will stop printing.

Printing is performed from the system disc enabling multiple copies to be printed without retransmission of data when on-line to a data channel. For off-line operation the operator can mount and feed a new tape while the system finishes the printing of the previous job. The system prints 2 pages per second or 120 pages per minute on plain paper. Unlimited font styles in sizes from 4 point to 24 point. Spacing is continuously variable from 3 to 18 lines per inch and from 4 to 30 characters per inch.

PUNCHED AND MAGNETICALLY ENCODED

9. Punched output. Early computers were predominantly punched card or paper tape input/output oriented but this type of input/output is now very rare as it has been superseded by much more flexible and faster magnetic media. It is therefore unnecessary to consider punched output further.

10. Magnetically encoded output. Output in this form is usually for the purpose of storing records and the media used for this purpose include floppy discs, exchangeable discs and magnetic tape. The nature of this media is extensively covered in Chapter IX.

VISUAL DISPLAY UNIT AND GRAPH PLOTTER

11. Visual display unit (VDU). A VDU is a dual purpose device which has already been discussed in detail (*see* V, **25**). It can be used as an input device for data, such as in an order-entry system, by means of the keyboard as well as being an output device for displaying text and graphical characters.

12. Graph plotter. In addition to the recently developed printer/ plotter extensively used on microcomputers, a dedicated graph plotter is used for the output of graphical information on large and small computers. A plotter provides a permanent hard copy of the graphical output as opposed to a VDU, which displays graphical output in a transitory manner on the video screen as it disappears when the machine is switched off. The output can be multicoloured.

COMPUTER OUTPUT ON MICROFILM (COM)

13. Nature of COM. Computer output by microfilm is an alternative to printed output, which is relatively slow even for the faster type of printer compared with the speed with which COM can be produced. COM not only produces output faster but also reduces stationery costs and the space needed for storing computer printouts. It is also an information retrieval system.

COM may be defined as a method which stems the tide of the "paperwork explosion" which has long been a feature of computerised batch processing systems. Hard copy output is not always required consequently, if all computer output is committed to paper, a problem soon arises, not only deciding *who* should have *what* reports but *where* they are all going to be stored *just in case they may be needed*. Copies of computer output can be stored on microfilm or microfiche at much reduced size compared to the size of computer stationery pages. This makes storage of output less of a problem particularly when it is supported by an effective information retrieval system.

14. Hardware and software requirements. A typical COM system is minicomputer controlled and produces alphanumeric or graphical output on imaged, cut and processed dry silver microfiche, either direct by means of a COM recorder connected directly to the host processor or via COM formatted magnetic tapes for off-line mode. Disc drives are used for storage of parameters and job details. Software provides facilities for forms drawing and outputting. Reduction ratios are typically $24 \times$, $42 \times$ and $48 \times$. Images can be stored either on film or 105mm microfiche. The COM system adds an index to each image for reference and retrieval purposes. Microfiche is more popular than roll film as images are more easily accessed by simply moving the microfiche under the viewer to the desired image. This facilitates the location of component parts for a particular unit so that it can be located in the stores of a spares organisation, for instance. Related images can be stored on the same microfiche. Fiche are more easily stored than rolls of film and fiche readers are less expensive than roll film readers, are capable of a much higher quality of image reproduction and are also less complex.

15. Information retrieval. Information stored as images on film or microfiche can be accessed for retrieval purposes by a microfilm or fiche viewer. If a hard copy is required then this is facilitated by a "demand" printer.

COMPUTER GRAPHICS

16. Graphics defined. Graphics may be defined as pictures in the widest sense including graphs, diagrams, charts and moving images on a video screen of a microcomputer, VDU or workstation. There exists three broad categories of graphics, i.e. block graphics, pixel and high resolution graphics (to which may be added sprite graphics). Graphics are widely used on home computers for playing computer games, for which there exists a profusion of programs available off the shelf ready to load from cassette or key in from programs published in computer magazines of which there are also a great many.

From a business point of view, graphical presentation of information is often more useful and has a higher impact than detailed printed reports. Images can be displayed on a screen and printed out on such devices as graph plotters, printer/plotters and on normal computer printers, as it is possible to print a copy of the display on the screen with some computers. Graphical presentation also embraces the display of forms and documents on a screen to enable basic office tasks to be performed in a similar way but using

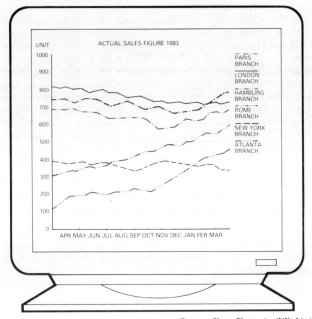

(Courtesy Sharp Electronics (UK) Limited)

FIG. 61   *Sharp MZ-3541 Business Computer displaying graphics.*

electronic technology. In addition, some computers have electronic desk top facilities which display files and documents on a screen for a variety of purposes (*see* Fig. 61 and XXIII, **8—12**).

17. Vector graphics. This is a technique, rather than a type of graphics, as it is a means of displaying graphical images using line drawings on a video screen. If the input is by keyboard then statements containing PLOT or DRAW commands define the plotting coordinates. The same results are achieved by the use of a light pen applied directly to the surface of the screen or by using a graphics tablet as an alternative to a light pen.

18. Light pen. A light pen is an electronic device in the form of a photo-diode on the end of a cable which is used in combination with a visual display unit or video screen. It is used to display, modify or detect images on the screen often in CAD (Computer Aided Design) applications. This is achieved by passing the light pen across the surface of the screen to trace the outline of the image to be displayed. The computer can detect the position of the pen on the screen by counting the number of vertical and horizontal synchronisation pulses (*see* Fig. 50).

19. Graphics tablet. Sometimes referred to as a digitising tablet which is constructed from a sensitive semi-conducting material which can trace the movement of a stylus forming graphical shapes. The shapes are converted into digital signals which are input directly into the computer. A mouse may be used as an alternative to a graphics stylus for achieving the same purpose.

20. Mouse. This is a small device (*see* Fig. 62) which can be moved by hand in any direction across a graphics tablet by means of a ball-bearing on its underside and which has one or two buttons on its upper surface. It can be used to plot images in defined locations on a screen, to select icons (*see* Figs. 149—51) representing particular office facilities in electronic desk top systems, and in word processing applications to rearrange the text on screen and for modifying the font used.

In an electronic desk top application (*see* XXIII, **8—12**) the cursor can be moved around the screen by moving the mouse in the direction required. When the cursor is correctly positioned a push of the button on the mouse will select the corresponding office facility. In this way, a "document" or "folder" icon on the "desk top" can be copied on to the "out basket" icon for despatch to an

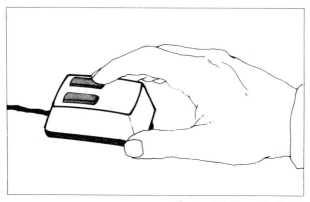

(Courtesy Rank Xerox (UK) Limited)

FIG. 62 *The "mouse"—hand-held cursor control device.*

electronic distribution list or sent for filing or printing by using the appropriate icons. With regard to electronic mail, documents on the screen can be selected for despatch to specific mail boxes stored in a file server. A small "envelope" appears in the "in-basket" on the screen of the receiver's workstation. This "envelope" can then be opened by the receiver.

PIXEL AND HIGH RESOLUTION GRAPHICS

21. Pixel graphics. The screen of a microcomputer or VDU is divided into small squares called pixels, i.e. picture elements or picture cells. The pattern of pixels which are activated make up the image displayed on the screen. The quality of the image depends on the number of pixels on the screen: the higher the number, the higher the resolution. Some micros have picture elements consisting of a 6×2 matrix of phosphor dots. Each pixel is stored in RAM in binary code and can be input by keyboard or from backing storage.

Pixel graphics fall in between block graphics and high resolution graphics. They give the user some control over each picture element as each can be called up individually and located in specified postions on the video screen. A pixel is the smallest pattern of dots that can be accessed for display.

22. High resolution graphics. Resolution is defined in terms of pixels which can be displayed on the video screen, the greater the number, the greater the sharpness of the image. The less expensive microcomputers with HRG capability have low definition compared to the more expensive business micros. The number of pixels which are typically displayed is 176×158 but the ICL PERQ computer has a screen capacity of 1024×768 pixels. The ACT Apricot computer has a capacity of 800×400 pixels and the ORIC-1 240×200 pixels.

Some microcomputers can be converted to high resolution capability by the addition of a special board, e.g. the PET can be enhanced by the Supersoft HR-40 board. Single dot resolution allows the drawing of smooth curves and accurate diagrams whereas block graphics tend to give images an uneven, chunky appearance. This particular board provides for 64000 individually addressable points, i.e. a resolution of 320×200.

Applesoft, for use on the Apple computer, has special commands which allows shapes to be drawn in high resolution graphics. Before they can be used however a "shape" must be defined by a "shape definition". This consists of a sequence of plotting vectors which are stored in the internal memory. One or more shape definitions with their index make up a "shape table" which can be created from the keyboard and saved for future use on disc or cassette. The shape definition is constructed in enlarged form on the screen by the plotting commands. The shape is formed by setting specific squares on the screen by cursor controls. (*see* **27** and III, **27–29**).

BLOCK AND SPRITE GRAPHICS

23. Block graphics. Some microcomputers have a display code containing a range of characters, including graphic shapes, specific to that machine. They may be displayed on the video screen by POKE statements. In addition to a display code some micros have a set of ASCII characters which can be displayed by a PRINT CHR$ (X) statement where CHR$ indicates that ASCII is being used and "X" is the code number of the specific character to be displayed (*see* II, **3** and Fig. 10). Graphic characters available direct from the keyboard can be displayed by a PRINT statement.

Block graphics allow displays to be generated without unnecessary complexity but do not provide any control over the individual dots making up the image. The "block" characters can be made to move on the screen by the use of vector graphic techniques, using SET and RESET and by modifying the display address on the screen in conjunction with a statement for clearing the screen of the previous display. The relocation of the graphic character simulates movement (*see* III, **27–29**).

24. Sprite graphics. Sprites are user definable graphical shapes used in computer games. Originally developed by Texas Instruments, sprite graphics are available on several home computers including the Texas Instruments T199/04A, the Commodore 64 and the Sord M5. Atari users know sprites as PMGs, i.e. Player Missile Graphics.

Sprites can be moved across the surface of the screen while the background remains static. This is accomplished by means of several screen planes. Conventional graphics pictures are built up on a single screen but with sprite graphics the computer has several planes or layers (the Sord M5 having thirty-two separate planes) each of which can have its own pictures which generates a three dimensional effect. The Commodore 64 has software available for defining sprites which consist of 24×21 pixel shapes which can be manipulated by a series of POKE commands.

TURTLE GRAPHICS

25. Turtle. A turtle, in the context of computers, is a mechanical device (a robot) which is connected to a computer by a cable. The turtle has two wheels and a pen and operates under the control of the computer using the LOGO programming language to draw lines on a sheet of paper to form squares, triangles, circles and other shapes. An alternative version of the turtle is a triangle of light on the video screen—the required shapes being formed by means of movement of the triangle.

26. Turtle graphics. Young children at school are often taught to use a computer by using a mechanical turtle (older children use the alternative version of the turtle in conjunction with a video screen and the LOGO language). The command FORWARD 20 causes the turtle to move forward 20 steps drawing a line behind it. The command RIGHT 90 causes the turtle to make a right angle and BACKWARD 10 causes the turtle to move 10 steps backwards. Various combinations of similar commands enables different shapes to be drawn. The turtle can also be instructed to remember the commands.

A square would be drawn by means of the following commands.

```
FORWARD 20
RIGHT 90
FORWARD 20
RIGHT 90
FORWARD 20
RIGHT 90
FORWARD 20
RIGHT 90
```

The same result can be achieved more simply by a BOX command:

```
TO BOX
REPEAT 4 [FORWARD 20 RIGHT 90]
END
```

USER DEFINED GRAPHIC CHARACTERS AND
COMPUTER AIDED DESIGN (CAD)

27. User defined graphics. Many computers have a set of graphics characters each consisting of a matrix of 8×8 phosphor dots. Each character occupies 8 bytes of storage. The ORIC-1 however forms graphics characters in a matrix of eight rows of six columns. Each row is a byte and the value of the last six "bits" (phosphor spots) determines the shape of the character. If a "bit" is set to "1" then a phosphor spot is "on" and if "0" it is "off". The screen has a capacity of 1K, i.e. 1024 bytes and can display 128 characters, i.e. 1024 divided by 8.

It is possible to generate ones own characters by means of a simple program containing POKE commands, e.g. using BASIC and the video screen locations of the ORIC-1 the program will appear as shown in Fig. 63.

```
10 POKE 46600,8
20 POKE 46601,20
30 POKE 46602,34
40 POKE 46603,20
50 POKE 46604,34
60 POKE 46605,20
70 POKE 46606,8
80 POKE 46607,0
```

FIG. 63 *Program for generating a graphic character.*

The numbers 46600 to 46607 shown in Fig. 63 are video screen addresses in which are POKED binary numbers, i.e. 8, 20, 34, 20, 34, 20, 8 and 0 respectively. These numbers form the desired chape as shown in Fig. 64.

Binary	Bit pattern
8	001000
20	010100
34	100010
20	010100
34	100010
20	010100
8	001000
0	000000

FIG. 64 *The effect of running the program shown in Fig. 63.*

If the "0"s are removed, the "1" bits generate the graphical shape shown in Fig. 65.

```
8          1
20         1 1
34        1   1
20         1 1
34        1   1
20         1 1
8          1
0
```

FIG. 65   *The output produced by the program shown in Fig. 63.*

Each "1" would be displayed as a square on the screen. In general shapes can be generated by PRINT statements when using ASCII characters and POKE statements when using a computer's display code. Graphics characters defined on the keyboard can also be displayed by PRINT statements.

28. Computer aided design (CAD). A technique for the development of graphical designs of various types using a computer equipped with sophisticated software and a light pen in conjunction with a video screen. These resources enable the initial design to be displayed on the screen and subsequently modified if necessary. The image on the screen can be rotated to obtain a three-dimensional view in order to assess its features from various aspects. The technique allows standard shapes to be stored on disc and accessed when required for incorporation in other designs. It saves considerable time in the design activity and improves quality as designs can be speedily checked to ensure compatibility with specifications. Errors can be corrected by light pen. The technique is widely used for the design of aircraft, cars and computers as well as a wide range of other products.

PROGRESS TEST 6

1. Summarise the different methods of producing computer output. **(1)**
2. Summarise the different ways of obtaining printed output. **(2)**
3. List the main features of a dot matrix and a daisy wheel printer. **(4)**
4. Outline the features of: (*a*) printer/plotter; (*b*) portable printer/printing terminal; (*c*) distributed electonic printer; (*d*) electonic printing system. **(5–8)**

5. Outline the nature of punched and magnetically encoded output   **(9, 10)**

6. Outline the nature of a visual display unit and a graph plotter. **(11, 12** and V, **25)**

7. The data processing manager of a large computer installation is concerned about the high volume of printout from the installation's two printers and the subsequent paper storage problems in the user departments. As a consequence he is considering the use of "Computer output on microfilm", COM (microfilm or microfiche). Explain what is meant by COM and the difference between microfilm and microfiche. Give the advantages and disadvantages of the systems.   **(13–15)** *(ICMA)*

8. What are computer graphics?   **(16)**

9. Define the meaning of the following terms: (*a*) vector graphics; (*b*) pixel graphics; (*c*) high resolution graphics; (*d*) block graphics; (*e*) sprite graphics: (*f*) turtle graphics; (*g*) user defined graphics.   **(17, 21–7)**

10. Define the meaning of the following terms: (*a*) light pen; (*b*) graphics tablet; (*c*) mouse.   **(18–20)**

11. Define the meaning of CAD and specify its purpose.   **(28)**

CHAPTER VII

Information Storage and Retrieval: Basic Concepts

MASTER FILES

1. Definition of a master file. A master file is a group of related records, e.g. stock file, customer file, employee file, supplier file. This type of file is periodically updated with current transaction data, in order to show the current status of each record in the file. Other types of master file contain reference information such as product prices, names and addresses and wage rates, etc. Such files may be used for general reference, or can form an integral part of data processing activities. Each record in a file is allocated an identification number or reference key and filed in ascending number order to facilitate ease of access or reference (*see* **2**).

There are also several types of master file, and the type used is also dependent upon the processing method employed.

(*a*) Loose leaf ledger or binder.
(*b*) Container of ledger cards.
(*c*) Reel of magnetic tape or exchangeable disc packs.
(*d*) Floppy discs.
(*e*) Cassette tape.

2. Record key. Accessing or referencing a record on a master file, whether on disc or other file media, is accomplished by means of a record key. This is a number assigned to a record for its specific, unique and unambiguous identification. The key field enables records to be matched with transaction data during file updating and provides the basis for sorting and merging related records. Some key fields contain a check digit for self-checking purposes using the technique of check-digit verification (*see* X, **24–8**). The technique detects transposed digits in key fields which is a common type of data preparation error.

The key field would be used to refer to a customer's name and address file when preparing invoices; refer to a product file to obtain the relevant price for invoice preparation; and refer to a wage rate file for computing gross wages for payroll requirements.

3. File conversion and creation. When applications are to be transferred to a computer the master files must be converted from their present form, perhaps ledger cards, to a computer compatible form, i.e. magnetic media. In effect this means the conversion of records from a visible form, on ledger cards, to an invisible form as magnetic spots on magnetic tape or disc (*see* Fig. 66).

Before conversion, it is necessary to reconcile the balances and other data on existing records before encoding the details of each record onto floppy disc or magnetic tape. New code numbers for

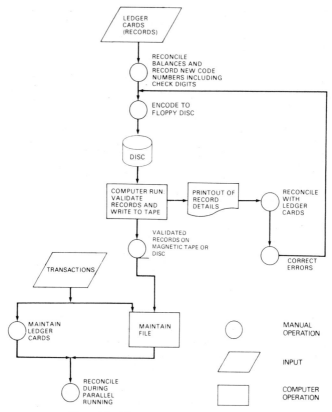

FIG. 66 *File conversion and creation.*

particular classes of records may be required particularly if they are to incorporate self-checking numbers with in-built check digits.

File conversion creates a high volume operation and suitable arrangements must be made for this commitment, especially as the records must also be verified to ensure they have been converted correctly.

During the file conversion run the new records are printed out and these must be manually reconciled with the old records to ensure there are no irregularities. All errors must be corrected. Most files are not static during the changeover period from the existing system to the computer system, as data is obtained from various sources within and without the organisation and data is for ever changing owing to the frequency of business transactions. Difficulties arise in the task of attempting to maintain files in phase during parallel running. During this phase it is necessary to update two sets of records, i.e. master files for reconciliation purposes to ensure the computer is producing accurate results.

4. File security. This important topic is dealt with in the chapter dealing with Checks and Controls in Computerised Systems (*see* X).

5. File updating. An important feature of data processing is file updating and in this respect it is important to appreciate that all data and the records, to which the data relates, must be stored in the internal memory of the processor before any data processing operation or file updating is possible. Records are transferred by means of the appropriate backing storage device, which is normally either a tape deck or disc drive, depending upon the media used for storing master files—magnetic tapes or discs (*see* Figs. 67 and 68).

Before processing commences the appropriate files are obtained

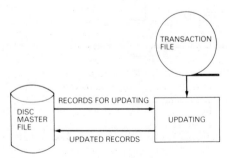

FIG. 67 *Disc updating.*

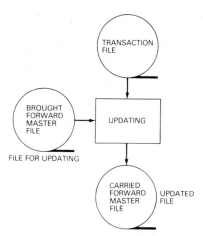

FIG. 68 *Magnetic tape updating.*

from the tape and disc library by the computer operator. After updating they are returned to the library for storage until they are required for the next updating run. In the meanwhile the files are stored off-line and are not accessible by the computer until the next run and this creates problems with regard to facilitating random enquiries from user departments unless the files are permanently on-line (*see* XI, **8, 9**).

File updating is performed systematically at pre-defined periods of time depending upon circumstances. In some instances the frequency of processing data and file updating is dependent to some extent upon the volume of transactions because of the necessity of avoiding a build-up of data on the one hand and the need to achieve a smooth work throughout on the other or the need for up to the minute information for business control.

The preparation of invoices and updating the sales ledger master file may necessitate a daily run because of the relatively high volume of transactions involved. If it is performed weekly the processing time may be so long as to preclude the processing of other important applications—the payroll for instance.

In some instances applications have natural updating and processing frequencies, a case in point being the factory payroll which has a natural weekly updating frequency. On the other hand a monthly staff payroll has a natural monthly updating frequency.

The frequency of updating is often dependent upon the information needs of management for business control. One instance of this is when the status of stocks is a key factor in running a business effectively, which necessitates daily updating because management require a daily schedule in order to be aware of shortages and excess stocks. Appropriate action is then effected in respect of purchase orders for raw materials and production orders in relation to sales orders.

6. File activity or "hit" rate. The proportion of records updated or referenced on each updating run in relation to the total number of records on a master file is referred to as the "hit" rate. This is a very important consideration in computer configuration deliberations regarding the type of storage media most suitable for specific applications, i.e. magnetic tape or magnetic disc.

In respect of magnetic tape files, it is necessary to access each record on the file serially, even though some of the records are not affected by current transactions. What is more, the whole of the file has to be rewritten on a new tape file. In this case, a file with a low "hit" rate can increase processing time and would be better stored on magnetic disc, which has direct access capability. Direct access requires only those records affected by transactions to be accessed for updating. In addition, records stored on disc do not have to be written to a different disc after updating since records are overwritten.

As a payroll has a high "hit" rate, there is no advantage in storing it on magnetic disc, as every employee's record needs to be updated each pay period. Magnetic tape has a high storage capacity and is cheaper than magnetic discs. On the other hand, a stock file may contain records which are only affected by transactions occasionally, therefore the whole of the file does not change each time a computer run is made. In this case, processing time can be reduced by storing stock records on magnetic disc (*see* Figs. 67 and 68).

7. File amendments. File amendments include the addition of new records or the deletion of obsolete records from a master file, for example the addition of new starters and the deletion of terminations from the payroll or employee master file (*see* XI, **4**). Reference files may require amendment occasionally in respect of changes of names and addresses, product selling prices and wage rates, etc (*see* Fig. 69).

From the following, illustrate and explain the effect of file amendments on a newly created forward master file on magnetic tape.

CUSTOMER MASTERFILE AMENDMENTS

Card code	Batch No.	Amend code	ACCOUNT	Card No.	Area	SYMBOL	Insured limit	Credit limit	Spec. acct.	Out	POINTER	MAP REF.	MILEAGE
E O				1									

Completion notes:

1) Always complete AMEND-code and ACCOUNT-no. on first card.
   For AMEND-code 1 = Insert new account
   2 = Amend account details
   3 = Delete account no.
2) For insertion of new account no. complete all of first card and complete other cards as necessary.
3) For amending of an account record complete details on cards 1–9 as required (if it is needed to delete one line of say delivery instructions, write the word DELETE in the relevant box-this must start at the beginning of the field and applies only to cards 2–9)
4) For deletion of an account record, no details (other than those in note 1 above) are required.

Card No.	1ST LINE OF INVOICE NAME & ADDRESS	2ND LINE OF INVOICE NAME & ADDRESS
2		

Card No.	3RD LINE OF INVOICE NAME & ADDRESS	4TH LINE OF INVOICE NAME & ADDRESS
3		

Card No.	5TH LINE OF INVOICE NAME & ADDRESS
4	

Card No.	1ST LINE OF DELIVERY NAME & ADDRESS	2ND LINE OF DELIVERY NAME & ADDRESS
5		

Card No.	3RD LINE OF DELIVERY NAME & ADDRESS	4TH LINE OF DELIVERY NAME & ADDRESS
6		

Card No.	5TH LINE OF DELIVERY NAME & ADDRESS
7	

Card No.	1ST LINE OF DELIVERY INSTRUCTIONS
8	

Card No.	2ND LINE OF DELIVERY INSTRUCTIONS

SALES DEPT.	DATE
Issued by:	
Credit Limit £	/ /
Approved:	/ /
ACCOUNTS DEPT.	
Approved:	

FIG. 69 *Customer masterfile amendment form.*

OLD MASTER FILE

	Record Number	Name	Credit Limit £	Balance due £
(1)	106075	Syson	5000	4275
(2)	106076	French	1000	450
(3)	106080	Bishop	2000	0000
(4)	106082	Osborne	4000	2500
(5)	106085	Corbett	8000	6350

AMENDMENT FILE

	Record number	Name	Transaction code	Credit Limit £	Balance due £
(A)	106076	French	1	7500	
(B)	106077	Green	3	4000	0000
(C)	106079	Ball	1	4250	
(D)	106080		2		
(E)	106082	Osborne	1	3000	

Transaction code: 1—Amendment
                     2—Deletion
                     3—Insertion

The solution to the question is outlined below:
The effect of applying the amendments to the file are shown as follows:

Record number	Name	Credit Limit £	Balance due £
106075	Syson	5000	4275
106076	French	7500	450
106077	Green	4000	0000
106082	Osborne	3000	2500
106085	Corbett	8000	6350

The following details provide an explanation of the amendments.

106075	Remains unchanged and is copied to the carried forward file
106076	Amendment to credit limit on carried forward file
106077	A new record to be added to the file
106079	Indicated as an amendment but does not exist on the file. The record is signalled as an error and excluded from the master file
106080	Deletion from the file

106082   Amendment to credit limit on carried forward file
106085   Remains unchanged and copied to carried forward
          file

Activities concerned with file amendments on magnetic tape include the reading in of a record to the processor's memory from the master file together with an amendment from the amendment file. The "key" fields are compared to establish if there is a match. Appropriate action is then taken either to write the record unchanged on the new file if it is not affected by an amendment, or, if it is affected by an amendment, to adjust it in the memory before it is written to the new file. If the amendment is a deletion, then the record is omitted from the new file but if it is a new record then it is added to the new file. All this must be effected before the master file is updated by transaction data. It is essential that records are amended before being used in processing.

RELATIONSHIP BETWEEN MASTER FILES, TRANSACTION FILES AND REFERENCE FILES

8. Master file. The nature of this category of file has already been defined and is also illustrated later in the chapter (*see* **1**). It is important to be aware of the relationship between files in a data processing environment. Sometimes a master file is consolidated to include reference information as well as information which is subjected to updating from a transaction file (*see* **5**). This is discussed below.

9. Transaction file. A collection of data relating to business transactions is referred to as a transaction file. This contains details relating to stock movements—stock transaction file, wages—wages transaction file, items required by customers—orders file, and so on. Such details are input for processing, including computing the value of stock movements, gross wages and the value of goods sold to customers. These values are then used as part of the information printed out on documents and schedules as well as being recorded on the relevant records in the appropriate master file to which they relate.

Transaction data may be collected for a period of time and processed in batches or may be processed as it arises on an interactive transaction processing basis. A file may not always be in evidence in such cases but if batches of transactions are dealt with as they arise then this process forms a transaction file dealt with on a transaction basis, i.e. on an individual rather than a batch basis.

10. Reference file. This is a file which contains reference information, i.e. information which is referred to during data processing operations, whether for random enquiries or for details required during batch processing. Such files contain details pertaining to product prices to be used for invoice computations, names and addresses of customers and suppliers to be used for the production of mail shots and for addressing documents such as invoices, statements and purchase orders, etc. Wage rates may also be recorded in this way.

If names and addresses are required predominantly for general mailing needs then the file may be structured separately, otherwise it may be integrated with the relevant master file, such as the customer or supplier file. If wage rates are reasonably stable then they may be incorporated in the payroll master file in respect of those employees paid on the basis of attended hours. The rates may otherwise be input as current wages data and omitted from the file completely.

FILE ORGANISATION

11. Logical and physical records. The records on a file are normally grouped by type whereby all similar records are stored on the same media. The individual records relating to a specific entity, e.g. account of customer X, the earnings and tax records of employee Y or the stock record of item Z, are logical records. The file media on which they are stored, i.e. the reel of tape or the specific disc pack is the physical storage media, therefore many logical records will be stored on a physical file (*see* Fig. 70 and VIII, **17, 18**).

The individual records are referenced, updated, amended and information is extracted from them according to the needs of the business. For effective file handling and processing a computer

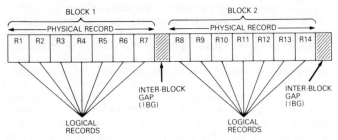

FIG. 70 *Blocked records illustrating the relationship of physical and logical records.*

handles physical records, i.e. groups or blocks of logical records. A block may be 512 bytes (characters) in length and the number of records in the block is determined by the systems designer on the basis of the number of characters in each record and the size of the block.

This achieves efficiency in the transfer of data from the physical file to the processor as it is impractical to stop/start a tape deck after transferring single records as there would be more stop/start time than data transfer time. A disc drive does not stop when transferring records but it does function on the basis of the "block" as blocks of records are transferred from the disc drive to the processor, not single records. The block containing a specific record for processing needs is searched after being transferred to internal memory to locate the record required (*see* **18, 19** and **24**).

12. Serial organisation. Both magnetic tape and disc files can be organised on a serial basis. Records are stored in ascending order of key field. Although the method is normally applicable to magnetic tape files because of the continuous nature of a reel of tape, it can be applied to disc files. With disc files, however, there is no way in which a record can be accessed directly and the method does not exploit the direct access capability of disc storage. Serial processing of disc files is similar to processing magnetic tape files (*see* **22**).

13. Indexed sequential. This method is applied to disc storage and is a modified version of serial organisation. It allows a sequential file to be processed serially as the records are stored in ascending order of "key" field. It is necessary to compile a cylinder and track index for direct access to records (*see* **24**). When processing a file on an indexed sequential basis it is normal practice to apply the "overlay" technique. The technique causes an overflow of records on a disc track which requires the use of an overflow area on the disc file. To overcome the problem of locating records in an overflow area, the cylinder/track index records the highest record key of records stored in the overflow area corresponding to each track indexed. The presence of the overflow address also indicates whether new records should be stored in the data area or the overflow area. It is important to maintain the sequence of records in the file and this is accomplished by "chaining". Using the technique of chaining, a record which has been displaced into the overflow area has its new location recorded within the record which logically preceded it. The displaced record also has the location of the next record in logical sequence. By this means, the sequential order of records is easily traced.

14. Partitioned file. With this method of file organisation on discs each record is located by reference to an alphabetic directory or index, which is useful for storing and locating sub-routines.

15. Random file organisation. Records are not stored on discs in any organised sequence (random), and so general rules for retrieving records cannot be applied. Random organisation requires the use of a full index or an address generation system.

With randomly organised files, it can take much longer to locate records than with a sequential file.

VIRTUAL STORAGE

16. Concept of virtual storage. Some computers incorporate a storage management technique known as "virtual storage". The technique increases the apparent capacity of internal storage by an amount many times its actual capacity. Concurrent processing of several programs, that would otherwise exceed the main internal storage capacity, is made possible.

17. Mode of operation. Virtual storage uses magnetic discs which are used to store programs required for processing. This is instead of loading them to internal storage (main storage), which is the normal method employed.

In order that the main storage available is used in the most efficient manner, the technique splits the program into small segments called "pages". Only those pages which are required for processing are called into main storage at one time. The remainder of the program stays in virtual storage.

The addresses within a page refer to virtual storage locations and when transferred to main storage the addresses must refer to main storage locations before processing can be executed. It is necessary, therefore, to effect address translation, which is achieved by a hardware-assisted table look-up.

FILE ORGANISATION—MAGNETIC TAPE

18. Blocking of records. A block of records consists of a number of records which are grouped together without intervening spaces between them, i.e. without inter-record gaps (*see* Fig. 71).

19. Block size. The size of data blocks has a direct bearing on the efficiency with which jobs are run on the computer.

Irrespective of the size of data blocks, a blank length of tape is

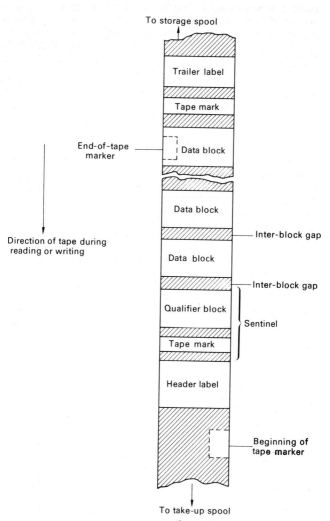

(Courtesy International Computers Limited)

FIG. 71 *Layout of a data file on magnetic tape.*

required between blocks. This is known as an "inter-block gap" and is used to allow the tape to slow down and stop after a block of data has been read or written, and to allow the tape to re-start and accelerate to the appropriate reading or writing speed for the next block of data to be input or output.

If data blocks are short, then the deceleration and acceleration of the tape between blocks can exceed the time actually taken in transferring data to and from the computer. In order to eliminate this unproductive time, the block size should be increased as much as the available internal storage locations will allow.

20. Fixed-length records. Fixed-length records consist of fields of a fixed length in a similar manner to fields of data on punched cards. Fixed length implies that the number of character positions allocated to each field of a record is constant, irrespective of the number of character positions required by the data. In circumstances when all the character positions are not required, it may be necessary to insert space characters to the right of indicative data, e.g. names and addresses.

Marker symbols are required, in order that the program may detect the end of records and blocks, the following are examples.

(*a*) *End of record marker* (*ERM*). Indicates that the end of one record has been reached and a new record is to commence.

(*b*) *End of block marker* (*EBM*). Indicates that the end of one block of data has been reached and a new block is to commence.

21.   Variable-length records. Variable-length records consist of fields of data in which the number of character positions in each field is allocated in accordance with the character positions actually required by the data. This method of recording data recognises that the same class of record does not always require the same number of character positions in each corresponding field, especially those relating to variable data such as quantities and values.

Records which vary in length and are recorded as such on magnetic tape increase the length of tape utilised for significant data. As the efficiency of using tape is increased, so is the speed of transferring data, and processing time is reduced accordingly.

Variable-length records require more program instructions to be written, however, as it is necessary to test for the end of fields. This is achieved by a further marker symbol known as an "end of field marker" (EFM). It is also necessary to indicate the end of records and end of blocks (*see* **20**).

With both variable- and fixed-length records, it is necessary to allocate sufficient storage locations to enable the maximum-length record to be stored prior to processing.

In general, the larger the size of block, the greater will be the amount of data recorded on tape, as the number of inter-block gaps will be fewer. As a result, the transfer of data in and out of the computer memory will be accomplished at a greater speed.

FILE ACCESS METHODS

22. Serial and sequential access. In respect of serial access, records are accessed in the order in which they are stored on the tape. Any specific record can only be accessed after all the preceding records have been. Sequential access and serial access mean the same thing in the context of magnetic tape files, as records are stored in ascending sequence of key field each of which is referred to serially.

There is a difference between serial and sequential access in the context of disc based files, however, as the records accessed serially may not be in a defined sequence. Sequential access refers to the process of accessing records in a file according to a specified sequence of keys.

23. Binary chop. It is possible to locate a record on a serially organised disc file without having to read each preceding record. This is achieved by the technique of "binary chop", also referred to as "binary search" and "dichotomising search". It is a speedy method of accessing specific records on a file or in a table. The method requires the various items on the file or in the table to be in a specific sequence; normally ascending order of key field.

The middle number or record key on a file or in a table is tested to determine whether it is above or below the one required. After the test one half of the file or table is discarded, i.e. the half which is below the desired record key. The process continues by examining the middle record or number of the remaining half of the file or table until the one required is located.

As an example of the functioning of "binary chop", how many comparisons are necessary to discover the number or record key 20 in the following array of record keys:

1 4 6 14 15 17 19 20 22

The data contains nine record keys, the middle one being 15. The lower half of the record keys is below that required, i.e. 20, therefore it is discarded. This leaves record keys 17, 19, 20 and 22. The middle of which comes between 19 and 20 therefore the left-hand side of the set is discarded. The next test refers to record keys 20 and 22. As the first number is equal to that required no further examination is necessary. Three tests were required to find the required record key. Without the binary search technique the file would have been accessed serially, necessitating eight tests before record key 20 was reached on the file.

24. Cylinder concept. A cylinder (*see* Fig. 72) is a hypothetical but highly practical notion comprising a set of data provided by each recording surface of the disc pack. It consists of the similar concentric tracks on all of the surfaces. Each track forms a ring or

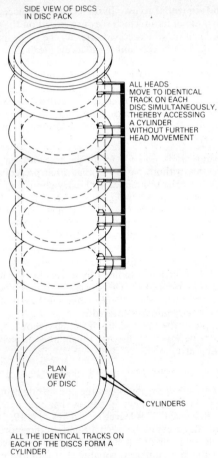

SIDE VIEW OF DISCS
IN DISC PACK

ALL HEADS
MOVE TO IDENTICAL
TRACK ON EACH
DISC SIMULTANEOUSLY,
THEREBY ACCESSING
A CYLINDER
WITHOUT FURTHER
HEAD MOVEMENT

PLAN
VIEW
OF DISC

CYLINDERS

ALL THE IDENTICAL TRACKS ON
EACH OF THE DISCS FORM A
CYLINDER

FIG. 72 *Cylinder.*

segment, in which records are stored in ascending order of key field, and to which are added the corresponding segments, i.e. the tracks of the other surfaces. The circular segments form a cylinder of records all of which can be accessed for a single positioning of the read/write heads. The cylinder is referred to as the "seek" area. This is an efficient way of accessing records as the delay encountered by continuously repositioning the heads is eliminated. It is only necessary to reposition the heads for each new cylinder of records and for a disc pack consisting of ten recording surfaces the cylinder contains ten tracks of records. Each surface has its own read/write head which makes the cylinder concept a practical proposition. If each disc surface contains a hundred tracks then the disc pack has a hundred cylinders.

It is necessary to compile an index indicating the highest record key in each cylinder, and the highest record key in each track. To access a specific record the record key is compared with the cylinder index which, by means of "high or equal" test, indicates the cylinder containing the record. The appropriate track (surface) is determined in a similar way. Disc surfaces are organised into a number of sectors, segments or buckets (often eight) which are in effect blocks. The block is the smallest unit of data transfer therefore it is necessary for each record key to consist of three elements, i.e. cylinder number, track (surface) number and block or bucket number. The storage location of a record may therefore consist of 99 (cylinder number), which is the penultimate track on a disc of 100 tracks; 4 (surface or track number) and 8 (block number), which is the last block on the disc track when each track consists of eight sectors. The location address of the record is therefore 9948.

When the block containing the required record is transferred to the internal memory the block is searched for the record key to be accessed either for reference or updating.

OTHER STORAGE ASPECTS

25. Volume. This term is often used to mean a unit of magnetic storage such as a set of exchangeable discs, i.e. a disc pack, or a reel of magnetic tape. Discs, hard and floppy, can be divided into multiple volumes each having a discrete entity, e.g. the sectors on a disc surface which effectively divide the surface of the disc into blocks. It is then necessary to specify the disc volume which stores the program required. This applies to Winchester discs in particular.

26. Formatting/soft and hard sectoring. A computer, by means of a DOS (disc operating system), keeps track of the location of records on a disc and can access any record by moving the head to the relevant track and then waiting for the sector (block) containing the required record to come into position. Two methods are used to indicate the location on a track where each sector starts:

(*a*) soft sectoring, whereby special signals are recorded on the disc surface and detected by the software; and

(*b*) hard sectoring whereby holes are punched through the disc around the central hole, one per sector.

These are referred to as formatted discs.

27. Archiving. The process of removing infrequently used files from the filestore. A filestore consists of files organised in a library under the control of an operating system. Archived files are omitted from the directory of current files and are normally stored on magnetic tape, reducing the number of discs required to be on-line. This effectively reduces operating costs and increases the efficiency of computer operations. Tape files can be converted to disc files when operational necessity requires it.

STRUCTURED MASTER FILES

The details which follow outline the contents of master files of various applications.

28. Payroll master file. Typical contents are summarised as follows:

(*a*) clock number;
(*b*) name;
(*c*) tax code;
(*d*) national insurance number;
(*e*) national insurance category;
(*f*) taxable gross to date;
(*g*) tax to date;
(*h*) taxable gross previous employment;
(*i*) tax previous employment;
(*j*) holiday credit to date;
(*k*) sickness holiday credit weeks to date;
(*l*) employee's National Insurance to date;
(*m*) total National Insurance contributions to date;
(*n*) fixed deductions:
　　(*i*) charities;
　　(*ii*) overalls;
　　(*iii*) savings;
　　(*iv*) loans;

(*o*) weekly salary amount (as appropriate);
(*p*) hourly rate (as appropriate);
(*q*) holiday credit flat rate;
(*r*) employee bank details;
    (*see* XI, **4–7**).

29. Customer file. Typical contents of this file include:

(*a*) account number;
(*b*) name and address;
(*c*) credit limit;
(*d*) account balance;
(*e*) category/discount rate;
(*f*) age analysis of account balance.

This file may also include details of customer sales history but can be structured separately to suit the needs of processing as shown below (*see* Fig. 73).

30. Customer sales history file. This file may be structured as follows:

(*a*) account number;
(*b*) representative code;
(*c*) customer type;
(*d*) area code;
(*e*) turnover this period—analysed by product;
(*f*) turnover to date since week 1—analysed by product;
(*h*) number of orders to date since week 1;
(*i*) discount received to date.

This file may be structured to include cost of sales and profitability or this requirement may be stored on a separate file.

31. Product file. This file could be structured as follows:

(*a*) product code;
(*b*) product description;
(*c*) pack size;
(*d*) price;
(*e*) VAT code;
(*f*) recommended retail selling price;
(*g*) location code;
(*h*) quantity in stock;
(*i*) reorder level;
(*j*) reorder quantity;
(*k*) ordered but outstanding;

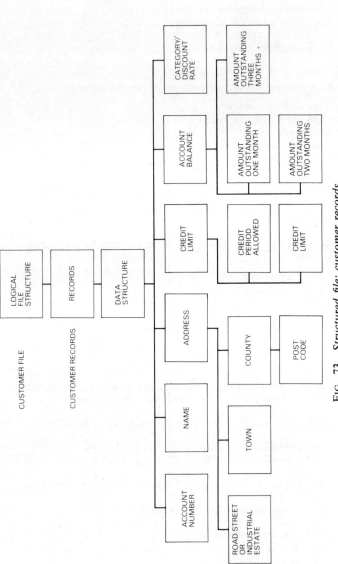

Fig. 73 *Structured file: customer records.*

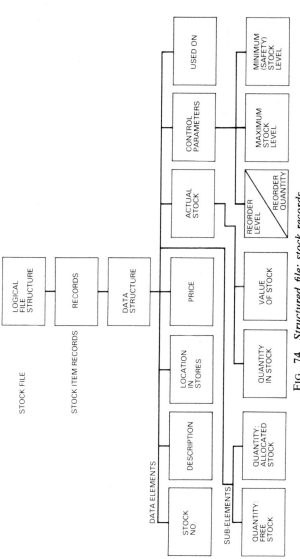

FIG. 74 *Structured file: stock records.*

32. Stock file: raw material or components. This file (*see* Fig. 74) may be structured in the following way:

(*a*) stock number;
(*b*) description;
(*c*) location in stores;
(*d*) price;
(*e*) actual stock;
(*f*) control parameters:
    (*i*) reorder level;
   (*ii*) maximum stock level;
  (*iii*) minimum stock level;
(*g*) used on;
(*h*) quantity: free stock;
(*i*) quantity: allocated stock.

33. Orders file. This file may be structured in the following way:

(*a*) order number;
(*b*) account number;
(*c*) product code;
(*d*) quantity.

The above details may be recorded on the orders file by direct input using a VDU in an on-line order entry system followed by details extracted from the customer file, viz.

(*e*) customer name;
(*f*) representative code;
(*g*) customer type.

Further information may be added from the product file (*see* **31**).

34. Plant register file. The contents of this file provide information for asset accounting requirements, giving details relating to specific items of plant and equipment.

(*a*) General information:
    (*i*) type of asset;
   (*ii*) plant code;
  (*iii*) supplier;
  (*iv*) manufacturer;
   (*v*) rating (horsepower(hp) or kilowatt (kW) rating);
  (*vi*) floor area;
 (*vii*) date of installation;
(*viii*) location;
  (*ix*) transfers.

(*b*) Accounting information:
- (*i*) date of purchase;
- (*ii*) original cost;
- (*iii*) installation cost;
- (*iv*) depreciation class;
- (*v*) annual amount of depreciation;
- (*vi*) cumulative depreciation;
- (*vii*) written-down book value;
- (*viii*) maintenance costs;
- (*ix*) cost of additions;
- (*x*) disposal value.

35. Problem relating to files. The details which follow relate to an ICMA question set in a MISDP paper:

Selected data from purchase invoices are punched into cards as follows:

supplier account number; purchase invoice number; purchase order number; quantity supplied; part number and/or expense code; value of invoice.

The above data are processed on the company's computer, which has magnetic tape backing storage, to produce numerous accounting and stock control reports included among which are the following:

Remittance advices containing supplier's name and address and details of invoices being paid;

Credit transfers containing the company's own and payee's banking details and amount of transfer.

Supplier analysis giving total expenditure for current month and year to date per supplier within each purchase classification.

It will be noted that this purchase classification is a broad group of expense codes with sub-sections. For example,

purchase classification, Raw materials—100

includes numerous expense codes, such as:

Steel—110, Copper—130, Zinc—160, etc.

Expense code analysis giving total expenditure for each expense code for the current month and year to date.

You are required to describe what files you would recommend should be maintained to produce the outputs given above and, for each of the files recommended, to state details of its sequence and minimum content.

36. Solution to file problem. An outline solution to the question is given below:

Purchase ledger file. This file would contain financial details relating to the suppliers dealing with the company as follows:

(*a*) Supplier account number.
(*b*) Supplier's name and address.
(*c*) Account balance.
(*d*) Details of invoices:
    (*i*) purchase invoice number;
    (*ii*) value of invoice.
(*e*) Details of remittance relating to invoices being paid:
    (*i*) purchase invoice number;
    (*ii*) value of invoice or amount being paid on account.
(*f*) Company's own and payee's banking details.

Details of invoices to be paid would have to be input so that they may be extracted from the appropriate accounts to update the account balance and for the details to be printed on the remittance advice.

The total amount to be paid would be printed on the credit transfers together with the company's own and payee's banking details.

Supplier history file. The punched cards could be sorted to supplier within purchase classification key for updating the history file by classification key by customer for the purpose of producing a supplier analysis as follows:

Supplier account number:
  Purchase classification:

Total expenditure	Steel—110—current month	year to date
Total expenditure	Copper—130—current month	year to date
Total expenditure	Zinc—160—current month	year to date
Grand total expenditure	—current month	year to date

Purchase history file. This file would contain details of expenditure for each expense code for the current month and year to date for the purpose of producing an expense code analysis as follows:

Expense code—Steel	110—Total expenditure	current month	year to date
—Copper	130—Total expenditure	current month	year to date

| —Zinc | 160—Total expenditure | current month year to date |
| | Grand total expenditure | current month year to date |

This file would be updated from details on the punched cards after they had been sorted to expense code. This information could be used for updating expense codes in the nominal ledger for the extraction of a trial balance and the preparation of final accounts.

ELECTRONIC DOCUMENT STORAGE AND RETRIEVAL

37. Storage of unstructured documents and records. The storage of logical structured records, relating to specific aspects of business activities, such as purchases, sales, stocks, production and employees has always been a routine element of data processing activities. Such records are stored on master files on physical storage media, such as magnetic tape or discs which are accessed for amendment and updating as required during processing runs.

The question now arises of how best to store and retrieve the data of an unstructured nature found in such documents as:

(*a*) stock reports;
(*b*) standard price schedules;
(*c*) estimates and quotations;
(*d*) sales summaries;
(*e*) budget reports—income and expenditure by department;
(*f*) labour turnover reports;
(*g*) candidate assessment forms;
(*h*) minutes of meetings.

The types of document outlined above normally reside in office filing cabinets in the relevant secretary's office but this area of business activity has been overtaken by the new electronic technology as electronic filing and retrieval systems using floppy disc based microcomputers are now becoming very common.

38. Electronic filing and retrieval systems. These systems are often referred to by various descriptive titles. However, it is confusing as to whether the nature of the systems under consideration differs or if it is a matter of a shovel being called a spade. The terms which may be encountered include those listed below:

(*a*) electronic document storage and retrieval systems;
(*b*) text filing and retrieval systems;
(*c*) file management systems;
(*d*) electronic retrieval of free text documents.

39. Electronic retrieval of free text documents. Systems which store documents electronically and which enable complete documents or sections of documents to be retrieved are predominant as floppy disc based microcomputers are being used instead of normal office filing cabinets. This is a good thing because even in the most efficient filing system documents tend to go astray and it is often difficult to trace them as they can be classified under various titles. Such electronically stored documents can be retrieved by specifying words or phrases that occur within the text. The words can be located anywhere within the text, eliminating the need for keyfields. Such systems require the ability to capture and retain documents electronically and retrieve them from a partial description of their contents.

Retrieval technique in general utilises "user friendly" language but more complex queries can be effected by using Boolean operators 'AND', 'OR' and 'NOT'. These can be applied when combining two factors, i.e. search terms which may be phrased as "find all documents which include both the words male AND single" or, "find all documents relating to personnel who have "O" level passes in Mathematics AND "A" level passes in English", or, "find those records of employees who are male AND staff NOT in the pension scheme",

Synonyms can be applied in a query to expand a search term when different words can have the same meaning or can be spelled differently. If the search term is "computer" it may have the synonym "electronic computer" or "digital computer". When applying the synonym facility the system automatically interprets the query as "computer" OR "electronic computer" OR "digital computer".

Truncation is applied for a root search whereby all subjects with a similar root are signalled by the system, very often by the asterisk sign, e.g. finance*, which could generate the following subjects—financial, financing, etc.

Masking may be applied when the user is not sure how a name should be spelled for searching purposes. This allows the middle characters of a word to be masked out, e.g. the name of a company Hindacem may be masked as Hind*cem if one is not certain whether it is Hindicem or Hinducem.

40. Inverted files. This type of file organisation may be applied to advantage for information retrieval purposes as it eliminates the need for serial searching and reduces the time to retrieve records possessing a specific attribute. Items possessing a specific feature are grouped together to form an inverted file. For example, a sales ledger file (customer master file) may have as an attribute "credit limit in the range £10 000–£25 000". All customer accounts possessing this attribute will be grouped on the basis of account number.

PROGRESS TEST 7

1. What is a master file? **(1)**
2. What is a record key? **(2)**
3. A critical stage in the implementation of any new computer-based system is initial computer file creation. You are required to explain: (*a*) the objectives and general approach to initial file creation; (*b*) the control and security procedures necessary at this stage; (*c*) the particular problems involved when the data for file creation emanate from various sources and how these can be overcome. **(3)** (*ICMA*)
4. Systems changeover and file conversion are two important stages in the implementation of a newly-designed computer system. Describe and comment on each of these activities. **(3 and XVI, 45)** (*ACA*)
5. An important activity in data processing is file updating. Discuss. **(5)**
6. (*a*) In the context of files on disc what is meant by the following terms: (*i*) block; (*ii*) record; (*iii*) key; (*iv*) address? (*b*) Describe, giving ONE example in EACH case, the difference between a high activity file and a low activity file. Describe a suitable method by which the high activity file may be organised, and how a particular record on this file is accessed. **(2, 6, 24, 26)** (*C & G*)
7 Outline the nature of file amendments. **(7)**
8. (*a*) Give a full definition of the word "file" as used in systems work and distinguish with a simple example of each, between a master file, a transaction file and a reference file. **(8, 9, 10)** (*b*) Identify and briefly explain FOUR of the factors a systems analyst will need to consider when designing a master file. **(6, 12, 13, 19–24, 26)** (*ACA*)
9. What are the functions of the following files in a computer system and what method of file organisation would be suitable to each on both tape and disc? (*a*) Master file; (*b*) transaction file; (*c*) transfer file; (*d*) work file. **(8, 9, 12, 13, 18–21 and XI, 7(*a*))** (*IDPM*)
10. Specify the difference between logical and physical records. **(11)**
11. Specify the meaning of serial file organisation and indexed

sequential file organisation indicating what method is most suitable for the storage of records on magnetic tape and magnetic disc. **(12, 13)**

12. Define the meaning of the terms: (*a*) partitioned file; (*b*) random file. **(14, 15)**

13. What is virtual storage? **(16, 17)**

14. How are records organised on magnetic tape files? **(12, 18−21)**

15. Describe the methods of serial and sequential access. **(22)**

16. Explain what is meant by a "binary search". How many comparisons are necessary to discover by this method the position of the number 18 in the following set of numbers? 1, 3, 5, 7, 13, 14, 17, 18, 21. **(23** outlines the means of solving this question) (*C & G*)

17. What is the significance of the "cylinder concept" in the context of file access? **(24)**

18. What is meant by the terms: (*a*) volume; (*b*) formatting/soft and hard sectoring. **(25, 26)**.

19. Describe briefly why archiving is necessary and how it is performed. **(27)** (*C & G*)

20. Define what is meant by data structures. (Fig. 73 and 74)

21. Specify the content of the following structured master files: (*a*) payroll file; (*b*) customer file; (*c*) customer sales history file; (*d*) product file; (*e*) stock file; (*f*) orders file; (*g*) plant register file. **(28−34)**

22. Outline the nature of electronic document storage and retrieval systems. **(37−9)**

23. What are inverted files and what purpose do they serve? **(40)**

CHAPTER VIII

Databases

DATABASE DEFINED

1. What is a database? A database or databank may be defined as a collection of structured data supporting the operations of the whole or major areas of a business. It may also be defined as a centrally located data file providing the foundations of a computer based management information system.

The concept of a database means something very specific and the collection of data must have certain qualities. The following definition was given by Floyd Johnson of Honeywell-Bull at an NCC conference on databases in 1973. "A non-redundant collection of all data serving one or more defined business applications, that data being structurally linked to and permitting access to all other data in that collection for which a natural or logical business relationship has been defined to exist, however complex."

An essential requirement of a database is not merely to store data efficiently but also to provide an effective means of retrieval. The objective of a database is to provide reliable up-to-date unambiguous information on demand. The centralisation of information in itself serves no purpose but if it can be retrieved more efficiently than is otherwise possible then the data structure of a business may be rationalised.

The term "data" in the context of a database refers to a collection of data elements which, when related in a logical manner, provides meaningful information.

A database to be of any use at all must be maintained in an up-to-date condition. In a large volume situation, such as the Driver and Vehicle Licensing Centre operations, this can present a formidable task regarding the number of transactions to be effected each day.

Similarly, file maintenance creates an additional work load for dealing with the deletion of obsolete, and the addition of new, records in respect of employees, customers and suppliers, etc.

2. Essential considerations for setting up a database. Traditionally functions have developed their own files to support their specific

165

operations. Such files are used for reference purposes or are updated with transaction data in order to provide the latest status of stocks, customer and supplier balances, etc. Such files often consist of records containing common data elements which are duplicated in several functional files. This situation creates redundancy as the same data elements in each of the files are updated separately. The personnel function, for instance, maintains a file of employee records containing data elements in respect of employee name, address, number, marital status, department number, grade and rate of pay, etc. Similar data elements are also stored on the payroll file used in the preparation of wages and maintaining a record of earnings and tax. An input of current transaction data is required to each application to update relevant data elements (*see* Fig. 75).

A database system aims at eliminating such duplication of storage and updating and providing the means for retrieving data elements for each of the application requirements in the required combinations. All data relating to a specific subject, employees in this case, is then consolidated rather than fragmented within several functional files (*see* Fig. 76).

When separate files are maintained with common data elements some are out of phase with others, which is due either to different

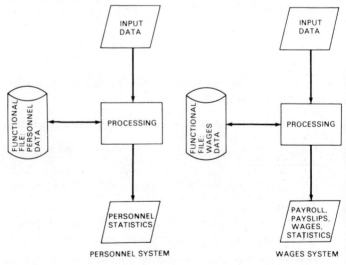

FIG. 75 *Functional (sub-system) approach to file structures.*

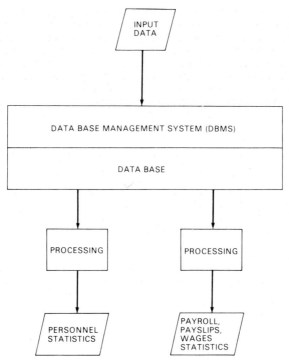

FIG. 76 *Database approach to file structures—integrated files.*

updating cycles or frequencies or even omitting to update a file completely.

Important factors related to the use of databases are summarised below:

(*a*) data should be input once only;

(*b*) redundant data should be eliminated;

(*c*) data should be capable of being speedily retrieved;

(*d*) files should be easy to maintain;

(*e*) files should be expandable;

(*f*) access to files should be restricted to authorised users by the use of passwords;

(*g*) restart and recovery procedures are necessary;

(*h*) selective printouts should be provided for the specific information requirements of managers;

(*i*) provision should be made for batch and on-line processing;

(*j*) new data structures should be capable of being incorporated into the database;

(*k*) distinction should be made between the physical and the logical storage of data;

(*l*) should be capable of contending with changing circumstances within the business;

(*m*) the cost of storing data should be optimised;

(*n*) should be self-monitoring including the provision of audit trails.

STRUCTURE AND PROBLEMS OF SETTING UP A DATABASE

3. Integrated file structure. A database is built-up on an integrated file structure basis to serve the needs of several functions. The ideal situation would be to have one large database serving the needs of the business as a whole but this leads to complexity in defining data relationships. A database need not be a single file, however, as it is often practicable to implement several small databases serving the needs of several integrated systems, that is several sets of functional groupings, in respect of functions which have direct relationships with each other. For example a sales accounting system may be integrated to provide for invoicing and stock control. A product file would provide data elements in respect of product code and description, cost price, selling price, VAT rate, stock balance, history of stock movements, etc. A customer file would provide data elements in respect of customer code number, name, address for invoicing and address for delivery if different to the invoice address, credit limit, account balance age analysis, sales history. The product file would enable stock schedules and re-order lists to be printed out on demand. The customer file would enable lists of account balances, accounts which had exceeded credit limit, age analysis of account balances, profitablity reports and statements of account to be printed out as required.

4. Problems and advantages of setting up a database. One of the problems of setting up a database for systems integration purposes is the classification of data elements as each must be allocated a data name for identification purposes. Data elements may be known by different names in the various functions and a data classification scheme is therefore essential before a database can be got off the ground. A data dictionary consisting of data definitions, characteristics and inter-relationships is therefore very necessary.

It is also necessary to specify data requirements for various functional needs, as indicated in the examples outlined previously, with regard to the personnel/payroll application and the integrated sales accounting system. The logical data relationships must also be defined. Only by this approach is it possible to design effective file handling methods, which must take into account the operating needs for accessing data rather than the manner in which data is physically stored.

The advantages of using a database are summarised below.

(*a*) Data is input once only, thereby eliminating duplication of input.

(*b*) Redundant data is eliminated as elements of data are stored only in one location. Access is attained as necessary for specific application requirements.

(*c*) Data can be retrieved very quickly.

(*d*) Confidentiality of information is attained by the use of passwords which restrict access to the whole, or part, of a database to authorised personnel.

(*e*) Data can be sorted at high speed and searched in accordance with defined parameters.

(*f*) Special report layouts can be generated according to specific needs.

(*g*) Labels and letters can be printed.

(*h*) Records can be browsed through on the display screen.

(*i*) Data can be subjected to calculations.

(*j*) A common database facilitates the integration of systems.

STRUCTURAL DATA RELATIONSHIPS

5. Data elements. In the every day use of our language it is well known that characters make up words. Words in the context of data processing may be classed as "fields" or data elements such as a customer's account number, quantity ordered, price and value, etc. A series of related data elements constitute "records". From this is can be seen that logical relationships exist between data elements which may be very simple or complex. In setting up a database it is essential to be aware of all such relationships. It is also important to appreciate logical relationships before making changes to particular data elements otherwise disruption will occur as certain functions will not be able to access data elements in the form they are required.

The Database Task Group (DBTG) initially recognised the three generally accepted definitions of structural data relationships as:

(*a*) sequential list structures;
(*b*) tree structures;
(*c*) complex network structures.

It was also considered that the totality of data in a business may be a combination of all three.

6. Sequential list structure. A structure in which each element is related to the element preceding it and the element following it.

7. Tree structure. A hierarchical structure in which each element may be related to any number of elements at any level below it but only one element above it in the hierarchy.

8. Network structure. Similar to a tree structure but with the important exception that any element may be related to any number of other elements. This type of stucture closely represents the logical data relationships which exist in the world of business.

9. Sets. The DBTG concept of "sets" may be used to define the structures indicated above. The concept of sets is fundamental to understanding any file management technique related to "lists".

(*a*) A set is a collection of named record types.
(*b*) Any number of sets may be defined in a database.
(*c*) A set must have a single "owner" type, i.e. a master record relating to a department for instance.
(*d*) A record type may be "owner" of one or more sets.
(*e*) A record type may be a "member" in one or more sets, e.g. details of employees may be a "member" of a personnel department set and a manufacturing department set.
(*f*) A record may be both owner and member but in different sets.
(*g*) A set must have a specified set order.

10. Relational structure. Data is stored in tables and the relationship of a record in one table to a record in another is indicated by having similar fields in each table. The data in tables is stored in record format. The tables are called "relations".

DATABASE AND DATA MANAGEMENT SYSTEMS

11. Database software. The control of a database is accomplished automatically by a software package which allows the user to define, amend, delete, add, sort, search, compute and print records. All this is achieved with a minimum of knowledge about computers on the part of the user as the programs guide the user through the various stages, often by means of a menu which lists on the video screen all the options. The menu may be defined as the "command centre" of the database and the required option is selected by keying in the option number.

Database or data management systems exist for all sizes of computer. The larger computers have very powerful systems costing several hundred pounds but less complex ones are available for microcomputers at relatively low cost, in fact one purchased by the author for the ORIC-1 cost no more than £4.95.

12. ICL Record Access to Program Independent Data. As an example of a database system for the larger computer ICL provide an integrated database manager on the ME29 computer which forms part of the TME(Transaction Machine Environment) modular operating system. The database system is known as TME-RAPID (Record Access to Program Indepenent Data). The database is set up and maintained interactively by the operating system allowing personnel with no previous experience of databases to manage their data effectively. Its features include COBOL file processing techniques. Data can be transferred to an IDMS system (*see* **13**) when the user has outgrown the facilities of TME-RAPID.

13. ICL Integrated Data Management System (IDMS). This system is run on the ME29 range for the creation, processing and administration of a database. IDMS is an implementation of a subset of the COBOL database facility proposed by the Codasyl Committee. The system manages data in the most natural way to match the business organisation and COBOL file processing techniques. A network structure is used to define relationships between types of record and is therefore free from the restrictions of conventional file structures.

IDMS consists of two main elements: a Data Description Language (DDL) for easy specification of data relationships and a Data Manipulation Language (DML) which provides statements for inclusion in COBOL programs to process the database as required.

14. Data management system facilities. Database or data management systems such as Compsoft's Data Management System have facilities for calculating, amending, sorting, searching, displaying, reorganising, linking, securing and printing. The system provides for the printing of circular letters (perhaps by word processors) and allows the merging of data, such as names and addresses, stored in the data management system. Self-adhesive labels can be produced to match any letter.

All programs offered by Compsoft have the following capabilities.

(*a*) *Data entry and amendments*. This can be done either through a standard screen display, or through formatted screens created to match individual needs. When you create your own screen formats you may expand your operator prompts, change the order of fields, miss new fields out or introduce new fields to hold sub-totals, etc. You may set up calculation routines to take place as new records are entered, and protect the files by passwords so that operators may do nothing more than enter or amend data.

(*b*) *Sorting*. This is the part of DMS that puts the records into meaningful orders, e.g. numeric or alphabetic, or combinations of these. Sorts are rapid and can be saved on disc.

(*c*) *Searching*. This is the part of DMS that finds all those records that meet various parameters. Up to eight search criteria can be used simultaneously. Special features include "free text" searching, range searching, less than, greater than, etc., and AND/OR searching. The search parameters can be saved on disc for future use or amendment.

(*d*) *Printing lists and reports*. DMS can print lists in sorted orders, using either the whole file of records, or only those records that meet various parameters. Printouts can be tailored to use standard stationery, and totals and sub-totals of numeric data can be produced automatically. Special report layouts may be stored on disc.

(*e*) *Letters*. DMS can write any number of letters for merging with the information contained in the records. Letters are storable and amendable.

(*f*) *Labels*. DMS can print on to label stationery up to five labels wide.

(*g*) *Screen display*. Records can be seen on screen, and "browsed" through, amending or "tagging" as you go.

(*h*) *Calculations*. You can add, subtract, divide, or multiply numeric data with constants or with other fields. Batches of records meeting various parameters can be processed separately, and batches of records deleted if required. Frequently used information can be stored in tables, e.g. currency rates, discount rates and dates.

(*i*) *File organisation*. Retaining existing data, you may add or remove fields from your record layout, or split or merge data files. DMS will reorganise your data to meet your changing requirements.

(*j*) *Links*. This is the automatic transfer of selected information into commercial word processing packages and user written software which uses sequential files.

(*k*) *Security*. Back up your program disc as often as you wish. Passwords may be used to protect confidentiality.

(*l*) *Machines/operating system*. Compsoft software will run on most machines operating on CP/M, MP/M or MSDOS using $5\frac{1}{4}$ inch (133mm) or 8 inch (200mm) diskettes, plus most Commodore machines.

EXPERT SYSTEMS

15. What is an expert system? Expert systems store knowledge relating to a specific field forming a database which can be accessed and processed by special software. Expert systems belong to that branch of information technology relating to artificial intelligence which deals with knowledge based systems.

16. Development of expert systems. The development of expert systems requires a high degree of coordination between researchers and experts. Researchers must possess a wide range of skills and knowledge relating to philosophy, statistics, psychology, computers and mathematics (this is indicative of the complexity of setting up expert systems). Experts from various fields of knowledge are interviewed by researchers to assess the best way of harnessing the knowledge they possess on plant life, medicine, engineering, electronics, nuclear energy, and so on into manageable computer based systems. This involves an analysis of how experts analyse a problem and their manner of deriving the required facts. Ultimately, this information will be used to develop computer programs for expert systems which follow similar thought processes and analytical technique as the human expert. The computer program has built-in rules for obtaining facts progressively until a suitable conclusion is attained. The program must be designed to ask questions systematically, applying the menu selection technique. Such systems may be used for diagnosing illnesses from symptoms indicated by a patient or diagnosing faults in complex machines such as computers, and for biological research into plant life etc.

LOGICAL AND PHYSICAL FILES IN A DATABASE

17. Logical files. "Logical files" is a term for files as they appear to a user who is concerned with the logical data relating to a specific application in the form of functional files.

18. Physical files. As a database is a collection of data serving one or more defined business applications, it is stored on a physical file. It loses the former specific identity of an application's logical file stored on a specific reel of tape or a specific disc pack. In other words, users can no longer pinpoint their own physical file as they could in non-database systems.

An operating system refers to a specific physical file and derives logical entities from physical entities by means of database management system software. The logical data of every function is stored within the various sub-schema (the separate uses of the totality of data in the database are referred to as a schema). Data independence allows physical files on which data is stored to be changed without affecting the application software using the data (*see* VII, **11**).

THE DATABASE ADMINISTRATOR

19. The database administrator as a coordinator. As the whole concept of a database is to rationalise business systems by the integration of such systems it follows that the data needs of an organisation must be coordinated at a very high level. This is basically the responsibility of a database administrator who may not yet exist in many organisations. Nevertheless someone has no doubt been vested with such responsibilities, perhaps a senior member of the systems staff.

When data is common to two or more applications then programmers are not allowed the freedom they previously enjoyed to name data elements and subject them to processing independently of other application requirements. This is where the database administrator assumes command, as it were, because he must consider the data needs of the several applications under consideration for consolidation into a database.

20. Duties of a database administrator. He must first of all be conversant with business policy and strategy, particularly for the long term, as the very fabric of a business is dependent upon an efficient and effective management information system of which a database is a fundamental part—the roots of such a system in fact. He should play an active part in the planning of information systems particularly with regard to feasibility studies.

He should be an expert in all file management techniques and be able to advise management and system planners of the capabilities and shortcomings of various file management systems with regard to the application under review. It is essential that he liaise and consult with project teams with regard to the development of design specifications, program specifications, systems documentation and programs, etc. It is imperative that he monitor the implementation of a database ensuring that time and cost constraints are adhered to. It is of extreme importance that the administrator ensures that system objectives are achieved. Also of importance is that the initial preparation and maintenance of a data dictionary should be the responsibility of a database administrator, as this is essential for the success of a database system.

PUBLIC DATABASE: PRESTEL

21. What is Prestel? Prestel is British Telecom's version of Viewdata, which is the name for textual information displayed on a television screen obtained via a telephone line, as opposed to teletext, which is the name for textual information displayed on a television screen but which is broadcast by a television company. The latter includes Ceefax of the BBC and Oracle of the IBA.

Prestel is a computer-based information system which provides information relating to a wide range of topics as outlined below. It is a "common carrier" public service over which other people supply and sell information. The system can be used for company use with built-in safeguards to retain confidentiality of information. The system provides the very latest information, as it is updated regularly (*see* Fig. 77).

22. Requirements to operate Prestel. A special Prestel television set is required, or else an adaptor can be fitted to an existing set. The set may be black and white or colour. The set may be a Prestel-only receiver or one capable of receiving Oracle and Ceefax as well. In addition, it is possible to have 26-inch or small screens. British Telecom connects the television to your telephone by a jack plug.

The system requires a small control pad with numbered buttons. By pressing selected buttons the Prestel computer is obtained via your telephone line. Prestel then announces itself by greeting your company on your television screen. When a second button is pressed, an index appears of the information available for access, which amounts to thousands of pages of information.

23. Information providers. Various organisations buy space on the Prestel computers to store and offer to the general public a wide variety of information. The organisations include *The Economist*, *Exchange and Mart*, Fintel, the Stock Exchange, *The Guinness Book of Records*, W.H. Smith, Data Stream, British Rail, *The Good Food Guide*, the English Tourist Board, the Government Statistical Service and many others.

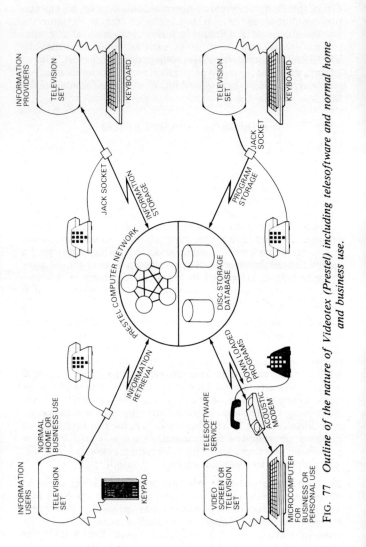

FIG. 77 Outline of the nature of Videotex (Prestel) including telesoftware and normal home and business use.

24. Information database. The type of information available is vast and includes information about companies, e.g. share prices, financial statistics and ratios, inter-company comparisons, company performance and so on. Information is also available relating to UK and international inflation rates, interest rates, travel, jobs, property and businesses for sale and wanted, business cards, tax guides, employment law, exporting, investments, business books and courses, currency exchange rates, economy indicators, industries, countries, weather reports, sports results and food prices, etc.

25. Cost factors. The costs relating to the Prestel service include a charge for each page of information displayed, which may be in the region of 15p, the cost of a local telephone call and a computer access charge.

26. Future developments. This type of service is likely to develop into television shopping whereby the television in the lounge may be connected to a supermarket warehouse for ordering goods to be delivered directly to your home. The shopping list would be keyed in, displayed on the television screen and then transmitted to the supermarket's computer. This is another version of catalogue shopping or mail order.

27. Response pages. As well as receiving information, users can send messages both to each other and to Information Providers using RESPONSE pages. These allow the user to order goods from a supermarket without leaving the house; book a hotel room or reserve a seat at the theatre. All this is achieved interactively making the system a very powerful communication facility.

It is also possible to use Prestel as an ELECTRONIC MAILBOX so that users can employ their local Prestel computer to send messages to the local computer of another user. The GATEWAY facility allows users to book flights directly on airline computers or book holidays with tour operators as well as checking account balances through the bank's computers.

PRIVATE DATABASE: TRAVICOM AND BULLETIN

28. Travicom. A company which operates a network for travel agents for the booking of airline tickets. It uses sixteen Videogate boxes as the foundation of the system. It is a user friendly viewdata network and each Videogate can handle four to thirty-two Viewdata systems. The nationwide network will initially handle bookings for six airlines building up to the full thirty-four in eighteen months from October 1983.

29. Bulletin—ICL's viewdata system. Bulletin is an interactive Videotex system which presents text, data and graphics on a television screen. The screen displays information from Bulletin's own database on viewdata pages. The pages are created by converting selected existing computer files. The information is amended when necessary and deleted when it has served its purpose.

It is possible to correspond with other users via the Bulletin screen and to access any public viewdata system such as Prestel. The system comprises specially adapted television sets linked to a central computer such as the ICL ME29 by a public or private telephone network.

The 26-inch Bulletin screen is operated by a remote numeric

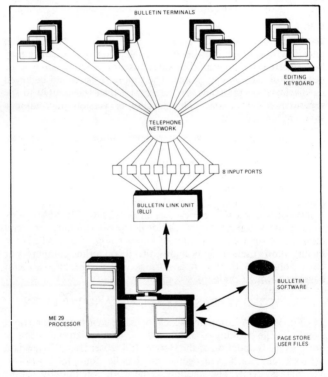

(Courtesy International Computers Limited)

FIG. 78   *Bulletin – ICL's Viewdata system.*

keypad. The 14-inch terminals are equipped with both numeric keypads and alphanumeric keyboards. Both types allow the Bulletin user to dial up the system automatically, to select screens, send messages to the ME29 and close down the system.

A Bulletin Link Unit (BLU) has eight ports and is connected to the ME29. Each port has its own telephone line which can be shared by a number of terminals. This is because the terminals are connected through a dialled telephone network and not permanently attached (*see* Fig. 78).

30. Bulletin software. The Bulletin system operates as an application program on the ME29 and its software has the following features.

(*a*) Editing software: individual pages can be created, amended or deleted from the database.

(*b*) Retrieval software: a user at a Bulletin screen can look at the pages on the database using a few simple commands.

(*c*) Formatting software: applications data held in existing files can be transformed into page data on the database.

(*d*) User window: users can look at conventional files held on ME29.

(*e*) Response frame: Bulletin users can send a limited amount of data back to the ME29 for further processing.

(*f*) Accounting facilities: records are kept of system usage by time and terminals so bills can be produced for each user.

31. The Bulletin database. The basic unit of storage is the "frame"; one or more frames relating to the same topic are grouped together as a "page". Each page has a page number and users can go straight to that page by typing in the number—providing they are allowed to look at it. The database is hierarchical in structure. This allows different parts of it to be allocated to different people known as "information owners". They are responsible for managing their data and deciding what it should look like on Bulletin.

32. Creating the database. Data already on the ME29 files using the special formatting software can be transformed into viewdata pages according to different user-defined screen layouts. An indexing structure may be automatically generated, making access to the information simple.

33. Security. The Bulletin system has elaborate security and privacy checks. A user must enter a user name before he can access information in the system. Optionally, where information is confidential or of a restricted nature, a password may be required. Access to some parts of the database can also be restricted to specific terminals.

Each information owner must explicitly list those user names allowed to access his data. The list may include other information owners who can look at, but not amend, his part of the database. Individual pages can also be restricted by giving them a list of user names. Where the information is of general interest, it can be made freely available by adding PUBLIC to the user name access list.

When a Bulletin user dials up the system and enters his user name, Bulletin will always check this name against the parts of the database the user wishes to access. If the user name is on either the list of the information owner or the page list, he will be allowed to look at that data.

34. Using the Bulletin screen. The system is designed to be self-guiding. When a user has entered a user name which is accepted by the system, he is presented with a screen listing the information available for selection. By following the instructions on the screen, he chooses a particular option and is "routed" to the information he has selected.

Since the database is hierarchical in structure, one page will point to further pages or to a previous index or selection. The user needs to know only a few simple commands to find his way round the database.

DATASTREAM

35. Nature of the service. Datastream is a financial information system available from Datastream International Ltd via their Datastream Business Research Services. The service provides access to financial information on UK and international unquoted and quoted company accounts, economic series and financial news.

36. Database. The system provides clients with a large database of financial, economic, stock market and company accounts information collected from sources around the world. The information is updated on a twenty-four hour basis with the latest available statistics.

37. Modus operandi. The manner in which Datastream functions is outlined below.

(a) *Dial-in*. Almost any teletype compatible terminal can access Business Research Services. Each client is allocated a password to restrict access to bona fide users only. Once connection has been made the Datastream service is displayed by selecting the program required which is transmitted at 300 or 1200 baud. The dialogue is user friendly enabling the system to be used without complexity.

(*b*) *Select required program and search the database.* Programs are selected from a comprehensive menu which perform specialised tasks in conjunction with specific databases. Search programs provide a powerful method of extracting information by drawing out data which meets with specific criteria.

(*c*) *Manipulate the data.* Datastream provides analytical tools for use with the raw data. Ratio analysis, for instance, combined with a dynamic flexi format program allows each individual client to specify his own spread sheet analysis and balance sheet extractions. It is possible to down-load data to a client's own mini or microcomputer and use in-house software which can convert information into graphical displays or be subjected to complex calculations created by the client.

(*d*) *Extract the information.* Any hard copy printer attached to the terminal can produce a permanent record of the information extracted in whatever form it is displayed.

(*e*) *Present the results.* Results in the form of printed reports are presented to management for executive decision making based on reliable facts.

PROGRESS TEST 8

1. What is a database? Give SIX advantages of the use of the database in a typical company. **(1, 4)** (*IDPM*)

2. What are the essential factors which must be considered when setting up a database? **(2)**

3. An organisation, which over the past ten years has developed computer systems for handling customer orders, invoicing, stock control, purchasing, accounting and payroll, is considering the installation of a database management system. What advantages might be gained from such a system, and what problems might be encountered? **(2−4)** (*C & G*)

4. Describe the organisation of a typical database system paying particular attention to its hardware, software and administrative features. **(3, 5−10, 11−14, 19, 20)** (*ACA*)

5. Outline the nature of structural data relationships. **(5−10)**

6. Give examples of database management systems specifying their functions. **(11−14)**

7. What is an "expert system"? **(15, 16)**

8. Specify the nature of logical and physical files in a database. **(17, 18)**

9. Outline the duties of a database administrator.   **(19, 20)**

10. You have been asked to prepare a report for the board of directors explaining the general features of Teletext systems (e.g. Ceefax and Oracle) and Viewdata systems (e.g. Prestel). Your report should also include an assessment of the likely commercial uses (if any) of the systems.   **(21–7)** (*ICMA*)

11. Give a BRIEF description of the facilities provided by an interactive viewdata service such as Prestel.   **(21–7)** (*C & G*)

12. Define the following terms: (*a*) information provider; (*b*) response pages; (*c*) interactive viewdata system.   **(23, 27)**

13. Outline the characteristics of a private viewdata system.   **(28–34)**

14. Specify the nature of an on-line financial information system.   **(35–7)**

CHAPTER IX

Backing Storage Devices and Media

THE NATURE OF BACKING STORAGE

1. External storage. Normal office filing cabinets are used for non-computerised systems for the purpose of storing records until they are required for reference, amendment or updating. The filing cabinets are an extension to the information stored in the memory of personnel performing activities in the system, as it would be impossible for a person to store information in his/her memory relating to all aspects of office activities which they deal with.

Although a computer could retain all business information in its internal memory it would be rather impractical to do so as it would require millions of bytes of storage capacity such as semiconductor memory in the form of RAMs, i.e. random access memory. It is usual to provide the computer system with off-line storage, referred to as auxiliary storage, for the storage of master files and programs relating to specific applications until they are required and transferred into the internal memory. Computers generally employ magnetic storage of one type or another but new developments are taking place such as optical discs which record data by means of a laser.

2. Types of backing storage. By far the most common types of backing storage are magnetic discs and tapes but these are now available in many different varieties to facilitate the needs of various types and sizes of computer, the volume of records to be held in backing storage, and data transfer speed requirements. The different types are summarised as follows:

(*a*) magnetic tape (reels);
(*b*) magnetic tape (cassette);
(*c*) hard discs:
    (*i*) exchangeable disc storage (EDS);
    (*ii*) Winchester discs;
    (*iii*) data module;
    (*iv*) high capacity fixed discs;

(*d*) soft discs:
  (*i*) 8 inch (200mm) floppy discs;
  (*ii*) $5\frac{1}{4}$ inch (133mm) mini-floppy discs;
  (*iii*) 3 inch (76.2mm) and $3\frac{1}{2}$ inch (88.9mm) microfloppy
discs;
  (*e*) integrated discs;
  (*f*) microdrive/cartridges;
  (*g*) personality module (used with discs);
  (*h*) silicon discs;
  (*i*) optical discs.

MAGNETIC TAPE (REELS)

3. General characteristics. Magnetic tape is widely used for backing storage, and is also used as a means of recording transaction data for input into the computer. Magnetic tape not only allows data to be entered into the computer at very high speeds, but also provides the facility for writing output data to tape at high speed. A further important feature is that it is a very compact means of storing programs and master files.

Magnetic tape in common use is $\frac{1}{2}$ inch (12.70mm) wide and 2 400 feet (731.52m) long, and is stored on a reel. A tape deck is used for writing data to magnetic tape from the processor and reading data from tape to processor. This is accomplished by read/write heads (*see* Fig. 79).

4. Magnetic tape codes.

(*a*) Data are recorded as magnetised spots which are known as *binary digits* or "bits".

(Courtesy IBM United Kingdom Limited)

FIG. 79   *IBM 3420 magnetic tape drive.*

(Courtesy International Business Machines Corporation)

FIG. 80 *Seven-track magnetic tape.*

(*b*) Data are recorded in *parallel tracks* along the length of the tape, the number of tracks may either be seven or nine.

(*c*) The tracks *across the width of the tape* provide one column of data, i.e. one character which may be either numeric, alphabetic or special.

(*d*) A character is represented by a code consisting of a *unique "bit" combination* of 0s and 1s. For example, a seven-track tape may use a code consisting of seven positions of binary notation divided into three divisions, as shown in Table VII (*see also* Fig. 80).

(*e*) The parity bit check is for ensuring that each character has the correct number of bits (*see* **7** and **8**). The zone bits are used in combination with numeric bits to represent alphabetic or special characters. The numeric bits are assigned the first four binary values of 8, 4, 2 and 1, which are used for representing, in binary coded decimal form, the decimal numeric digits 0–9. Seven-track tape therefore consists of six data tracks and one parity track (*see* Fig. 80). Nine-track tape consists of eight data tracks and one parity track for recording bytes.

TABLE VII   STRUCTURE OF SEVEN-TRACK TAPE CODE

Position	Designation	Number of bit positions
1	Parity check	1
2 and 3	Zone	2
4, 5, 6 and 7	Numeric	4

5. General features of magnetic tape.

(*a*) It is possible to record 800, 1 600 and 6 250 bpi (bits per inch), this is referred to as the packing density. However, the row of bits across the width of the tape forms a character or byte, which means that bits per inch may be translated as also meaning bytes per inch to avoid confusion in expressing data transfer speeds (these are defined in terms of bps, i.e. bytes per second). The speed at which data is transferred from the tape deck to the processor is dependent upon two factors: the packing density and the speed at which the tape moves past the read/write heads. This is in the region of 45–200 inches per second (ips) depending upon the model of tape deck in use. Speeds for a packing density of 1 600 bytes per inch (bpi) vary between 72K and 320K bytes per second. For a packing density of 6 250 bpi the speed increases to 1.25MB/s, i.e. Mega (million) bytes per second. This compares very favourably with the earlier disc drives which had a transfer speed of about 200KB/s. At the higher end of the speed range of 1.25MB/s (1.25 million bytes per second) this is equivalent in some instances to the speeds of modern disc drives which range from 600KBs to 1.2MB/s. Typical speeds for older tape units are 60, 120 or 200K bytes per second for 9-track tape and 30K bytes per second for 7-track tape.

(b) The capacity of a standard reel of magnetic tape is in the region of 100 Megabytes for the higher packing density but this may fall to 20MB for tape with a low packing density.

(c) Characters are grouped into fields, examples of which are account numbers, names and addresses, quantity, price and value.

(d) Related fields constitute a record.

(e) Records on tape may be fixed or variable length.

(f) Records on tape are stored in blocks and the number of records within a block may be fixed or variable.

(g) Reels of tape may be used repeatedly:
    (i) old data may be erased and the tape reused;
    (ii) old data may be overwritten by new data.

(h) The process of writing to a magnetic tape which already holds data destroys the data already recorded, therefore control procedures are necessary to ensure that current data is not over-written in error.

(i) Data on magnetic tape can be *used repeatedly*, because the process of reading tape is non-destructive.

(j) As records held on magnetic tape (especially master files) are normally *in sequence with regard to a particular field* (account number or part number, for instance) the records are stored serially (*see* VII, **12**).

6. Uses of magnetic tape. Magnetic tape may be used for a number of different purposes, but in general it is used as a media for input, storage and output. This aspect differed from the use of punched cards and paper tape, which were usually only used as a means of input even though it was possible to use such media for output of an intermediate nature. Specific uses of magnetic tape are indicated below.

(*a*) *Input for processing.* Transaction data may be encoded directly to magnetic tape, thereby dispensing with the need to use punched cards for recording such data. Alternatively, a small computer may be used for converting transaction data in punched cards to magnetic tape for input to a larger, more powerful computer. Historically data was first punched into cards and input to the computer in random order; then validated and written to magnetic tape for further processing to take advantage of magnetic tape transfer speeds and flexibility.

(*b*) *Storage of master files.* Magnetic tape provides a compact means of storing records which are either subjected to updating or used for reference purposes.

(*c*) *Storage of programs.* Computer programs are often stored on magnetic tape, as it provides a fast media for their transfer to the internal memory of the computer in readiness for processing.

(*d*) *Storage of intermediate processing results.* Very often the output from one run is recorded on magnetic tape, which becomes the input for the next run.

(*e*) *Output for conversion.* The output from a powerful computer may be in the form of magnetic tape, which is subsequently converted to printed output by off-line operations to avoid holding up the processor by slow printing speeds.

PARITY CHECKING OF MAGNETIC TAPE CHARACTERS

7. Odd or even parity. When data is being written to magnetic tape, in the form of magnetised spots (bits), an additional magnetised spot is written to each row of spots (representing characters) when necessary to conform to the mode of parity used—"odd" or "even".

Odd parity may be used for seven-track tape, which provides for six data bits per row and one parity bit. When using this parity mode the number of bits representing a character will have a parity bit recorded if they come to an even number, in order to make them add up to an odd number.

When using even parity, the number of bits representing a character will have a parity bit recorded if they come to an odd number in order to make them an even number.

8. Purpose of parity checking. Parity checking is used to ensure that data (in the form of characters) have the correct number of bits written on tape. Parity is automatically checked after being recorded by a read-after-write parity check.

When data is being read into the computer from tape, the parity is again checked and the parity bit is then discarded, as it is not stored in the internal memory. If parity checks indicate invalid characters (incorrect number of bits) then the data are subjected to either re-reading or re-writing and if, after several attempts, the parity check fails, an error is indicated in the data.

ADVANTAGES AND DISADVANTAGES OF MAGNETIC TAPE

9. Advantages of magnetic tape.

(*a*) It is perhaps the most widely used form of backing storage, because it is *relatively inexpensive* and has a *large data storage capacity*.

(*b*) It is capable of *transferring* data to and from internal storage at *very high speed*.

(*c*) Data held on magnetic tape can be *sorted by the computer* into the sequence required for updating master files.

(*d*) Transaction data can be *recorded directly on to magnetic tape* by means of magnetic tape encoding machines.

(*e*) Old data may be erased and the *tape used repeatedly*.

(*f*) Records held on magnetic tape do not *take up much storage space* as compared with records held on punched cards.

10. Disadvantages of magnetic tape.

(*a*) It is only possible to *access records serially*, which necessitates the reading of all records until the one required is reached.

(*b*) Input data relating to transactions must always be sorted into the *sequence of the master file* before updating can commence. This is unnecessary with random access devices such as magnetic drums and magnetic disc units.

(*c*) Data can be *accidentally erased or overwritten* unless stringent control procedures are used.

(*d*) Updated information cannot be *written back to the same location* on the same tape. It must be written to a different tape, thus necessitating an additional tape deck. With random access devices it is possible to write updated information to the same storage location.

(*e*) *Visual reading of records* is not possible.

(*f*) *Stringent environmental control* is necessary to eliminate dust and static electricity from the atmosphere, which otherwise could adversely affect the quality of data recorded on the tape, thereby affecting the capacity to read the data accurately.

CASSETTE TAPE

11. General outline. This type of storage (*see* Fig. 25) provides for serial access to records or programs which are stored sequentially, one after the other, along the length of tape in the same way that music tracks are stored on musicassettes in an audio system. It is necessary to read all the records to reach the one required, which takes a considerable time compared with the time required for magnetic discs. The same considerations apply to programs—lengthy programs seem to take hours to load and, what is more, all programs which precede the one required must be accessed first.

12. Important rules. A number of rules must be observed to ensure that tapes are used efficiently; these may be summarised as follows:

(*a*) Recorder and recording head must be kept clean.

(*b*) Tapes should be stored in a plastic box in a clean environment: no excessive dust and free from damp.

(*c*) Tapes should be kept away from electric or magnetic fields otherwise data or programs may be erased or distorted (corrupted).

(*d*) Tape should not be placed on top of the cassette recorder (handler) as it contains an electric motor.

HARD DISCS

13. Exchangeable disc storage (EDS). This type of storage is used on mainframe computers because of its high storage capacity, high data transfer speed and fast access time. Its records can be retrieved very quickly by directly addressing their location on the disc surfaces. In batch processing applications only those records affected by transactions need to be accessed for updating. Records unaffected by transactions remain unaltered and there is no need to rewrite them. This is an advantage relative to records stored on magnetic tape which have to be rewritten during updating runs.

Exchangeable discs are so called because they can be removed from the disc drive and exchanged for others in accordance with the programs and master files required for subsequent processing operations. This type of storage media is referred to as "hard" discs because they are produced from a light alloy which is coated on both sides with a layer of magnetisable oxide. A number of discs are combined to form an integrated disc pack. The number of discs in a pack varies between six and twelve and the capacity varies accordingly between 60MB and 300MB (million bytes) per drive depending upon the model. Some discs have a capacity of 30MB on each surface providing a total capacity of 300MB for a disc pack containing ten recording surfaces. The total capacity available to a computer is dependent upon the particular disc capacity being used and the number of disc drives available at one time via a disc controller. If a disc pack has a capacity of 300MB and 4 disc drives are on-line then the total capacity is 1 200MB or 1.2GB (gigabytes).

Discs have an access time in the region of 40–50ms (milliseconds, i.e. thousandths of a second) but this can vary for individual disc drives. A typical data transfer speed from the disc drive to the processor is in the region of 600KB/s to 1.2MB/s. These figures may be compared with those of the IBM 3380 Direct access storage device, 3MB/s (*see* **16**).

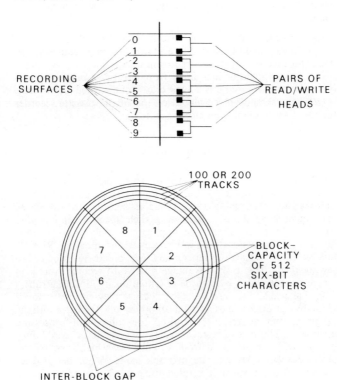

FIG. 81   *Exchangeable discs.*

FIG. 82   *Exchangeable disc pack.*

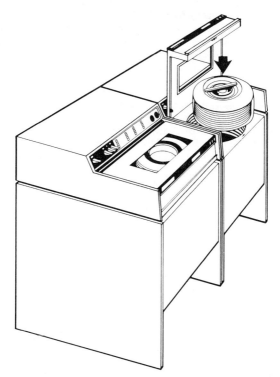

FIG. 83   *Exchangeable disc drive.*

Exchangeable disc drives are free standing and fairly large in physical size relative to the disc units of a microcomputer which are mounted on the top of a desk and sometimes integrated with the microcomputer itself. The disc drive on which the discs are loaded rotates the discs. The discs are accessed as they revolve by means of read/write heads which float over the disc surfaces. The disc drive has built-in heads set in pairs all moving together over a set of discs (see VII, 24). Each disc is fourteen inches (355.6mm) in diameter. A disc pack of six discs contains only ten recording surfaces as the upper surface of the top disc is for controlling the read/write heads and the bottom disc only utilises its upper surface (see Figs. 81–3).

14. Winchester discs. These discs are tending to replace floppy discs in some microcomputer applications as they have a much greater storage capacity (typically 5,10 and 20MB), compared with the capacity of floppies which is in the region of 200 to 700K but new and smaller versions of floppy discs have ever increasing capacities up to 6MB. These will not match the capacity of the Winchester discs however, apart from the smaller version (i.e. 5MB).

A Winchester disc is rigid and is sealed in a case with recycled filtered air to ensure the disc is free from dust and moisture. The newer versions of floppy discs are being protected from air pollution by a rigid plastic casing with a sliding shutter, (see 19) but the earlier versions of floppy discs are quite prone to attract dust from the atmosphere as they are stored in sleeves with an open aperture which can attract contaminating particles.

Winchesters rotate at extremely high speed, much faster than a floppy, which allows data transfers to be effected at a higher speed. The discs cannot be removed from the disc drive and anything up to six discs is possible. The contents of discs are copied on to tape for security purposes.

15. Data module. This is a multi-platter disc unit with in-built read/write heads housed in a transparent plastic case. This differs from standard disc systems whereby read/write heads are part of the disc drive. The data module is more expensive than the standard disc pack but the drive is correspondingly less expensive. Disc surfaces are kept cleaner and if a head crash occurs the consequences are localised compared with standard disc packs, where head crashes can be more drastic. Up to 140MB can be stored on a dual-spindle unit with a transfer speed up to 885K bytes per second.

16. High capacity fixed disc units. The IBM 3380 is a fixed disc storage unit for large computer systems. Each unit consists of two spindles (drives) each with a capacity of 1 260MB, a total of 2 520MB, i.e. 2.52 gigabytes (billion bytes). The data transfer speed is 3MB/s (megabytes per second) with an average access time of 16ms.

This type of storage allows current data to be on-line which improves the effectiveness of data processing operations. It eliminates the need to change exchangeable discs or magnetic tape reels as is necessary in lower capacity storage systems according to the requirements of specific jobs being run on the computer.

SOFT DISCS

17. 8 inch Diskette (floppy discs). Diskettes are used for storing master files, operating systems and application programs in smaller computer systems. They are also used for encoding transaction data for input to a computer and for receiving output from a computer. Diskettes are light in weight and non-rigid in construction which is why they are referred to as "floppy" discs. This is in distinction from the exchangeable discs made from metal which are referred to as "hard" discs. The "floppy" nature of the discs makes them suitable for mailing to a central computer without risk of damage.

Diskettes are housed in eight inch (approximately 200mm) square covers or sleeves and may be single- or double-sided, single or double density. The single sided double density discs have a capacity in the region of 250K bytes (equivalent to approximately 3 000 punched cards) and the double sided double density a capacity in the region of 500K bytes. The data transfer speed is in the region of 31K bytes per second. NCR tend to define these discs as flexible discs whereas the term diskettes was originated by IBM.

This method of data recording and storage has tended to be used instead of the more traditional methods in some cases, but it is considered to have a challenger in the form of bubble memory (*see* II, **37**).

18. $5\frac{1}{4}$ inch mini-diskette (mini-floppy discs). Mini-diskettes are smaller versions of the 8 inch discs, being $5\frac{1}{4}$ inch (approximately 133mm) square and stored in a cover or sleeve. These mini-floppies tend to be used on microcomputers and have a capacity in the region of 89K bytes for single density discs or 170K bytes for single sided double density discs. Later versions have capacities similar to those of the 8 inch disc, i.e. 400–500K bytes for double-sided double density depending upon the number of recording tracks per surface.

More recent versions of the $5\frac{1}{4}$ inch disc have a capacity of 700K bytes, another has a capacity of 10MB and yet another consists of five discs, each of 1.2MB capacity, in a pack, i.e. a total of 6MB per pack.

Discs are available in various versions including single side/single density, single side/double density, double side/double density, single side/quad density, and double side/quad density. The number of tracks per disc surface varies also, 35, 40, 48, 80 and 160 are typical of those available. All of which has a bearing on disc capacities and transfer speeds (*see* Fig. 24).

19. 3 inch and $3\frac{1}{2}$ inch Microfloppy discs. These discs are a recent development designed to protect the media stored on disc from dust in the atmosphere. They are housed in a rigid plastic casing having a sliding shutter which automatically closes when the disc is removed from the disc drive. The 8 inch and $5\frac{1}{4}$ inch discs of older design have an open aperture in the storage cover, allowing the disc surface to be contaminated by dust in the atmosphere, which can cause the data to be corrupted. The capacity of one version of the 3 inch disc is 250K bytes per surface in double density format and 125K bytes in single density. Another version of $3\frac{1}{2}$ inch disc has a capacity of 1MB (one million bytes) on a disc of 135 tracks per inch. The disc is also double sided. Discs are becoming available with 1.5MB capacity.

PERSONALITY MODULE, SILICON DISC AND OPTICAL DISC

20. Personality module. This is a very small device located inside a connecting cable linking a computer to a disc drive. In general, microcomputers are restricted to disc drives specifically designed for them. Consequently it is necessary, without this facility, to change disc drives when changing to a different computer. However, a CYBORG "personality module" allows you to upgrade your micro without having to change the disc drives. It is only necessary to change the connecting cable containing the "personality module" for the micro in question. In addition, it is necessary to obtain what is referred to as a System Nucleus floppy disc.

21. Silicon disc. This is a method of using a RAM card as if it were a disc. This allows much faster access to information than with an actual disc, as it is unnecessary to position read/write heads over

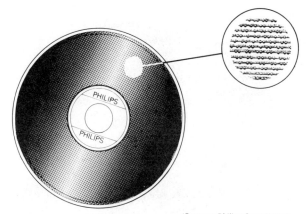

(Courtesy Philips Organisation)

FIG. 84 *Philips (optical) disc.*

tracks and sectors and for information to be transferred from backing storage to internal memory.

22. Optical disc. A mass storage device which takes the form of a plastic disc on which information is recorded and read by a laser. Digital information can be recorded at rates of twenty-four million bits per second. A single disc can store in the region of 50 000–100 000 pages of information depending on the average content. It has been stated that a single disc can store the equivalent information to fifty magnetic tapes or two thousand floppy discs (*see* Fig. 84).

INTEGRATED DISCS AND MICRODRIVE

23. Integrated discs. Some modern small computers have integrated discs stored in the same cabinet as the processor and memory. The discs are mounted in a pull-out unit and a single spindle unit holds one fixed two-surface disc and one removable two-surface disc. Each disc has a capacity of approximately 4.9 million bytes and a transfer speed in the region of 312 kilobytes per second (*see* Fig. 7).

24. Microdrive. Sinclair Research Limited's mass storage device (*see* Fig. 85) for the Spectrum microcomputer. The drive does not use a disc but an endless tape cartridge, sometimes referred to as a "Stringy Floppy', containing approximately twenty feet of tape.

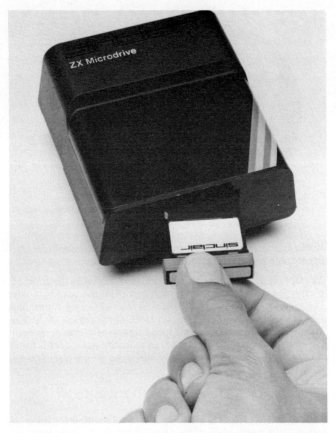

(Courtesy Sinclair Research Limited)

FIG. 85   *ZX Microdrive and magnetic cartridge.*

The tape is driven over a magnetic head at great speed, many times faster than cassette tape. A special interface is used—Interface 1—and a ribbon cable connects up to eight microdrives to the interface (*see* Fig. 86). The interface has an RS 232 interface which enables sixty-four Spectrums to be linked in a network for data transfers and the sharing of peripherals, providing they are not more than a hundred metres apart. The industry standard 232

(Courtesy Sinclair Research Limited)

FIG. 86 *ZX Microdrives connected to ZX Spectrum microcomputer.*

interface will allow the Spectrum to be linked to other computers and printers. Access time of the cartridge is in the region of 3.5 seconds—one particular program which normally required six to seven minutes to load from cassette was loaded by cartridge in nine seconds. The capacity of a cartridge is 85K bytes providing a total capacity of 680K bytes when eight microdrives are connected to the Interface 1.

Each cartridge can contain up to fifty files. The microdrive controller inside the interface expands Sinclair BASIC to include file handling and communication facilities. It is claimed that a 48K program can be loaded in approximately 3.5 seconds.

ADVANTAGES AND DISADVANTAGES OF DIRECT ACCESS STORAGE

25. Advantages.

(*a*) Any item of data can be directly addressed depending upon the method of the file organisation used.

(*b*) High data transfer speed.

(*c*) Input data can be input in random order (without the need for sorting).

(*d*) Discs may be used for real-time remote enquiry systems.

(*e*) Latest discs have a high storage capacity.

(*f*) Data may be erased and new data recorded on data tracks.

(*g*) Different discs or disc units are not required for updating records as the existing records may be amended by overwriting.

(*h*) Sub-routines, tables and rates may be called in as required during processing.

26. Disadvantages.

(*a*) Storage devices are rather expensive.

(*b*) Data may be accidentally erased or overwritten unless special precautions are taken.

(*c*) Problems of locating overflow records on discs.

(*d*) Relative complexity of programming.

(*e*) Some discs have a lower storage capacity than magnetic tape.

PROGRESS TEST 9

1. Why is it necessary to have backing storage? **(1)**

2. Summarise the types of backing storage available which are used on micros, minis and mainframes. **(2)**

3. Outline the general characteristics of magnetic tape. **(3–10)**

4. Discuss the factors which determine the time it will take to update a magnetic tape master file containing 50 000 records with a transaction file, also on magnetic tape, containing 5 000 records. **(5 and VII, 6)** (*C & G*)

5. Specify the uses of magnetic tape and state the purpose of parity checking. **(6–8)**

6. State the advantages and disadvantages of using magnetic tape as a file media. **(9, 10)**

7. Describe the characteristics of cassette tape. **(11, 12)**

8. Define the following terms in respect of hard discs: (*a*) exchangeable disc storage (EDS); (*b*) Winchester discs; (*c*) data module; (*d*) fixed discs. **(13–16)**

9. Increasingly, the choice of backing storage for computer systems, particularly at the micro or mini level, is between "floppy discs", "Winchester-type discs" or some combination of the two. You are required to describe: (*a*) the characteristics and facilities offered by these disc systems and give advantages and disadvantages of each; (*b*) the concepts of "hard sectoring" and "soft sectoring" as applied to disc backing storage. **(14, 17–19 and VII, 26)** (*ICMA*)

10. What differences are there likely to be between a disc storage unit attached to a large mainframe computer and one attached to a microcomputer? The answer should include diagrams and give

approximate details of physical size, transfer rates and data capacities.   (**13, 14, 17–19**) (*C & G*)

11. Define the term "soft discs".   (**17–19**)

12. Specify the nature of the following types of disc: (*a*) personality module; (*b*) silicon disc; (*c*) optical disc; (*d*) integrated disc; (*e*) microdrive.   (**20–4**)

13. Specify the advantages and disadvantages of direct access storage. (**25, 26**)

PART THREE

CHECKS, CONTROLS AND PROCESSING TECHNIQUES

CHAPTER X

Checks and Controls in Computerised Systems

SPECTRUM OF CONTROL

1. Analysis of areas of control. If one views a large data processing department as a small business, which in effect it is, this will provide some indication of the range of checks and controls which need to be applied. A data processing department is a subsystem of a larger system which must be coordinated within the framework of corporate strategy and company policy. It can be seen then that even more checks and controls must be applied as the activities of a data processing department have a bearing on the efficiency and effectiveness of all, or nearly all, functions of a business.

The areas of control may be analysed very broadly within the following categories; they are purely arbitrary as they may be defined in different ways and referred to by different terms. If it is considered that a data processing department plays a major part in the operations of a business, then the relevant checks and controls must be applied to maximise its performance however they may be defined. The categories are:

- (*a*) organisational;
- (*b*) administrative;
- (*c*) environmental;
- (*d*) technological;
- (*e*) sociological;
- (*f*) procedural and operational;
- (*g*) development.

2. Organisational controls. These may be summarised as follows.

(*a*) The data processing department in the larger organisation should function through a policy-formulating steering committee in order to ensure that only those projects are undertaken which will provide maximum benefit to the business as a corporate entity rather than merely maximising or optimising the performance of individual functions. This does not preclude the data processing manager gaining direct access to his immediate superior, the managing director for instance, as this is often essential during the course of day to day operations to resolve immediate problems.

(b) In addition to the remarks made in (a) above, the data processing manager should report to a higher authority than the functional level, as he himself is a functional manager. It is necessary for him to report to, and receive instructions from, a superior such as the managing director, so that overriding authority may be implemented in conflicting circumstances.

(c) The various activities of a data processing department should be organised to allow for the implementation of "internal check" procedures to prevent collusion to perpetrate fraudulent conversion of data and master files regarding the transfer of funds to fictitious accounts, for instance. This course of action necessitates a separation of duties, as in the accounting function, but in this case instead of separating the cash handling from the cash recording it is necessary to separate systems development from systems operation. It also necessitates the independence of a data control section even though it is normally structured within the operations section under the control of the operations manager. The preparation of input should be shielded from the influence of operations staff as data must maintain the utmost integrity. There must also be independence of the computer file library, as in a large data processing complex chaos can occur if stringent controls are not applied to the movement of master files and program files. Strict control procedures are required to ensure "purge" dates are adhered to, to avoid premature overwriting or prolonged storage.

3. Administrative controls.

(a) Access to data relating to business transactions should be restricted to functional and data preparation staff in the data processing department.

(b) Access to the computer room, if a centralised department, must be restricted to authorised personnel only (see 29).

(c) Master files and programs must only be released from the library on the presentation of an authorisation slip and they must not be allowed to leave the data processing department unless by special authority for processing at a bureau in the event of a systems breakdown.

(*d*) Internal check procedures must be implemented as indicated above (*see* **2** (*c*)).

(*e*) Adequate security measures must be incorporated to prevent fraudulent entry of data to perpetrate fraud by the use of passwords and Datakeys (*see* **13** and **29**).

(*f*) Projects must be controlled to ensure they are implemented to time schedules as far as is possible (*see* **32**).

(*g*) Projects must be formally approved by management prior to systems development perhaps as a result of the deliberations of a steering committee.

(*h*) Budgeted levels of expenditure should be adhered to and controlled by means of a formal budgetary control system.

(*i*) Control of performance standards (*see* **34**).

4. Environmental controls. Some computer installations require critically controlled conditions of temperature, power and humidity as well as the level of dust in the atmosphere. These factors must be continuously monitored to ensure trouble free operations. For example, dust in the atmosphere can corrupt magnetic files if it settles on the recording surfaces, and excessive heat can cause malfunctions in the hardware. This is not so critical as with the early mainframes but nevertheless must be controlled. Dust extracting mats and double doors as well as monitoring equipment achieve these requirements.

5. Technological controls. The controls to be applied in this area are mainly to ensure that the most suitable equipment is being used for all data processing activities. If an installation is still operating with punched card or paper tape input then it is certain that it is technologically obsolete and perhaps not so efficient as it could be using other methods of input, such as that achieved by the use of magnetic tape (standard reels or cassette tape) or magnetic discs (hard discs or floppies according to circumstances). Direct input methods requiring the use of workstations in the form of VDUs for order-entry systems may need to be installed to replace the older batch processing technique. Distributed processing using networks of minis or micros may be more suitable than the current centralised system using a second generation mainframe.

6. Sociological controls. With the continuing and expanding use of automation in the administrative environment it must not be overlooked that this, in effect, is a "dehumanising" of tasks traditionally performed by people. We all know the consequences of this—REDUNDANCY. When developing computerised systems it is imperative that the "human" aspect of operations is dealt with in the most humane way possible. People are not machines and need more than a little "maintenance" to keep them motivated to their tasks. These tasks need restructuring in many instances as their former work is "relegated" or "farmed out" to a computer. This has the effect of "deskilling" their work which can have a demoralising effect and needs careful control to avoid having staff with "moronic" tendencies (*see* I, **26–9**).

PROCEDURAL AND OPERATIONAL CONTROLS

7. Summary of controls. The controls in this area embrace:

    (*a*) input controls;
    (*b*) hardware controls;
    (*c*) file security;
    (*d*) batch controls;
    (*e*) auditing and audit trails;
    (*f*) confidentiality of information;
    (*g*) software (program) checks:
        (*i*) validation checks;
        (*ii*) check digit verification.

8. Input controls. In batch processing applications in particular, source data is recorded on source documents by clerical staff and errors are often made. Such errors cannot be allowed to enter the computer system so it is necessary to correct obvious errors before releasing the documents to the batch control section of the data processing department (*see* **14**).

Checking would be concerned with detecting missing data fields or transposed digits. Assuming that data is to be recorded (encoded) on magnetic tape or disc to produce a transaction file, this will be done by an operator using a magnetic tape encoding machine or key-to-disc by means of a keying station. It will be necessary to verify the data in both instances and validate the data in the case of the key-to-disc system. In both instances it is advisable to utilise a different operator to avoid similar errors being made at both times, i.e. the initial recording and the verifying stages.

9. Hardware controls. Initially it is of paramount importance to ensure that all hardware is maintained regularly, perhaps by a maintenance contract, to ensure a minimum of down-time. It is necessary to "check-out" the computer circuitry to ensure that all characters consist of the correct number of binary digits (bits) and this is accomplished during processing operations by parity checking (*see* IX, **7, 8**). Check bits are automatically recorded on tape and disc during initial encoding and it is essential to detect data corrupted due to a parity failure otherwise the computer system will produce a high degree of error.

FILE SECURITY

10. Purpose of file security. The purpose of a file security system is to provide a basis for reconstituting master files containing important business information, as it is possible to overwrite or erase a file in error.

It is essential that file security precautions be incorporated in those electronic computer data processing systems which store master files on a magnetic media, to safeguard against the consequences of loss of data, errors or corrupted data.

Without such precautions, it would be necessary to reprocess data, in the event of loss or corruption, from the last run when the file was known to be correct.

The reprocessing of data for a number of previous runs is very disruptive to the work scheduled for the computer, and consequently has an adverse effect on the productivity of the electronic data processing (EDP) department. It is therefore imperative that the reprocessing of data is kept to a minimum.

11. The generation technique of file security. In respect of master files recorded on magnetic tape, the technique of file security applied is known as the "generation" technique because files relating to two previous periods are retained transiently in addition to the current updated file and the current movement file. The two previous period files plus the current file comprise three generations, which are referred to as Grandfather—Father—Son. The technique operates as follows.

(*a*) The first master file produced is referred to as the "Son tape".

(*b*) The "Son tape" produced during the following updating run replaces the first "Son tape", which becomes the "Father tape".

(*c*) The next updating run produces a new "Son tape", the first "Son tape" (at present the "Father tape") becomes the "Grandfather tape". The previous "Son tape" now becomes the new "Father tape".

(*d*) On the next updating run, the original "Son tape" (now the "Grandfather tape") is overwritten, and can in fact be used for producing the new "Son tape" (*see* Fig. 87).

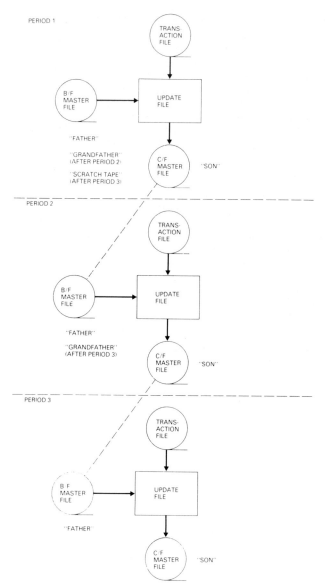

FIG. 87   *Generation technique of file security.*

205

12. The dumping (copying) technique of file security. With regard to master files recorded on magnetic discs, the existing records are overwritten during updating, and consequently the previous records are destroyed.

File security in respect of disc files is often achieved by the technique of "dumping", which involves copying the updated records from one disc to another disc or to magnetic tape. In the event of loss of data on one disc, the situation is resolved by using the records for further processing from the spare disc or the magnetic tape reel on which the records were "dumped".

The records are retained in this manner until the next dump is carried out and proved to be free of errors and corrupted data.

It is also possible to apply the "generation" technique to disc files, by the retention of three generations of records either on one disc or on separate discs.

13. File safety and ensuring the confidentiality of information. The records retained for regeneration purposes are filed for safety away from the computer centre, in case of damage by fire, etc. Thus even if the files retained in the computer centre are damaged or destroyed the records will still be available in the remote filing location.

Other physical precautions which may be used to protect files from loss or damage include the following.

(a) Use of a write-permit ring to prevent overwriting of information on magnetic tape. When the ring is removed from the tape reel the file can only be read. When the ring is placed into position it depresses a plunger on the tape deck allowing the tape to be overwritten.

(b) Prevention of unauthorised access to computer room.

(c) Implementation of suitable security measures to prevent sabotage if this is a possibility. This may require security guards patrolling regularly and perhaps the installation of alarms connected to the local police station to signal a break-in.

(d) File labels encoded on the header label of magnetic files to indicate the date when the information may be overwritten. The "purge" date validation programs are used for this.

The confidentiality of information is largely achieved by means of software and includes the following aspects.

(a) Particularly in time sharing systems it is normal practice for each authorised user to be provided with a password which is entered on the keyboard of the terminal and transmitted to the computer. The password is not printed or displayed on the terminal, however, so that it cannot be observed by anyone in the vicinity. The password allows access to specific files related to the user of the system (*see* Table IX).

(*b*) Information on a file may be stored in a "scrambled" format which can only be decoded by providing the system with the decoding key to unscramble the information.

(*c*) Specific terminals may be prohibited from receiving transmitted information by lock-out procedures. In this way only designated terminals will actually receive file information.

BATCH CONTROL

14. General considerations of batch control. It is one thing to process data, quite another to know that all the necessary data required for processing has been received, processed, errors signalled and corrections made. In order to control the flow of data in and out of the data processing system, it is normal practice to incorporate a data control section in the data processing organisation.

The data control section receives all incoming data for processing from internal operating departments or outlying branches. The data may already be batched when received in readiness for data preparation operations, unless the data is already in a form suitable for direct input to the computer. Each batch of data has a batch control slip attached, on which is recorded batch number, department or branch number, document count (number of documents in the batch) and other control totals if relevant such as hash or meaningful totals.

Each batch is recorded in a register in the control section for maintaining a record of the date when the batch was received. The batches may be vetted for correctness and completeness of data in general terms and then sent to the data preparation section for encoding on magnetic tape. Data are, of course, verified to ensure the accuracy of data preparation operations before being sent for processing. After processing, the batches of documents and the printed output from the computer are sent to the data control section, where they are entered in the register as a record that all batches have been processed or otherwise. It is then necessary to check for errors discovered during processing, as outlined below.

15. Errors correction routine. When the printed documents from the computer are received by the control section, they are checked for errors, signalled by an error diagnostic code or alternatively a separate error list is printed.

One of the first tasks undertaken by the control section is to compare the control totals with those generated by the computer, as it is possible that documents may have been overlooked during data preparation and not presented for processing and it is therefore essential that the fugitive documents are identified, traced and presented for processing.

After errors have been identified, it is necessary to extract the appropriate input document from the batch for correction. Corrected errors are then re-assembled in a batch with a batch control slip attached for re-punching and processing. The new batch number is recorded on the print-out for cross-reference and control. The control of corrections is carried out in a similar manner to the control of original data.

AUDITING AND THE COMPUTER

16. The approach to auditing computer applications. The work of both internal and external auditors is affected by the introduction of an electronic computer. While they need not be computer experts, they should be familiar with the mode of computer input, processing and output in order that they may conduct test checks with understanding. Auditors should also be familiar with computer programming so that they may recommend adequate controls to be built into the programs when they are being prepared. It is difficult and costly to amend programs once they have been completed, especially as they take a great deal of time to prepare initially. Computer programs are becoming very complex with the development of integrated systems and exception reporting, which often eliminate intermediate result print-outs.

An earlier approach was known as the "Black Box" technique; the auditor extracted a sample of records and had them calculated manually. The results were then compared with the output from the computer and if there were no differences it was assumed that everything was satisfactory. In this respect, the "Black Box" was the computer and in order to audit records it was not necessary for the auditor to know anything about how the computer processed the data or about the programming techniques.

The auditor may, however, assume wider duties in the present electronic data processing era. He must as before observe the principles of *internal check*, the separation of functions to prevent collusion and fraudulent intent. This includes the separation of data origination, control of input by means of "batch totals", data preparation and processing, systems and programming.

17. Audit trail. The introduction of a question on this topic will assist the reader in appreciating the significance of the computer in the provision of an audit trail. The question to follow was set in a MISDP paper of the ICMA:

> Your organisation is about to install a computer system but your auditors have written to you expressing their concern over the proposal as they fear that the audit trail may be lost. Draft a reply to your auditors responding to their concern and, in addition, point out ways in which the computer can assist the audit process.

The reply to the auditors could intimate that the audit trail would certainly not be lost as a list of transactions processed each period can be printed out after each computer run, providing a complete record for auditing purposes. In addition, the total of the transactions can be compared with pre-calculated batch control totals on a control slip attached to the source documents—this total is fed into the computer and any difference is printed on a control report.

Copies of documents can also be retained on file for audit trail purposes and, if required, the contents of master files can be printed out for audit control purposes. This would enable the state of various suppliers', customers', stock and employees' records to be inspected on a random basis, perhaps using an audit package.

18. Documentation of procedures. Other controls required are that procedures should be documented and routed through the internal audit department. This may consist of:

(*a*) procedure narrative;
(*b*) flowcharts (indicating processing steps);
(*c*) coded program together with a printout from the computer;
(*d*) operating instructions for the computer operator;
(*e*) error routines;
(*f*) log sheets for recording computer operating and down-time;
(*g*) program modifications.

19. Checks and controls. It must be ensured that adequate control totals are kept before entry into the computer, which is usually done by the control section. Sometimes hash totals are used as a safeguard against data being lost or corrupted during processing (*see* **14, 15**).

Validity checks are usually incorporated to test data against pre-determined limits:

(a) date check—number of days in month;
(b) weekly wage level earned by employees;
(c) weekly tax level by employee.

Sequence checking is also done to ensure that records are in the correct order.

20. Testing of transactions. The testing of transactions may be achieved by means of:

(a) samples;
(b) statistical samples;
(c) spot checks;
(d) test data (a set of data for a test run of a computer: the results are compared with pre-calculations);
pre-calculations);
(e) enquiry programs (Auditfind).

21. Computer time for checking purposes. Computer time must be placed at the disposal of the auditor for conducting such checks as necessary. It may also be necessary to have a printout of static information contained in master files for example:

(a) material prices;
(b) product prices;
(c) wage rates;
(d) discount rates;
(e) credit limits;
(f) account details of suppliers and customers.

22. Original documents. Original documents should be held on file for further checks as necessary, i.e. clock cards, piecework tickets, despatch notes and orders, etc. There could be pressure, however, from personnel responsible for systems design to eliminate as many as possible of these original documents since the data could be prepared automatically as direct inputs by means of electronic counters, mark-sensed cards or magnetic tape from cash registers and time records, together with other data recorders, retail terminals using laser scanning.

SOFTWARE (PROGRAM) CHECKS

23. Data validation. The objective of a data validation system is to detect errors at the earliest possible stage, before costly activities are performed on invalid data. It is therefore essential to ensure that source data is correctly recorded initially before data preparation (punching or encoding) takes place. Similarly, it is important to check the accuracy of data preparation operations before data is processed, and this is achieved by verification procedures.

When data is input for processing, it is subjected to a vetting procedure by means of an edit program which allows valid data to be written to the media to be used in subsequent processing—magnetic tape or disc.

Invalid data either may be written to another magnetic tape, or may be printed out on the line-printer as a special report, or errors may be indicated on the main report. The choice of method depends upon individual circumstances, and the manner in which the system is designed.

During the various stages of processing on the computer several types of check may be performed.

(*a*) Check to ensure that data are of the *correct type* in accordance with the program and master file.

(*b*) Check to ensure that data are for the *correct period*.

(*c*) Check to ensure that master files have the *correct generation indicator*.

(*d*) Check digit verification detects transposition errors when recording "key" fields on source documents in respect of customer account codes, stock codes or expenditure codes, etc. (*see* **24–8**).

(*e*) Check to ensure that each character has the *correct number of bits*—parity check (hardware check) (*see* **9**).

(*f*) Check to ensure that records and transactions are in the *correct sequence and all are present*.

(*g*) Check to ensure that fields contain the *correct number and type of characters of the correct format*—format (or picture) check.

(*h*) Check to ensure that data *conforms to the minimum and maximum range of values*, for example, stock balances, gross wages and tax deductions, etc. As the range of specific items of data may be subject to fluctuation, the range limits may be input as parameters prior to a run instead of being incorporated in a progam.

(*i*) In a nominal ledger computer application the validation of nominal ledger codes would be accomplished by reference to a nominal description file as an alternative to using check digits.

(*j*) In an order-entry system product codes would be validated by reference to a product file and customer account codes by reference to a customer file as an alternative to using check digits.

(*k*) Some errors may be detected by various types of check, e.g.

a five-digit product code being used instead of a six-digit salesman code could be detected by a check on the type of transaction (*see* (*a*)). The difference in the number of digits could be detected by a field check (*see* (*g*)).

(*l*) An error in the quantity of raw material being recorded in tonnes instead of kilograms could or should be detected by visual inspection rather than a computer validation program. The unit of weight is normally pre-recorded on transaction data and weight designations are pre-defined in the program.

(*m*) Compatibility checks are used to ensure that two or more data items are compatible with other data items. For instance, discounts to customers may be calculated on the basis of order quantity but a discount may only apply if a customer's account balance is below a stated amount.

(*n*) Probability checks are used to avoid unnecessary rejection of data as data can on occasions exceed normal values in a range of purely random causes. If this arises with an acceptable frequency (probability) at a defined level of confidence (normally 95 per cent), then the data need not be rejected. This would tend to reduce the level of rejections and the time expended on investigating causes of divergences.

(*o*) Check to ensure "hash" and other control totals agrees with those generated by the computer.

24. Check digit verification. It is important to appreciate that the accuracy of output from data processing can only be as accurate as the input from which it is produced. Errors often occur in the initial recording and transcription of numerical data, such as stock numbers and account codes, frequently through transposition.

Check digit verification is a technique designed to test the accuracy (validity) of such numerical data before acceptance for processing. The data vet program performs check digit verification as part of the editing routine. Data is rejected as invalid when the check digit is any other number than the correct one. The data must then be re-encoded and represented for processing.

25. Check digit. A check digit is a number which is added to a series of numbers (in the form of a code number for stock or customer identification) for the purpose of producing a "self-checking" number. Each check digit is derived arithmetically, and bears a unique mathematical relationship to the number to which it is attached. The check digit is normally added in the low-order position.

26. Modulus. Before indicating the way in which a check digit is calculated, it is necessary to understand what is meant by a "modulus". A modulus is the figure used to divide the number for which a check digit is required. Moduli in common use are 7, 10, 11 and 13.

27. Check digit calculation.

(*a*) Assume modulus 11 is selected for the purpose of calculating a check digit.

(*b*) Assume the number for which a check digit is required is 2323.

(*c*) Divide 2323 by 11 and note the remainder. Remainder is 2.

(*d*) Obtain the complement of the remainder and use as the check digit. $11 - 2 = 9$ (complement = check digit).

(*e*) The number including its check digit now becomes 23239.

28. Calculation of a check digit using weights. A weight is the value allocated to each digit of a number according to a specified pattern, to prevent acceptance of interchanged digits. A more refined method of obtaining a check digit is achieved by the use of weights.

(*a*) Assume the same number and modulus as in the above example, i.e. 2323 and 11 respectively.

(*b*) The selected series of weights are 5, 4, 3, 2.

(*c*) Multiply each digit of the number by its corresponding weight as follows:

		Weight	*Product*
Units digit	3	2	6
Tens digit	2	3	6
Hundreds digit	3	4	12
Thousands digit	2	5	10
		Sum of products	34

(*d*) Divide sum of products by modulus 11 and note the remainder. Remainder is 1.

(*e*) Obtain the complement of the remainder and use this as the check digit: $11 - 1 = 10$ (assigned the letter **x**).

(*f*) The number including its check digit is 2323**x**.

A check may be applied to confirm that 10 or **x** is valid as follows:

Sum of the products	34
Add calculated check	10
	44

Divide by modulus 11 and note any remainder.
As there is no remainder, the check digit is valid.

DATAKEY: THE KEY WITH A MEMORY

29. What is a Datakey? A Datakey is an electronic memory circuit (EAROM) embedded in plastic and moulded to the shape of a key. It is a personal, portable information device which utilises alterable semiconductor memory. It is reusable and has an unlimited read/write life span.

Another device called a Keyceptacle Peripheral Subsystem is the interface between a Datakey and a higher level host system. It acts as the electronic liaison for the Datakey. The Keyceptacle access component incorporates the contact and routing circuitry which provides the physical exchange between the Datakey and the

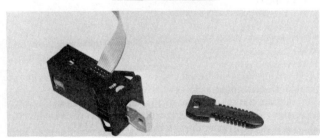

(Courtesy Data Card (UK) Limited)

FIG. 88   *(a) Datakey and Keytroller. (b) Close-up of Datakey.*

Keytroller electronic module. The Keytroller incorporates the intelligence for interchange between the Datakey and the host system. It consists of an encapsulated microcomputer with serial input/output communications. The firmware is the heart of the Keytroller (*see* Fig. 88).

30. Applications. An access controller interfaced with a user's equipment enables a Datakey to serve as a restrictive data filter assimilating and distributing information on an authorised basis. The Datakey can simultaneously record these transactions which effectively provides an additional method of monitoring a data security system.

Selective access can also be applied for personnel to gain access to buildings and data files, credit/debit systems as well as other applications. When personnel or customers are provided with a programmed Datakey, a perpetual, updatable record can be maintained for practically any information gathering purpose in a user's system.

As can be seen Datakey is a product that has an almost endless list of uses for applications including data capture, security system control, data input and data retrieval. Applications already using Datakey include shop floor data capture (where operator identity is an important factor) computer terminal security; software protection; physical access control systems; operator identity in photocopier systems; pre-payment in vending systems, as well as other applications in hotel accounting terminals and automatic test equipment.

In these particular applications the Datakey is used for a variety of purposes. In certain instances for a particular operation but in others carrying out a number of functions, e.g. identifying the operator to the host system, enabling specific accounts to be debited with the charge for the service, protecting the host system from unauthorised use and enabling any revised information to be written back to the Datakey.

SYSTEMS DEVELOPMENT CONTROLS

Before developing computerised systems it is necessary, particularly in the larger installation, to obtain the relevant authority from the board of directors which may be based on recommendations of the data processing steering committee. The committee provides guidance to management on the basis of the results obtained from the conduct of a feasibility study, which indicates the points for and against a specific course of action. It is these factors which guide management in making decisions to pursue one course of action as opposed to another. Important factors which need to be subjected to some form of control or monitoring include those listed below.

31. Important factors to be controlled. The list which follows is meant to convey the important factors as a guideline for effective control of computerised projects, rather than being a complete list of all factors.

(*a*) Periodic reviews need to be undertaken to ensure that projects conform to laid down time schedules as far as is possible and that resources are not used excessively.

(*b*) It is necessary to assess the problems encountered during the course of investigations or design stages which were unforeseen during the preliminary survey.

(*c*) The highest degree of coordination must be sought between "user" department staff and systems development staff to ensure a workable system is subsequently implemented.

(*d*) Design philosophy must be discussed before procuring expensive hardware and software. It is a matter of deciding the nature of processing facilities to suit the requirements of the system. Similarly it is pointless designing a real-time system which requires expensive hardware and systems support when all that is necessary is more frequent reporting cycles. This may apply to stock management situations. Of course, it is possible to implement on-line systems using terminals for direct entry of data, such as customer order details, without going to the extreme of making it a real-time system as on-line entry can be supported by effective batch processing systems at lower cost.

(*e*) Systems documentation must be prepared and maintained during the course of developing systems, to ensure it readily portrays the status of the system at any time. This is essential for continuity of development projects, as staff may leave and be replaced by personnel unaccustomed with the stage the system had reached and with the details of the system generally. Documentation should be developed on the basis of data processing and programming standards (*see* **34** and XVIII, **3**).

(*f*) Systems must be implemented with a minimum of disruption to current operations. Parallel running must continue until the computerised system proves to be adequate for its defined purpose and seen to be attaining projected levels of performance.

(*g*) Access to databases must be controlled by the use of passwords so that only authorised personnel can gain access to the system or to specific files (*see* VIII, **33**).

(*h*) Effective fail-safe procedures must be implemented in the case of lengthy processing tasks or important operations such as the real-time control of a major or critical operation, e.g. airline seat reservation systems and stock management systems.

(*i*) Accounting records must be checked after being converted to magnetic file media to ensure that they contain correct information.

32. Critical path method for project control. Critical path analysis is a very useful technique for controlling computer development projects, whether for the initial implentation of a computer into an organisation, or for the development of complex systems for an existing computer.

The technique indicates the interrelationships of each activity including those which can be performed simultaneously and those which must be performed sequentially. "Event times" are also computed, enabling the "critical path" to be identified as it consists of those activities which form the "longest route" through the network. Any "delay" on this path will delay project "completion time" therefore it is imperative to be aware of which are the "critical project activities" so that they may be constantly monitored. Activities with "slack time" can be identified as this will enable "resources", typically manpower, to be "redeployed" to more critical activities if these are falling behind schedule.

The network must be continuously updated to enable planned times for systems analysis, document design, test runs, etc., to be compared with actual times achieved, so that appropriate action can be taken as circumstances decree.

It may be necessary to revise original time schedules (guesstimates) as more factual details come to light during the course of systems development, as unexpected complications may arise. In any event it is difficult to be precise in the time required for the various stages of a project.

DATA PROCESSING STANDARDS

33. Types and purposes of standards in general. There exist many types of standards for many different purposes covering procedural regulations, forms and paper sizes, screw sizes, electrical and building standards, flowcharting symbols and terminology in various professions, such as the Terminology of Management and Financial Accountancy, of the IMCA. Standards are contained in army manuals, British Standards and International Standards, etc.

Standards attempt to provide a code of practice or to reduce variety thereby providing a framework of best practices and the basis for rationalisation.

34. Standards and data processing. It follows that standards should be adopted in data processing activities for the purpose of providing a code of practice. In this respect it is prudent policy to adopt standard practices for the preparation of systems documentation and the operation of data processing systems. Of particular importance is the adoption of a Data Processing Standards Manual containing details in respect of:

(*a*) the contents and format of a systems specification (*see* XVI, **34, 35**);

(*b*) computer operating instructions;

(*c*) program preparation and documentation;

(*d*) program testing procedures;

(*e*) validation procedures;

(*f*) systems evaluation procedures.

A manual of this type provides the means for familiarising new systems staff with the code of practice required and assists in the recognition of the design philosophy adopted by their predecessors. The manual also provides the means for staff training and continuity of systems development. It would also be of great assistance for inter-disciplinary communications if data processing terminology was standardised because a variety of terms are used to define similar aspects.

Data processing performance standards are necessary for controlling efficiency in the same way that it is essential to control the activities of all departments in the organisation. Such standards are used to assess the utilisation of resources relating to men, money and machines.

Performance standards are required for controlling output; labour turnover; time spent on projects such as systems analysis, systems development and programming; efficiency of operations—achievement of job schedules; cost effectiveness; program efficiency; machine utilisation/time lost due to breakdowns and maintenance; timeliness of providing reports to management; cost of data preparation; level of errors and so on.

Standards may be defined in a number of ways such as budgets indicating levels of expenditure allowed for defined activity levels; job schedules specifying project duration time and run time estimates and schedules for operational requirements outlining time periods allowed for specific applications to be run on the computer; and standard costs for comparison with actual costs of data preparation, computer operations and other related operations (*see* XVIII, **3**).

PROGRESS TEST 10

1. Indicate the main areas of control in a data processing environment.   (**1**)

2. Specify the nature of organisational control relevant to the data processing function.   (**2**)

3. A manufacturing company which utilises batch processing has a computer-based inventory control system. Source data are input by key to disc encoder and output is produced by a line printer. You are required; (*a*) to describe briefly four typical source documents which would be used as input to the computer system, taking care to identify the source of each item of data on the documents; (*b*) to select one of the documents described in (*a*) and trace the passage of the document from its origin to the processing of the data from the document to the computer; at each stage you should describe the operational/system/programming checks which should apply to the document and the data items it contains. (The following references will provide some guidance but not a complete answer to this question: (**2**(*c*), **3**(*e*), **8, 9, 14, 15, 17, 23, 24,** and XI, **3** in respect of part (*b*) and XV, **11** in respect of part (*a*)).   (*ICMA*)

4. Specify the nature of administrative controls relevant to the data processing function.   (**3**)

5. Outline the features of environmental and technological controls which should be incorporated into the data processing activity.   (**4, 5**)

6.(*a*) Describe the sequence of checks, (human, hardware and software) involved in producing an accurate transaction file on magnetic tape from source data. (*b*) Describe what is meant by a check digit and illustrate how a modulus 11 check digit is calculated.   (**8, 9, 23–8**) (*C & G*)

7. Specify the nature and purpose of input and hardware controls.   (**8, 9**)

8. What precautions would you adopt to ensure the security and confidentiality of master files?   (**10–13**)

9. In relation to magnetic tape files, explain how each of the following contributes to secure and accurate processing: (*a*) horizontal parity using the longitudinal check character; (*b*) the write-permit ring; (*c*) the purge data in the header label; (*d*) the trailer label; (*e*) grandfather—father—son processing. (The

following references will answer most parts of the question: **11,** **13**(*a*), (*d*), **VII** and **IX**) (*IDPM*)

10. Describe in detail the checks and controls that can be applied to input data before it is used to update a master file. Assume a batch processing system. **(14, 15, 23–8)** (*ACA*)

11. What is an audit trail and why is it necessary? **(17)** (*C & G*)

12. What is data verification and how is it accomplished in a direct data entry system? **(23** and **23**(*j*) specifically) (*C & G*)

13. List the typical checks applied to input data to ensure its integrity. **(23)**

14. (*a*) What is the role of the Validate Program in a typical commercial batch processing system? Your answer should include a diagram. (*b*) Explain how the Validate Program could use FOUR of the following checks, giving an example of each: (*i*) a format (or picture) check; (*ii*) a presence test; (*iii*) a size test; (*iv*) a range (or limit) test; (*v*) a hash total. (The following references will provide guidance: **23** and Fig. 89) (*IDPM*)

15. Specify the nature of check digit verification. **(24–8).**

16. What are the important factors to be controlled when developing computer based systems? **(31, 32)**

17. Describe briefly the role of critical path analysis in project control. **(32)** (*C & G*)

18. Outline the nature and purpose of data processing standards. **(33, 34)**

CHAPTER XI

Processing Techniques (1)— Batch Processing

GENERAL OUTLINE OF TECHNIQUE

1. Definition of batch processing. The technique of batch processing is very widely applied in clerical, mechanical and electronic data processing systems. It is concerned with processing batches of related data for a defined period of time as the basis for obtaining processing efficiency. Many businesses have high volume routine data processing requirements and have installed batch processing computer configurations to obtain the benefits of high speed accurate data processing. The main features of a batch processing configuration are automatic input and output devices, which operate with a minimum of manual intervention under the control of a stored program after the devices have been loaded with transaction data and appropriate print-out stationery.

2. Applications. Batch processing operations relate to specific applications such as payroll, stock control, invoicing and sales ledger, purchases and purchase ledger and the nominal ledger, etc. Each application consists of a number of computer runs each of which is designed to accomplish a defined stage of processing in respect of each transaction (*see* Fig. 89).

3. Stages of batch processing: Job titles and tasks. When a job is processed in a batch processing environment, it passes through many stages between data collection and job completion. The job titles of the personnel involved with data processing and the tasks they undertake are important.

(*a*) *Clerical staff—user department.* As transactions occur in the business relating to: goods sold to customers; units produced by specific employees in the factory; items received into the stores; items issued from the stores to production; transfer of personnel between departments; and other similar events, it is necessary to "record" the relevant details on "source" documents. These are the

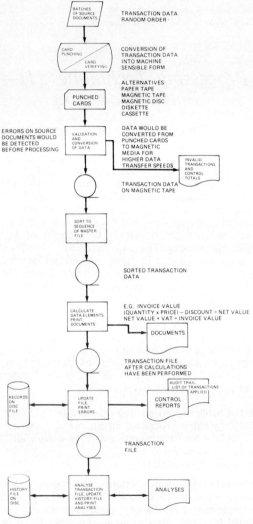

FIG. 89 *Cycle of activities in a typical computer-oriented batch processing application.*

routine documents used by a business for recording routine transactions so that a record is available for accounting and data processing purposes. It is then necessary to "batch" related documents in readiness for processing. Each batch has a "control slip" attached on which are recorded various details (*see* X, **14**). The batches are then sent to the "data control" section.

(*b*) *Data control clerk.* The contents of batches are checked for obvious errors, either for immediate correction if they can be dealt with locally or for return to the originating department. The batches are then sent to the data preparation section (*see* X, **15**).

(*c*) *Data preparation operator.* Data on the source documents is converted into "machine sensible" media by relevant techniques and methods such as "key-to-disc", "key-to-diskette" or "key-to-cassette" (*see* V, **9–11**). The data is then verified to ensure there are no data conversion errors, as it is essential that errors do not enter the computer for processing otherwise GIGO ensues, i.e. garbage in, garbage out.

(*d*) *File and program librarian.* Issue the disc or tape files required for processing on the computer. These must be recorded in a register in order that a strict control can be maintained on their movements.

(*e*) *Computer operator.* The computer operator consults the run diagram and the system documentation in the manual, which provides guidance on how the relevant computer "runs" are to be set up. He then obtains the necessary master files and programs from the librarian. Each run is then set up and executed. When a run is completed the operator inspects the output and reports inconsistencies to the operations manager to enable the relevant action to be taken. "Control totals" provided with the input data are compared with the computer generated control totals and differences are investigated. This comparison indicates if any documents have been omitted from the run or whether any data has been corrupted.

Subsequent runs may require a changeover of stationery on the line printer or the insertion of new stationery with preprinted headings for payroll and invoices, etc. Programs, as well as master files when relevant for file updating must be loaded for each separate run.

Details of processing are automatically recorded on a "log". Messages from the operator to the operating system and responses from the operating system are displayed on the video display screen. The operator also acts upon messages displayed on the screen by the system. Typical runs include those for data validation, sorting data into a defined sequence, computing values, updating files, printing documents and reports and resorting of data for various analyses.

(*f*) *File and program librarian.* When files and programs are returned they are recorded in a register. Those which should have been returned but have not been remain outstanding in the register and this provides the means for "chasing them up". They have probably been left in the computer room and this carelessness must not be allowed to persist.

(*g*) *Data control clerk.* The output from the computer, i.e. printed documents, reports and analyses are recorded in the batch control register thereby maintaining control over the throughput of batches (*see* X, **14**).

STAGES OF PROCESSING A FACTORY PAYROLL

The typical stages for processing a factory payroll are shown below.

4. Amendments to master file. It is essential to ensure that the payroll master file containing details of each employee in respect of earnings, tax and other deductions is up to date before current pay data is processed. Amendment data includes:

(*a*) details relating to new starters;

(*b*) details pertaining to leavers;

(*c*) amendments to National Insurance rates;

(*d*) tax code changes;

(*e*) changes of name (in respect of a female employee getting married);

(*f*) changes of address;

(*g*) changes of department;

(*h*) changes to rates of pay;

(*i*) changes to method of payment—cash to credit transfer direct to bank;

(*j*) additional deductions, i.e. wages advance or court orders, etc.

(*k*) changes to miscellaneous deductions, i.e. National Savings, repayment of loans, etc.

5. Collect current data. This relates to what may be defined as "variable" data, i.e. pay details which can vary each pay period relating to:

(*a*) hours worked by each employee paid on hourly basis or, alternatively, variations from "standard" working hours;

(*b*) number of units produced by each employee paid on the basis of "payments by results" (PBR) schemes including "bonus" schemes.

6. Conversions, computations and printouts.

(*a*) Convert data into machine sensible form.

(*b*) Compute gross wages:

(*i*) hourly earnings: hours worked × hourly rate;

(*ii*) piecework earnings; units produced × piece rate or terms of bonus scheme;

(*iii*) overtime premiums for evening or week-end work in excess of standard hours.

(*c*) Check computations and correct errors.

(*d*) Compute holiday credits.

(*e*) Compute cumulative tax to date and current tax to be deducted or refunded.

(*f*) Compute net pay, i.e. gross pay less tax to be deducted or plus tax to be refunded (+ standard deductions + advance of wages + court orders + holiday credit + National Insurance deductions (employee)).

(*g*) Print payroll and pay advice notes including note and coin analysis.

(*h*) Print bank credit transfer slips for employees paid by this method.

7. Computer runs for payroll preparation.

The amendments and current pay data will be converted into machine sensible form by an appropriate data preparation method such as "key-to-disc", "key-to-diskette" or "key-to-cassette". The data is then sent to the computer room for processing in batches. The payroll may be departmentalised in order to produce payrolls and payslips for each separate department. This is a convenient way of breaking the job into sections and it also facilitates audit trails and accounting routines as well as localising errors. Batch control totals are computed. The payroll may be structured into a series of runs as follows (*see* Fig. 90).

(*a*) *Run 1.* Payroll data is validated and a printed report is produced on the line printer or displayed on a video screen, indicating those details containing errors. Such errors need to be referred back to the originating department for correction. Correct or valid data is written in random order to a work file which may be on magnetic tape or disc.

(*b*) *Run 2.* This run is concerned with sorting employee pay data into employee number within department number to facilitate

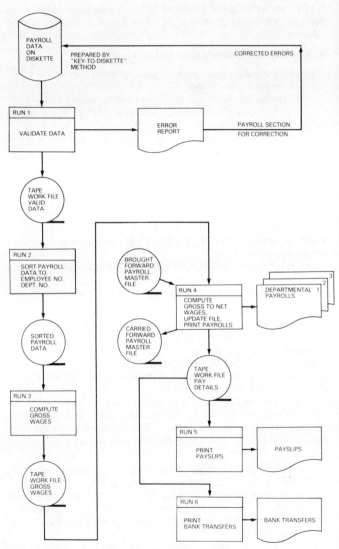

FIG. 90 *Payroll run chart.*

file reference and updating of the payroll master file in a subsequent run.

(c) *Run 3*. Gross wages are computed and recorded on a work file (either magnetic tape or disc).

(d) *Run 4*. This run is largely concerned with tax computations and calculating holiday credits, National Insurance deductions, fixed deductions and other deductions such as court orders. The payroll master file is referred to for various details of tax to date. National Insurance category, holiday credit to date and other related details. The master file is also updated to record taxable gross pay to date, total National Insurance contributions to date and tax to date, etc. Payrolls are also printed out in this run together with a note and coin analysis if relevant. Pay details are recorded on a work file for the next run.

(e) *Run 5*. The work file containing pay details is input and payslips and envelopes are printed out. These may be combined pay slips/envelopes containing a carbon insert to enable printing to take place inside the envelope maintaining confidentiality of pay details as nothing is visible on the outside of the envelope.

(f) *Run 6*. When appropriate this run prints bank credit transfer slips for employees paid by this method.

The general processing routine is outlined in the section dealing with the stages of batch processing (*see* **3**).

PROBLEMS OF DEALING WITH RANDOM ENQUIRIES IN BATCH PROCESSING ENVIRONMENTS

8. Off-line storage of master files. The off-line storage of master files creates problems in respect of random enquiries from user departments. To deal with such enquiries on an individual basis is not economically viable, as it would necessitate the setting up of runs specially for each enquiry which would be very disruptive. If enquiries are sufficiently numerous, however, it may be viable to schedule a special enquiry run to deal with batches of enquiries. In this case, access to appropriate records such as customer or supplier accounts can be facilitated by an enquiry package program. When an application is run daily then the details printed out may be adequate to deal with enquiries and this avoids the necessity of arranging a special run thereby saving important processing time. A 24-hour run-round time for dealing with enquiries may be suitable in most business instances but if this is inadequate an on-line enquiry system may be developed. In this instance, files must be stored on a direct access media such as discs, accessible by user departments by means of local enquiry terminals.

9. Absence of human-sensible records. The main problem of dealing with enquiries on a batch processing computer configuration is the absence of human-sensible records, as these are stored on magnetic media which are only machine-sensible. In clerical (manual) and mechanised systems access to records for enquiry purposes is facilitated by loose leaf records and ledger cards. All that is necessary to deal with an enquiry is to refer to the appropriate record in the file.

PROGRESS TEST 11

1. Define the term batch processing indicating when it is most suitable for use. **(1)**

2. Briefly outline the nature of batch processing applications. **(2)**

3. When a job is processed in a data processing environment, it passes through many stages between data preparation and job completion. Give the job titles and describe the tasks undertaken by the personnel involved in processing such a job. **(3)** (*C & G*)

4. List the data elements which may need to be amended in a payroll application. **(4)**

5. Indicate the data to be processed and the main processing activities required to produce a factory payroll. **(5, 6)**

6. Describe briefly a payroll system in a large manufacturing firm and give overall system flowcharts. **(4-7)** (*C & G*)

7. At 9.30 a.m. on Tuesday in a normal working week, the wages section of XYZ Ltd sends its transaction and amendment data to the computer department. At 4.00 p.m. (1600 hours) on Wednesday, the wages section receives paylists, payslips and other printed results back from the computer department. Give a detailed account of the activities which would typically take place in the computer department between the receipt of the payroll data and the despatch of results back to the wages section. (The following references provide guidance on the solution to this type of question.) **(4-7)** (*ACA*)

8. What are the problems of dealing with random enquiries in batch processing applications? **(8, 9)**

CHAPTER XII

Processing Techniques (2)—On-line, Real-time, Multiprogramming and Time Sharing

ON-LINE PROCESSING

1. Definition of on-line processing. The technique of processing data by computer by means of terminals connected to, and controlled by, a central processor. In this way, various departments in a company can be connected to the processor by cables. If operating companies are a number of miles away from the processor then they are linked by means of telegraph or telephone lines (*see* Fig. 91).

This type of processing provides multi-access to information files by terminal users and also enables them to update files with transaction data. Such systems are often used as a more efficient alternative to batch processing. In this case, instead of preparing data in a machine-sensible form for processing in batches at predefined periods of time, input of transaction data is effected by many terminals at random time intervals.

2. On-line applications. Systems are being developed or are already in use for a wide range of applications in different types of industry including electricity and gas boards, banking, building societies, tour operators, retailing and stock exchanges, etc.

(*a*) *Electricity and gas boards.* By means of terminals situated in showrooms it is possible to inform prospective customers of the availability of appliances in response to their enquiries.

(*b*) *Banking.* It is possible to inform bank customers of the status of their account in response to an enquiry by accessing the relevant file using an on-line terminal.

(*c*) *Building societes.* The use of terminals to enter details of clients' transactions in respect of savings, investments and mortgage repayments from branches to the central computer.

(*d*) *Tour operators.* Reservation offices accept telephone

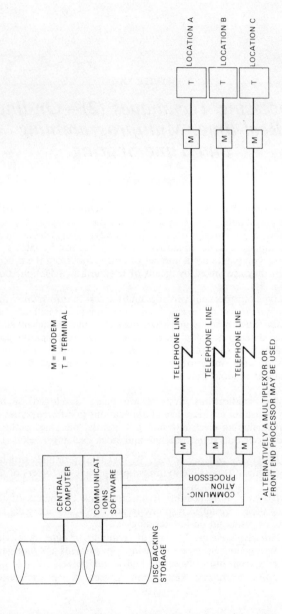

FIG. 91 *On-line data transmission system.*

enquiries from travel agents regarding the availability of holidays in respect of clients' enquiries. By means of terminals the availability of the required holiday can be checked and booked immediately.

(e) *Stock exchanges.* Terminals located in major stock exchanges throughout the country and the offices of participating brokerage firms enable the speedy processing of share dealings.

(f) *Stock control.* Terminals located in warehouses provide the means for automatic re-ordering of stocks, updating of stock records, reservations, follow-up of outstanding orders and the printing of picking lists, etc.

3. Remote job entry. "Remote job entry" or "remote batch processing" is a technique which enables batch processing to be employed by remote operating units by sharing a centrally located computer. For this purpose the remote operating units are equipped with data transmission facilities in the form of a bulk communications terminal for transmitting data in punched cards, paper tape or magnetic tape. The data is then processed at the central computer and the results may either be transmitted back to the remote operating units and printed on a local printer or they may be printed at the computer installation and despatched by post or messenger service to the remote units.

4. Comparison of on-line and real-time processing. Real-time systems process transactions in a time-scale that permits the effective control of business operations enabling them to optimise their performance. Computer based real-time systems are of necessity on-line systems as terminals connected to a remote processor are a basic requirement of such systems.

On-line systems are not necessarily real-time systems, however, as they are sometimes used as a more efficient alternative to batch processing. The use of on-line systems for up-dating files alleviates one of the problems associated with batch processing, regarding the problem of dealing with random enquiries. In this instance, files are updated continuously and the latest status of records in respect of customer accounts and stocks can be provided by direct access instant response facilities.

5. Communications software. On-line terminal operations are controlled by communications software, which controls messages being transmitted by various terminals simultaneously. The software assembles and checks the messages before passing them to the computer, either for information retrieval requests or for file updating. For this purpose the communications software must communicate terminal requirements to the operating system so that it can call in the necessary programs from backing storage.

Communications software monitors communication lines and terminals for the detection of faults and requests retransmission of messages when errors are detected. It also modifies the priority of terminals as necessary. In addition, it facilitates the transmission of messages from the computer system to the individual terminals which may necessitate re-routing in the event of line or terminal faults being discovered.

6. Benefits provided by on-line systems. On-line systems provide a number of benefits all of which assist in improving administrative efficiency which is essential in the inflationary economy in which businesses operate. A number of benefits are outlined below.

(*a*) *Integration of clerical staff with the computer.* A computer should not operate in isolation to the business as a whole but should be an integral element of the systems which support business operations. In this respect, on-line systems assist in harnessing the activities of clerical staff to the computer by the use of terminals. They then have access to the information they require for the efficient performance of their jobs in dealing with customer enquiries and order processing, etc.

(*b*) *Elimination of tedious tasks.* Routine clerical tasks are replaced by terminal operations providing a greater degree of job interest. The benefits provided by this are a greater degree of operating efficiency and job satisfaction.

(*c*) *Reduction in paper work.* The volume of paper work generated by normal clerical systems and batch processing systems is relatively high. On-line systems reduce the volume of printouts required for management reports as information may be displayed on terminal screens on demand. To reduce the volume of paperwork assists in stemming the tide of increasing administrative costs.

(*d*) *Improved accuracy.* As terminal messages are checked for accuracy before being transmitted to the computer by data validation programs the quality of information in a system will increase as input errors are reduced. As a result information will be more reliable.

(*e*) *File updating improved.* Master files are more easily updated by terminal keyboard with regard to transaction data, as special runs do not require to be set-up as in the case with batch processing applications.

(*f*) *Management information more readily available.* Management information becomes more readily available by direct access facilities, which enables managers to obtain a greater degree of control of the operations for which they are responsible.

(*g*) *Improved customer service.* Improvements in the level of customer service can be expected in those systems concerned with appliance sales, holiday bookings and account enquiries, etc.

(*h*) *Reduced data preparation costs.* On-line systems dispense with the need to convert human-sensible data into machine-sensible data thereby eliminating punching and verifying operations. This saves time and the costs associated with such operations. Data is input in a shorter time-scale as a result and processing as a whole becomes more cost effective.

DIALOGUE DESIGN

7. Dialogue. A dialogue enables computer users to converse with a computer system for the interchange of data in the form of messages between the computer and individual users by means of a terminal. The terminals are interactive, allowing conversational processing between the computer and the user via the keyboard and printer of a teletype or the keyboard and screen of a VDU.

8. Dialogue design. Dialogue design is of extreme importance in the development of teleprocessing networks because it is the principal means of interfacing the user with the computer. If the terminals are at a distance from the processor, which they often are, then the responses on the terminal are the only means of contact. The user of a microcomputer however actually sees the computer he is using so the situation is a little more tangible.

If the dialogue is too simple (say baby talk) then this does not assume any intelligence on the part of the terminal user and accordingly they may not accept the system and refuse to operate it. On the other hand, if the dialogue is too complex then it will be difficult to learn and be very off-putting. This will create many error situations, particularly in the entry of data due to not having a clear appreciation of what is required. Dialogues need to be user friendly, guiding the user through the routines in a simple step-by-step manner. If the user is a specialist computer operator or programmer then this is a different situation and such a person will be capable of handling a more complex dialogue structure.

In determining what is a suitable dialogue it is necessary to establish the experience and calibre of the operator. The operator is not likely to be a computer specialist, but a person from the department whose work has been transferred to the computer, or managers who have been put "on-line" for enquiry purposes so that they may access information on demand for control purposes.

9. Dialogue techniques. There are numerous dialogue techniques including those which are natural language based, those which use keywords, menu selection, panel displays, form outlines, and displayed formats, etc.

10. Factors which influence the choice of dialogue technique. The purpose of an application is an initial consideration and other factors include response time requirements, volumes of data and complexity of processing. The type of operator also has an influence on the technique because, for instance, a former accounting machine operator is likely to be more conversant with business routines and applications than a typist and is able therefore to apply a greater degree of intelligence. The type of terminal also determines the manner in which dialogue is presented, whether displayed on a screen or printed.

REAL-TIME PROCESSING

11. Real-time concept. Some businesses are dependent for efficient operation on up-to-date information being immediately available on request. This is particularly the case in respect of businesses with geographically dispersed operating units, such as airlines with dispersed booking offices and tour operators.

The term "real-time" refers to the technique of updating files with transaction data immediately the event to which it relates occurs. This is in distinction to "batch processing", which processes related data in batches at pre-defined periods of time.

A real-time computer system is communications-oriented, and provides for random enquiries from remote locations with instantaneous responses; because of this characteristic, this type of operation is referred to as on-line or "conversational" processing.

Real-time processing is suitable when it is necessary to have the latest possible information in the following types of business operations:

(*a*) wholesale suppliers and manufacturers—availability of stocks;
(*b*) airlines—flight seat availability (*see* Fig. 92);
(*c*) steel making—yield optimisation;
(*d*) manufacturing—status of production orders.

It is important to appreciate that the use of a computer for real-

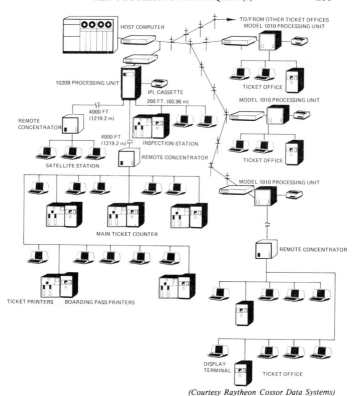

(Courtesy Raytheon Cossor Data Systems)

FIG. 92   *Typical airline reservations and ticketing real-time system.*

time processing, although often a practical necessity, is not automatically implied. If, for instance, a perpetual inventory technique is applied to a clerical stock control system and all stock transactions recorded immediately they occur, rather than at defined periods of time then, in effect, it is a real-time system. This type of system, however, may have a slow "response time" in the provision of management information and the updating process may be slow due to the volume of transactions. Therein lie some of the reasons why a computer is necessary, particularly as some types of business have dispersed operations such as airlines with dispersed booking offices.

Some computer systems are dedicated to real-time operations and others are designed to operate in both batch and real-time modes.

12. Master files. In real-time systems, master files containing operating information are normally stored on magnetic disc and need to be permanently on-line to the processor for updating and retrieval requirements. Whereas with batch processing applications the master files are stored off-line between processing runs.

13. Output. Real-time systems display information on the screen of VDU terminals in a transitory manner, which contrasts with batch processing systems which have a predominance of print-outs. Even while information is being displayed on a VDU screen in response to a request for such information, its status can be seen to change as events occurring in other dispersed locations are updated on the information file, e.g. airline seat bookings.

14. Operating systems. An essential element of a real-time system is software in the form of an operating system which, in respect of a combined batch and real-time computer configuration, provides interrupt facilities to deal with real-time requirements. The interrupted batch program(s) is temporarily transferred to backing storage and the program required to deal with the real-time operation is called into the processor's memory. After the real-time operation has been dealt with the interrupted program is transferred back to internal storage from backing storage and processing is recommenced from a "restart" point. All of which takes but a few seconds.

15. Processing steps. Real-time processing processes each transaction or message through all relevant steps, whereas batch processing processes all transactions through specific steps before proceeding with other steps. The structure of processing steps is stipulated in the run sequence.

16. Dynamic nature of real-time systems. Real-time systems are dynamic as they accept random input at random time intervals and the status of files changes dynamically as a result. It is this characteristic which makes it difficult to audit or recover the system in the event of system failure. Both of these factors are provided for by means of periodic check points, say every two to three minutes, at which point all relevant restart and audit information are dumped to magnetic tape. The dumps can be used to restart the system.

MULTIPROGRAMMING

17. Definition of multiprogramming. A small computer installation may process one program at a time and find that it is quite adequate for its processing load. In such instances the running of the application programs is controlled by an operating system.

Eventually as more applications are transferred to the computer, it may be found that there is insufficient processing capability operating on the present basis of one program at a time. Multiprogramming may then need to be considered whereby two or more programs can be processed concurrently. This enables overall processing time for all programs to be reduced even though the time required to process individual programs may be increased due to switching between programs. Such operations are still controlled by the basic control program but the computer operations staff are responsible for determining the program mix, that is the programs which are to be run together, and the order in which they are to be run. This is referred to as work scheduling and in a large installation it becomes a complex and time consuming task. (*See below.*)

18. Operating system. As the purpose of multiprogramming is to increase the utilisation of the computer system as a whole, there is a need to employ more powerful software in the form of an operating system incorporating automatic work scheduling features. A programmer may then specify scheduling factors in a "job description" which allows the operating system to perform work scheduling activities automatically. A "job description" specifies the name of the job, the peripherals (input and output devices) required, priorities, the streams of data to be input and output and the time programs take to run.

TABLE VIII   COMPARISON OF BATCH AND REAL-TIME PROCESSING SYSTEMS

Batch processing	*Real-time processing*
1. Routine high volume applications: —Invoicing —Payroll —Sales ledger updating —Stock ledger updating —Nominal ledger updating	1. Busines control applications: —Steel making —Stock control —Airline operations and aircraft seat reservations

Table Continued

TABLE VIII *Continued*

Batch processing	Real-time processing
2. Data collected for a defined period of time and processed in batches	2. Random data input at random time intervals as events occur
3. No direct access to system by user departments	3. Direct access to system by user departments using terminals
4. Files only on-line during a processing run	4. Files permanently on-line
5. Magnetic tape files may be used for sequential access to records. Disc files may be used as an alternative to increase processing productivity by restricting access to records affected by current transactions—particularly useful means of storage for low hit-rate files	5. Direct access files only—usually magnetic discs
6. Information on master files only as up to date as last updating run	6. Information on master files updated dynamically as events occur
7. Detailed documents, reports and transaction lists printed	7. Information normally displayed on a VDU screen as messages. As an alternative, messages may be printed on a teletype terminal
8. Audit trails facilitated by printing out lists of transactions applied during updating and by printing out file contents using an audit package	8. Audit trails not so well provided for as control is centred around the number of messages input rather than details of transactions
9. All transactions recorded on source documents which must be converted to machine-sensible input by costly and time consuming data preparation operations	9. Transaction details input directly by terminal keyboard, sometimes from source documents, sometimes not, depending upon the system. Absence of costly and time consuming data preparation operations
10. Information from computer files only accessible during a specially set-up run	10. Information permanently accessible on demand

19. Mode of operation. Multiprogramming operates in the following way—when processing is interrupted on one program, perhaps to attend to an input or output transfer, the processor switches to another program. This enables all parts of the system, the processor and input and output peripherals, to be operated concurrently thereby utilising the whole system more fully. When operating on one program at a time the processor or peripherals would be idle for a large proportion of the total processing time even though this would be reduced to some extent by buffering. Buffering enables the processor to execute another instruction while input or output is taking place rather than being idle while the transfer was completed. Even so, when processing one program at a time, basic peripherals are used for input and output such as card readers and line printers which, being mechanical, are slow compared with the electronic speed of the processor and this causes imbalance in the system as a whole.

20. Off-lining. Multiprogramming employs the technique of "off-lining" which requires the transfer of data from punched cards (or paper tape) to magnetic media, such as discs, before programs are run. Similarly, output from some programs would also be output to magnetic media for printing when the printer becomes available. In this way it is possible to process the payroll and prepare invoices by loading both programs into the main memory. While the line printer is printing an invoice line the processor switches to the payroll. Afterwards the processor reverts back to the invoice application. As the printer is being used for printing invoices, payroll data would be recorded on magnetic media for later conversion when the printer is available.

TIME SHARING

21. Time sharing defined. Time sharing is an on-line processing technique which enables many users to gain access to a centrally located computer by means of terminals. Users are geographically remote from the computer and from each other. Each user is also unaware that the computer is being accessed by anyone else, which creates the impression of having a computer for one's sole use. This is made possible by the computer continually switching between the various terminals at extremely high speed under the control of an operating system. These facilities may be provided either by an in-house installation or by a computer time sharing bureau.

22. Terminals. There are many types of terminal used in business applications, two of which are used for time-sharing. These are the teletype and the visual display unit (VDU) which are outlined in V, **24** and **25**.

23. Accessing the computer for time sharing operations. The stages outlined below indicate the various activities necessary for accessing and using a centrally located time sharing computer by a remote terminal.

(*a*) Plug in terminal and acoustic coupler to power supply, perhaps using a two-way adaptor.

(*b*) Switch on mains power supply.

(*c*) Switch on acoustic coupler—a red light glows.

```
TSL FILES A/B
WHICH SYSTEM ?




                     B
TSL FILES B TSLB11 15:40:58 TTY141

.LOGIN
JOB 15 TSL FILES B TSLB11 TTY141
ID: 2663,10025
PASSWORD:

ACCT REF: RHODES,STAFF
1542    11-MAY-76         TUE

.YBASIC

NEW OR OLD--NEW
NEW FILE NAME--PRINT
READY
100   PRINT 23.2,23.2+2,23.2+3
110   END
RUN

PRINT   11-MAY-76        15:44:43



 23.2           538.24         12487.2

READY
SYSTEM

EXIT

.KJOB
CONFIRM: F
JOB 15, USER [2663,10025]  LOGGED OFF TTY141   1546  11-MAY-76
CONNECT TIME 00:03:49 PRU 1
```

FIG. 93 *Logging in and out of a time sharing system.*

(*d*) Set acoustic coupler to full duplex operation.

(*e*) Set terminal (teletypewriter) to full duplex operation.

(*f*) Use telephone to dial computer direct or via a regional office multiplexor of the time sharing bureau. Gaining access to the computer, say in London, direct incurs long distance call charges, whereas going via the regional office only involves local call charges.

(*g*) When contact is established with the computer it responds by transmitting a high-pitched whistle.

(*h*) Place telephone in acoustic coupler and close lid—a green light glows.

(*i*) Log into the system (*see* **24**).

(*j*) Use the system for required purpose (*see* Fig. 93).

(*k*) Log out of the system (*see* **24**).

(*l*) Switch off power supply, remove telephone from acoustic coupler and replace.

24. Logging in and logging out procedure. Figure 93 shows a terminal record of the stages undertaken for logging in and out of a time sharing system. To assist the reader in understanding the printout Table IX will serve to illustrate the various responses of the computer and system user. 1, 2, 3, etc. are steps in the procedure.

TABLE IX   ANALYSIS OF RESPONSES OF THE
COMPUTER AND SYSTEM USER

Computer responses	*User responses*	
1. TSL FILES A/B WHICH SYSTEM?	2. B	(CR)
3. TSL FILES B TSLBII 15:40:58 TTY141	4. LOGIN	(CR)
5. ID:	6. 2663, 10025	(CR)
7. PASSWORD:	8. (Password entered on keyboard but not printed for security purposes)	(CR)
9. ACCT REF:	10. RHODES,STAFF	(CR)
11. 1542 11-MAY-76 TUE	12. XBASIC	(CR)
13. NEW OR OLD—	14. NEW	(CR)
15. NEW FILE NAME—	16. PRINT	(CR)
17. READY	18. 100 PRINT 23.2,23.2↑2,23.2↑3	(CR)
	110 END	(CR)
	RUN	(CR)

Table Continued

TABLE IX *Continued*

Computer responses	User responses	

19. PRINT 11-MAY-76
    15:44:43
    23.2   538.24   12487.2
    READY
	20. SYSTEM	(CR)

21. EXIT	22. KJOB	(CR)
23. CONFIRM:	24. F	

25. JOB 15, USER [2663, 10025] LOGGED OFF
    TTY141   1546   11-MAY-76
    CONNECT TIME 00:03:49 PRU 1
	}	Computer
		response

Observations on computer and user responses:

1. WHICH SYSTEM?	This is an enquiry which system the user wishes to be connected to as the time sharing bureau has several systems.
2. (CR)	The user must depress the carriage return key (CR) on the terminal after entering each line as shown on the printout.
3. TSLBII	Assigned job number.
4. 15:40:58	Time of logging in.
5. TTY141	Channel number.
6.	Monitor dot which indicates that the user can go ahead.
7. ID:	Request for user's account code.
8. PASSWORD:	Request for user's password which enables the user to gain access to computer files and programs.
9. ACCT REF:	Details of job to be entered on invoice charging for the services provided by the time sharing bureau. Used for reference purposes.
10. 1542 11-May-76 TUE	The time, date and day the user was connected to the system.
11. XBASIC	Connects the user to the system for using BASIC programming commands and instructions. XBASIC means extended BASIC language.
12. NEW OR OLD—	The system is asking the user whether a previous program held in backing storage is to be used or whether a new one is to be developed.

Table Continued

TABLE IX *Continued*

Computer responses	User responses
13. NEW FILE NAME—	The system is asking the user to provide a name for the file to be developed.
14. READY	BASIC system awaiting commands or instructions from the user.
15. 100 PRINT, 110 END, etc.	User developed program.
16. PRINT 11-MAY-76, etc.	File heading, i.e. title of report printed out containing results of processing.
17. 23.2 538.24, etc.	Calculated results.
18. SYSTEM	Transfer to system monitor in readiness for logging out after completing job.
19. EXIT	User informed that he has left the BASIC system.
20. KJOB	Terminate connection—kill job.
21. CONFIRM:	Requires user to confirm that he wishes to leave the system.
22. F	Response to CONFIRM—achieves a fast log out from the system.
23. 00:03:49	The time connected to the system— hours, minutes and seconds. (Basis of charging.)
24. PRU 1	Processor time used—processor units. (Basis of charging.)

25. Time sharing operations. Time sharing facilities provide direct access to a computer for obtaining instant responses to questions asked of statements made in an interactive conversational mode. This means that both the user and the computer converse by transmitting messages to each other. The user types messages or commands on a terminal keyboard which are then transmitted to the computer. The computer responds by transmitting messages to the terminal which are either printed or displayed on the screen depending upon the type of terminal used.

By this means accountants, corporate planners and managers are assisted in their activities concerned with planning and problem solving involving sensitivity analysis, network planning, linear programming, capital budgeting and trend forecasting, etc. These requirements are facilitated by library programs which may be called in for use as required. Alternatively, it is possible to develop one's own programs. In either case the computer calculates the data input by the user and provides the results in the format required—

either a printed report format or, in some instances, a graphical display.

26. Programming for time sharing. As most users of time sharing systems are not computer programmers, relatively simple languages have been developed to enable users to converse with the computer at command level. One such language is known as BASIC—*B*eginners *A*ll purpose, *S*ymbolic *I*nstruction *C*ode (*see* XVIII, **10**(*b*), (*c*), (*d*)).

PROGRESS TEST 12

1. Define and give examples of on-line processing applications. **(1–3)**

2. Distinguish between the terms "multi-access" and "multiprogramming". **(1, 17, 21)** (*C & G*)

3. Explain the distinction between real-time processing and remote job entry data. Describe an application appropriate to each technique justifying your choice of method. **(3, 11)** (*IDPM*)

4. Distinguish between on-line and real-time processing. Give an example of a commercial data processing application where real-time processing would be applicable and explain what characteristics make it necessary to consider this type of processing. **(4 and Table VIII)** (*ICMA*)

5. Indicate the nature of software for the control of on-line terminals. **(5)**

6. (*a*) What is meant by the term "real-time" processing? (*b*) Explain the hardware and software facilities which are required for the operation of a real-time system. **(5 and II, 12)** (*ACA*)

7. Outline the benefits provided by on-line processing applications. **(6)**

8. Dialogue enables computer users to converse with a computer. State important considerations of dialogue design. **(7–10)**

9. Distinguish between the following methods of computer operation: (*a*) batch processing; (*b*) real time processing; (*c*) time sharing. Your answer should include a discussion of the necessary hardware (particularly storage devices) and a description of typical situations in which EACH method could be used to advantage. **(11–16, 21–5 and XI)** (*C & G*)

10. Distinguish BRIEFLY between time sharing and real-time systems. **(11, 21)** (*C & G*)

CHAPTER XIII

Processing Techniques (3)—Interactive Processing Applications

BASIC CONSIDERATIONS

1. Nature of interactive processing. There is a tendency at the present time for many computer applications to be processed using the interactive processing technique. The technique is interactive in the sense that the user and the computer communicate with each other in a conversational mode by means of a terminal, usually a VDU with a keyboard. The technique is also referred to as "transaction-driven" processing as transactions are dealt with completely on an individual basis through all the relevant processing operations before dealing with the next transaction. This is in distinction to batch processing which processes transactions in batches through each processing stage, i.e. validation, sorting, calculating, updating and printing, etc.

Transaction data is input either by a computer operator using a terminal or, alternatively, from remote points such as sales offices, warehouses, factory departments or accounts office according to the needs of a given application. Interactive processing allows files to be updated as transactions occur and enquiries to be dealt with on an immediate response basis.

Although on-line processing has already been outlined in XII and interactive processing falls into this category, or may even be classified as real-time, the technique is outlined separately in this chapter to define the specific nature of on-line processing, as some on-line applications are not fully interactive. For instance, some on-line order entry systems only enter order details into the system via a terminal—the transactions are not fully dealt with as they occur but are stored on backing storage for subsequent batch processing (*see* Fig. 118).

INTERACTIVE GENERAL LEDGER SYSTEM

2. Application philosophy. The Interactive General Ledger System incorporates traditional accounting control and comprehensive financial reporting in a completely automated application. It channels all accounting transactions into an integrated information base that serves as the control module for the complete system. It can be implemented as a stand-alone system or utilised in conjunction with other general accounting applications such as payables, receivables, and payroll. It can handle any current account numbering scheme in either a single-client or multi-client environment.

Basic accounting data, including comparative budget data and previous years' history, is accumulated in a single master file that reflects both current and future needs with the ability to extract reports by department, division, and cost centre for budget and cost analysis. Complete audit control is provided by debit/credit balancing at all levels of processing, and the reports produced comply with general accounting practices.

The general ledger application is an interactive, transaction-oriented processing system. It employs double-entry bookkeeping methods, balancing each debit and credit entry with either an offsetting entry or control total, and immediately updating all related master files. A trial balance at either the detail or control total level may be taken at any time. Balances are maintained by account for each period, providing a means of creating a trial balance for any previous period. Detail debit and credit transactions may also be retained by account at the user's option.

The system is easy to install, operate, and maintain. As an interactive system, the clerical workload is significantly reduced and the possibility of transcription errors, bookkeeping errors, and the unauthorised use of the general ledger accounts is eliminated.

3. Direct data display. The screen display is the control centre for the system. At a glance, the operator can read program instructions, system messages, data to be input, and data file information. A position indicator informs the operator what information may be required to complete a posting or answer a question. The operator enters the requested information and visually checks the data before it is processed.

Account posting is completed in a matter of seconds—it is fast and easy; it is verified; it is correct; and the entry will appear on all affected reports. Correction procedures are just as easy—operator merely replaces the character and/or digits with the correct value.

The general ledger application accepts both automatic postings from other related applications and general journal entries initiated by the operator. All automatic postings and general entries include complete source document reference information for internal audit and control. New accounts can be easily added to the integrated data base, and existing accounts deleted. Changes to account information can be performed during routine maintenance operations.

4. Master menu. General ledger processing operations are concise, straight-to-the-point; the operator merely follows the instructions on the video display. From the master menu display (*see* Fig. 94), the operator selects one of five processing functions such as Daily Processing or End-of-Period. Before continuing the operator must enter employee number and/or security code. After security code verification by the program, the selected processing function is displayed—G/L Daily Menu.

FIG. 94   *Screen display: general ledger master menu.*

FIG. 95   *Screen display: general ledger daily menu.*

FIG. 96 *Screen display: security code/employee number.*

FIG. 97 *Screen display: general ledger account posting.*

5. Daily menu. The G/L Daily Menu schedule displays seven functions (*see.* Fig. 95): Enquiry, Account Posting, Batch Posting, Account Maintenance, Company Deletion, Interface Maintenance and End-of-Day Processing. Again, before any entries are processed the operator's security code must be verified (*see* Fig. 96). Then, the operator can follow the position indicator and enter the data requested under the G/L Account Posting display (*see* Fig. 97). Before transferring data to memory and updating the account, the display is visually verified for accuracy.

6. Control. The general ledger system incorporates a variety of validating, auditing, and control techniques to ensure the accuracy of the financial reports. The monthly trial balance and monthly reporting transactions detail constitute the traditional accounting tools. All posting functions accumulate total of debits and credit entries and must be equal before end-of-run processing can be performed.

When trial balance is performed, any difference between debits and credits is posted to an error account. This account balance must be cleared before financial statements are prepared.

7. Period/year-end closing. During the period cycle, the current period totals are closed and transferred to history totals. A general journal is printed and details of posted entries purged from the system. After a period is closed, the account totals can be revised or updated through file maintenance.

Year-end close-out is completely automatic and transfers revenues and expense account balances to capital account before financial reports are prepared.

8. Enquiries. The system provides for instantaneous on-line enquiry into the integrated data base and the master files of the interfaced applications. Enquiries are initiated at the console by the operator and displayed on the screen. Enquiry security codes restrict access to the information in the system data base.

The general ledger application offers a complete selection of enquiries, ranging from current data and budget information to historical data, for any and all accounting periods. The operator merely selects and enters the identifying code or account number for the desired information (*see* Fig. 98).

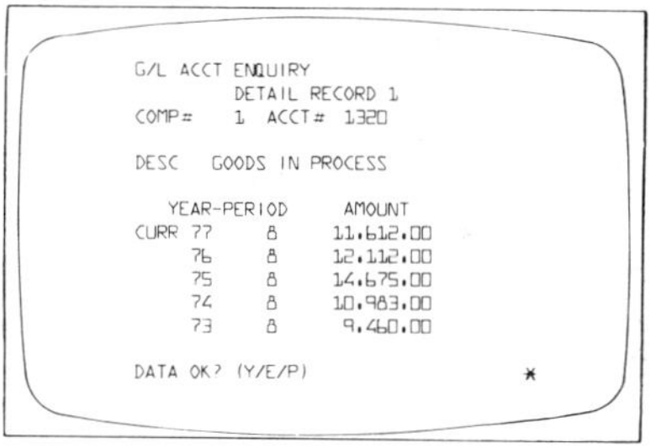

```
     G/L ACCT ENQUIRY
              DETAIL RECORD 1
     COMP=   1  ACCT# 1320

     DESC   GOODS IN PROCESS

          YEAR-PERIOD    AMOUNT
     CURR 77      8   11,612.00
          76      8   12,112.00
          75      8   14,675.00
          74      8   10,983.00
          73      8    9,460.00

     DATA OK? (Y/E/P)              *
```

FIG. 98   *Screen display: on-line enquiry/general ledger.*

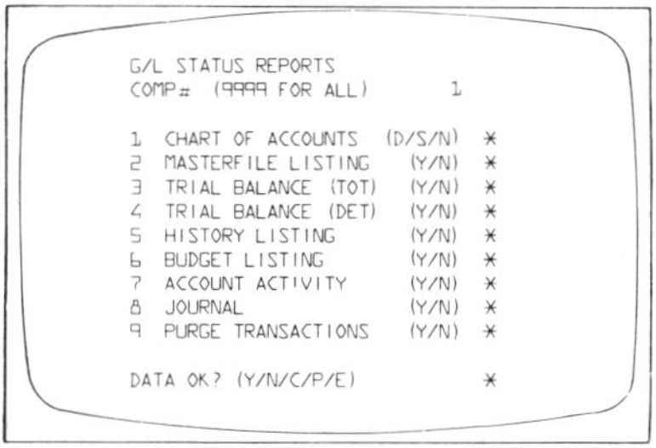

```
     G/L STATUS REPORTS
     COMP=  (9999 FOR ALL)      1

     1  CHART OF ACCOUNTS   (D/S/N)  *
     2  MASTERFILE LISTING   (Y/N)   *
     3  TRIAL BALANCE (TOT)  (Y/N)   *
     4  TRIAL BALANCE (DET)  (Y/N)   *
     5  HISTORY LISTING      (Y/N)   *
     6  BUDGET LISTING       (Y/N)   *
     7  ACCOUNT ACTIVITY     (Y/N)   *
     8  JOURNAL              (Y/N)   *
     9  PURGE TRANSACTIONS   (Y/N)   *

     DATA OK? (Y/N/C/P/E)             *
```

FIG. 99   *Screen display: general ledger status reports.*

9. Management control and financial reports. A complete range of audit, control, and financial reports is provided. The reports follow accepted accounting practices, and the audit, transaction, and control reports can be printed at any time (*see* Fig. 99). The range can include:

(*a*) chart of accounts listing;

(*b*) master file listing;

(*c*) transaction journal;

(*d*) account activity/journal report;

(*e*) maintenance audit trail;

(*f*) trial balance;

(*g*) history/budget listing;

(*h*) comparative balance sheet;

(*i*) income/expense report;

(*j*) comparative income/expense report.

10. Income/expense report.

(*a*) The report is prepared automatically and summarises activity for current and year-to-date periods.

(*b*) Revenue/expense account percentages are based on gross revenue/sales (*see* Fig. 100).

11. Comparative income/expense.

(*a*) Report lists revenue and expenses for current/prior/to-date periods, budget allocations, and variance percentages.

(*b*) Current period and year-to-date section compare revenue/expense balances to either prior period balances or budget allocations and list applicable variance percentages (*see* Fig. 101).

12. Trial balance.

(*a*) Report is prepared automatically, with operator supervision, from the integrated general ledger data base.

(*b*) Beginning and ending debit or credit balance is listed for each account.

(*c*) Total debit/credit balances and net difference are summarised for the current and four previous periods (*see* Fig. 102).

13. Comparative balance sheet.

(*a*) Report is prepared in its entirety without operator intervention.

(*b*) Current period is compared to previous year period. Increase/decrease amount is listed with percent of variance.

(*c*) Minor/major distribution totals are computed for assets, liabilities, and capital (*see* Fig. 103).

```
           THE NATIONAL CO              1  INCOME-EXPENSE REPORT              15 JAN 19——        PAGE 5
              DIVISION 1

PERIOD 1                                         PERIOD                              YEAR-TO-DATE

CO NO. ACCT NO.  DESCRIPTION                 AMOUNT        %                    AMOUNT          %

1  4000000000 SALES PRODUCT 1               96,723.42     38.02               531,978.70       38.02
1  4010000000 SALES PRODUCT 2               89,559.34     35.21               492,576.15       35.21
1  4020000000 SALES PRODUCT 3               68,087.13     26.77               374,479.05       26.77
1  4500000097 .TOTAL SALES                 254,369.89    100.00             1,399,033.90      100.00

1  6010000000 PURCHASES                    178,058.91     70.00               979,323.74       70.00
1  6200000000 SALARIES — OFFICE             10,800.00      4.25                57,950.00        4.14
1  6210000000 SALARIES — SALES STAFF         7,500.00      2.95                34,800.00        2.49
1  6220000000 SALARIES — PLANT              18,414.10      7.24               107,287.95        7.67
1  6300000000 UTILITIES                      1,129.73       .44                11,021.97         .79
```

Fig. 100 *Income/expense report.*

THE NATIONAL CO   1 COMPARATIVE INCOME-EXPENSE REPORT   28 FEB --   PAGE 2

PERIOD 2									
							YEAR-TO-DATE		
CO NO.	ACCT NO.	DESCRIPTION	PREVIOUS	CURRENT	BUDGET	VAR%	ACTUAL	BUDGET	VAR%
1	4250000000	SALES – DIVISION 1	4,128.00	4,450.00	4,000.00	11.25	8,400.00	8,000.00	.05
1	4260000000	SALES – DIVISION 2	3,850.00	4,395.00	3,750.00	17.20	8,420.00	7,500.00	12.27
1	4270000000	SALES – DIVISION 3	3,975.00	4,350.00	3,900.00	11.54	8,105.00	7,800.00	3.91
1	4280000000	SALES – DIVISION 5	4,695.00	4,895.00	3,700.00	32.30	8,370.00	7,400.00	13.11
1	4500000097	.GROSS SALES	16,648.00	18,090.00	15,350.00	17.85	33,295.00	30,700.00	8.45
1	6010000000	SALARIES – DIVISION 1	925.00	1,000.00	900.00	11.11	2,000.00	1,800.00	11.11
1	6020000000	SALARIES – DIVISION 2	900.00	900.00			1,800.00		
1	6030000000	SALARIES – DIVISION 3	900.00	900.00			1,750.00		
1	6040000000	SALARIES – DIVISION 5	900.00	900.00			1,800.00		
1	6500000097	.SALESMAN'S SALARIES	3,625.00	3,700.00	900.00	311.11	7,350.00	1,800.00	308.34

FIG. 101 *Comparative income/expense report.*

THE NATIONAL CO 1 TRIAL BALANCE 30 SEP 19–– PAGE
DIVISION 1

CURRENT PERIOD 9

CO NO.	ACCT NO.	DESCRIPTION	BEGINNING BALANCES DEBITS	BEGINNING BALANCES CREDITS	ENDING BALANCES DEBITS	ENDING BALANCES CREDITS
1	1110000000	CASH	50,750.92		49,605.92	
1	1120000000	SECURITIES, STOCKS	800.00		800.00	
1	1130000000	SECURITIES, BONDS	700.00		700.00	
1	1210000000	ACCOUNTS RECEIVABLE	32,278.00		35,287.00	
1	1220000000	ALLOW. FOR UNCOLL. A/R	820.00		787.00	
1	1310000000	FINISHED GOODS	7,491.00		7,216.00	
1	1320000000	GOODS IN PROCESS	12,112.00		11,612.00	
1	3330000000	MATERIALS	9,923.00		9,923.00	
1	1720000000	FACTORY BLDGS. AT COST	65,000.00		65,000.00	

FIG. 102 *Trial balance.*

THE NATIONAL CO — 1 COMPARATIVE BALANCE SHEET — 15 SEP 19— — PAGE 12

DIVISION 1

CURRENT PERIOD 8

CO NO.	ACCT NO.	DESCRIPTION	CURRENT BALANCE	PRIOR YEAR BALANCE	DIFFERENCE	VAR %
1	1110000000	CASH	49,605.00	50,750.00	1,145.00–	2.26–
1	1120000000	SECURITIES, STOCKS	800.00	800.00	.00	.00
1	1130000000	SECURITIES, BONDS	700.00	700.00	.00	.00
1	1190000000	.CASH ASSETS	51,105.00	52,250.00	1,145.00–	2.19–
1	1210000000	ACCOUNTS RECEIVABLE	35,287.00	32,278.00	3,009.00	9.32
1	1220000000	ALLOWANCE FOR UNCOLL.A/R	787.00	820.00	33.00–	4.02–
1	1290000097	.ADJUSTED RECEIVABLES	36,074.00	33,098.00	2,976.00	8.99
1	1290000098	..LIQUID ASSETS	87,179.00	85,348.00	1,831.00	2.15

FIG. 103 *Comparative balance sheet.*

14. Summary. The NCR Interactive General Ledger System is completely documented, including implementation and operation procedures. It can be readily installed as a stand-alone system or in conjunction with other accounting applications. It is an effective and versatile application for processing and controlling the general ledger. The system:

(*a*) maintains clearly-defined audit trails and internal control for all levels of processing;

(*b*) employs double-entry bookkeeping methods for balanced, up-to-date general ledger control;

(*c*) offers complete flexibility in single-client and multi-client processing with individual or multiple financial reports;

(*d*) produces general ledger reports completely independent of a chart of accounts;

(*e*) performs fiscal year accounting independent of the calendar year;

(*f*) provides for up to thirteen accounting periods in a year;

(*g*) maintains account summary totals as historical data for all periods in a year;

(*h*) maintains budget information on all valid accounts for comparative analysis;

(*i*) posts journal entries for the current period and to any of four open future periods;

(*j*) provides nine levels of total accumulation for reporting purposes;

(*k*) transfers account balances and control information automatically at year-end closing;

(*l*) improves financial control over all business activity without a major restructure of accounting procedures or retraining efforts.

PROGRESS TEST 13

1. Outline the nature of interactive processing. **(1)**

2. Specify the basic philosophy and processing features of an interactive general ledger system. **(2–14)**

CHAPTER XIV

Processing Techniques (4)—Centralised and Distributed Processing

CONCEPTS OF CENTRALISED PROCESSING

1. The computer as a centralised service in a single operating unit. When a business comprises only one factory or office as opposed to a group of factories or other business units, and a computer is implemented in the organisation, then the way in which it is used requires careful consideration. Sometimes the computer, under such circumstances, may be used only for processing routine accounting applications such as payroll, sales ledger, stock control and purchase ledger, etc.

To obtain the maximum benefit however, the computer should be used to aid management in problem-solving and decision-making by the use of quantitative application packages for linear programming, statistical stock control, production planning, network analysis and discounted cash flow, etc. When a computer is used for all the functions within the business it is a centralised facility in the form of a data processing and information system.

2. The computer as a centralised service in a group of operating units. When a business organisation is a widely dispersed conglomeration of various types of operating unit, including factories, warehouses and sales offices and a computer is in use, it is usually located at the head office of the group. In these circumstances the objective would be to provide the best possible service for the data processing and information needs of all functions and operating units in the group.

The benefits to be derived from a centralised service may be summarised as follows.

(*a*) Economy of capital expenditure due to the high cost of computers (in the 1960s and early 1970s) through having only one computer for use by the group instead of several located in the various units.

(*b*) If one large powerful computer is implemented, the resultant advantages are: increased speed of operation, storage capacity and processing capability.

(*c*) Economy in computer operating costs due to the centralisation of systems analysts, programmers, computer operators and other data processing staff as compared with the level of costs that would be incurred if each unit in the group had its own computer on a decentralised basis, i.e. avoiding the duplication of resources.

(*d*) Centralisation would also facilitate the standardisation of applications but this would depend upon the extent of diversity in the dispersed operations regarding payroll and invoicing structures, etc.

If the computer is also communications oriented, whereby all operating units are equipped with transmission terminals connected to the central computer, then basic data may be speedily transmitted for processing by remote job entry and the results transmitted back and printed on a local printer. This would reduce any time delay in receiving computer output through the post or messenger service. The possibility of an integrated management information system then becomes feasible, as data from dispersed

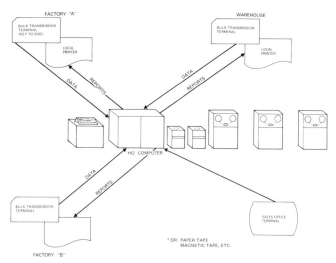

FIG. 104 *The computer as a centralised service in a group of operating units: communications-oriented remote job entry.*

units is speedily processed for local use and information becomes available at head office by means of the computer files for corporate planning (*see* Fig. 104).

Such a centralised computing service should be structured in the organisation at a level which enables the data processing manager to report to a higher level of management than the department level or functional level for which he is providing a service. This enables policy matters to be established at Board level, rather than at functional level, which establishes the use of the computer on a corporate strategic basis in order to optimise its use. If the data processing manager reports to the managing director, he is free from direct inter-functional conflict as problems are resolved at a higher level.

CONCEPTS OF DISTRIBUTED PROCESSING

3. Systems architecture. Distributed processing must not be confused with decentralised processing, even though decentralisation is a feature of distributed processing. Prior to the advent of the computer, different companies in a group may well have used their own data processing installation, i.e. a decentralised facility. The centralisation of data processing, as outlined in **1** and **2** above, was the trend of the 1960s, but the tendency of the late 1970s and early 1980s has been a reversal of this situation, largely due to the development of workstations, mini and microcomputers. These cost much less than mainframes, which makes it a viable proposition to install them in departments and branches on a distributed processing basis. This is the philosophy of providing computer power where it is most needed, instead of concentrating all processing in a single centralised computer system. Systems architecture is a design philosophy whereby small computers in dispersed operating units may be connected by a communications network to each other and also to a large, centrally-located mainframe. The mainframe may support a large database, which would allow information of a strategic nature to be retrieved on demand for corporate planning. This would be a distributed processing network.

The mini and microcomputers may be dedicated machines being used for a single main purpose and, in some instances, may be used as stand-alone processing systems when appropriate. This situation allows a high degree of autonomy at the local operating level which encourages motivation, flexibility and a greater acceptance of responsibility by the local management.

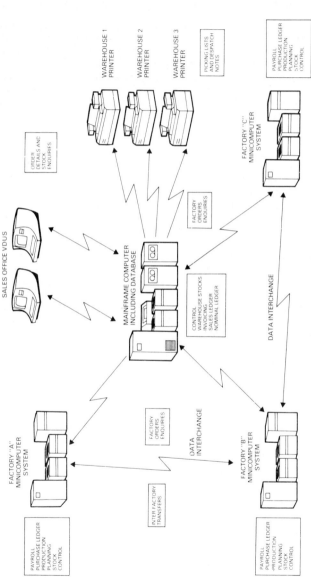

SALES OFFICE VDUS

ORDER DETAILS AND STOCK ENQUIRIES

WAREHOUSE 1 PRINTER

WAREHOUSE 2 PRINTER

WAREHOUSE 3 PRINTER

PICKING LISTS AND DESPATCH NOTES

MAINFRAME COMPUTER INCLUDING DATABASE

CONTROL
WAREHOUSE STOCKS
INVOICING
SALES LEDGER
NOMINAL LEDGER

FACTORY ORDERS ENQUIRIES

FACTORY "C" MINICOMPUTER SYSTEM

PAYROLL
PURCHASE LEDGER
PRODUCTION
PLANNING
STOCK
CONTROL

DATA INTERCHANGE

FACTORY "A" MINICOMPUTER SYSTEM

PAYROLL
PURCHASE LEDGER
PRODUCTION
PLANNING
STOCK
CONTROL

INTER FACTORY TRANSFERS

FACTORY ORDERS ENQUIRIES

DATA INTERCHANGE

FACTORY "B" MINICOMPUTER SYSTEM

PAYROLL
PURCHASE LEDGER
PRODUCTION
PLANNING
STOCK
CONTROL

FIG. 105 *Outline of characteristics of a distributed processing network.*

4. Coordinating influence of distributed processing. Simplicity of gaining access to a computer by relevant operating personnel at all levels of an organisation is not an easy matter to accomplish even within a single unit business organisation equipped with terminals. This problem is accentuated when there are many dispersed units within the organisation, many of which may be interdependent, e.g. marketing and manufacturing functions, as all units must be fully aware of the operational status of each other's sphere of operations.

It becomes even more of a problem when a business is a multi-national organisation with widely-dispersed subsidiaries. With the implementation of distributed processing systems, this is not so much of a problem because it is of no consequence whether the small computers are located in the same building as a mainframe computer or whether they are situated the other side of the oceans. Distributed processing allows a business to select the level of processing autonomy in respect of depots, factories, warehouses or sales offices.

Distributed processing also includes the use, on a decentralised basis, of intelligent terminals, i.e. terminals with processing capabilities which may be used on a local basis for off-line operation or for on-line operations linked to a host computer. The choice of terminal may be selected according to local needs and may include badge readers and data collection terminals in factory departments, tag readers and point-of-sale terminals in retail sales outlets, visual display units (VDUs) for offices; VDUs and/or printers for warehouses and video units in the sales department for on-line entry of order details (*see* Fig. 105).

DISTRIBUTED OFFICE SYSTEMS: ICL DRS 20

For the purpose of defining specific facilities in a distributed resource system, the following details are based on the ICL DRS20 series of Distributed Resource Systems (*see* Fig. 106) which may be defined as workstations.

5. Basic philosophy. The basic philosophy of distributed systems is to make offices more productive; to provide individuals and departments with the facilities with which to do their jobs faster and more accurately; to improve the quality of decision making by improving access to information; and to achieve economy of operation by sharing resources when appropriate.

To achieve these results a system is required which is capable of distributing computing power throughout every office, linking

(Courtesy International Computers Limited)

FIG. 106   *ICL DRS 20 Model 20 and Model 25 intelligent
desk-top workstations.*

workstations in the same way that office activities are structured for achieving a specified activity.

6. Three levels of computing facilities. The ICL DRS20 range of workstations has been designed to provide computing facilities at three levels in the organisation compatible with the way in which work is performed. The various levels may be analysed as follows.

(*a*) Computer power for the individual. The workstation is used as an independent desk top computer using software packages.

(*b*) *Computer power for the department: person to person.* Provides for people working as coordinated groups using common information and sharing resources such as disc storage and printers. The workstations are designed to be linked together to form a departmental network consisting of up to sixteen workstations. This arrangement allows common information files to be available to every authorised user. Data is input to the network once only. Each workstation in the network can use the processing power, storage capacity and communications facilities of any other workstation.

(*c*) *Computer power throughout the organisation: office to office, building to building and company to company.* It is normal

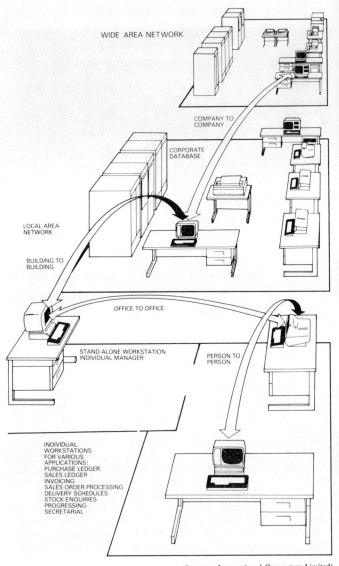

WIDE AREA NETWORK

COMPANY TO
COMPANY

CORPORATE
DATABASE

LOCAL AREA
NETWORK

BUILDING TO
BUILDING

OFFICE TO OFFICE

STAND-ALONE WORKSTATION
INDIVIDUAL MANAGER

PERSON TO
PERSON

INDIVIDUAL
WORKSTATIONS
FOR VARIOUS
APPLICATIONS:
PURCHASE LEDGER
SALES LEDGER
INVOICING
SALES ORDER PROCESSING
DELIVERY SCHEDULES
STOCK ENQUIRIES
PROGRESSING
SECRETARIAL

(Courtesy International Computers Limited)

FIG. 107 *Networks.*

practice within an organisation to exchange information between the various parts of an organisation as part of daily routine; to coordinate activities with other departments—some local, some remote requiring local and remote communications with local and wide area networks, mainframes and minicomputers for random enquiry and data transfer purposes (*see* Fig. 107).

7. Non-intelligent. A DRS20 workstation can act as a non-intelligent terminal when connected to a mainframe for data entry, transaction processing, program development and running software held on the mainframe.

8. Dissipation of computing power. With the normal type of centralised system supporting on-line terminals, the more terminals connected to the mainframe the more dissipated the computing power becomes. The opposite is true in respect of workstations as additional ones increase a network's capabilities.

9. Multi-processors. Each workstation has several micro-processors, the number of which varies for each model, but each one has a dedicated task including the running of programs, file handling, communicating with other computers, controlling the input and output of data and managing the workstation. This fact enables each workstation to handle a number of tasks simultaneously, i.e. concurrently. Micros with only one processor can perform only one function at a time.

10. Range of models. DRS20 workstations are available in a range of models offering a balance between facilities, power, capacity and cost. They also have their own range of software for business and accounting applications, text processing, financial and project planning. Networking is a standard feature achieved by means of the DRX operating system (Distributed Resource Executive). Less expensive models are designed to function as terminals in a wide area network. They do not have extensive processing capability.

(*a*) *Model 50.* This model supports up to fifteen workstations and has a 1MB floppy disc drive and a hard disc of 16 or 27 MB. Its options include a streamer tape; microprocessor for wide area communications through telephone lines and an extension cabinet with extra hard disc storage giving a total of 81MB.

(*b*) *Model 25.* This is an intelligent workstation equipped with integral fixed and flexible disc drives. It can be used as a stand-alone unit or linked to other workstations in local and wide area networks.

(*c*) *Model 20.* This model is also an intelligent workstation equipped with two integrated flexible disc drives. It may be used on a stand-alone basis or used within local and wide area network systems.

(d) *Model 10*. This is an intelligent workstation but it does not have its own file storage and may be used as an element in a local area network.

11. Peripherals. Peripherals include line, matrix and correspondence printers.

12. Cluster controller. When an office has a large number of terminals it is both convenient and economical in the use of lines to install a "cluster controller" which links the terminals to a mainframe by a single line. Up to twenty-four terminals can be connected by this means.

PROGRESS TEST 14

1. Indicate the nature of centralised data processing. **(1,2)**

2. How may a centralised computer be utilised in an organisation? **(1,2)**

3. (a) Describe the characteristics of centralised data processing and decentralised data processing. (b) Compare the advantages for a large organisation of centralised and decentralised data processing arrangements. **(1–4)** (*ACA*)

4. Define the term distributed processing, and examine the case for and against the use of distributed processing as a means of organising information systems. **(3–12)** (*ACA*)

CHAPTER XV

Computer Bureaux and Computing Services

COMPUTER BUREAUX

1. Definition of and factors to consider in selection of a bureau. A computer service bureau is a company which operates a computer to process work for other companies, particularly those which cannot justify a computer of their own. A number of factors need to be considered when choosing a computer bureau as it is necessary to select one which is both reliable and efficient. The following factors provide a reasonable assessment of a bureau's capability relative to others:

(*a*) reputation;
(*b*) integrity;
(*c*) efficiency;
(*d*) competitiveness;
(*e*) number of years established;
(*f*) financial stability;
(*g*) turnround time-reliability;
(*h*) calibre of staff employed;
(*i*) market standing;
(*j*) approach to technological developments.

2. Types of computer bureaux. There are basically three types:

(*a*) *independent companies* specially formed for the provision of computing services to clients;

(*b*) *computer manufacturers* with separately structured computer bureaux, a notable example being BARIC Computing Services Ltd., which is a joint venture between Barclays Bank Plc. and International Computers Ltd;

(*c*) computer users with *spare capacity* who allow other firms to use their computer system either for standby facilities or for program testing prior to the installation of a simple computer system.

3. Services available from computer bureaux. In general, the range of services provided by computer bureaux is as follows.

(*a*) *Data preparation or conversion.* This service consists of the conversion of source data into a machine-sensible form for processing by computer. Conversion may be in the form of floppy disc, cassette tape, magnetic tape or optical characters. A bureau may be used for the initial conversion of master files when changing procedures to EDP.

(*b*) *Systems investigation and design.* This consists of the analysis of existing procedures and their conversion for processing by computer.

(*c*) *Program preparation and testing.* This service provides an addition to the service indicated in (*b*) above.

(*d*) *Hiring computer time.* Here the service to the client consists of processing the client's data using the programs supplied by the client. The hire charges usually vary according to the time of day the service is provided and the length of time the bureau's facilities are used.

(*e*) *Do-it-yourself service (DIY).* The provision of computing facilities to allow the clients' computer operators to process data with their own programs. The service is usually available during off-peak periods.

(*f*) *Time sharing.* Access to the bureau's computer by means of communication links, which in effect provides each user with computing facilities as if he had an in-house computer.

4. Reasons for using bureaux. Any particular company will of course have specific reasons for using a computer bureau, but in general the following reasons are common:

(*a*) to obtain valuable initial experience of processing by computer before deciding whether or not to install an in-house computer;

(*b*) to provide standby facilities, by arrangement, in case of breakdown of the in-house computer;

(*c*) to provide facilities for coping with peak data processing loads owing to insufficient capacity of the in-house computer;

(*d*) non-availability of finance for the installation of an in-house computer;

(*e*) space restrictions for accommodating a computer installation;

(*f*) to avoid the responsibility of operating an in-house computer;

(g) insufficient volume of work to justify the installation of a computer;

(h) to obtain the benefit of computer power at reasonable cost;

(i) to provide more information for management control;

(j) to test and prove programs to be run on a similar computer, when installed, to that used by a bureau;

(k) to obtain the skill and experience of bureau operating staff in the processing of data;

(l) recognition that a bureau is likely to have powerful, up-to-date equipment, made economical by processing a wide variety of work at high volumes;

(m) recognition that bureau will be using, as far as possible, the most efficient techniques and software aids;

(n) to process jobs that cannot be processed economically by an in-house computer.

5. Disadvantages of using bureaux. One of the main disadvantages of using a bureau is the loss of control over the time taken to process data (turn-round time) suffered by an organisation, because of the competing requirements of other clients of the bureau.

In some instances, an organisation may be better served by an in-house computer but may be reluctant to take the plunge; as a result, no experience is gained directly in operating a computer installation. This may create indirect benefits to competitors, especially in the problem-solving applications for which a computer is so valuable. This means that competitors who use computers for their problem-solving needs probably generate optimum solutions, whereas a business without a computer may lose this advantage.

DATA PROCESSING BY COMPUTER BUREAU

6. Computer bureaux and the smaller business. The administrative efficiency of smaller businesses may be increased by utilising the data processing services of computer bureaux. Such services may be used for computing the payroll, wages analysis, purchase analysis and maintenance of the purchase ledger, sales analysis and maintenance of the sales ledger and the control of stocks, etc.

Smaller firms have data processing requirements similar to those of larger firms but they cannot justify the installation of an in-house computer due to the relatively low volumes of data involved. This situation may change with the advent of the low cost microcomputer. Nevertheless, by using a computer bureau the smaller firm can harness electronic computer power to its data processing requirements and become administratively more efficient as a result.

Computer bureau charges are based on the level of service provided, therefore the cost of processing low volumes of data will be relatively low, which makes this course of action an economic proposition. The alternative would be either to increase the number of staff to process the data so as to provide management information for business control or to retain present staff levels and dispense with the provision of important information to management.

It is, of course, essential to obtain estimates of bureau charges for specific data processing requirements for comparison with existing costs but even if bureau charges are higher the additional information provided may create benefits, by being able to control the business more efficiently, in excess of the extra costs.

Bureaux often provide standard computer programs for processing clients' data which may be used to advantage providing they are compatible with the needs of the business. On occasions it may be a prudent course of action to modify existing systems to comply with the features of package programs because by doing so, outmoded systems may be completely updated, and create additional administrative efficiency.

There now follows an outline of various bureau applications indicating the type of data to be submitted and the output which can be provided.

7. Computer bureau payroll application. Initially the bureau must produce a payroll master file either on magnetic tape or disc and this is facilitated by recording relevant information on input forms provided by the bureau. Other data requirements include the following.

(*a*) Standard data:
    (*i*) wage rates (unless provided as initial employee data);
    (*ii*) overtime premium rates;
    (*iii*) piecework rates;
    (*iv*) standard working hours.
(*b*) Amendment data:
    (*i*) new starters;
    (*ii*) leavers;
    (*iii*) changes to deduction rates;
    (*iv*) changes to overtime premiums;
    (*v*) changes to wage rates.

(*c*) Variable transaction data—supplied weekly:

(*i*) hours worked by employees on hourly rates or, alternatively, variations from standard working hours;

(*ii*) details of units produced by employees.

The information which would be received back from the bureau would typically include: pay advices, payroll, national insurance schedules, lists of deductions, various analyses and annual tax returns.

8. Computer bureau purchase accounting. Initially, the bureau must produce a supplier master file which is facilitated by recording relevant information on input forms provided by the bureau. This information would include the name, address and current balance of each supplier. Other data requirements include the following.

(*a*) *Amendment data.*

This basically consists of:

(*i*) addition of new suppliers' names and addresses;

(*ii*) deletion of names and addresses of suppliers not now applicable;

(*iii*) change of address of suppliers.

(*b*) *Variable transaction data*:

(*i*) suppliers' invoices;

(*ii*) suppliers' statements of account;

(*iii*) details of remittances to suppliers;

(*iv*) suppliers' credit notes and other adjustments.

The information which would be supplied by the bureau would typically include a list of creditors at the end of each accounting period, purchase analysis, list of purchases to date from each supplier, purchase ledger accounts and remittance advices for each current supplier, VAT analysis and an audit trail. If required the bureau could also print cheques for payment or credit transfer slips. In addition the purchase ledger would be updated.

9. Computer bureau and sales invoices. A bureau may be employed for the preparation of sales invoices and for this purpose it would be necessary to supply relevant information on input forms supplied by the bureau. This information would include the name and address of each customer and product details in respect of descriptions and code numbers, prices and VAT rates. Product details may already exist at the bureau if they are processing the finished stock accounting application.

The variable transaction data in respect of sales may be supplied to the bureau in any convenient form. From the combination of customer and product details and the variable data in respect of sales, invoices are produced ready for despatch. This application could either stand alone or provide the input of invoice data to the sales accounting application.

10. Computer bureau sales accounting. Initially the bureau must produce a customer master file which is facilitated by recording relevant information on input forms provided by the bureau. This information would include the name and address of each customer and other relevant information. Other data requirements include the following.

(*a*) *Amendment data*:
    (*i*) addition of new customers' names and addresses, credit limit, discount rate and area code, etc.;
    (*ii*) deletion of names and addresses of customers not now applicable;
    (*iii*) change of address of customers.
(*b*) *Variable transaction data*:
    (*i*) copy of sales invoices (or extended advice notes);
    (*ii*) details of remittances from customers;
    (*iii*) customers' credit notes and other adjustments.

The information which would be supplied by the bureau would typically include a list of debtors at the end of each accounting period, sales analysis, statements of account for each customer, credit control reports, VAT analysis and an audit trail. In addition the sales ledger would be updated.

11. Computer bureau stock accounting. The bureau must first produce a stock master file unless this is already in existence for sales invoicing purposes. Other data requirements include the following.

(*a*) *Amendment data*:
    (*i*) addition of new product details;
    (*ii*) deletion of details in respect of discontinued products;
    (*iii*) changes to selling prices, unit cost price, control parameters and VAT rate, etc.
(*b*) *Variable transaction data*:
    (*i*) despatches to customers.
    (*ii*) receipts into stock;
    (*iii*) returns from customers;
    (*iv*) returns to suppliers;
    (*v*) journal adjustments.

COMPUTING SERVICES

Many computing services' organisations originally started out as computer bureaux, providing data processing facilities to small businesses which could not justify the use of a computer. This has now changed to some extent due to technological developments which have already been discussed. Many bureaux have expanded the range of services they provide and may now be defined as computing service companies (*see* **12-16**).

12. Supply and installation of computing equipment. Some organisations now supply hardware including micro, mini and mainframe computers either to function as "in-house" systems or as "front-end" processors linked to other mainframes. They may also supply networked micros, intelligent terminals, multi-user and multi-processor systems.

13. Supply of software. In addition to providing software support with computing equipment as a complete package, some companies also function as software houses developing software packages for distribution through a dealer network or developing "custom" (bespoke) software for individual companies to their specification.

14. Facilities management. This is an arrangement whereby a company transfers all or part of its data processing facility, including hardware and staff, to a contractor, i.e. a computing services organisation and then purchases back the processing requirements of the company. A specific level of service is guaranteed. Contracts vary according to specific needs of individual customers and may involve providing all operational and development staff to run an existing data processing installation or the transfer of the installation to the premises of the computer service company.

Facilities management can provide an efficient service at less than the equivalent "in-house" costs. It is useful when it is necessary to limit capital expenditure for upgrading or replacing an existing system.

15. Consultancy. Some companies will require the services of a consultant before embarking on the installation of computerised systems, and others will need advice on specific problems of a data processing nature. Consultancy services covering these needs are often provided by computing services organisations.

16. Turnkey services. Turnkey services may be defined as "the supply and installation of a computer system in such a complete form that the user need only "turn a key" as it were to commence using the system". Such a service is provided by external consultants. The user figuratively turns a key to gain access to the system for whatever purpose it is designed. This requires the initial identification of a client's needs, the selection of the most suitable hardware (computer system) and the relevant elements of software support. The service covers systems design, program coding, testing and debugging until the system is suitable for handing over to the client.

A business with very little data processing experience using sophisticated machines, or no computer specialists on the staff, would find this service of the utmost benefit as it would enable the changeover of systems to be accomplished by experts without too much involvement by management.

PROGRESS TEST 15

1. Define the term computer bureau. **(1)**

2. (*a*) Describe the range of services offered by computer bureaux. (*b*) List the major features which should be considered when choosing a computer bureau. **(1,3)** (*ACA*)

3. Specify the types of computer bureau available. **(2)**

4. List FOUR services offered by a typical computer bureau. **(3)** (*C&G*)

5. For what reasons would you consider using a computer bureau? **(4)**

6. What are the disadvantages of using a computer bureau? **(5)**

7. How may the services of a computer bureau assist a small business to become more proficient? **(6)**

8. Briefly outline the nature of processing the following applications at a bureau: payroll, purchase accounting, sales invoicing, sales accounting and stock accounting. **(7-11)**

9. Many bureaux have expanded the range of services they provide and become in effect computer service organisations. What services would you expect them to provide? **(12-16)**

10. Define the following services: (*a*) facilities management; (*b*) turnkey services. **(14,16)**

PART FOUR

DEVELOPMENT OF COMPUTER SYSTEMS

CHAPTER XVI

Implementing a Computer

INITIAL CONSIDERATIONS FOR SUCCESSFUL IMPLEMENTATION OF A MAINFRAME COMPUTER

1. Feasibility study. A mainframe computer cannot be plugged in and away she goes, as it were—its successful implementation depends upon a number of factors among which is the need to conduct a thorough "in-depth" feasibility study. Management must make a decision on the basis of a feasibility study report either to implement or not to implement a computer. Whichever decision is made can have far reaching effects on the future efficiency of the business.

The correct decision is crucial because it is possible to make an incorrect decision in either of two instances. In the first instance management may decide not to implement a computer when they should or, in the second instance, to implement a computer when they should not. The consequences of failure to implement a computer when it is necessary is a reduction in administrative efficiency. On the other hand, the consequences of implementing a computer when it is not needed is chaos as systems will be disrupted, unnecessary costs will be incurred and organisational changes will be made needlessly (*see* **8-13**).

2. Top management support. The time, effort and finance required for the initial implementation and development of computerised systems may deter the most enlightened managers unless the feasibility study report makes refusal difficult. This is a further pointer to the value of an accurate feasibility report. It is imperative for top management—the board of directors and functional managers—to show interest at the outset, otherwise projects will have little chance of success once a computer is installed.

Any dissension on the part of top management will filter through the organisation to the lower management levels and this in itself will detract from the successful implementation of systems. Departmental managers in charge of systems to be computerised will not, in all probability, provide the required level of support to systems staff which is so essential for the efficient operation of new systems. User departments need to participate in the design of systems with which they are concerned and for which they are responsible.

3. Education and training programme. The reason for any lack of enthusiasm on the part of management may be ignorance of computers—or even fright—and this should be dispelled by means of a short induction course. Such a course may be conducted by internal systems staff if any are already employed in the organisation or, if they are not, selected managers and staff may attend a computer manufacturer's or college based computer appreciation course. The contents of a computer appreciation course may consist of the following:

 (*a*) definition of a computer;
 (*b*) the place of the computer in the organisation;
 (*c*) duties of systems analysts and programmers;
 (*d*) responsibilities of the data processing manager;
 (*e*) outline of computer applications;
 (*f*) benefits of using computers related to present systems if relevant;
 (*g*) data preparation methods;
 (*h*) processing techniques, batch, on-line, real-time and multi-programming, etc.

4. Communication. Before a large computer is implemented within the organisation the fact that this is under consideration should be communicated to all personnel, particularly those who are likely to be the most affected once a computer becomes operational. This course of action will dispel distorted rumours circulating within the organisation which could have a damaging effect on morale.

It is also necessary to communicate company policy with regard to possible redundancies when systems are transferred to the computer. Of particular importance are the arrangements to be made for retraining staff and possible redeployment.

In most companies it will be the responsibility of the managing director to formally communicate these factors and he should also stress the importance of obtaining the fullest cooperation of staff in the difficult transition period ahead, in respect of systems development and changeover.

5. Recruitment of effective data processing staff. A computer installation will only be as efficient as the personnel who manage, develop systems and program the computer. It is essential to obtain the services of an effective data processing manager who, first and foremost, should be a good manager. He should have a wide knowledge of business systems particularly of the business in which he is employed and due to this essential requirement he is often appointed from within the business. Former organisation and methods specialists and line managers have been appointed to the post of data processing manager on the basis of their knowledge of key systems in the organisation.

The data processing manager should have a considerable knowledge of computers, particularly of the model in use, or about to be implemented, but he need not be an expert in programming. He is responsible for interpreting and executing the policy of the steering committee, planning, organising, coordinating and controlling projects to ensure they achieve objectives.

Systems analysts should be recruited from within the organisation whenever possible to take advantage of their knowledge of the business which is of extreme importance for the development of computer systems. They must be aware of the needs of the operating functions and departments particularly the purpose and objectives of the systems they operate. This is the reason why O & M investigators often become systems analysts when a computer is implemented into a business.

A system analyst must have many talents and be capable of viewing the business as a total system and yet be able to analyse it into its constituent elements (sub-systems). He must be able to appreciate the interactions which occur between sub-systems and the effects computerisation is likely to have on them. He should design systems without unnecessary complexity as the simpler the design the more effective they are likely to be (*see* **30, 31**).

Programmers are required who are capable of writing simple, efficient programs. Unnecessary complexity in programs is likely to increase computer running time and produce documents and reports which are too complex for system needs. This situation requires a higher degree of coordination between programmers and systems analysts to ensure that ambiguity does not enter into programming as this will result in systems failing to meet their objectives.

6. Data processing steering committee. A steering committee should be formulated with responsibility for appraising the viability of computer projects, to ensure they are cost effective and would be of benefit to the business as a whole, to optimise corporate performance rather than functional performance. Such a committee enables the data processing needs of the business as a whole to be coordinated with other functional activities within the framework of corporate plans.

Membership of a steering committee should consist of representatives of the various functions which will be affected by the installation of a computer into the business. The committee is likely to be chaired by the chief executive, which would enable him to have an overview of proposed computer projects and assess whether they accord with the future strategy and policy of the business. The interest of functions in a typical manufacturing business would probably be represented by the production controller, stock controller, chief accountant, sales manager, chief buyer and of course the data processing manager. The data processing manager is then in a position to be aware of company policy and can interpret its requirements more objectively before executing the needs of such policy.

7. Main stages in developing computer applications. Many details need to be appraised when developing computerised applications amongst which are those included in the list below.

(*a*) Identify the nature of the problem, i.e. the type of application.

(*b*) Plan the project, i.e. the use of resources and time schedules.

(*c*) Conduct feasibility study:

(*i*) technical feasibility: demands on the system, speed of response, hardware capability, software availability;

(*ii*) economic feasibility: annual operating costs, development costs and annual equipment costs, anticipated benefits including staff reduction, more timely information flows, improved cash flows, increased customer satisfaction and improved production scheduling.

(*d*) Systems analysis: collect, record, verify, and examine facts.

(*e*) Systems design:

(*i*) specify design philosophy;

(*ii*) prepare a detailed written description of the proposed system including clerical, data preparation, data control and computer operating procedures;

(*iii*) prepare system flowcharts, procedure charts, block diagrams, computer run charts, decision tables and data structure charts, etc;

(*iv*) define reports to be produced by the system;

(*v*) define the master files to be used;

(*vi*) specify the checks and controls to be built-in to the system;

(*vii*) define the primary input and output documents;

(*viii*) develop a glossary of terms for communication purposes between systems and user department staff.

(*f*) Specify arrangements for converting current files.

(*g*) Present proposals to management.

(*h*) Discuss proposals with management and user department staff.

(*i*) Implement management decision either to abort project or selected alternative design philosophy.

(*j*) Programming:

(*i*) prepare program flowcharts;

(*ii*) code programs;

(*iii*) compile programs;

(*iv*) test and debug programs.

(*k*) Implementation:

(*i*) plan for system changeover from current to computerised system;

(*ii*) conduct pilot schemes or parallel running of current and computerised system;

(*iii*) monitor performance by comparing results of both systems and noting variations in computations, etc;

(*iv*) modify system as appropriate to correct errors or faults in the design of the system;

(*v*) finalise job procedure manuals and operating manuals for data preparation staff and computer operations staff;

(*vi*) live operation having disposed of the current system;

(*vii*) maintain system to accord to changing circumstances and development of systems integration.

FEASIBILITY STUDY

A number of important considerations concerned with conducting a feasibility study are summarised below.

8. Objectives of study. At the outset it is important that objectives of the study should be clearly defined in order that the study team have a clear understanding of the requirements of the study. The objectives may be to determine if all or some of the following factors are feasible using a computer:

(*a*) reducing the number of staff in specific administrative functions because of cost;

(*b*) avoiding the need to increase clerical staff because the calibre of staff required is in short supply;

(*c*) improving the flow of information for management;

(*d*) providing problem solving facilities for management;

(*e*) improving cash flows by producing invoices and statements of account earlier;

(*f*) reducing the cost of processing each unit of data;

(*g*) streamlining accounting routines;

(*h*) providing the means for effective systems integration;

(*i*) improving the accuracy of information and data on business documents.

9. Choice of areas for improvement. In order to achieve the designated objectives it is necessary to select the areas of the business most likely to achieve them. Possible areas may be chosen on the following basis:

(*a*) those involving procedures which process a large volume of data, forms or documents;

(*b*) those involving procedures with a high proportion of repetitive operations;

(*c*) those involving procedures with a large number of clerical staff;

(*d*) those involving procedures which suffer from delays due to bottlenecks in processing perhaps due to insufficiently planned procedures, inadequate methods of processing or high-volume posting or calculating operations.

10. General considerations of a feasibility study. A number of important factors must be taken into account before any conclusions can be established and before the feasibility study report is presented to management. They include the following aspects:

(*a*) the alternative types of computer configuration available;

(*b*) the availability of standby facilities in case of breakdown of the computer;

(*c*) business trends and their likely impact on data processing commitments;

(*d*) the extent to which the organisation would need restructuring with the advent of a computer;

(*e*) the availability of experienced computer personnel, systems analysts and programmers, etc;

(*f*) the feasibility of using a computer bureau instead of installing an in-house computer;

(*g*) the feasibility of using several microcomputers instead of a mainframe computer;

(*h*) the incidence of redundancy in respect of clerical staff;

(*i*) the time necessary to develop computerised systems;

(*j*) the need for computer appreciation courses for management and staff.

11. Cost considerations of using a computer. Some of the elements of cost which must be considered by a management accountant, for instance include:

(*a*) the cost of purchasing or renting a computer perhaps compared with the cost of using a computer bureau;
(*b*) the cost of developing computer systems;
(*c*) the cost of computer accommodation;
(*d*) the cost of recruiting and training computer staff;
(*e*) the manual cost of operating the computer system;
(*f*) the comparative costs of alternative methods of processing;
(*g*) the cost of writing off current equipment;
(*h*) the availability of finance to purchase a computer system;
(*i*) the cost of obtaining finance to purchase a computer system;
(*j*) the cost of converting master files to magnetic tape or disc.

12. Expected benefits of using a computer. The possible benefits are numerous if computers are planned and used effectively. Some typical benefits are summarised below:

(*a*) more effective administrative procedures and accounting routines;
(*b*) more timely and relevant information for management decision making and control;
(*c*) improved cash flows by earlier production and despatch of invoices and statements of account or revision of product prices or maintenance contract terms;
(*d*) more effective control of stocks;
(*e*) more optimal solutions to administrative problems such as production planning and capital budgeting;
(*f*) increased level of systems integration providing economy and increased efficiency;
(*g*) improved forecasting techniques;
(*h*) facilities for simulating business operations before embarking on costly changes to the physical systems concerned;
(*i*) random enquiry facilities for the retrieval of information on demand;
(*j*) real-time control of key operations.

13. Feasibility study in an organisation possessing a computer. When a computer already exists in the organisation it is still necessary to conduct a feasibility study for any proposal to computerise a business system. The objectives and stages of feasibility study for

a proposed system may be based on the following outline of action
to be taken:

(a) define objectives of system to be studied;

(b) define objectives of the feasibility study (see 8);

(c) collect facts relating to the current system, including types
and volume of input, types and volume of output, frequency of
processing, time for performing each main activity, number of staff
employed on the system, type of files used, number of records in
files, frequency of referring to files, frequency of updating files, file
activity ratio ("hit rate"), problem areas and operating costs, etc;

(d) anticipated system development costs, including costs of file
conversion;

(e) estimate run times;

(f) anticipate costs of computer operations;

(g) assess expected benefits (see 12);

(h) prepare feasibility study report;

(i) submit and discuss report with appropriate management;

(j) make decision to computerise and proceed with more
detailed systems analysis if management consider proposals
satisfactory; otherwise continue with existing system perhaps with
minor modifications.

SYSTEMS ANALYSIS

14. Systems analysis defined. Systems analysis is the term used to
describe the process of collecting and analysing facts in respect of
existing operations, procedures and systems in order to obtain a
full appreciation of the situation prevailing so that an effective
computerised system may be designed and implemented if proved
feasible.

The difference between an organisation and methods investigation (a review of clerical procedures and methods) and a systems
analysis project is one of objective rather than one of principle.

An O & M investigation sets out to improve the existing situation
by the most suitable means, chosen from a number of possible
alternatives. Systems analysis, however, has as its objective the
design of an effective computerised procedure which will create
benefits in excess of those possible by other means.

Systems analysis also embraces systems design, which is an
activity concerned with the design of a computerised application
based on the facts disclosed during the analysis stage. Both
activities are carried out by the same person who is known as a
systems analyst.

15. Duties of systems analyst. The duties may be summarised as follows.

(*a*) Collect, record and anlayse details of existing procedures and systems.

(*b*) Develop ideas for a computerised system superior to the existing methods in use—improve system performance.

(*c*) Design system input, file and output requirements.

(*d*) Specify checks and controls to be incorporated in conjunction with audit staff.

(*e*) Define actions required to deal with various conditions arising in the system by means of decision tables.

(*f*) Specify the structure of computer runs.

(*g*) Specify the most appropriate processing technique for the prevailing circumstances.

(*h*) Estimate run timings.

(*i*) Prepare computer operating instructions.

(*j*) Define error messages to be incorporated in the system.

(*k*) Specify test data to be used for proving programs in conjunction with audit staff and programmers.

(*l*) Arrange for test runs in conjunction with programming staff.

(*m*) Document all aspects of the system in a system specification.

(*n*) Implement parallel operation of old and new system.

(*o*) Monitor results.

(*p*) Maintain system to accord to changing circumstances.

(*q*) Communicate with user department, systems staff and programmers as appropriate.

16. Systems analysis team. Some projects require a team of analysts, the size of which is dependent upon the complexity and type of system to be investigated. It is good policy to recruit suitable personnel from existing staff, as it is important that they should have a sound knowledge of the business which often takes many years to obtain in sufficient depth to analyse systems effectively.

The team should also include representatives from the various departments of the organisation that will be affected by the investigation. This approach ensures that personnel with an intimate knowledge of the systems being reviewed for computerisation have the opportunity to record facts which may otherwise be overlooked and which are important for the effective design of the computer system.

After the project is concluded the personnel on secondment go back to their department (unless recruited for systems work on a full-time basis due to their experience) and take an active part in the newly installed computerised system. By this means the best results are obtained, as personnel who have been brought into the picture are more likely to co-operate and accept the changes which have been implemented.

17. Problems posed by resistance to change.

(*a*) Overmanning.
(*b*) Inefficiency.
(*c*) Low productivity.
(*d*) Failure to meet objectives.
(*e*) Out of date methods.
(*f*) Out of date procedures and systems.
(*g*) High processing costs.

18. Ways of overcoming resistance to change.

(*a*) Inform staff of reasons for change.
(*b*) Enlist the co-operation of staff.
(*c*) Allow staff to participate in systems development.

19. Systems analysis and O & M. In general, the same stages of investigation are conducted for a systems analysis project as for an O & M investigation. The main differences are the types of document used for recording facts (in some respects) and the greater depth of analysis which is required with regard to the number and type of characters contained in documents, records and reports.

During the design stage, however, the technical details differ greatly because an O & M investigator may assess the viability of using word processing equipment instead of normal typing services, for instance. A systems analyst, on the other hand, will be concerned with the best way of designing the system in accordance with the characteristics of the computer configuration installed or to be installed.

The reader is referred to the author's HANDBOOK, *Organisation and Methods*, which covers the stages of conducting a systems investigation in depth. It is now proposed to deal with those aspects which have a direct bearing on the facts required prior to computerising a procedure or system. It is emphasised, however, that the basic stages of collecting, recording, verifying and examining the facts are common to any type of systems investigation as are the types of facts collected in respect of resources used, operating data, quantitative data, operating costs, organisation structure of application areas, company policy and external influences, etc.

COLLECTING FACTS

20. Interviewing. This technique collects facts by interviewing personnel connected with the system under investigation as it is considered that they possess vital information relating to the systems with which they are concerned. The interviewer should encourage the staff to give their point of view of how they consider the system may be improved and accordingly the interviewer should be prepared to listen rather than dominate the interview. He should possess sufficient tact, however, to steer any discussion in the desired direction.

There should be no mystery surrounding an interview and the purpose of conducting it should be stated as it must be appreciated that personnel become very apprehensive of pending changes. An interview should be concluded amicably and in such a manner that any further assistance will be forthcoming freely.

21. Questionnaire. A questionnaire may be used as an aid to interviewing as it has the advantage of containing pre-formulated questions, answers to which are essential for the development of the system under consideration. This approach avoids the possibility of overlooking important facts. Questions should be framed as simply as possible to avoid ambiguity, should be asked in a logical sequence, should not be too numerous and leading questions should not be asked. The answers obtained may be verified by interviews after the questionnaire has been completed or it may be used during the course of an interview.

22. Observation. This technique is used to obtain an overall visual impact of a systems environment. It takes into account details relating to the movement of personnel and forms, types of machines and equipment being used, the speed of operations, working conditions, idle time, numbers of staff, bottlenecks and delays, etc.

23. Inspection and examination. This entails the examination and inspection of documents regarding number of entries made, their general state, how they are filed and the effectiveness of the filing system. The state of machines and equipment will also be examined as will the general working conditions in the systems environment.

RECORDING TECHNIQUES USED IN SYSTEMS ANALYSIS

24. Procedure chart. A chart used for analysing the activities and their relationships within a defined procedure. It portrays the various activities in the procedure and by means of symbols indicates the type of activity performed. This type of chart is used in systems investigations to record the details of the existing procedures so that they may be subjected to further analysis. The symbols used in the construction of this type of chart are shown in Fig. 108. A typical procedure chart is illustrated in Fig. 109.

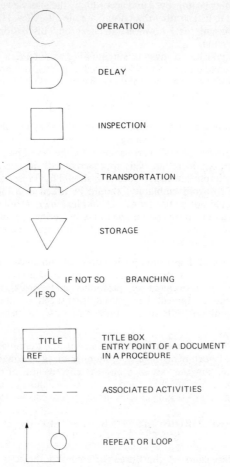

FIG. 108 *Symbols for the construction of procedure charts.*

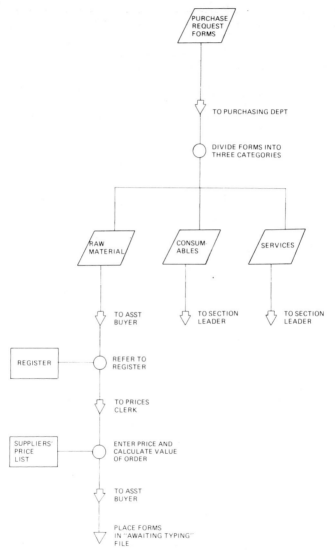

FIG. 109 *Typical procedure chart.*

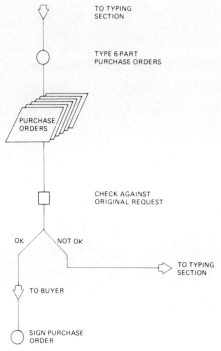

TO TYPING
SECTION

TYPE 6-PART
PURCHASE ORDERS

PURCHASE
ORDERS

CHECK AGAINST
ORIGINAL REQUEST

OK   NOT OK

TO TYPING
SECTION

TO BUYER

SIGN PURCHASE
ORDER

FIG. 109   *(Contd.)*

25. The grid or X chart. This chart is used to define the relationships which exist between the various documents in a system. It is very useful when used in combination with document classification to determine the relationship between input and output documents.

The chart also assists the identification of unnecessary documents and elements of data.

In addition, the chart is useful for establishing which documents can be combined or those which may have the number of copies reduced.

The relationship between the various documents is indicated by an X in the relevant box.

26. Document analysis form—output. This form assists the analysis of the documents in the existing system and provides information for the design of a new system.

A document analysis form should be prepared for every document in the existing system and for documents required in the new system which do not exist in the present system.

The form is essential for describing the output from the system, and includes the following information.

(*a*) *Identification* of the form:
> (*i*) form title;
> (*ii*) form number.

(*b*) *Distribution and use.* Each person who receives a copy of the output (report) should be interviewed and the following facts established:
> (*i*) job title, function and responsibility;
> (*ii*) reason for receiving the report;
> (*iii*) information used from the report;
> (*iv*) action taken from the report;
> (*v*) additional information required;
> (*vi*) information not required;
> (*vii*) suitability of report layout;
> (*viii*) establish whether copy is filed, passed on or destroyed (for subsequent follow-through if necessary).

(*c*) *Frequency of issue:*
> (*i*) daily;
> (*ii*) weekly;
> (*iii*) monthly;
> (*iv*) quarterly;
> (*v*) annually;
> (*vi*) on request.

(*d*) *Elements of data and their sequence:*
> (*i*) control keys or fields, e.g. customer account number, etc.;
> (*ii*) filing sequence, e.g. invoice number, customer account number, pre-printed number on pads of documents, etc.;
> (*iii*) reason for preparing the report in a specific sequence;
> (*iv*) identify the source of each element of data shown on the report;
> (*v*) elements of data produced during processing and the manner of their production;
> (*vi*) maximum, average and minimum size of each element of data and its percentage occurrence.

(*e*) *Volume:*
> (*i*) maximum and average number of documents;
> (*ii*) maximum and average number of lines of data per document;

(*iii*) assess growth rate for elements of data and reports together with seasonal variations.

(*f*) *Format*:

(*i*) consider if the layout of the document requires amendment or whether suitable in the existing format;

(*ii*) assess whether all the data need be preprinted or whether suitable for printing by the line printer.

27. Document analysis form—input. This form is useful for describing the source documents within the system, that is those documents which contain basic data to be input for processing.

The information contained on the analysis form may consist of the following.

(*a*) *Identification*:

(*i*) form title;

(*ii*) form number.

(*b*) *Purpose* of the document.

(*c*) Where *originated* and by what means:

(*i*) allows a check to be made for duplication of documents;

(*ii*) determines the extent to which various similar documents may be combined;

(*iii*) the content of similar documents may be rationalised;

(*iv*) enables an assessment to be made on the adequacy of the present methods of preparation;

(*v*) an assessment is made to ensure if it is originated in the best possible location under the circumstances.

(*d*) *Elements of data* and their *sequence*:

(*i*) description of each data field;

(*ii*) sequence of each data field;

(*iii*) pre-printed fields;

(*iv*) fields which may be required but not presently included;

(*v*) size of each of the fields indicated, specifying whether fixed or variable length, maximum, average and minimum size of each field;

(*vi*) an indication of the percentage of occurrence of each field is useful for assessing the average size of the complete input data for each transaction, which is an important aspect in the design of punched cards for input.

(*e*) *Volume*:

(*i*) maximum and average number of source documents;

(*ii*) possible future changes in volume;

(*iii*) seasonal variations in volume.

(*f*) *Frequency of preparation*:

(*i*) at present;

(*ii*) foreseeable or prospective changes in frequency.

(*g*) *Files affected* by the input:

(*i*) determine the type of file affected by the input (transaction) and the applications concerned;

(*ii*) assess the adequacy of the file organisation and content of records compared with the fields contained in the source document.

28. File analysis form. This form is used for defining the construction of files and may contain the following information.

(*a*) *Identification:*

(*i*) file name;

(*ii*) application in which used.

(*b*) *Purpose* of the file.

(*c*) *Records constituting the file:*

(*i*) maximum, average and minimum size of each record;

(*ii*) names of different records contained in the file;

(*iii*) percentage occurrence of each type of record in the file.

(*d*) *Volume* of records in the file:

(*i*) maximum, average and minimum number of records contained in the file;

(*ii*) maximum and average transaction volumes affecting the file;

(*iii*) assess future size of file;

(*iv*) indicate future volumes of transactions affecting the processing of the file;

(*v*) indicate seasonal variations of transactions affecting the processing of the file.

(*e*) *File organisation:*

(*i*) sequence of records;

(*ii*) control key;

(*iii*) adequacy of present sequence;

(*iv*) suitability of present keys.

29. Output analysis chart. This chart assists in examining the outputs from the current system to establish the information content of reports, their source and the relationships which exist between source documents and reports.

The chart is constructed as follows.

(*a*) Output documents are listed down the left-hand side of the chart.

(*b*) Information fields contained in reports are listed along the top of the chart.

(*c*) The type of character contained in files is classified as follows.

(*i*) N = numeric.

(*ii*) A = alphabetic.

(*iii*) A/N = alpha/numeric.

(*d*) Information fields derived from records are indicated by the designation R, and those derived from source documents by S.

(*e*) Information fields derived from calculations are indicated by the designation C.

(*f*) The maximum and average field size in characters is also indicated.

(*g*) Appropriate designations are entered in columns at the point of intersection of the document column and the appropriate information field.

(*h*) Fields marked R must be contained in master records.

(*i*) Fields marked S are the transaction details which must be contained in source documents.

SYSTEMS DESIGN

30. Objectives of systems design. The design of a computer-based system (and any other type of system) is a creative task which has as its objective the implementation of a system creating benefits and improvements superior to those achieved by other methods.

The system must therefore be designed so that basic business documents and reports are produced as effectively as possible in accordance with the needs of the business.

Provision should be made for automating decisions of a routine nature whenever possible, which may be incorporated in the program in the form of standard formulae, thereby assisting the various levels of management by freeing them from routine decision-making.

During the process of designing a system, it should be borne in mind that the system(s) under review should not be considered in isolation from other systems, as many systems are inter-related either by the need for basic information or by the output from one system being the input to other systems.

The processing requirements of the total system—the organisation—should be considered, even though it may be decided to design separate systems—"sub-systems"—initially. Even so, the separately designed systems should be planned in such a way that they may be developed with a minimum of amendment and disruption at a later date after gaining experience in the design and processing of separate applications.

31. Essentials for the effective design of systems. A well-designed system should take into account the following factors:

(*a*) production of the desired information, at the right time, in the right amount, with an acceptable level of accuracy and in the form required at an economical cost;

(*b*) incorporation of checks and controls which are capable of detecting and dealing with exceptional circumstances and errors;

(*c*) need to minimise the cost and the time spent on recording source data;

(*d*) need to minimise the cost and the time spent on data preparation;

(*e*) need to minimise the cost and the time spent on processing data;

(*f*) effective safeguards for the prevention of fraud;

(*g*) effective security measures in order to avoid loss of data stored in master files;

(*h*) efficient design of documents and reports;

(*i*) efficient design of computer runs;

(*j*) design of suitable coding systems to aid identification, comparison, sorting, verification and the elimination of ambiguity;

(*k*) policy matters and their effect on business systems;

(*l*) legal matters and their relationship with business systems;

(*m*) adequate handling of exceptions to normal situations.

While a system can be designed to process all possible variations or exceptions on a computer, this may create a considerable degree of complexity in programming and extend processing time to an unacceptable level. Consequently it may be more efficient to design clerical systems instead of computer systems to handle them.

32. Basic principles of designing a form. Forms are an integral part of business procedures whether clerical or computer based and care must be taken in their design as this has an effect on operational efficiency regarding compiling the forms and in their interpretation for business administration and control. Basic principles which must be considered in the design of forms are outlined below.

(*a*) The paper must be of suitable quality for the purpose it is to serve.

(*b*) The form should be as simple as possible to understand and compile.

(*c*) Entries should flow in a logical sequence.

(*d*) Data boxes should be of sufficient size for the details to be entered in them.

(*e*) Layout and form sizes should be standardised as far as is practicable.

(*f*) Ensure they can be completed in the shortest possible time.

(*g*) Eliminate possible ambiguity.

(*h*) Combine related forms when feasible.

(*i*) The duplication of data on several forms should be avoided when possible.

(*j*) Sprocket feed holes must be provided for computer continuous stationery.

(*k*) Natural spacing characteristics of line printers must be allowed for.

33. Form design question. The following question is part of a question set by the Association of Certified Accountants.

XYZ Ltd maintains its sales ledger system on a minicomputer. The sales ledger master file is held on magnetic disc. Accounts, which contain the usual standard data, are kept on a brought forward balance basis with the total balance analysed over current month, month 1, month 2, month 3 and month 4 and over. Visual display units are employed for the entry of transaction data and for the retrieval of data for aswering enquiries. A variety of printed reports is produced on the line printer.

Draft, with TWO lines of sample entries, the Credit Limit Excess and Aged Balance report which is produced monthly for the Accounts Manager. Your answer should be in the format of a typical computer-produced line-printer report.

SOLUTION

A suggested layout for the report is shown in Fig. 110.

SYSTEMS SPECIFICATION

34. Purpose of a systems specification. The systems analyst having developed a computer based system must specify in writing the features and operating requirements of the application. Initially it is presented to management for their scrutiny and approval prior to implementation. The document also provides a programmer with the details he requires for writing the programs for each run.

(a)

TRANSACTION DATA:

1. INVOICES (SALES)
2. CREDIT NOTES (RETURNS)
3. CASH REMITTANCES, TRADERS CREDIT TRANSFERS, ETC.
4. CASH DISCOUNTS
5. ADJUSTMENTS (CORRECTIONS)

(b)

ACCOUNT NUMBER	ACCOUNT BALANCE	CREDIT LIMIT	CREDIT LIMIT EXCESS	CURRENT MONTH	AGED ACCOUNT BALANCE			
					1 MNTH	2 MNTH	3 MNTH	4 MNTH AND OVER
	£	£	£	£	£	£	£	£
12345	1000	800	200	500	200	300	–	–
12346	2000	1800	200	600	400	300	500	200

FIG. 110 *Credit Limit Excess and Aged Balance Report.*

It also provides formal documentation for system maintenance and general reference. It is the counterpart of a procedure manual prepared by O & M staff.

35. Structure of a systems specification. A typical systems specification may be arranged into six sections as follows.

(*a*) Introduction:

    (*i*) terms of reference;

    (*ii*) objectives;

    (*iii*) expected benefits;

    (*iv*) annual operating costs, development costs and annual equipment costs.

(*b*) Systems definition:

    (*i*) written description of system embracing clerical and computer procedures;

    (*ii*) system flowcharts, procedure charts and computer run charts (*see* **37, 39, 40**).

(*c*) Equipment:

    (*i*) schedule of equipment required to operate the system including ancillary equipment for data preparation;

    (*ii*) possible alternative equipment.

(*d*) Detailed specification:

    (*i*) input specification and layout (*see* **43**);

    (*ii*) output specification and layout (*see* **42**);

    (*iii*) file record specification (*see* **44**)

    (*iv*) source document specification and layout (*see* **43**).

(*e*) Program specification:

    (*i*) details of test data and testing procedures;

    (*ii*) checks and controls.

(*f*) Implementation (*see* **45**):

    (*i*) file conversion;

    (*ii*) parallel running and pilot schemes during program and system testing;

    (*iii*) job procedures for user departments;

    (*iv*) job procedures for data preparation and computer departments.

DIAGRAMS, CHARTS AND FLOWCHARTS

36. Block diagram. A block diagram is sometimes referred to as a "system outline" or "system function" diagram. The diagram is used to outline the whole system in respect of inputs, files, processing and outputs independent of operation details.

The computer is not shown in such a diagram, as it is only required to show the flow of information through the system and the output produced.

37. Systems flowchart. This chart is prepared from the block diagram and introduces the computer, which is shown as a box. The chart is mainly designed to illustrate the flow of documents around the computer and the processing performed by the computer.

Some essential aspects of its construction are:

(*a*) the name of each department concerned with the system is recorded along the top of the flowchart;

(*b*) inputs to the system are shown on the left-hand side of the chart;

(*c*) outputs from the system are shown on the right-hand side of the chart;

(*d*) processes are shown by the appropriate symbol in the relevant column, and contain a reference code;

(*e*) each symbol contains a brief description;

(*f*) symbols are connected by lines and arrows.

38. Procedure narrative. A procedure narrative is a written description of the new system, and expands the restricted details shown on the systems flowchart. The narrative and systems flowchart combined form the most important part of the initial specification presented to the chief programmer.

39. Computer run chart. Computer run charts are prepared from the systems flowchart, and show the sequence of computer operations to be performed.

The chart expands the detail of each computer box on the systems flowchart showing inputs, files and outputs relevant to each run.

It is good practice to support the chart by a written description of the processing stages (*see* Figs. 113, 114, 115, 117, 118).

40. Clercial procedure chart. This type of chart is also prepared from the system flowchart and outlines the clerical operations necessary to support computer operations. (*see* Fig. 109).

41. Computer procedure flowchart. This is the most detailed flowchart prepared by the systems analyst during the design stage, and is used to support the written program specification.

It is used to show the sequence of operations and decisions in a computer procedure.

The chart is prepared from a computer run chart.

INPUT, OUTPUT AND FILE SPECIFICATIONS

42. Output specification and layout. When designing the output from the system, it is necessary to consider the needs of the user in order that the output should serve a useful purpose. The size of a document and/or report must not be decided upon without first considering the limitations of the equipment used in their production.

For each printed output it is necessary to consider the following aspects.

(*a*) Use *standard planning chart* for indicating:
- (*i*) system identification—name and number;
- (*ii*) program name and number;
- (*iii*) number of print lines per sheet;
- (*iv*) maximum size of fields;
- (*v*) field content;
- (*vi*) lateral and vertical spacing requirements.

(*b*) Prepare a *written description of the output* in respect of:
- (*i*) purpose of document or report;
- (*ii*) number of copies;
- (*iii*) type of stationery, e.g. size, pre-printed or blank and quality;
- (*iv*) special considerations;
- (*v*) distribution;
- (*vi*) frequency of issue (allied to frequency of computer run).

(*c*) Provision of samples.

43. Input specification and layout. It is necessary to consider both the original source document and the input media to the computer.

Source documents are the forms used for the initial recording of data and they are usually pre-printed. The design of such documents should take into account the layout of the punched card or other media used for input so that data fields appear in the most convenient order for transcription—that is, punching or encoding.

Data of a fixed nature, that is non-variable, can be pre-printed to avoid unnecessary entry of details each time the form is compiled.

It must not be overlooked that some source documents are originated outside the business, which means that their design cannot be changed.

Source document specifications contain the essential elements recorded on the input document analysis form together with any amendments that are deemed necessary (*see* **27**).

Samples of source documents and input media must be provided.

44. File record specification. The construction of files is based on the information recorded on the file analysis form, suitably amended for the needs of the computer system.

The following details are extremely important in the design of files for computer processing.

(*a*) Specification for *all files:*
    (*i*) medium to be used;
    (*ii*) file name;
    (*iii*) labels;
    (*iv*) size of records—maximum and average;
    (*v*) names of different records contained in the file;
    (*vi*) sequence of records;
    (*vii*) block size—unit of transfer—applicable to magnetic files;
    (*viii*) field names, descriptions, field lengths and maximum values.

(*b*) Specification for *card files:*
    (*i*) card types;
    (*ii*) punching code.

(*c*) Specification for *magnetic tape files:*
    (*i*) packing density and gap size;
    (*ii*) number of reels constituting the file;
    (*iii*) file security arrangements;
    (*iv*) retention period.

(*d*) Specification for *direct access files:*
    (*i*) method of storage—random, serial, sequential, partitioned or indexed sequential;
    (*ii*) method of access—random, serial, sequential, selective-sequential or partitioned.

It is important to note that the method of storage refers to the manner in which the file is organised and the method of access refers to the manner of referencing, updating or amending the file.

    (*iii*) bucket size.

SYSTEMS IMPLEMENTATION, MONITORING AND MAINTENANCE

45. Systems implementation. Before a new computer system is implemented it may be necessary to conduct "pilot" runs with test data to ensure that the system achieves its defined purpose and objectives. Programs must of necessity be subjected to trial runs with test data, consisting of both valid and invalid data for the purpose of ensuring that the program can contend with all possible eventualities. Corrections are then made either to the programs or to the system, which are then subjected to further trials. When the situation appears to be satisfactory "parallel" running of the new system and the existing system can commence. The results produced by both systems can then be compared and any notable differences investigated and corrected. This is a "fail-safe" procedure as it would have drastic consequences on the business if the old system was dispensed with before the new system had proved to be satisfactory. It is not unknown for "bugs" to appear after parallel running has been dispensed with even after detailed trials have been conducted.

46. Monitoring performance. Computer systems must be monitored to detect any deviations from planned results and performance, so that suitable amendments can be effected and staff subjected to further training if necessary.

47. System maintenance. The term updating is sometimes referred to as maintenance in the context of ensuring that a system meets current requirements. Systems must be adjusted for the needs of change either for fundamental reasons, e.g. the introduction of VAT or for systems development in respect of integration or the introduction of on-line processing. When packages are used, amendments to programs may need to be effected perhaps for more efficient running of the relevant programs.

BENCHMARK TESTS

48. Benchmark tests defined. Benchmark tests are used to assess the performance of different computer systems for the selection of the system which best fits the requirements of the business's data processing commitment. The tests are applied to representative data and processing functions such as reading and writing records, sorting operations and multiplication, etc. The actual times obtained can be compared with manufacturers' published performance data for evaluating the various computer systems under consideration. Tests are conducted by benchmark programs which also provide valuable information in respect of the amount of internal storage used during processing.

49. Advantages of benchmark tests. These are summarised below:

(*a*) assists in selecting the most suitable computer system for businesses' data processing requirements;

(*b*) performance data is known in advance which assists in formulating job schedules.

CODING SYSTEMS

50. Purpose of coding systems. Code numbers are allocated systematically to specific entries on a planned and coordinated basis in order to provide a unique identity of customers, stocks, expenditure items, suppliers and employees, etc. A code number is a compact means of defining a specific entity as only a few digits are required rather than lengthy descriptions. Descriptions are still required however for the purpose of describing items on despatch notes, sales invoices and purchase orders, etc. Such descriptions are complementary to code numbers and they must, of course, be matched by validation checks. Code numbers are referred to as "key" fields on transactions and records.

Computer processing systems in particular utilise code numbers for locating specific records on master files and matching them with transaction data prior to updating the records.

51. Centralised control of coding systems. It is good practice for series of code numbers to be planned and allocated centrally to avoid conflict. If this is not done, duplicated code structures could be implemented causing chaos in the identification of various transactions types. This could be overcome to some extent, however, by validation checks on the type of transaction. Systems staff usually accept responsibility for the design of coding systems as it is an integral element of systems design.

52. Important features of coding systems. The following summary will serve to indicate the main factors to consider for effective coding systems.

(*a*) *Uniqueness*—Each entity should have a unique unambiguous code number for specific identification.

(*b*) *Useful purpose*—Code numbers in general serve a useful purpose as they assist sorting of transactions which can be done much faster by computer than any other method. It is also much easier to sort by numeric codes than alphabetic descriptions. Code numbers also facilitate the comparison of data items, perhaps for matching purposes, either for updating master files or for comparing actual and budgeted expenditure, etc.

(c) *Compactness*—Code numbers require fewer digits or characters than descriptions which complement each other but at the same time allow descriptions to be abbreviated in certain instances to eliminate redundancy, i.e. unnecessary characters. For example, "FASTENER" may be abbreviated to "FSTNR" by eliminating the vowels.

(d) *Meaningful*—Although not always possible or desirable, specific parts of a code when relevant should relate to particular facets of the item to which it relates, e.g. size, shape, type, location and specification of component parts held in store (*see* **53**).

(e) *Self-checking*—Codes should contain self-checking facilities when necessary in the form of check digits for validation purposes (*see* X, **24-8**).

(f) *Expansibility*—Codes should facilitate expansion by allowing flexibility in the coding structure to allow insertions by leaving gaps between blocks of code sequences.

(g) *Standard size*—All codes of a given type relating to a specific entity should contain the same number of digits to facilitate field checks.

53. Faceted code. Each position in the code number has a specific meaning, for example, if it is required to develop a code for basic raw materials used in manufacturing it may be based on the following structure.

> *Type of material*—1st digit
> > 1—Steel
> > 2—Copper
> > 3—Brass
>
> *Section*—2nd digit
> > 1—Rod
> > 2—Strip
> > 3—Sheet
>
> *Size*—3rd digit
> > 1 ⎫
> > 2 ⎬   Appropriate range
> > 3 ⎪   of sizes
> > 4 ⎭

Location in stores—4th digit

$\left.\begin{matrix} 1 \\ 2 \\ 3 \\ 4 \end{matrix}\right\}$ Appropriate storage location

54. Serial code. Sequences of code numbers may be allocated to specific types of record to identify specific entities. No information is conveyed by the code number itself. For example, a range of numbers may be allocated for departmental codes, expenditure codes, stock codes, customer account codes, etc.

These codes numbers may be applied in the following way.

(*a*) Departmental code:
Direct:
  1—Press shop
  2—Machine shop
  3—Assembly shop
  4—Finishing shop
  5—Inspection shop

Indirect:
  6—WIP stores
  7—Finished product stores
  8—Consumable stores
  9—Toolroom
  10—Maintenance department

(*b*) Expenditure codes:
Operating labour:
  20—Tool setters
  21—Labourers
  22—Shop clerks
General operating overheads:
  25—Scrap
  26—Rectification
  27—Waiting time
  28—Shift premium
  29—Small tools
  30—Consumable materials
  31—Lubricants
  32—Works stationery

(*c*) Combination of codes may be used as follows:
  1/29—Press shop/small tools
  9/31—Toolroom/lubricants
  10/20—Maintenance department/tool setters

55. Block coding. A block is a set of serial or code numbers analysed into smaller groups which may be based on some general characteristic of the entities, for example:

Steel rod	0001–0170
Steel strip	0171–0340
Steel sheet	0341–0500
Copper rod	0550–0670
Copper strip	0671–0840
Copper sheet	0841–1000
Brass rod	1050–1200
Brass strip	1201–1400
Brass sheet	1401–1550

PROGRESS TEST 16

1. Why is it essential to attain top management support when systems are being computerised? **(2)**

2. Why is management and user education so important in an organisation whose operations are being computerised for the first time? As a data processing manager, how would you plan the progressive education of the staff of the data processing department? **(3)**(*IDPM*)

3. Before a large computer is implemented within an organisation the fact should be communicated to all relevant staff. Discuss. **(4)**

4. Why is it essential to recruit effective data processing staff for the operation of a computer installation? **(5)**

5. What are the responsibilities of a data processing steering committee? **(6)**

6. Why is it important to conduct a feasibility study either to implement a large computer initially or into the transfer of systems to a computer already installed subsequently? **(8-13)**

7. (*a*) List the stages in the life cycle of a systems project. (*b*) Describe the activities carried out by a systems analyst in TWO of these stages. **(7)** (*C & G*)

8. (*a*) Outline the main sections of a feasibility report and briefly explain the purpose of the typical contents of each section. (*b*) An important part of any feasibility report is a section giving a financial justification for the proposed system. Describe in detail the matters dealt with in this section and the role of the management accountant in its preparation? **(8-13)** (*ICMA*)

9. Describe fully the work carried out by a systems analyst during the investigation and analysis of a business system. **(14, 15)** (*ACA*)

10. Describe the work of a systems analyst. Pay particular attention to his working relationships with users and programmers. **(14,15)** (*C & G*)

11. State the problems posed by resistance to change and ways of overcoming them. **(17, 18)**

12. In spite of the growth in computer-based information processing, many office procedures are carried out by conventional clerical means, either completely manually or by some combination of manual and mechanised systems. The person who deals with the planning and installation of such systems is usually called an Organisation and Methods (O & M) specialist. You are required: (*a*) to explain the scope of O & M, the methods by which an O & M investigation is carried out and the relationship (if any) between O & M and systems analysis; (*b*) to discuss how advances in technology are causing changes in the systems, procedures and equipment which the O & M specialist recommends to deal with the particular problems of office correspondence. **(19** and XXII)(*ICMA*)

13. Specify four ways of collecting facts during a systems invesigation. **(20-3)**

14. Specify the recording techniques which can be used by a systems analyst. **(24-9)**

15. Indicate the objectives of systems design and the essential requirements for the effective design of systems. **(30, 31)**

16. Prepare a check list for the guidance of systems analysts when designing forms for use in computer systems. **(32)** (*ACA*)

17. (*a*) Briefly summarise the main purposes served by a systems specification. (*b*) Tabulate the main sections of a typical systems specification and give details of the principal contents of each section. You are to assume that a computer is already installed and that no further computing equipment will be required. **(34, 35)** (*ACA*)

18. Specify and describe briefly the contents of a system specification. **(34, 35)** (*IDPM*)

19. Define the following terms: (*a*) block diagram; (*b*) system flowchart; (*c*) procedure narrative; (*d*) computer run chart; (*e*) clerical procedure and computer procedure flowchart. **(36-41)**

20. Define the following terms: (*a*) output specification; (*b*) input specification; (*c*) file record specification. **(42-4)**

21. Indicate the activities concerned with systems implementation. **(45)**

22. What is the purpose of coding systems? **(50)**

23. Identify and briefly comment on EIGHT of the desirable, if not essential, features of a coding scheme. **(52)**(*ACA*)

CHAPTER XVII

Flowcharting Computer Applications

RUNS, ROUTINES AND SYMBOLS

The purpose of this chapter is to illustrate by means of flowcharts (computer run charts) a number of computer applications.

In general, computer applications consist of "runs" and "routines", and it is now proposed to indicate some of the more important considerations (*see* **2**).

1. Flowchart symbols. When designing computer run charts, flowchart symbols are used. The various computer manufacturers and the National Computing Centre use different symbols, but Fig. 111 serves to indicate basic symbols and Fig. 112 the symbols recommended by the NCC.

2. Computer run. A run is a unit of processing consisting of a number of operations applied to each transaction item within a batch. Each item is processed in accordance with a program which loops back to the next item after completing the processing on the preceding item.

It is normal for each run to have its own program consisting of a series of instructions to be performed on each transaction item.

The number of operations performed in a single run should be as high as possible, and it is necessary to consider the following factors which have a bearing on the constituent elements of each run.

(*a*) The *size of internal storage* and the capacity available for storing the program, which may consist of many instructions.

(*b*) The *feasibility of segmenting programs* and storing the various segments in direct access backing storage devices to be called in when the previous segment has been completed. This technique overcomes the non-availability of internal storage for storing the whole program.

(*c*) The *number of devices* (such as magnetic tape units or

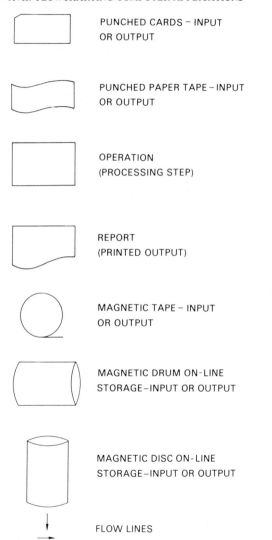

FIG. 111 *General flowchart symbols for the construction of computer run charts.*

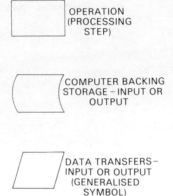

FIG. 112 *NCC flowchart symbols for the construction of computer run charts.*

printers) required in a run should be no more than those which comprise the computer installation.

(*d*) The *complexity of the run* in respect of the number of different activities to be performed (such as calculating, printing and updating) within the run.

(*e*) The ability of the run to deal with *exceptions and errors* within the data being processed.

3. Processing routine. A routine may form all or part of an application consisting of a number of computer runs usually interconnected by the output from a preceding run forming the input to the succeeding run. For example, the output from a wages calculation routine includes the updating of the payroll master file which forms the input to the next run for printing payslips and pay envelopes.

Some routines consist of combinations of on-line and batch operations whereby data to be processed is input directly by the keyboard of a VDU. The data is validated by reference to specific master files before being stored on a work file ready for processing in batch mode.

Each stage of processing is controlled by a VDU operator who loads the appropriate program for performing relevant operations such as sorting, printing and updating. (*See* ICMA November 1980 at the end of this chapter).

In addition, specific segments or sections of a system have

different processing frequencies, some segments being performed daily, weekly or monthly. This is partially outlined in ICMA November 1979.

In other instances, routines are processed on an interactive transaction basis, dealing with each transaction individually through all relevant processing stages before dealing with the next transaction (*see* XIII).

APPLICATIONS

4. Types of applications. There are many other computer applications, depending upon the nature of the business, for example, insurance, banking, tour operation, building societies, supermarkets, warehouses and so on. It is interesting to note that many organisations of a seemingly different nature have similar systems relating to payroll, purchasing, sales and stock control, etc.

It is also of interest to appreciate that seemingly different systems in different types of organisation have a great deal in common, for example: controlling the booking of rooms in a hotel chain, controlling the reservation of seats on aircraft, controlling banking transactions and the movement of commodities in a warehouse: all have one thing in common—the control of stocks of one type or another, i.e. rooms, seats, money and commodities.

5. Integrated nominal ledger application. Figure 113 illustrates the computer runs for an integrated nominal ledger system which may be performed by a nominal ledger package providing for the production of profit and loss statements, balance sheet and variance reports. The latter is achieved by incorporating budgetary control and budget flexing. Other forms of nominal ledger applications may not be so comprehensive and incorporate only sales and purchase transactions. Yet other applications may not produce profit and loss statements or balance sheets but restrict their output to accounts schedules or trial balance for the preparation of final accounts and balance sheets by normal accounting methods.

Run 1. Input is derived from data produced by the separate computer applications in respect of stocks, payroll, sales, purchases, plant and machinery including depreciations, accruals and pre-payments, accounting adjustments and cash. The data on the transaction files is deemed to have been validated in the relevant runs of the appropriate applications. The run is concerned with consolidating all nominal ledger data on relevant nominal ledger codes.

Run 2. The input to this run is the consolidated file from run one. This run is for the purpose of updating the nominal ledger

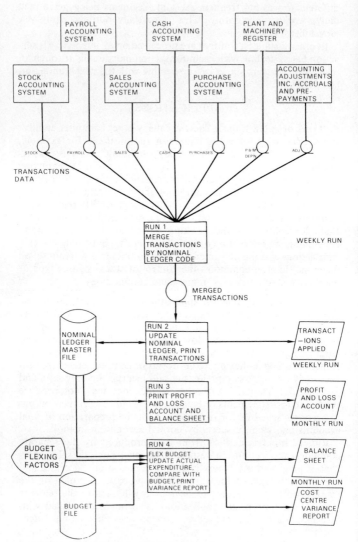

FIG. 113   *Integrated nominal ledger flowchart.*

master file and printing out a list of transactions applied for the purpose of providing an audit trail. The master file is stored on disc to facilitate direct access to relevant nominal ledger records.

Run 3. At the end of the month the nominal ledger master file is used for printing a profit and loss account and balance sheet.

Run 4. The nominal ledger master file records are input together with a budget file and budget flexing factors. The budget file is updated with actual expenditure for the period to obtain the cumulative expenditure to date for comparison with budgeted expenditure. This provides the basis for printing out a cost centre variance report.

Figure 114 outlines the structure of an integrated stock control, invoicing and sales ledger system.

ICMA QUESTION ONE SOLUTIONS

6. November 1979

G Manufacturing Limited has decided to computerise its purchase accounting system. It is expected that extensive expenditure analysis will ultimately be included but initially this aspect of the system will be restricted.

The computer configuration available comprises a medium sized central processor with punched card reader, line printer and two exchangeable disc drive units (each of 30 million characters).

An outline of the new system is as follows:

Source document

A source document will be created clerically from purchase invoices passed for payment. The contents of this document will be

    source document reference number
    supplier identification code number
    supplier's own reference number
    invoice date

expense code   minimum × 1
amount   occurs average × 1.2
value added tax rate   maximum × 5

Output

This source data will be processed to produce these outputs.

(*i*) Purchase daybook, being a daily listing of all prime data input, in source document reference number sequence.

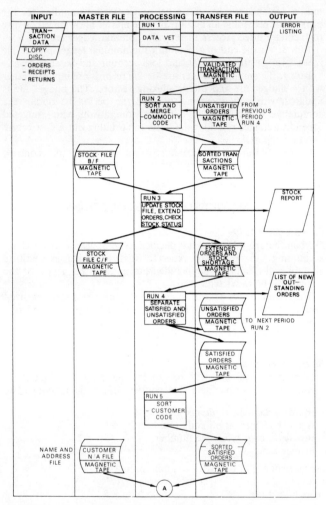

FIG. 114 *Computer run chart—integrated stock control, sales invoicing and sales ledger system (using NCC symbols).*

The system illustrated assumes that complete processing is carried out once a month. In practice, certain parts of the processing may be performed daily, weekly or monthly.

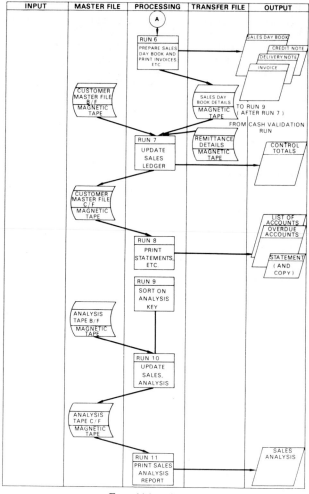

FIG. 114 *(Contd.)*

(*ii*) Remittance advices, containing supplier name and address and full details of invoices being paid in supplier identification code number sequence.

(*iii*) Credit transfers, containing payer and payee bank details and amount, in supplier bank reference number sequence.

(*iv*) Supplier analysis giving total expenditure for this month and this year to date per supplier, in supplier identification code number sequence within supplier category (note: suppliers are categorised according to the type of goods supplied, e.g. raw metal, stationery, lubricating oils).

(*v*) Expense code analysis giving total expenditure per each expense code.

It will be noted that (*i*) above will be produced daily, while (*ii*), (*iii*), (*iv*) and (*v*) will be produced at the month end.

Predicted volumes

Purchase invoices per day	200
Suppliers	2000
Expense codes	70

Any facts or figures not given may be assumed provided each assumption is clearly stated.

You are required to submit the following:

(*a*) computer system run flowchart(s) with brief narrative for the purchase accounting/expenditure analysis system;

(*b*) a description of the main files required;

(*c*) a suggested lay-out for print-out (*iv*) above, the monthly supplier analysis.

SOLUTION

Part (*a*). This part of the question required a runchart to be submitted for the system outlined. The runchart must obviously be based on the computer configuration available, which includes a card reader. This intimates that source data is to be punched into cards and subjected to batch processing operations. A runchart should be prepared (*see* Fig. 115).

Part (*b*). A description of the main files required is outlined below:

Supplier file. This will contain details as follows.

(*a*) Supplier identification code number.

(*b*) Name and address.

(*c*) Payee bank details.

(*d*) Invoice date and amount (each invoice).

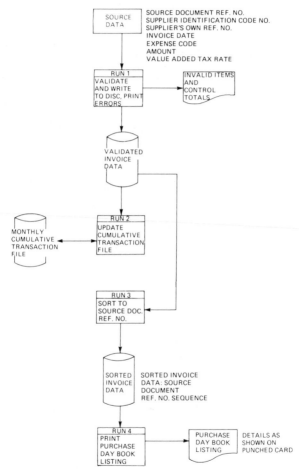

FIG. 115 (a) *Run chart: purchase accounting—daily routine.*

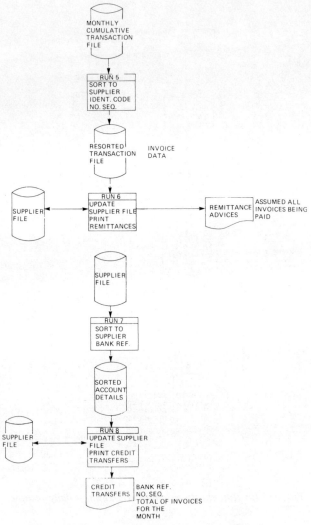

FIG. 115 (b) *Run chart—monthly routine.*

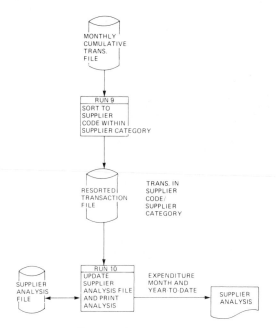

FIG. 115(b)   *(Contd.).*

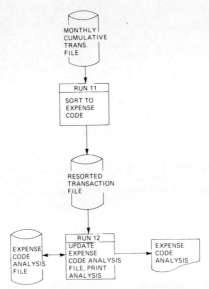

FIG. 115(c)   *Run chart—computerised purchase accounting system.*

Monthly cumulative transactions file. The details contained in this file are summarised below.

(*a*) Source document reference number.
(*b*) Supplier identification code number.
(*c*) Supplier reference number.
(*d*) Invoice date.
(*e*) Expense code.
(*f*) Amount.
(*g*) Value added tax rate.

Expense code analysis file. The details in this file are as follows.

(*a*) Expense code.
(*b*) Total expenditure for each expense code.

Supplier analysis file.

(*a*) Supplier identification code number.
(*b*) Supplier category.

SUPPLIER IDENTIFICATION CODE NO.	SUPPLIER CATEGORY	EXPENDITURE FOR MONTH £	TOTAL EXPENDITURE YEAR TO DATE £
123	10	100	1000
	20	300	4000
TOTAL		400	5000
125	10	200	1200
	20	400	3600
	30	—	1000
TOTAL		600	5800
GRAND TOTAL	10	5000	10000
	20	6000	12000
	30	1200	3000
	40	800	5000
		13000	30000

SUPPLIER ANALYSIS   MONTH . . . .

FIG. 116 *Suggested layout for monthly supplies analysis printout.*

(c) Total expenditure, for the month.

(d) Total expenditure, year to date.

Part (c). See Fig. 116.

7. May 1980

A company is to introduce a computer based production control system.

As part of the overall system the weekly production activities are to be planned as follows.

(a) The production controller determines quantities for each assembly to be manufactured for the following week. This is termed the "assembly build programme" (ABP).

(b) For each assembly on the programme (approximately 300 per week) the assembly number and quantity are entered to magnetic tape on a key/tape system.

(c) The data processing procedure is as follows.

    (i) Input data are read and validated and an error report is produced.

    (ii) Input data are checked for the feasibilty of ABP, to determine components requried for each assembly and to access/update component stock to produce the following two reports:

        (1) made-in components in short supply report, showing components needed for ABP, in component number sequence;

        (2) bought-out components report, in component number sequence.

(d) Updated component stocks are processed to produce two reports:

    (i) made-in component manufacturing programme, showing economic batch quantity for each component that has less stock than minimum stock level;

    (ii) similarly, a bought-out components purchasing programme.

(e) Check made-in component manufacturing programme data for feasibility, to determine the raw material requirements and availability of raw material for each component, to update raw material stock file and to produce the following reports:

    (i) made-in components with raw materials shortage report, in component number sequence;

    (ii) raw materials in short supply report, in raw material code sequence.

(f) Process updated raw material stocks and produce stock report for items having less stock than minimum stock level.

It may be assumed that the main files have already been determined as follows:

Assembly master file on disc pack A. Indexed sequential form in assembly number sequence containing the breakdown of components per assembly for 3 000 assemblies.

Component master file on disc pack B. Indexed sequential form in component number sequence sub-divided into bought-out and made-in component sub-files. There are 6 000 bought-out component records containing details of suppliers, prices and other information. Also there are 12 000 made-in component records containing details of raw materials, production processes, tools required etc.

Component stock file on disc pack C. Indexed sequential form in component number sequence sub-divided into bought-out and made-in component sub-files. The file contains details of current stock balances, re-order levels, batch quantities, stores location etc.

Raw material stock file on disc pack C. Indexed sequential form in raw material code sequence containing current stock balances, re-order levels, batch quantities, stores locations etc.

The computer configuration consists of a medium sized central processor, two magnetic tape units, three exchangeable disc units and a line printer.

You are required to:

(*a*) Design and flowchart a system for processing the information and producing the results specified above. (Your answer should contain sufficient narrative to explain adequately the system you have designed).

(*b*) Note that the system flowchart requested in (*a*) above is but one part of the documentation required for a full specification of the system. Describe, briefly, three other items which would be required for the complete recording of the system, but do not fully specify them.

SOLUTION

Part (a). The computer configuration stated in the question is typical for batch processing operations and the runchart required for processing the information and producing the results specified must be designed accordingly (*see* Fig. 117).

Part (b). Other items which would be required for a full specification of the system include:

(*i*) input, output and file specification and layout;

(*ii*) program specification including details of test data to be used; testing procedures and checks and controls to be implemented for the validation of data;

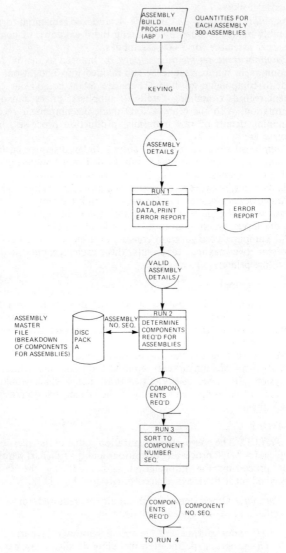

FIG. 117 *Run chart—computer-based production control system.*

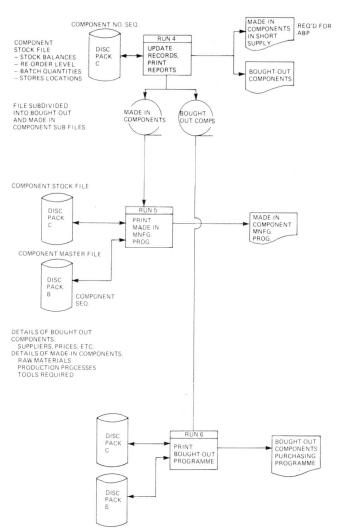

FIG. 117 *(Contd.).*

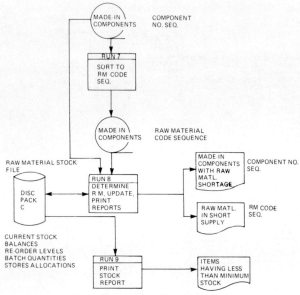

FIG. 117   *(Contd.).*

(*iii*) implementation requirements, including: file conversion, changeover plans (parallel running of old and new system) and job procedures for data preparation, data control, computer operations staff.

8. November 1980

A manufacturer wishes to maintain a computer based file of all customers' orders outstanding. A typical order from a customer comprises the following information:

	Maximum number of characters
customer's name	30
date of order	9
delivery date requested	9
customer's order number	10
product group	9
size code	9
description	30
quantity	3

(product group, size code, description, quantity grouped with 6 ×)

Each week the master file of outstanding orders will be updated by:

	Approximate number per week
(*a*) addition of new orders	200
(*b*) deletion of despatches including partial despatches	220
(*c*) order amendments including cancellations	50

The outstanding orders master file will contain approximately 1000 outstanding orders.

You are required to specify a complete data processing system which will provide the following facilities:

(*a*) weekly updating of master file;

(*b*) weekly report of all outstanding orders in order number within customer number within product group sequence;

(*c*) weekly report showing total value of new orders for each product group;

(*d*) weekly report of despatches for week showing total value per customer for each product group:

(*e*) monthly report showing the total value of outstanding orders per size within delivery date.

At a minimum your specification should include:

(*a*) an outline of the computer configuration required, listing the main items of equipment;

(*b*) a systems flowchart containing or supported by brief narrative;

(*c*) details of the file(s) you intend to maintain;

(*d*) details of the minimum inputs necessary.

Any facts or figures not given above, which you feel are necessary in designing your system, may be included in your answer but must be clearly specified.

SOLUTION

Part (*a*). With regard to the type of computer configuration required, this may be determined by examining the features of the system: e.g. the volume of transactions are not very great and this intimates that on-line data entry should be considered for the input of order details, despatches and amendments. A suitable configuration is a minicomputer system outlined below.

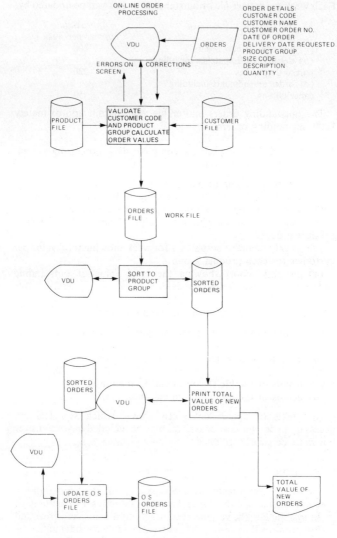

FIG. 118(a) *Weekly updating of outstanding orders file and weekly report showing total value of new orders.*

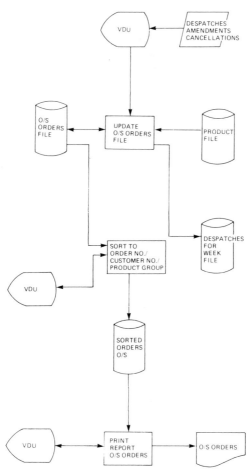

FIG. 118(b)   *Weekly report showing all outstanding orders.*

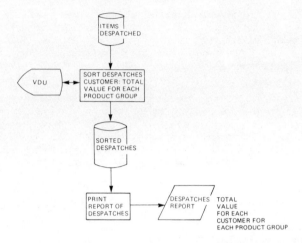

FIG. 118(c)   *Weekly report of despatches.*

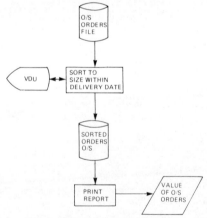

FIG. 118(d)   *Monthly report showing value of outstanding orders.*

(*i*) Processor with memory of 64K bytes or more.

(*ii*) Integrated disc units (housed in processor cabinet) for backing storage.

(*iii*) Visual display unit (work station) for data entry and system control.

(*iv*) Line printer for printing reports.

Part (*b*). A system flowchart should be prepared defining the features of the proposed system and indicating that order details are to be collected on an *orders file* for batch processing, the order details having been entered by the workstation. The orders file is used as a basis for printing a weekly report, showing the total value of new orders. The orders file is also used to update the *outstanding orders file*. The file is also updated with despatches, amendments and cancellations. A weekly report of outstanding orders is printed from this file. The despatches are stored on a *despatches for week file* which is printed out weekly. The outstanding orders file is used to produce a monthly report showing the total value of outstanding orders per size within delivery date (*see* Fig. 118).

Part (*c*). Details of the files required include the following.

(1) Product file:
- (*i*) product group:
- (*ii*) size code;
- (*iii*) description;
- (*iv*) cost price;
- (*v*) selling price;
- (*vi*) VAT code;
- (*vii*) discount rate;
- (*viii*) quantity in stock;
- (*ix*) value of stock.

(2) Orders file:

Details entered via VDU:
- (*i*) customer code;
- (*ii*) order number;
- (*iii*) delivery date;
- (*iv*) product group and size code;
- (*v*) quantity;
- (*vi*) date or order.

Details read from product file:
- (*vii*) product description;
- (*viii*) cost price;

    (*ix*) selling price;
    (*x*) VAT code.

Details read from customer file:
    (*xi*) customer name;
    (*xii*) discount rate.

(3) Outstanding orders file:

Details read from orders file for new orders and entered via VDU regarding despatches, amendments and cancellations:

    (*i*) customer code;
    (*ii*) customer name;
    (*iii*) order number;
    (*iv*) date of order;
    (*v*) delivery date;
    (*vi*) product group;
    (*vii*) size code;
    (*viii*) product description;
    (*ix*) quantity.

(4) Customer file:

    (*i*) customer code;
    (*ii*) name and address;
    (*iii*) discount rate;
    (*iv*) minimum value to receive discount;
    (*v*) credit limit;
    (*vi*) account balance;
    (*vii*) ageing of account balance;
    (*viii*) area code;
    (*ix*) turnover details.

(5) Despatches for week file: *see* Part (*b*) notes.

Part (d). Minimum input requirements include those entered via the VDU in respect of new orders (*see* Part (*c*) (2)) and those details also entered via the VDU with regard to despatches, amendments and cancellations. This requires the operator to input the order number and amended product details; the order number and product number of cancellations and details of items despatched.

The question also states that "any facts or figures not given above ... may be included in your answer but must be clearly specified."

A useful item which could be incorporated into the system is either the computation of gross profit margins or contributions. It would be a simple matter to calculate the relative profitability of the various products sold by incorporating the variable cost of each item as well as the selling price on the Product file. Management would then be in a position to make decisions either to discontinue unprofitable products or attempt to sell greater quantities of the more profitable ones.

PROGRESS TEST 17

1. Specify the symbols used for constructing computer run charts. **(1)**

2. Specify the factors which must be considered in the design of computer runs. **(2)**

3. Define the nature of processing routines. **(3)**

4. Specify the nature of computer applications. **(4)**

5. Outline the characteristics of an integrated nominal ledger application. **(5)**

6. ICMA Question One MISDP, Nov. 1979. **(6)**

7. ICMA Question One MISDP, May. 1980. **(7)**

8. ICMA Question One MISDP, Nov. 1980. **(8)**

CHAPTER XVIII

Computer Programming: Principles and Concepts

PROGRAM SPECIFICATION, DOCUMENTATION AND STANDARDS

1. Program specification. Before programming can commence it is essential that the programmer is aware of the nature of the system to be programmed, its purpose and objectives. The programmer must be aware of the various conditions which exist within the system under consideration and actions required to deal with them. This information is contained in the systems specification prepared by the systems analyst which also includes the types of checks and controls to be built into the system; routine decision making needs to be integrated within the program for automatic stock re-ordering, for instance; and the test data to be used during program testing.

2. Program documentation. After programs have been prepared all the relevant documentation is held in the systems folder or manual which is referred to as a "systems specification" because it contains all the details of the relevant system. The documentation includes low-level flowcharts indicating the broad characteristics of the system; decision tables outlining the logic of the system regarding the nature of the conditions to be provided for and the actions required to deal with them when they arise; program coding sheets of the source program prepared by the programmer together with the subsequent source program listing obtained from the compilation (or assembly) run; operating instructions for running the program specifying breakpoints in the program and stationery changeover needs, etc. In addition, the documentation contains input, output and file formats; data structure charts; charts consisting of sections relating to input, processing and output. The input and output sections are concerned with input, output and files whereas the processing section describes the processes necessary to convert inputs to outputs; program network diagrams are also included which illustrate interactions between data and the various processing operations.

3. Programming standards. If programs are produced within the framework of data processing standards this will aid the continuity of program development in the event of programmers leaving the company. New programmers will be in a position to assess the documentation as far as it has been developed and continue from that point on the basis of laid down standards relating to the construction of flowcharts, decision tables and coding, etc. Accordingly, they will attain an acceptable level of productivity and expertise much sooner than otherwise would be possible.

Standards have been developed by the National Computing Centre (NCC); the British Standards Institution (BSI); IBM and other major computer manufacturers; the International Organisation for Standardisation (ISO), the American National Standards Institute, Inc. (ANSI) and the European Computer Manufacturers' Association (ECMA). The BSI represent the UK in international organisations concerned with the preparation of international standards. Standards have been established for flowchart symbols and computer languages. The standards relate to file organisation methods, checkpoint/restart routines, job control programs, routines for label writing and checking on file media. Standardisation also includes the use of standard coding sheets and modular programming (*see* **13**).

NATURE OF COMPUTER PROGRAMMING

4. Computer instructions. Each operation performed by a computer (on transaction data relating to a specific application) is in accordance with a pre-defined instruction.

Each instruction defines a basic operation to be performed, identifies the address of the data to be processed, the location of the data affected by the operation and the input or output device to be used. The complete set of instructions necessary to process a job is known as a "program".

Instructions are of five basic types as follows.

(*a*) *Arithmetic/logic.* Add, subtract, multiply, divide, shift, round-off, collate and compare, etc.

(*b*) *Data transfer.* Read from input, read to output, read a character, read a word, read a block of data, print a line, transfer data to different locations in the memory, etc.

(*c*) *Conditional branch or jump.* The presence of specific conditions in the data being processed is established by a comparison of data factors or the testing of a counter which causes the computer to branch or jump to the next appropriate instruction (*see* Fig. 121).

(*d*) *Unconditional branch or jump and loop.* When it is necessary to execute an instruction which is not the next in sequence in the internal memory, this is achieved by an instruction known as an unconditional branch or jump. This provides the means of creating a loop in the program for executing a common sequence of instructions repeatedly to various units of data. A loop is terminated by a conditional branch after effecting a test (*see* Fig. 121).

(*e*) *Counter.* A counter is a memory location (unit of storage) used for the purpose of storing a control parameter for automatically controlling a processing sequence. A counter may be set with a specific number which is decremented by "1" after each event being controlled. The counter may then be tested to detect whether it reads "0", for instance. If a "0" is detected then a conditional branch is executed to a specific set of instructions. If the counter does not read "0" then a conditional branch is executed to a different set of instructions, perhaps to execute a further loop in the program (*see* Fig. 121).

5. Main stages of program preparation. A lot depends on the nature of the processing technique to be applied and the nature of the computer configuration to be used, as a different approach will be necessary for programming a system to run on a batch processing configuration from one to run on an interactive basis on a microcomputer. The stages outlined below apply in general.

(*a*) Define the nature of the problem by studying the system specification which contains details of the program specification.

(*b*) Decide on the type of language to use; assembly code (low-level language) or high-level language, which in the case of a mainframe computer may be COBOL, and in the case of a microcomputer BASIC.

(*c*) Determine sub-routine requirements, print format and layout, whether data is to be input via the keyboard of the console or microcomputer or within the program and the checks and controls to be incorporated etc.

(*d*) Prepare decision tables and program flowcharts as appropriate to the complexity of the problem.

(*e*) Determine programming strategy relating to the approach to developing programs, whether to adopt monolithic, modular or structured programming (*see* **12–14**).

(*f*) Specify breakpoints (*see* **6**).

(*g*) Code each statement (instruction) of the program in the relevant programming language. This stage produces the SOURCE program.

(*h*) If a microcomputer is being programmed the statements may be input via the keyboard. They will then be interpreted directly into machine code. For a batch processing configuration the "source" program together with the assembler or compiler are then input to the processor for conversion into a machine code "*object*" program.

The process of assembling or compiling records the "object" program on either magnetic tape or disc and prints out details of the source program including errors at the same time—this is known as a program listing. The programmer checks the list for errors and corrects them accordingly.

(*i*) The program is tested using test data as defined in the program specification. Any errors are noted and corrected.

(*j*) The program is stored on a suitable backing storage media for future use. For a mainframe computer this would be either magnetic disc or tape, for a microcomputer either floppy disc or cassette tape.

6. Breakpoint. A programmer must determine the point in a program where it is necessary to insert a breakpoint when applicable. This is the point where a program is interrupted for a specific reason, perhaps for the operator to input a parameter or to change the type of stationery on the printer. For interactive processing by microcomputer it may be defined as the point in the program where a message is displayed on the screen asking the user to enter specific data to allow processing to continue.

DEVELOPMENT OF PROGRAMMING LANGUAGES

7. Low-level language—machine code. At one time, in the early days of computers, all computer programs were written in machine code, i.e. an instruction (operation) code specific to a particular manufacturer's computer. Programs of instructions had to be written in a form that the computer could interpret and execute and accordingly this type of programming was classified as "machine-oriented" as the instructions were in a form required by the computer but not in a form to assist the programmer to solve the problems under consideration, i.e. not "problem-oriented".

As computers operate by pulses of electricity representing data in binary code the instructions were written as a series of 0s and 1s in accordance with the "bit " pattern of the instruction to be performed, e.g.

00101	00110	10100	00100	(binary)
5	6	20	4	(decimal)

The programmer was required to have a detailed knowledge of the computer with regard to core storage locations, registers and the function (operation) code, etc. He had to keep track of all core storage locations for data input, working areas, output assembly and the locations occupied by the program. However, the programmer's task is now made easier as these functions are performed automatically by software in the form of translation programs known as "assemblers and compilers".

As program instructions were written as a series of 0s and 1s far removed from basic English, it was classified as low-level language programming. However, not all computers used the same function or operation code, or indeed the same instruction format, which meant that a programmer probably had to learn a different function code and the operating details of another type of computer if he changed his job.

8. Low-level language—assembly code. To overcome these difficulties and to avoid the laborious task of writing programs in machine code, each computer manufacturer devised his own assembly code or assembly language. The advantage of an assembly language is that it enables a program to be written much more easily, at the same time allowing the same degree of flexibility that was available when writing programs in machine code. This means that programs can be prepared much more quickly than is possible with machine code, without the sacrifice of machine-running time when processing a job, which is not so with the high-level languages to be discussed later.

An assembly language enables program instructions to be written in mnemonic or symbolic code, that is in pseudo-code (a language which is not machine code). Programs written in this type of language are known as "source" programs and they have to be translated into a machine code program by a programming aid (software) known as an "assembler". After assembling, the object program is input each time the job to which it relates is to be processed. The process of writing instructions in mnemonic or symbolic code is known as "autocoding".

Instead of writing 5 for "add" and possibly 10 for "compare", the programmer writes "ADD" and "COM" in accordance with the symbolic code for a particular computer. Also, instead of specifying actual storage addresses (internal memory locations) symbolic addresses are indicated in each instruction, i.e. OLDBAL, which is the symbolic address for "old balance".

An instruction in assembly language, for a single-address type computer, would take the form:

LDX 1 OLDBAL

This instruction means "load the item of data named 'OLDBAL' to accumulator 1". The assembler automatically assigns a core store location to OLDBAL, which is indicated in the object program.

Assembly languages are still rather complex, and generally the number of instructions which have to be written are still the same as for machine code programming unless "macro-coding" is used. Such a language is also biased towards the machine rather than the problem.

HIGH LEVEL LANGUAGES

9. Portability of languages. Digital Research Inc. develop languages which allow the user to design applications programs, which can then be applied to various processors and operating systems allowing full portability from 8-bit to 16-bit or 32-bit environments: from microcomputer to mini or mainframe. Programming productivity has been enhanced by Digital Research as they provide the most important commercial programming languages in sophisticated compiler implementations which are portable. Some aspects of these programs are outlined in the following text.

10. High level language defined. A high level language is any problem orientated programmer's language which allows instructions to be written in a form with which the user is conversant, such as the use of mathematical equations for a mathematician and plain English-style statements for business applications. This is as distinct from machine-orientated languages which relate to a specific machine rather than the type of problem to be solved. Examples of high level languages are outlined below.

(*a*) *Algol.* Algol is an acronym for *ALGO*rithmic *L*anguage which is a high-level problem oriented language for mathematical and scientific applications using algorithms. The language defines algorithms as a series of statements and declarations in the form of algebraic formulae and English words. Each operation is represented as a statement and each unit of data is known as a variable each of which is assigned a name by the programmer. An

instruction or assignment statement of the form—$b: = a + c + 5.0$;
effectively adds 5.0 to the numbers in the locations a and c and
places the answer in location b. The statement consists of the name
of a variable followed by: $=$, followed by any arithmetic expression whose answer is put into the left hand side variable.

Example of a programming problem extracted from the City and Guilds of London examinations.

Lorries making deliveries on the continent may leave their home base in England at any time of the day or night. Each driver has a log book in which he writes:

the name of his destination;
the departure time from base;
the arrival time at the British port;
the departure time from the continental port;
the time of arrival at the continental destination.

All times are recorded using a standard twenty-four hour clock. Design and write a program which will read batches of the data and print a list of those destinations which involve a total driving time exceeding eight hours. It may be assumed that all journeys are completed within twenty-four hours of leaving home, and that no lorry leaves unless a sailing is guaranteed. Design your own formats

```
10  PRINT "C"
20  REM "DRIVING TIME"
30  PRINT/P"DESTINATIONS WITH TOTAL DRIVING TIME IN EXCESS OF EIGHT HOURS"
35  PRINT/P
40  FOR I = 1 to 54
50    PRINT/P" ■ ";
60  NEXT I
65  PRINT/P
70  INPUT"NUMBER IN BATCH?";B
75  FOR I = 1 TO B
80  INPUT "NAME OF DESTINATION?";D$
90  INPUT"DEPARTURE TIME FROM BASE?";TB
100 INPUT"ARRIVAL TIME AT BRITISH PORT?";AB
110 INPUT"DEPARTURE TIME FROM CONTINENTAL PORT?";TC
120 INPUT"ARRIVAL TIME AT CONTINENTAL DESTINATION?";AC
130 IF AB< TB THEN AB = AB + 24
140 X = AB - TB
150 IF AC< TC THEN AC = AC + 24
160 Y = AC - TC
170 Z = X + Y
180 IFZ = <8 THEN GOTO200
190 PRINT/PD$
200 NEXT I
```

FIG. 119(a)   *Program to produce printout in Fig. 119(b).*

DESTINATIONS WITH TOTAL DRIVING TIME IN EXCESS OF EIGHT HOURS

PARIS

BRUSSELS

PARIS

FIG. 119(b)   *Program printout.*

for input and output, and ensure that your documentation includes details of your proposed testing procedure. The solution is outlined in Fig. 119 (*a*) and (*b*). The prgram was written in BASIC and run on the author's Sharp MZ-80K.

(*b*) BASIC. A programming language widely used for time sharing applications and for programming mini- and micro-computers. It is a high-level language relatively simple to learn by non-computer specialists. The term BASIC is an acronym for *B*eginners *A*ll purpose *S*ymbolic *I*nstruction *C*ode. A simple program for adding two numbers and displaying the result on the screen of a terminal (such as a VDU) or microcomputer is outlined below:

```
10 INPUT A
20 INPUT B
30 C = A + B
40 PRINT C
50 END
```

For further details of BASIC refer to the HANDBOOK *Microcomputing* by the same author.

(*c*) CBASIC *Compiler.* This is the Digital Research Inc. industry standard commercial dialect of BASIC suitable for the business environment. CBASIC Compiler is a direct enhancement of CBASIC that is five to ten times faster in execution than most versions of BASIC. It is possible to write, test and combine separate modules for creating complete programs applying the modular, top-down approach (*see* **13, 18**). It includes facilities for graphics, expanded file processing techniques, supports multi-user operating systems and is compatible with CP/M Graphics.

(*d*) *Other versions of* BASIC. Microsoft BASIC which is very widely used; XBASIC which is a British engineering and mathematic orientated version with matrix-handling and XTal BASIC another British version which has a choice of screen or line-based editors.

(*e*) COBOL. This is an acronym for *CO*mmon *B*usiness *O*riented *L*anguage. It is a high-level programming language designed to assist the task of programmers by enabling them to write programs in a more simple form than is possible with assembly code. The language is largely used for mainframe computer applications. It is problem-oriented rather than machine-oriented as it is designed to assist the solving of business problems for such applications as stock control, payroll, sales and purchase ledger accounting.

COBOL consists of four divisions, these are:

   (*i*) identification division;
   (*ii*) environment division;
   (*iii*) data division;
   (*iv*) procedure division.

(*f*) CIS COBOL. This version of the language is that of Micro Focus Ltd. The CIS stands for *C*ompact, *I*nteractive and *S*tandard. It is a complete system for compiling, testing, debugging and executing standard COBOL programs. It has become the most widely favoured version of the ANSI 1974 COBOL language. It can be used for running existing mainframe and minicomputer programs on a microcomputer. A micro can also be used to develop COBOL software for larger computers.

(*g*) *Level II* COBOL. This version of the language is also attributable to Micro Focus Ltd. It provides the full facilities of mainframe COBOL on 8-bit or 16-bit microcomputers allowing the user to develop mainframe programs with the interactive facilities of a microcomputer. It allows portability of software between mainframe and microcomputers. Employs dynamic paging to allow implementation of programs greater than 64K on 8-bit microcomputers. Provides for interactive screen handling.

(*h*) *Pascal*. This is a high level programming language which is highly structured, enabling programs to be written more efficiently without the problems of writing long programs using monolithic structure (*see* **12**).

It executes programs quickly, much faster than interpretative languages like BASIC, but it is more complex and time consuming to learn initially. When preparing a program Pascal words are typed in boldface such as PROCEDURE, BEGIN, END, PROGRAM and WRITE. Modules consist of separate procedures each of which is an element of the main program. The main program "calls" the procedures in the order they are to be executed.

(*i*) *Pascal/MT +* . This is a version of Pascal by Digital Research Inc. It provides speed and accuracy for developing microcomputer programs. It is a direct-compiling dialect of the full ISO standard Pascal—greatly enhanced and extended to maximise the inherent versatility and portability of the language. Pascal/MT +

Native code compiler executes much faster than traditional p-code Pascal compilers. The programming system includes a compiler, a linker, run-time support library, disassembler and a symbolic program debugger. It is compatible with CP/M Graphics.

(*j*) *PL/1.* A powerful all-purpose language which rivals Fortran for scientific applications and COBOL for commercial applications. Digital Research Inc. have developed a version of the language for implementation on microcomputers. It is based on the ANSI Standard Subset G. It is easily transported from micro to mini to mainframe or from mainframe to mini to micro. The Digital Research Inc. PL/1 program development system includes an optimising native code compiler, an assembler, a linker, library manager, cross-reference generator and a comprehensive library of built-in functions. It supports CP/M Graphics.

(*k*) C. An advanced programming language built for coding power and speed of execution with a minimum of constraints. It allows skilled software developers to take full advantage of the inherent structure of the computer. C is ideal for applications which must achieve a high level of performance and for systems level programming. The Digital Research Inc. C programming development system includes a compiler, linker, run-time library containing a wide range of utilities which handles everything from transcendental functions to input-output.

(*l*) LOGO. A structured programming language which is becoming popular in the field of education as it is designed to allow very young children, in the four or five years' age group, to program a computer. The language was developed at the Massachusetts Institute of Technology in the late 1960s by a team led by Seymour Papert. LOGO takes the form of a "turtle", i.e. a mechanical device or a triangle of light on the screen of a computer. Both forms provide the means for drawing lines either on a sheet of paper or on the screen (*see* VI, **25, 26**).

(*m*) *Fortran.* An acronym for *FOR*mula *TRAN*slation. It is a high-level language for scientific and mathematical use. The language was introduced by IBM in 1957 but has since developed into different forms. It has been replaced to some extent by BASIC and other high-level languages.

(*n*) *Lisp.* This language is designed to process data in the form of lists which is indicated by the name of the language, viz. *LIS*t *P*rocessing language. It is based on Algol.

(*o*) *Coral.* A high-level porgramming language for real-time applications developed by the Royal Radar Establishment at Malvern, England.

(*r*) *Forth.* A high-level programming language designed for small computers having the advantage of requiring a small amount of memory and being independent of a specific machine.

MONOLITHIC, MODULAR AND STRUCTURED PROGRAMMING

11. Choice of language. High-level languages are not so efficient with regard to machine running time as those written in an assembly language. The reason for this is that a language such as COBOL or BASIC produces generalised sets of instructions from high-level statements which are required in more detail at the machine code compilation stage. Assembly codes on the other hand allow the programmer more flexibility in determining the series of instructions to achieve the desired results. It goes without saying that tasks may be processed in a number of ways, some of which are dependent more on the skill of the programmer than the language he is using.

12. Monolothic programming. The National Computing Centre publication *Program Design Methods* states that the term "monolothic programming" relates to the largely undisciplined and non-formalised approach to the development of computer programs in which the programmer is allowed a completely free rein. Programs produced in this way reflect the programmer's own experience and personal interpretations.

13. Modular programming. This approach to programming adopts the technique of developing suites of related programs. The overall program is divided into modules, each of which is developed separately but on a coordinated basis. This enables the complete suite of programs to be prepared by a team of programmers if appropriate and programs become available more quickly as a result. It is also easier to debug programs and maintain them when they are constructed in this way. Modules include those for housekeeping, input, processing, output and the closing of files.

14. The nature of structured programming. Structured programming requires the development of a program as a series of independent sections designed to perform only one specified task. This enables program errors to be localised in one section only and assists in the maintenance of each section. Each section must have only one entry point and one exit point. There should not be any jumps to statements in other sections as this would violate the requirements of entry points and exits. The use of this form of programming is an attempt at standardising programming methodology. Structured programming includes such facilities as REPEAT ... UNTIL and WHILE ... WEND which are used to set up loops and complement the standard FOR ... NEXT facility.

15. REPEAT–UNTIL. This facility allows repeated execution of a group of statements as a loop. A Boolean expression, c, is evaluated after each execution of the statements to establish whether the loop should be terminated or repeated. The loop is repeated until the expression, c, after the UNTIL is true e.g.

```
10 REPEAT
20 A = A + INT(RND(1)*6 + 1)
30 PRINT A
40 UNTIL A ⇒ 30
50 END
```

The program computes random numbers and adds them together until the total is 30. In this instance it would not be possible to know the number of loops required which precludes the use of the FOR/NEXT loop.

16. WHILE–WEND. A facility which allows a loop to be executed as long as a logical expression, c, is true. This is the opposite of the REPEAT–UNTIL facility which continues while the condition is untrue.

17. IF–THEN ELSE. A statement which provides for branching to a specified statement if the relation is true ELSE do as directed otherwise. A simple program will make this clear:

```
10 CLS
20 INPUT A
30 IF A > 10 THEN PRINT "OUTSIDE RANGE OF VALUES" ELSE PRINT
   "NUMBER ACCEPTABLE"
40 FOR I = 1 TO 200:NEXT
50 GOTO 10
```

The program compares the value assigned to variable A to test if it is greater than 10 and if it is to print a message "Outside range of values", ELSE print a message "Number acceptable" when it is less than or equal to 10.

APPROACH TO PROGRAM DESIGN

18. Top-down approach to program design. It now tends to be standard practice to adopt a "top-down" approach to program design which requires a specific objective to be defined for a program. This is then analysed into subsidiary functions in increasing levels of detail. Each module should ideally consist of 50–100 instructions, which simplifies the detection of errors and program testing.

19. Functional decomposition. This is a method for segregating a monolithic program into specific modules. The approach is to partition a list of program activities into separate functions on the basis of the frequency of processing, the type of input and output and processing activities.

A basic functional decomposition applicable to many programs would comprise the following elements.

    (*a*) *Program set-up*:
        (*i*) data input;
        (*ii*) define constants;
        (*iii*) define work areas;
        (*iv*) open files;
        (*v*) define accumulators;
        (*vi*) define variables.
    (*b*) *Inner loop*:
        (*i*) input data;
        (*ii*) compute;
        (*iii*) print/display output;
        (*iv*) update files.
    (*c*) *Program termination*:
        (*i*) print control totals;
        (*ii*) close files.

Larger programs would subdivide the inner loop which converts a single level structure into a tree structure or a modular hierarchy.

20. Data-driven design. This is an alternative method for segregating a monolithic program into specific modules. This approach is based on the philosophy that the structure of a program should be determined by the structure of the data which it processes. The approach consists of a number of stages as follows.

    (*a*) *Data stage*. This requires the preparation of a data structure diagram for each set of data to be processed (*see* Figs. 73 and 74).

    (*b*) *Program stage*. The separate data structure diagrams are combined into a single program structure diagram based on the details indicated above in respect of program set-up, inner loop and program termination.

    (*c*) *Operation stage*. The operations required to produce the output are defined and listed and each operation is structured in the program according to the logical requirements.

TABLE X   MAJOR DIFFERENCES BETWEEN HIGH AND LOW LEVEL LANGUAGES

Low-level language	*High-level language*
(*a*) Known as "assembly, symbolic or mnemonic code"—operaton codes are defined as mnemonics, e.g. LDA for load accumulator; operands are allocated labels or symbolic addresses, e.g. REC or ISS for receipts and issues.	(*a*) Uses expressions with which the user is conversant when problem solving without the aid of a computer. Various languages allow the use of normal scientific and mathematical notation in respect of Algol and Fortran, for instance. On the other hand COBOL allows the use of English style statements for business applications. Operation codes are referred to, depending upon the language, as "keywords" such as LOAD, LIST and PRINT in the case of BASIC. Operands, known as variables in BASIC, are allocated identifying letters and sometimes a number such as A or A1 to represent specific operands. COBOL, as an example, allocates a name to operands such as RECIN for receipts into store and ISSIN for issues from store.
(*b*) Machine oriented as the language is specific to a particular manufacturer's computer.	(*b*) Problem oriented as high-level languages are not "machine specific".
(*c*) Object programs are "assembled" by software known as an "assembler" (*see* XXI, **35–8**).	(*c*) Object programs are "compiled" by software known as a "compiler" or firmware known as an "interpreter" depending upon the type of computer as mainframes normally compile and micros interpret (*see* XXI, **39–43**).
(*d*) The translation from program code to object program in machine code is normally on a one for one basis where one machine code instruction is generated for each assembly code instruction.	(*d*) Translation from high-level language to object program in machine code is normally on the basis of many for one, i.e. many machine code instructions are generated for each high-level statement.

TABLE XI ADVANTAGES AND DISADVANTAGES OF HIGH
AND LOW LEVEL LANGUAGES

Low-level language	High-level language
Advantages	*Disadvantages*
(*a*) Runs faster because it is machine specific (the features of a particular machine have been taken into account within the structure of the language).	(*a*) Runs slower due to the generality of the statements and the fact that they are portable between different machines providing a suitable compiler is available. Such languages are machine independent.
(*b*) Requires fewer instructions to accomplish the same result.	(*b*) Requires more storage overhead as programs require more instructions, due to their generality, to accomplish the same result.
Disadvantages	*Advantages*
(*a*) Programs take longer to code because of the more complex nature of the language.	(*a*) Programs can be written more quickly, in general, as the coding is easier to learn. Applications become operational much sooner.
(*b*) Lack of portability of programs between computers of different makes.	(*b*) Portability between computers of different types (*see* Disadvantages(*a*).
(*c*) Languages take longer to learn.	(*c*) Languages easier to learn.
(*d*) Programmers have to learn new languages when moving to installations using different machines with different low-level languages.	(*d*) Programmers can move to different installations using high-level languages without having to learn new languages.

PROGRAM DUMPS AND RESTART PROCEDURES

21. Program dump. When programs are tested it is usual either to print out sections of the program from memory or to display them on a video screen for the purpose of tracing sequence errors which prevent the execution of the program. Sometimes when editing program errors on the screen of a micro they are not always effected in memory so it is advisable to print out the program or list it on the screen to verify whether the corrections have been implemented.

22. Dump and restart procedures. To avoid the consequences of hardware or software malfunctions a fail-safe procedure is adopted, particularly for lengthy or critical programs which are essential for the control of a real-time system. In such instances it is usual to implement checkpoint/restart routines. These provide for the periodic dumping of the contents of the internal memory which signifies the status of the system at that moment of time. Dumping is usually effected to disc or magnetic tape, thus enabling the system to be restarted from the point of the last dump without having recourse to the beginning of the program (which would be impossible to do in any event when controlling dynamic systems). It would however be possible to recommence from the beginning jobs running in batch mode but this would hardly be a practical proposition.

COMPILE TIME AND EXECUTION TIME ERRORS

23. Compile time errors. When a source program is being compiled from a high-level language to a machine code object program, the compiler generates error diagnostics indicating the type of error in the various instructions—particularly syntax errors. Such errors must be corrected before progressing with program testing. Interactive compilers produce error diagnostics after every statement or instruction, whereas batch compilers list the errors at the completion of the compilation run.

24. Execution time errors. These may be defined in two different ways as follows.

(*a*) *Program error.* Microcomputers programmed in BASIC have interpreters, in ROM chips, for converting BASIC statements into machine code at execution time, i.e. at the time the program is run. It is only then that syntax and other types of error—logical errors—are signalled. This can be very frustrating as it can delay the running of the program. Errors should be detected and corrected during program testing prior to running the program on live data. The unexpected error may still arise at the most inopportune moment.

(*b*) *Data errors.* Data errors are detected when a program is run. These may be detected interactively when using a microcomputer, from validation checks built into the program. The computer automatically indicates if the incorrect type of data is being input, i.e. whether numeric data instead of alphabetic characters, or vice versa. When batch processing on a mainframe computer, the initial run is for validation purposes to detect errors before the data is subjected to processing (*see* X, **23**).

CLOSED AND OPEN SHOP PROGRAMMING

25. Closed shop programming. This is a restriction whereby programmers are not allowed to test programs on the computer themselves but must allow the computer operations staff to do this on their behalf and provide the test results. The reason for this restriction is to curtail the use of the computer to the operations staff in order to minimise the time the computer occupies on program testing and to avoid disrupting routine processing schedules.

26. Open shop programming. This is a facility provided to programmers for program testing, which allows them to use the computer themselves, providing they are suitably experienced. This provides flexibility in program testing and does not rely on the good offices of operations staff to get the job done. If on-line programming facilities are available then there need not be any disruption to routine processing.

CLOSED AND OPEN SUBROUTINES

27. Open subroutine. An open subroutine is inserted into the main sequence of instructions, rather than transferring control to a subroutine, in a specific part of a program when it is required. When this definition is analysed the following considerations must be made. If it is a common subroutine then it will be repeated frequently throughout the program—this may apply when rounding values to one decimal place—which will increase the storage space required in the internal memory. On the other hand processing time may be saved by not having to branch to the subroutine each time it is required.

28. Closed subroutine. A closed subroutine is one which is inserted in the program once and is referred to when required by a GOSUB or CALL instruction. After execution of the subroutine, control is returned to a specific part of the program automatically. A "stack" keeps control of subroutine operations and a branch back to the main routine is accomplished by a RETURN instruction, which automatically returns control to the instruction following the GOSUB instruction last executed.

29. Subroutine library. Subroutines can be stored in backing storage in a subroutine library, and can then be accessed by a CALL command when required for execution at a specific stage of processing the main program.

30. Link editing. The process of link editing can be applied for combining both external subroutines—those stored in a subroutine library on disc—and those specifically prepared for a particular application by the programmer. The input/output routines and other routines when combined form a complete suite of programs for a particular application. Consolidated programs can then be stored on disc ready for loading and execution at the appropriate time, i.e. run time.

PROGRESS TEST 18

1. What is the nature and purpose of a program specification? **(1, 2)**

2. Specify the nature and purpose of programming standards. **(3)**

3. Indicate the nature of computer instructions. **(4)**

4. Describe the stages in creating a working program in a high-level language. **(5)** (*C & G*)

5. Describe the stages carried out by a programmer in the development of an application program. **(5)** (*IDPM*)

6. List FOUR factors which are important in producing an efficient computer program. **(5(a)–(f))** (*C & G*)

7. What is the purpose of a breakpoint in the context of programming? **(6)**

8. Outline the nature of low and high level languages. **(7–10)**

9. (*a*) Describe the following program design techniques: (*i*) modular; (*ii*) structured. (*b*) Draw a comparison between these design techniques. **(13–17)** (*IDPM*)

10. What is meant by STRUCTURED PROGRAM? What advantages are claimed for structured programming? **(14)** (*C & G*)

11. Define the nature and purpose of the following approaches to program design: (*a*) top-down approach; (*b*) functional decomposition; (*c*) data-driven design. **(18–20)**

12. List the MAJOR differences between high level and low level languages. Explain, with the aid of examples, the advantages and disadvantages of BOTH types of language. (Tables X and XI) (*C & G* (part of a question))

13. Explain the difference between compile time errors and execution time errors. Explain how a program dump may be used to rectify certain programming errors. Distinguish between a program dump and a dump used in dump-restart procedures. **(21–4)** (*C & G*)

14. Describe briefly the difference between closed shop and open shop programming. **(25, 26)** (*C & G*)

15. Distinguish between open and closed subroutines. **(27, 28)** (*C & G*)

16. What is a closed subroutine? What arrangements must be made to link it with the calling program? **(28, 30)** (*C & G*)

CHAPTER XIX

Flowcharting Computing Problems

PROGRAM FLOWCHARTS

1. Flowcharting. This is a technique adopted by system designers and programmers to aid them in portraying specific characteristics of a system and developing systems or programs to solve the particular problem under consideration.

2. Flowchart. A flowchart is a pictorial representation of a system prepared on the basis of symbols and relational (flow) lines. The term flowchart is used in the widest sense to indicate any type of diagram showing the sequence of events or activities in a procedure or system. Program flowcharts, sometimes referred to as computer procedure flowcharts, are often prepared as a preliminary to program coding to assist in determining the logical aspects of a problem and the correct sequence of statements required. Program flowcharts also show input operations, setting of counters, testing of counters, loops and branching, etc.

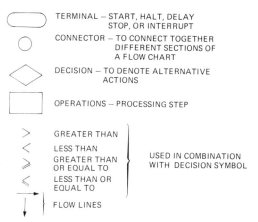

FIG. 120 *Program flowchart symbols.*

349

3. Flowchart symbols. By convention there exist a number of standardised symbols used for the draughting of flowcharts of all types (*see* Fig. 120). The symbols used for program flowcharts distinguish between an operation, i.e. a basic processing step, and a test including logical tests for establishing whether certain conditions exist in the data to be processed which determined the conditional branching requirements of a program.

PROGRAM FLOWCHARTING EXERCISES

Questions relating to flowcharting problems arise quite frequently in examinations. The following are examples.

4. Program flowcharting exercise 1. This is an ICMA question which requires in the solution the setting and decrementing of a counter, program loops, conditional and unconditional branching.

Draw a program flowchart to read cards and accumulate the quantities read into 10 fields in core, depending on the code in the card and print out the 10 totals, each on a separate line.

Card layout	Columns
Code	1–2 (range of 01–10)
Quantity	3–5 (max. 999, min. 001)

SOLUTION
Figure 121 provides the solution to this question.

5. Program flowcharting exercise 2. This is a question set by the Association of Certified Accountants. The solution necessitates testing for the end of a record and the end of a file; computing and accumulating values.

Data from a batch of customers' orders is held on magnetic tape and, for each customer, consists of: (*i*) customer account number; (*ii*) quantity of each product ordered; (*iii*) price per unit of product.

Where a customer orders more than one product, quantity and price are repeated for each item until all his requirements have been included. The end of customer marker is "0" and the end of file marker is "−1". You are required to draft a program flowchart to print out:

    (*a*) the value of each separate product sale on each order;
    (*b*) the total amount to be charged to each customer;
    (*c*) the total value of the entire batch or orders.

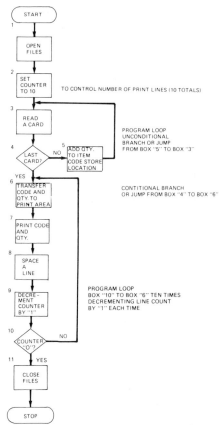

FIG. 121 *Program flowcharting exercise 1.*

SOLUTION
Figure 122 provides the solution to this question.

6. Program flowcharting exercise 3. This is an ICMA question relating to file updating, necessitating the use of program switches.

Draw a program flowchart to update a stock master file held on a magnetic disc in item reference order. The input to update the master file includes receipts and issues and is held on magnetic

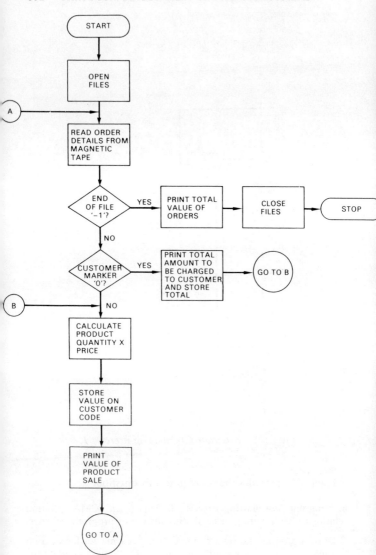

FIG. 122   *Program flowcharting exercise 2.*

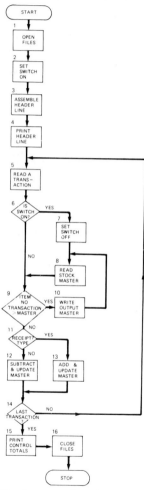

FIG. 123   *Program flowcharting exercise 3.*

tape which has been sorted by a previous program into the following sequence: (*a*) item reference; (*b*) receipts; (*c*) issues.

The control totals are the only items to be printed by this program.

SOLUTION
Figure 123 provides the solution to this question.

7. Program flowcharting exercise 4. The following question was set in a former IAS examination now AAT.

Illustrate by drawing a program flowchart the logic to be applied to produce the results shown in the last two columns of Fig. 124, if the record was held on a computer-based file.

SOLUTION
The missing information is the number of units in respect of the various transactions, i.e. orders, receipts and issues. It is necessary to obtain the missing units by deduction, i.e. logical assessment. Units ordered increase O/S orders; receipts reduce O/S orders and increase bin stock and issues decrease bin stock. The details are shown in Table XII.

STOCK ITEM NO _____			BIN LOCATION _____	
DESCRIPTION_____				
			BALANCES (UNITS)	
DATE	D O C U M E N T	PARTICULARS	OUTSTANDING ORDERS	BIN STOCK
1.1.–8 2.1.–8 4.1.–8	1 2 3	BALANCE B/F ORDERS RECEIPTS ISSUES	10000 12000 9000 9000	15000 15000 18000 16000

FIG. 124   *Program flowcharting exercise 4: extract of information appearing on a stock master card.*

TABLE XII   MISSING TRANSACTION INFORMATION

Date	Document Code	Particulars	Transaction (Units)	Balances O/S Orders	(Units) Bin Stock
1.1.−8	—	Balance B/F	—	10 000	15 000
1.1.−8	1	Orders	2 000	12 000	15 000
2.1.−8	2	Receipts	3 000	9 000	18 000
4.1.−8	3	Issues	2 000	9 000	16 000

The program flowchart required to show the logic to be applied to produce the results shown in the last two columns, if the record were held on a computer based file is shown in Fig. 125.

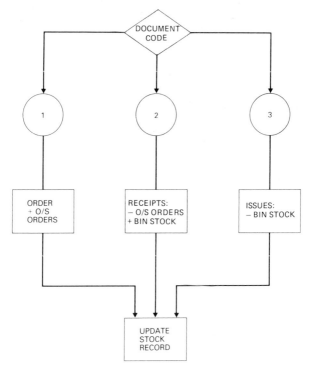

FIG. 125   *Program flowcharting exercise 4: simplified program flowchart.*

8. Program flowcharting exercise 5. The following question was set in the former IAS examinations now the AAT and it outlines a typical data processing procedure which should demonstrate to the student the logical aspects involved in defining the steps required to produce the required output.

Input

A card file is fed into the card reader, data punched in the following fields:

Card columns	1–6	Product Code	
"	"	7–11	
			Order No.
"	"	12–14	Order Quantity
"	"	15–17	Unit Price
"	"	18–19	Discount (%)

Processing

Order value = Order quantity × Unit price
Discount   = Order quantity × Unit Price × $\dfrac{\% \text{ Discount}}{100}$
Net value   = Order value—Discount

Output

A listing under the following headings is required.

Product No.	Order No.	Order Quantity	Unit Price	Order Value	Net Order Value
xxxxxxx	xxxxx	xxx	xxx	xxxxxxx	xxxxxxx

The listing should provide a final total order value and total net order value.

NOTE: The last card will have 999999 punched in card columns 1–6 and blanks in all other fields.

Draw a PROGRAM flowchart to show the steps required to produce the output required.

SOLUTION

The solution is given in Fig. 126

PROGRESS TEST 19

1. What is the purpose of flowcharting? **(1)**
2. What are flowcharts and what characteristics do they possess? **(2)**
3. Define the nature of the symbols used for constructing program flowcharts. **(3)**

Refer to text for examples of flowcharting exercises.

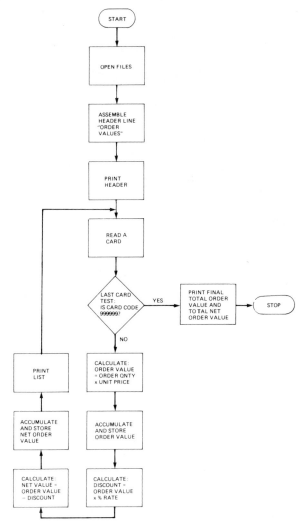

FIG. 126   *Program flowcharting exercise 5.*

CHAPTER XX

Decision Tables

GENERAL CONSIDERATIONS FOR THE CONSTRUCTION AND USE OF DECISION TABLES

1. Use and construction of decision tables. Decision tables are used in the process of analysing the factors involved in a problem, which necessitates defining the conditions specific to the problem and the actions to be taken when the various conditions arise.

A computer program written for a specific application must provide for branching to appropriate parts of the program when specified conditions in data are discovered after testing.

A decision table enables the branching requirements of a program to be precisely specified.

Decision tables may be used to assist the preparation of a complicated flowchart to ensure that all conditions and actions have been catered for and that cause and effect relationships are clearly visible.

A decision is divided into four parts:

(*a*) condition stub   ⎫
(*b*) condition entries ⎬ condition statement
(*c*) action stub   ⎫
(*d*) action entries   ⎬ action statement

The condition stub and condition entries define the conditions to be tested.

The action stub and action entries define the actions to be taken dependent upon the outcome of the testing.

The "rules" consist of a set of outcomes of conditions tests, together with the related actions.

A decision table may be prepared from a procedure narrative by underlining all conditions present with a solid line and all actions with a broken line. The conditions and actions are then recorded on the decision table.

The features of a decision table are as follows.

(*a*) Each condition and action stub contains a limited entry, that is to say an entry complete in itself.

(*b*) The entry part of the table in respect of the condition stub indicates if a particular rule satisfies the condition.

(*c*) The entry part of the table in respect of the action stub indicates the action required in respect of the condition entry.

(*d*) Three symbols are used in the condition entry part of the table.

    (*i*) Y (yes) if the condition is satisfied.

    (*ii*) N (no) if the condition is not satisfied.

    (*iii*) - (hyphen), if the condition is not relevant to the rule.

(*e*) In the action entry part of the table an **x** is recorded to signify a required action. If no action is required the column is left blank.

2. When to prepare and use a decision table. A decision table may be used to assist the preparation of a program flowchart when the detailed logic involves a number of complex decisions. This ensures that all possible combinations and actions are met. The program flowchart is then prepared on the basis of one rule at a time working through the decision table. Decision tables may be used when programmer time is limited and the available software permits the direct input of decision tables.

DECISION TABLES AND PROGRAM FLOWCHARTS

3. Decision table and flowchart exercise 1. This is an ICMA question.

Stockists Limited calculates discounts allowed to customers on the following basis:

Order quantity	% Normal discount
1–99	5
100–199	7
200–499	9
500 and over	10

These discounts apply only if the customer's account balance is below £500 and does not include any item older than three months. If the account is outside both of these limits, the above discounts are reduced by 2 per cent. If only one condition is violated, the discounts are reduced by 1 per cent. If a customer has been trading with Stockists Limited for over five years and conforms to both of the above credit checks then he is allowed an additional 1 per cent discount.

You are required to:

(*a*) construct a limited entry decision table illustrating the above situation; and

(*b*) draw a flow chart illustrating the above situation.

SOLUTION

The solution to this question is illustrated in Figs. 127 and 128.

4. Decision table and flowchart exercise 2. For additional practice in the preparation of decision tables and flowcharts the reader may wish to attempt the following question set by the former IAS, now the AAT.

A soft drinks manufacturer sells to three sales outlets,

(*a*) supermarkets and large departmental stores
(*b*) retailers
(*c*) hotels and catering establishments.

Dependent upon the sales outlet and the value of sales, the following chart indicates the discounts allowed to customers.

Supermarkets and large departmental stores: Discount Allowed %

For orders less than £50	5
For orders £50 and over but less than £100	8
For orders £100 and over	10

Retailers: *Discount allowed %*

For orders less than £50	3
For orders £50 and over but less than £100	7
For orders £100 and over	10

	RULES											
CONDITION STUB	1	2	3	4	5	6	7	8	9	10	11	12
	CONDITION ENTRIES											
ORDER QUANTITY < 100	Y	Y	Y	Y								
ORDER QUANTITY < 200	–	–	–	–	Y	Y	Y	Y				
ORDER QUANTITY < 500	–	–	–	–	–	–	–	–	Y	Y	Y	Y
ACCOUNT BALANCE > £499	Y	Y	N	N	Y	Y	N	N	Y	Y	N	N
ANY ITEM OLDER THAN 3 MONTHS	Y	N	Y	N	Y	N	Y	N	Y	N	Y	N
TRADED FOR OVER 5 YEARS	–	–	–	Y	–	–	–	Y	–	–	–	Y
ACTION STUB	ACTION ENTRIES											
NORMAL DISCOUNT 5%	X	X	X	X								
NORMAL DISCOUNT 7%					X	X	X	X				
NORMAL DISCOUNT 9%									X	X	X	X
NORMAL DISCOUNT +1%				X				X				X
NORMAL DISCOUNT −1%		X	X			X	X			X	X	
NORMAL DISCOUNT −2%	X				X				X			

FIG. 127 *Decision table and flowchart exercise 1: decision table.*

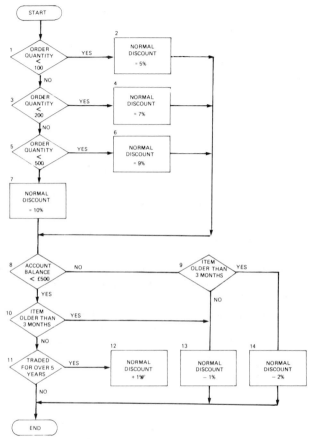

FIG. 128 *Decision table and flowchart exercise 1: flowchart.*

Hotels and catering establishments:	*Discount allowed %*
For orders less than £50	4
For orders £50 and over but less than £100	$7\frac{1}{2}$
For orders £100 and over	10

(*a*) From the information given, construct a "limited entry" decision table and flowchart.

CONDITION STUB	1	2	3	4	5	6	7
	CONDITION ENTRY						
ORDER ≥ £100	N	N	N	N	N	N	Y
RETAILER	Y	Y	N	N	N	N	–
HOTEL & CATERING	–	–	Y	Y	N	N	–
S & L	–	–	–	–	Y	Y	–
ORDER < £50	Y	N	Y	N	Y	N	–
ACTION STUB			ACTION ENTRY				
DISCOUNT							
3%	X						
4%			X				
5%					X		
7%		X					
7½%				X			
8%						X	
10%							X

FIG. 129 *Decision table and flowchart exercise 2: decision table.*

(*b*) What advantages are there from the use of decision tables?

NOTE: The question has been slightly amended.

SOLUTION
The solution to the question is outlined in Figs. 129 and 130.

5. Decision table and flowchart exercise 3. The question which follows was set in the examinations of The Association of Certified Accountants (ACA).

The following is a description of the procedure for dealing with delivery charges for goods bought from AB Ltd:

For the purpose of determining delivery charges, customers are divided into two categories, those whose Sales Region Code (SRC) is 50 or above, and those with an SRC of less than 50.

If the SRC is less than 50 and the invoice amount is less than £1 000, the delivery charge to be added to the invoice total is £30. But if the invoice value is for £1 000 or more, the delivery charge is £15.

If the SRC is equal to or greater than 50 and the invoice total is less than £1 000, the delivery charge is £40. For invoices totalling £1 000 or more, however, the delivery charge is £20.
Required:

(*a*) prepare a decision table of the above procedure;
(*b*) prepare a flowchart of the above procedure.

NOTE: The question has been slightly curtailed.

SOLUTION
The solution to the question is outlined in Figs. 131 and 132.

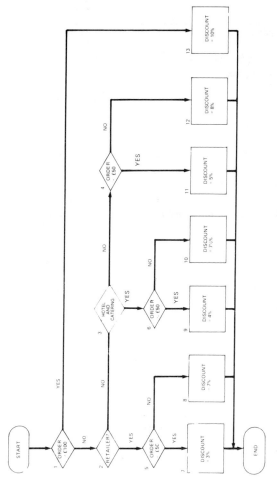

FIG. 130 *Decision table and flowchart exercise 2: flowchart.*

	RULES			
	1	2	3	4
CONDITION STUB	CONDITION ENTRY			
SALES REGION CODE ≥ £50	Y	Y	N	N
INVOICE AMOUNT ≥ £1000	Y	N	Y	N
ACTION STUB	ACTION ENTRY			
DELIVERY CHARGES:				
ADD £15 TO INVOICE TOTAL			X	
ADD £20 TO INVOICE TOTAL	X			
ADD £30 TO INVOICE TOTAL				X
ADD £40 TO INVOICE TOTAL		X		

FIG. 131   *Decision table and flowchart exercise 3: decision table.*

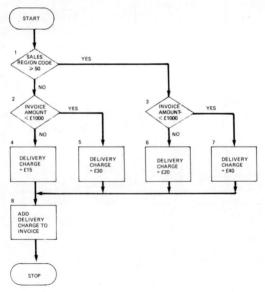

FIG. 132   *Decision table and flowchart exercise 3: flowchart.*

6. Decision table and flowchart exercise 4. This question was set in the ICMA examinations.

A warehouse operates the following stock control procedures.

A free stock balance (physical stock plus outstanding replenishment orders less unfulfilled orders) is compared with the re-order level and if it is at or below re-order level a replenishment order is placed. If a replenishment order has already been placed, a standard progressing letter is sent.

If the free stock balance is at or below the emergency level, any replenishment order will be subject to the emergency progressing procedures. If no replenishment order is outstanding a rush order will be sent. If the free stock balance is greater than re-order level but below maximum level and a replenishment order is outstanding, the delivery of the replenishment order is delayed for one week.

If the free stock level is at or above maximum level, any replenishment order outstanding is cancelled. If the free stock level goes above the maximum level more than once in any month, all levels and re-order quantities for that item are reviewed.

You are required:

(*a*) to construct a limited entry decision table covering the above procedures;

(*b*) to state the circumstances in which systems analysts would prefer to use decision tables rather than flowcharts.

SOLUTION
The solution to the question is outlined in Figs. 133 and 134. Part (*b*) of the question is not dealt with but Fig. 134 illustrates the flowchart of the problem although not required in the question.

```
CONDITIONS = 5
ACTIONS    = 8
RULES      = 9
```

		RULES								
	CONDITIONS	1	2	3	4	5	6	7	8	9
1	FREE STOCK BALANCE ≤ RE-ORDER LEVEL	Y	Y	Y	Y	N	N	N	N	
2	REPLENISHMENT ORDER PLACED/OUTSTANDING	Y	Y	N	N	Y	Y	Y	N	E
3	FREE STOCK BALANCE ≤ EMERGENCY LEVEL	Y	N	Y	N	–	–	–	–	L
4	FREE STOCK BALANCE < MAXIMUM LEVEL	–	–	–	–	Y	N	N	N	S
5	FREE STOCK BALANCE > MAXIMUM LEVEL PREVIOUSLY THIS MONTH	–	–	–	–	–	Y	N	Y	E
	ACTIONS									
1	START EMERGENCY PROGRESSING PROCEDURE	X								
2	SEND STANDARD PROGRESSING LETTER		X							
3	SEND RUSH ORDER			X						
4	PLACE REPLENISHMENT ORDER				X					
5	DELAY DELIVERY OF REPLENISHMENT FOR ONE WEEK					X				
6	REVIEW ALL LEVELS AND RE-ORDER QUANTITY						X		X	
7	CANCEL REPLENISHMENT ORDER						X	X		
8	DO NOTHING (TAKE NO ACTION)									X

FIG. 133   *Decision table and flowchart exercise 4: decision table.*

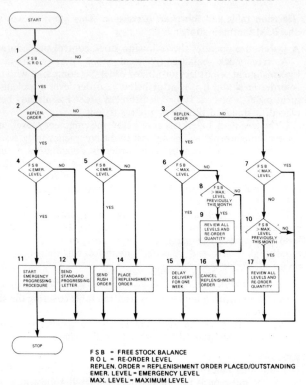

FIG. 134 *Decision table and flowchart exercise 4: flowchart.*

	RULES											
CONDITION STUB	CONDITION ENTRY											
	1	2	3	4	5	6	7	8	9	10	11	12
> 5 YEAR'S SERVICE	Y	Y	Y	Y	Y	Y	N	N	N	N	N	N
LONDON SALESMAN	Y	Y	Y	N	N	N	Y	Y	Y	N	N	N
MONTHLY SALES:												
£0-2500	Y	N	N	Y	N	N	Y	N	N	Y	N	N
£2501-5000	–	Y	N	–	Y	N	–	Y	N	–	Y	N
> £5000	–	–	Y	–	–	Y	–	–	Y	–	–	Y
ACTION STUB	ACTION ENTRY											
BASIC SALARY	X	X	X	X	X	X	X	X	X	X	X	X
ADD 10% BASIC SALARY	X	X	X	X	X	X						
ADD £100	X	X	X				X	X	X			
ADD: 0.5% SALES	X			X			X			X		
1.0% SALES		X			X			X			X	
1.5% SALES			X			X			X			X

FIG. 135 *Decision table and flowchart exercise 5: decision table.*

7. Decision table and flowchart exercise 5. The following question was set in the ACA examinations.

The gross remuneration of a company's salesmen comprises a basic salary and certain additional payments and bonuses as follows:

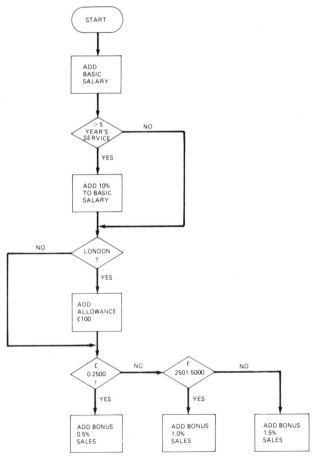

FIG. 136 *Decision table and flowchart exercise 5: flowchart.*

salesmen with over 5 years' service receive a 10 per cent addition to their basic salary each month;

London salesmen receive an addition allowance of £100 per month;

monthly bonus payments are made and calculated as follows:

Monthly sales	Bonus as a percentage of monthly sales
£0–2,500	0.5%
2,501–5,000	1.0%
> 5,000	1.5%

You are required to:

(*a*) prepare a flowchart and a decision table to calculate the gross monthly remuneration of a salesman;

(*b*) outline FOUR major advantages associated with the use of decision tables.

SOLUTION
The solution to the question is outlined in Figs. 135 and 136.

PROGRESS TEST 20

1. Decision tables are used in the process of analysing the factors involved in business applications regarding inherent conditions and the necessary actions to deal with them which, of necessity, must be included in computer programs. Discuss. **(1, 2)**

2. How are decision tables constructed? **(1, 2)**

Other exercises are included within the text.

CHAPTER XXI

Software Profile

THE NATURE OF SOFTWARE

1. Definition. Software is the term used to describe program support which enables computer hardware to operate effectively.

A computer system consists of both hardware and software, and it is only by the intelligent combination of both that the best results are obtained. Hardware is a collection of machines which can only perform tasks when directed to do so by the software.

Software enables a general-purpose computer configuration to be transformed into a special-purpose system for carrying out a unique series of tasks for a number of different applications.

In general, software consists of the programs used by a computer prepared either by the manufacturer or user, but, specifically, the term embraces the operating systems and application programs supplied by the computer manufacturer.

2. Types of software. The nature of software is as wide and as varied as the nature of the work performed by computers. Software includes programs for accounting, financial planning and control, managerial planning and control, communications, word processing and utility programs. To some extent the nature of the computer determines the tasks to be performed, which in turn determines the type of software required. A small home computer will have a need for games programs or home utilities such as money management, budgeting or letter writing programs. Small business and mainframe computers will necessitate the need for software relating to accounting matters in respect of payroll processing, stock control and integrated accounting systems, etc. Most computers can utilise some form of word processing or database/records management software.

The types of software available for computers in general may be summarised as follows.

TABLE XIII   SPECTRUM OF SOFTWARE

Nature of software	Type of software	Typical examples
System control	Operating system– general	Disc operating systems (DOS) UCSDp system CP/M UNIX DME/3 VME/K
	Operating system– networking	Designed to access local and networked resources (CP/Net)
Accounting packages	Application processing	Integrated accounting system General ledger Order processing Invoicing Payroll Stock control Sales ledger (sales accounting) Purchase ledger (purchase accounting) VAT records Business graphics
Managerial planning and control	Problem solving and optimising packages	Bill of materials (BOMP) Production control (OMAC) Project planning and control (PERT) Deployment of scarce resources (optimiser) Linear programming (LP) Simulation
Financial planning and strategy	Financial modelling packages	General financial planning (The financial director) Financial strategy (Busicalc) Financial planning by use of spread-

Table Continued

TABLE XIII *Continued*

Nature of software	Type of software	Typical examples
		sheet (VisiCalc, Micro Plan, Supercalc) Integrated spreadsheet modelling, Graphics, WP, database and communications (Silicon office)
Communications	Communications software	Access to Prestel and private viewdata systems (Owltel) Teletype communications (Micro-Linkline) Downloading (Interlink)
Various applications	Word processing packages	Text processing (WORDPRO, WORDSTAR)
	Various	Letter writing Diary planner Mailing list Card index
	Database/data management systems	Data and records management systems (many and varied)
System utility programs	Systems software aids	Editing Media conversion card or floppy disc to disc tape to disc Dumping files Job control language (JCL) Sorting/merging Report generators Housekeeping Debugging/trace routines Disassemblers Assemblers and compilers

Table Continued

TABLE XIII *Continued*

Nature of software	Type of software	Typical examples
Sub-routines	Standard routines	PAYE routine for payroll processing
		Routines common to several programs
Home finance	Home management packages	Money management
		Budgeting
Games	Mainly for home computers	Many and varied
Miscellaneous	Programs for special purposes	Property management
		Civil engineering
		Builders
		Farm management
		Airline operations including seat reservation systems
		Hotel management and reservation systems
		Insurance
		Banking
		Building society administration
		Tour operators
		Electricity and gas boards, etc.

All computers whether mainframes, minis or micros, including those defined as "home", "personal" or "business" computers require software. The degree to which software is used however, is dependent upon the processing power of the particular computer. Some computers operate on the basis of a standardised operating system which provides access to a wider range of software than would otherwise be possible. Other computers have large internal memories which is an essential prerequisite for the running of large, complex programs, and others have high resolution graphics facilities which widen the software horizons further.

No distinction is to be made between the various types of computer in relation to software as it is considered appropriate to outline the general nature of software. Each job or application requires a set of instructions to accomplish purpose and objectives of the system whether it is payroll processing, sales invoicing and sales ledger updating or stock control, etc. An essential element of software is the operating system.

OPERATING SYSTEMS

3. Definition of operating system. An operating system is the primary element of software as it is a master control program which controls the running of all other programs. It is a powerful unit of software without which the hardware is inanimate. This type of software controls multiprogramming on the larger mainframe and mini computers and assigns control to the various programs on a priority basis. It controls data transfers between the various peripherals, and generates system messages on the video screen and reacts to commands input by the keyboard, etc.

It is important when considering the purchase of a computer for business use to know what operating system it runs under as the more efficient the operating system, the more effective is the computer. Many manufacturers have their own operating system but others adopt specific operating systems such as the industry standard CP/M, an abbreviation for Control Program for Micros. CP/M is the trademark of Digital Research Inc. It is a disc operating system and a large number of software houses develop CP/M compatible programs which allows portability of programs between different computers providing they all operate under CP/M. One of the dangers when selecting a micro is the availability of software, particularly application packages, as this reduces the potential power of the computer if there is not much software available for the specific machine. This factor is related to the software support available for a particular micro and whether it is CP/M compatible because if it is, there is no problem as software is freely available—otherwise there may be a problem until a new micro becomes established.

Another version of the CP/M operating system is available from Digital Research. It is stored on a chip, thus avoiding the need to load the operating system from disc backing storage each time the microcomputer is to be used. Other operating systems are available such as Disc Operating System (DOS) and UCSDp-System.

DOS controls all the operations of a disc drive, allowing direct access to programs for transfer to the internal memory. It avoids the need to store the whole of the operating system internally as it is stored on disc until the required sections are called in.

UCSDp System is an operating system designed for use with Pascal programs. Programs written for the "p" system can be run on different machines without amendment. It is available as an option for such machines as the Apple II and is standard on some machines such as the Sage II. It can run on 8, 16 and 32-bit machines.

A bootstrap loader is a small program which facilitates the loading of the operating system from backing storage into the internal memory on some of the larger computers. Without a bootstrap loader it would not be possible to load the operating system, and processing could not be activated. Some small computers have the operating system built into a ROM chip, which is located on the main circuit board, so that the operating system is available immediately the power is switched on.

The primary tasks performed by an operating system depend upon the type of computer because the larger mainframes are capable of processing several jobs in multiprogramming mode and others are used for real-time processing tasks, all of which are controlled by the operating system.

The normal tasks performed by an operating system include:

(*a*) communicating with computer operator by means of the console unit or typewriter;

(*b*) loading and unloading of programs;

(*c*) supervising multi-programming operations, including:

(*i*) supervising the running of each program;

(*ii*) allocating control to each program according to its priority and the operating state of its peripheral units;

(*iii*) protecting each program's working store from overwriting;

(*d*) allocating peripherals to programs and checking their availability;

(*e*) controlling and monitoring all information transfers;

(*f*) warning the operator when peripheral units require attention;

(*g*) automating the logging of time relating to computer operations.

Regarding the larger type of computer, the ICL 2950 has a choice of operating system, either the DME/3 (Direct Machine Environment) and VME/K (Virtual Machine Environment). The operating systems used by IBM's large processors are MVS/SP (Multiple Virtual Storage/System Product) and VM/SP (Virtual Machine/System Product). It is now proposed to outline some of the features of MVS/SP.

4. MVS/SP (Multiple Virtual Storage/System Product). IBM provides two versions of MVS/SP. Version 1 is designed for IBM System/370, 4341, 303X and 3083/81 installations. Version 2 is an option for the IBM 3083/81 family and is designed to support installations with large networks, databases and applications. The systems resources manager is in control of all the work being processed. The resource usage of all operators is controlled and priority given according to the specifications agreed and set by the installation. Individual applications and transactions can be given order of priority. System resources— processor, input/output and storage can be balanced between testing and production work. MVS/SP schedules and priorities work automatically across multi-processors. If one processor becomes unavailable the other can continue processing without operator intervention. It prevents unauthorised access to data in main memory. The RACF (Resource Access Control Facility) provides protection of an installation's data. Access to any protected resources can be limited to authorised users. Personal passwords allow access to specific applications and information. Fast response times are provided to users of the TSO (Time Sharing Option) while handling other work. Job networking allows work, data and commands to be passed between central processors that may be remote from each other or connected in the same location. This allows for off-loading of work from one centre to another or the facility to send the job to the location of the data.

5. VM/SP (Virtual Machine/System Product). This system is supported on IBM System/370,4300, 303X and 3083/81 processors. It is designed to enhance other IBM system control programs. With VM/SP each user appears to have his own dedicated computer, as all users have their own virtual machines.

6. Choice of operating system. Some manufacturers are offering a choice of operating system for their machines such as MSDOS,CP/M86 and Concurrent CP/M. It is possible to switch automatically between processors depending upon the specific application of those machines which are also providing both an 8-bit and 16-bit processor.

JOB CONTROL LANGUAGE (JCL)

7. Purpose of JCL. The purpose of JCL is to control the running of jobs on a computer. Often on a large computer several jobs are run concurrently in multiprogramming mode. The JCL enables the names of jobs, the files to be used, the peripherals required, priorities of the various jobs and interrupt procedures to be specified. It enables a computer operator to communicate with the operating system by means of the console for the purpose of controlling the processing of the various jobs.

8. Job control language. Job control commands are written in a job control language. In batch processing applications the job commands are usually predefined and input with a source or object program with the relevant data, or are stored in a "command file". Special symbols distinguish commands from program instructions. Examples of job control commands are listed in Table XIV below.

TABLE XIV JOB CONTROL COMMANDS

Mainframe computers	BASIC for use with microcomputers	Timesharing systems
Compile	Run	Login
Execute	Load	Logout
Delete	Save	EOJ (End of Job)
Start	Verify	
Sort	Clr	
Dump	List	
Edit	New	

The BASIC commands may be defined as follows:

(a) Run—the computer executes the program resident within the internal memory.

(b) Load—the computer loads a program from backing storage into the internal memory.

(c) Save—records a program stored in the internal memory to cassette or disc backing storage.

(d) Verify—ensures that a program has been "saved" correctly.

(e) Clr—clears the screen.

(f) List—lists a program stored in internal memory on the screen.

(g) New—clears the internal memory of program and variables ready for a new program.

UTILITY PROGRAMS

9. Utility programs defined. Utility programs are also referred to as "service" or "general-purpose" programs, as they are used for applications in general regardless of the nature of specific application programs. All processing activities require the support of utility programs, particularly when processing data in batch mode. This type of processing requires operations of a routine nature such as "sort/merge" for the purpose of arranging transactions into the sequence of the master file to which they relate prior to file updating; the conversion of data from one media to another, e.g.

the conversion of data in floppy discs to magnetic tape or high speed discs after being validated. This arrangement enables data to be processed faster; copying of files for security purposes usually applies only to disc files which are copied to magnetic tape; reorganising disc files periodically to eliminate overflow conditions on the tracks; housekeeping routines including such tasks as the writing of header labels on magnetic tape files, the blocking and deblocking of records and zeroing memory locations to ensure garbage is eliminated; and input/output routines and so on.

10. Examples of utility programs. In addition, other utilities include "toolkit" which is a program for enhancing the BASIC language by additional commands, such as TRACE, AUTO and RENUMBER, all of which assist the tasks of programming and debugging of programs. Toolkits are loaded either from backing storage or they reside on a chip. "Trace" is a software facility which enables programs to be checked for the detection of errors. Each step in a program is monitored by the software and displayed on the video screen while the program is running. A "disassembler" is software which converts machine code into assembly code, i.e. mnemonic code. It enables machine code programs to be stepped through one instruction at a time for editing purposes. "Report program generators" such as NCR's PICO (Parameter Input/ COBOL Output) allows programmers to custom-design report programs by simply entering report parameters through a video display terminal. PICO generates the report from the program with or without user code identification. The parameters permit data access from up to ten data files providing versatile report design.

Other facilities allow programmers to develop programs from remote terminals on-line to a computer. This allows programs to be created, modified, tested and debugged interactively without interrupting routine processing, as both can run concurrently (*see* XVIII, **25, 26**).

A software tool, known as Visual Information Processor (VIP), allows software companies to write programs with a common user interface. It is written in the systems language—C and has a collection of link utilities which allows the software companies to adapt their programs to run on different machines. Programs that use VIP have many of the benefits associated with Apple's Lisa (*see* XXIII, **11**).

Sub-routines consist of instructions to perform tasks common to many different applications, an example being the PAYE routine which effects all payroll programs. This is called into the main program when the relevant stage of processing is reached. Whether the main program is a software package or an internally developed program, the PAYE routine would be obtained from the computer manufacturer. Its use avoids the necessity of writing the routine for every installation running the payroll application. In other instances, entirely different programs require a similar sub-routine for performing a common series of instructions; this may relate to statistical computations or the printing of column headings at the top of each page of a report, etc. They are stored in a library until required, when they are called into the internal memory. This subject is discussed further in the chapter relating to programming (*see* XVIII, **27**, **28**).

APPLICATION PACKAGES

11. International Directory of Software. This is a publication by Computing Publications Ltd which assists the selection of software packages. It describes 5 100 software products under 107 categories and 24 industry groupings. The publication also provides Quarterly Bulletins. The products contained in the directory include Accounting, Administration and Banking, Communications, CAD/CAM, Data Management, Development Aids, Distribution, Insurance, Microprocessor Systems, Modelling and Statistics, Production and Utilities.

12. Source of packages. Packages are available from a number of sources depending upon the type of computer. Programs for microcomputers, for instance, are available from mail order sources as advertised in computer magazines; or over the counter from retail shops and stores. Packages are also available from dealers in microcomputers, who provide hardware and software, and directly from the computer manufacturer in some instances.

Software for the larger computer, i.e. mainframes, is available from a number of sources including the manufacturer of the hardware who also develops the software, from specialist organisations known as software houses, and from private organisations who have developed programs for their own use which they make available to other users for an appropriate fee. Packages are also available from a number of computer bureaux who have expanded their activities.

13. Cost of software. Sometimes a minimum of software is supplied free of charge when the hardware is purchased, this is referred to as being "bundled" and would include the operating system, utilities and applications software. Other software has to be purchased as required on an "unbundled" basis, it is charged separately.

Microcomputer manufacturers often have a sales promotion policy of providing extensive software with the machine at no extra cost, in order to generate sales of the hardware. This is dependent upon the economic circumstances which prevail at the time and whether a new model is to be launched or new software is becoming available, etc.

14. Package defined. Packages are pre-written computer programs which are widely used for common applications in order to avoid unnecessary duplication of similar programs by many users. It is a means of rationalising programming effort but this does not imply that the same type of package is not available from more than one source. They are sometimes provided to suit the needs of different models of computer and sometimes in competition. The need to shop around is no less than with competing sources of supply of other commodities and products.

A package consists of a suite of programs, sometimes on the same storage media, for the different routines required to achieve the purpose of the specific application. It consists of documentation in the form of a program/systems manual, containing details of how to set up the program and run it on the computer. The package also includes the relevant media on which the program is stored. This is usually tape or disc.

15. Package compatibility. Whether a package is suitable for a particular model of computer depends upon a number of factors. Packages for a specific make of computer are designed to run on the model with a defined memory capacity, therefore packages will not run on machines with less than the specified memory capacity. Some micros have 16K or 48K memory, the Oric-1 and the Sinclair Spectrum, for instance have software designated to run on the particular models. Compatibility also depends on the operating system being used (i.e. whether it is standard, such as the CP/M operating system). Standard operating systems have a wide range of packages available which can run on any machine using that particular operating system, regardless of the make of machine (*see* **3-6**).

When manufacturers of the larger mainframe computers launch a new model they normally provide for a migration path from one machine to another by making software compatible for the older model and the later model.

In other instances packages are designed to be run on disc based systems and others on cassette or magnetic tape (large reels) based systems. Once again the type of operating system is important because disc operating systems vary, i.e. some discs are soft-sectored and others hard-sectored (*see* VII, **26**).

In other instances a package may be compatible with the system but incompatible with regard to the hardware, so it is important initially to choose a computer that can accomplish system requirements on specific hardware. Dialectical variation in a programming language such as BASIC is also a determining factor, as many machines have their own versions of the language and programs will run only on machines using a specific version.

OUTLINE OF ACCOUNTING PACKAGES

As an example of the facilities offered by accounting packages, the details outlined below are based on the packages available from MPSL who distribute BOS (Business Operating Software).

16. Sales ledger. This provides facilities to maintain customer accounts from the entry of invoices, credit notes, payments and journals through to credit checking, production of statements and cash forecasting. Both balance forward and open item accounting are available.

17. Invoicing. This provides facilities to produce invoices and credit notes and sales analyses by customer, product, territory and salesman. Invoicing automatically maintains stock records and sales ledger accounts. The invoicing package requires the sales ledger package.

18. Inventory control. This provides facilities to maintain stock records, to record and control stock issues and receipts, to check reorder levels and lead times and to provide total financial management of stock.

19. Purchase ledger. This provides facilities to maintain all aspects of a company's purchase ledger; from the logging of transactions and the approval of payments, through to the calculation of discounts, scheduling of payments, printing of cheques and credit transfers and the maintenance of supplier details.

20. Nominal ledger. This provides facilities to maintain all aspects of a company's accounts. The package accepts input directly or from the sales ledger package, purchase ledger or fixed assets package and produces profit and loss statements, trial balances, balance sheets and detailed schedules by company, department and account type.

21. Payroll. This provides facilities to produce payslips, credit transfers and management reports for a company payroll. The package fulfills all Inland Revenue requirements for the calculation of tax deductions, contracted-in and contracted-out National Insurance and covers SSAP reporting (UK).

22. Order processing. This handles all aspects of multi-warehouse sales order processing: back orders, forward orders, regular orders, picking lists, delivery notes and invoices. Order details per product and per client can be displayed on demand. This package requires the sales ledger package and operates in conjunction with the inventory control package and microsafes.

23. Fixed assets. This maintains a complete register of the fixed assets of a company or group of companies, and automatically calculates depreciation either by historical cost or current cost conventions. Current cost accounting conforms to SSAP 16(UK).

24. Menu driven packages. Many package programs, especially for microcomputers, function on an interactive basis allowing the user to select the required option. In a stock control package the user can select the code for the required option from the "menu" displayed on the screen (*see* Fig. 137). The various codes provide for item creation, item change, item deletion, stock enquiry, stock posting, printing of a stock list or reorder list, etc. A return to the

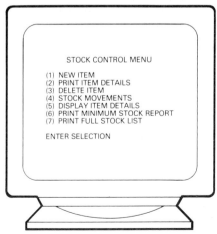

FIG. 137   *Screen display: stock control menu.*

menu is achieved by pressing a defined key indicated by the program. A different option can then be selected. This interactive mode enables newly created records containing errors to be corrected by keying in the code for "item change", followed by the key field of the item to be corrected.

25. Electronic office software. Graffcom has a new package called O-MAN which incorporates all the features required for word processing, financial planning, data manager, diary, calculator, telephone book, business graphics and printing. It will run under Concurrent CP/M and includes a mouse interface.

TAXCOMP: SPECIALIST TAX SOFTWARE FOR PRACTISING ACCOUNTANTS

26. General outline. A tax computation package available from Integer Computer Systems is designed to eliminate the effort in making tax computations, to increase office efficiency, and to reduce errors and costs. The programs are user friendly and can be used without difficulty by staff at all levels. Screen layouts are designed to inform the user where and how data is to be entered. Calculations are performed automatically in all locations, e.g. as data is entered for Stock relief the adjusted profit is automatically updated. Clients' tax data is maintained on disc which can be accessed as required. The package also has built-in word processing functions for the production of tax letters, client letters and bills. In addition, an annual updating service is provided. If desired the package can be tailored to specific customer requirements (*see* Figs. 138 and 139).

27. Built-in features. These include the following.

(*a*) *Profit adjustment.* This section adds back and deducts automatically the data as it is entered. It includes: special "loss adjustments" section which sets off trading losses against the appropriate gains, etc., in the correct order; a register of previous years' profits which is automatically updated; a facility to alter the narratives, for example, "Motor Expenses—$\frac{1}{2}$"; and automatic updating of the other computations and the results of the adjusted profit computation as these are carried out.

(*b*) *Stock relief.* This section stores stock indices on the program disc and can be easily updated manually from published figures. This performs an automatic stock relief calculation from the appropriate information, whether it is for an existing or new business.

Harris
Corporation Tax Computation based on the Accounting Period
for the year ended 31st January 19–2

Loss as per Accounts		(11442)
Add Back		
Motor Expenses (1/2)	254	
Entertaining	875	
		1129
		(10313)
Deduct		
Bank Interest Received	1234	
Rent Received	1000	
Stock Relief	2102	
Capital Allowances	8022	
Industrial Building Allowances	3500	
		15858
Adjusted Loss		(26171)
Allocation		
Case III	1234	
Schedule A	1000	
Carried back s177(3)	5245	
		7479
		18692
Losses B/Fwd		5555
Losses C/Fwd		24247
Case III	1234	
Less s177(2)	1234	
		Nil
Schedule A	1000	
Less s177(2)	1000	
		Nil

(Courtesy Integer Computer Systems)

FIG. 138 *Printout of TAXCOMP package.*

(*c*). *Capital allowances.* This section provides up to twenty different asset categories including pools. Columns can be added or deleted as required with adequate space for full descriptions. Private usage is catered for. The rows for additions, disposal and computations form a grid with the columns which can be worked on as required. If disposal value is greater than original cost, the

Harris
Corporation Tax Computation based on the Accounting Period
for the year ended 31st January 19–2

Stock Relief Computation

Stock at 1.2.–1	25456
Less: de minimis deduction	2000
	23456
Movement in all stocks index for the year 8.96%	
Stock relief	2102

Capital Allowances Computation

	Pool	Motor Van Pool	Vauxhall Cavalier ABC 259X	Austin Allegro SRE 589Y	Ford Escort GHU 123Y	Cla
B/FWD	943	4263	6000		7000	
Additions	2245			8500		
	3188					22
FYA	2245					
WDA	236	1066	1500 R1/4	2000 R20%	1750	57
C/FWD	707	3197	4500	6500	5250	80

Industrial Building Allowance Computation

Narrative	Date of Acquisition	Original Cost	Balance B/Fwd	Allowance	Balance C/Fwd
430 Bury New Road	1.1.–0	125000	57500	3500	54000
				3500	

(Courtesy Integer Computer Systems)

FIG. 139   *Printout of TAXCOMP package.*

program makes the appropriate calculation for efficient tax planning and the use of restricted allowances. All calculations may be manually overruled.

(*d*) *Industrial building relief.* This section caters for all the requirements relating to such computations. Again, by the use of a grid of rows and columns and manual and automatic calculations, a system for entering data with ease and observing the results has been made available.

(*e*) *Letters.* This section makes use of many typical word processing features. Various items of information are extracted from the working section of the program and symbolised for easy and automatic insertion. All the names and addresses of the tax offices are stored away on the program disc for instant recall. Letters can be standardised (over fifty standard letters) to suit all clients' needs. By means of a simple editing function anyone in the office can enter, alter, amend and print out letters and bills.

28. Disc storage. When computing is completed all the information is stored away on disc for future use, for amendments, updates or next year's tax computations. The computer automatically brings forward to subsequent years the maximum amount of information: dates, stock, asset written down values, losses brought forward, name and address, and letters.

MICROBROKER: SPECIALIST SOFTWARE
FOR INSURANCE BROKERS

29. Microbroker: main features. This is a software package available from Intelligence (UK) PLC designed for use by insurance brokers. The main features of the package include:

(*a*) password controlled access;

(*b*) full client and policy records;

(*c*) range of policy screens;

(*d*) no limit on policies per client;

(*e*) legal protection policy option;

(*f*) claims information storage;

(*g*) client and policy searches even on partial information;

(*h*) rapid retrieval of historic data;

(*i*) a word processor for generating any letter to any client on file;

(*j*) a marketing system for generating sales information from any data in Microbroker;

(*k*) policy confirmation letters to client/insurance company;

(*l*) automatic generation of renewals, reminders, cover notes and lapse letters;

(*m*) alternative quote and/or instalments choice with renewal reminders;

(*n*) an actions list detailing all policies/clients requiring action;

(*o*) diary system;

(*p*) cash, invoice and credit note posting;

(*q*) direct debits;

(*r*) insurance company statement reconciliations and premium/commission reports;

(*s*) invoice and statement generation;

(*t*) complete integrated nominal and purchase ledgers;

(*u*) outstanding debtors report wherever required;

(*v*) placement of business analysis;

(*w*) motor quotations.

30. Power of package programs. The details outlined above clearly indicate the power of package programs for specific applications, without which computing would not be so widely practised in the smaller administrative unit or business.

ELECTRONIC CARD INDEX AND ELECTRONIC DIARY

31. Electronic card index. With the advance of technology into the office it is foreseeable that the normal office cabinet will tend to be less frequently used and will perhaps disappear completely in the not too distant future. The reason for this is the prevalence of databases and smaller versions of databases called electronic card index systems. With the aid of a microcomputer and a software package, records can be created and stored electronically on cassette or disc. One such system allows for up to ten lines per card and up to 255 cards. Records can contain one to twenty-five cards. The records can be searched, browsed through and printed. Facilities are also provided for calculations on any two fields. A mailing list can also be printed.

32. Electronic diary. Some microcomputers have diary software available to assist the business executive in keeping track electronically of his appointments. The software has facilities which enable details of appointments to be input, sorted, browsed through on the video screen and edited. Data can also be stored in backing storage. One can immediately have the day's appointments to hand by displaying the contents of the diary file each morning.

ARGUMENTS FOR AND AGAINST THE USE OF PACKAGES

33. Arguments for the use of packages. These are summarised as follows.

(*a*) Programmers are able to concentrate their efforts on applications for which no suitable packages exist due to the special nature of a particular task.

(b) It is unnecessary to employ specialist programmers, particularly when using microcomputers, as packages are available for most requirements.

(c) Applications can be up and running (operational) much more quickly than would be the case when developing one's own computer systems, including the writing of programs.

(d) Expertise is "built-in" when using packages which, in effect, deskills the use of computers, particularly the use of micros.

34. Arguments against the use of packages. These may be summarised as follows.

(a) Package programs may take longer to run than specially written programs, but this depends on the relative skill of programmers and whether machine code is used rather than high-level languages. Compiled programs usually take longer to run because they contain more instructions than machine code requires to achieve a specific task.

(b) It may be necessary to modify a package, as it may not be compatible with system requirements in all instances and this fact will increase the cost of the package.

(c) Purchased programs may cost more than internally written programs but this is dependent upon the expected volume of sales of the package since the larger the sales volume the lower the cost to the ultimate user, as the development costs are spread over a greater volume of sales.

ASSEMBLER

35. Definition. This is a program which translates a "source" program, written in an assembly or programming language, into a machine code "object" program.

The translation process is performed by the computer itself, and this is known as "automatic programming".

36. Purpose. The purpose of such a procedure is to simplify and speed up the task of programming by enabling the programmer to write programs in a language much simplified compared with that used for writing programs in machine code. Therefore, instead of writing a program which is immediately compatible to the computer, a program is written which is more compatible to the programmer for solving the problem and the computer is used for the conversion of the program to one which it can interpret and execute.

37. Translation. The assembler translates symbolic or mnemonic function codes into the equivalent machine codes and symbolic addresses into actual internal store locations. Each mnemonic instruction is normally converted into a machine code instruction on a one-for-one basis, but it is possible to use the technique of "macro-coding", which enables a complete sub-routine to be incorporated into the object program by means of writing a single "macro-instruction". Once again, the objective is to simplify the task of programming.

38. Object program. The term object program is used to define the program which is generated by the translation process and which is then used for processing the data of a specific application. The term source program is self-explanatory, as it is the original program written for processing the data of a specific application but which is not directly usable by the computer.

After translation, the object program is retained either in magnetic tape or magnetic disc. In addition, a print-out is produced by the line-printer of both the source and the object program instructions, for comparison and error checking. It is also possible to have a print-out of diagnostics as an aid to error checking.

COMPILER

39. Definition. This is a program which translates a source program, written in a high-level language, into a machine code object program.

A compiler performs the task of assembling the object program, but is generally more complex than an assembler because each source program instruction in a high-level language such as COBOL generates a number of machine code instructions, i.e. a macro-instruction generates a number of micro-instructions.

As a result of the increased complexity, the compiler is larger in terms of the translation instructions it contains, and this produces a problem of internal storage capacity, as a large amount of storage is required, to accommodate the compiler during the compilation run. It is sometimes necessary to compile a program on a computer which is different to that on which the compiled program will be run on account of this factor. As a matter of interest, this is the reason for stating the source computer and object computer in a COBOL program.

40. Purpose. Compiling is performed for similar reasons as for assembling—to reduce the complexity and time involved in writing programs.

41. Storage requirements. To give some idea of the core storage required for both assembling and compiling, it must be appreciated that during translation the internal store must hold the source program, the compiler or assembler and the resulting object program.

INTERPRETER

42. General features. Interpreters are usually used by personal or small business computers, whereas mainframes utilise compilers. Interpreters and compilers are translation programs which, in respect of small computers, convert statements written in BASIC into machine code. When the command "run" is keyed in, each statement in the program is interpreted and if any statement does not conform to the rules or grammar (known as syntax) of the language then a syntax error is displayed on the screen. This can be a disadvantage as it slows down the execution of the program until the errors are removed. In addition, each statement is interpreted each time the program is executed and this also tends to slow down its execution.

43. Switch to compilers. Many small computers now have compilers available, which means it is only necessary to translate the program once, during the compilation run, and the compiled program is then stored on tape or disc backing storage until the relevant application is to be run. As each statement does not have to be translated at "run time" the program runs faster than an interpreted program. An interpreter is more "firmware" than "software" as it is stored on a ROM (read only memory) chip which is part of the electronics of the computer.

TELESOFTWARE AND CABLE GAMES

44. Telesoftware. A facility for downloading programs from a central source (database) to users via their intelligent terminal or microcomputer equipped with an acoustic modem and associated software. The ORIC-I has this facility which enables users to download software direct from Prestels' (British Telecom's Viewdata system) ALADDIN'S CAVE via the user's own telephone, either very cheaply or free of charge. Other computers have similar facilities.

A system being marketed at the present time is Micronet 800

which is a joint project of British Telecom-Prestel. EMAP Computer & Business Publications Telemap Limited, ECC Publications Limited and Prism Microproducts. Most micros can be connected to the Micronet 800 database for a small fee. The fee covers all the hardware and software for connecting to the system and for downloading software. Prospective users need to inform Micronet of the type of micro they use because each micro has different software. All major micros are scheduled to be added to the system progressively. To use the system snap your telephone receiver into the acoustic modem and call Micronet's number from your keyboard. The system asks the user to enter an identification number. The Welcome to Micronet message then appears on the screen which indicates the user is on-line to one of the world's largest databases. When the user has the required information or downloaded programs to the micro's memory the keyboard is used to switch off the telephone link. The receiver is then replaced. The system allows the user to choose from hundreds of free games from Micronet's Aladdin's Cave. The games are changed often and the user selects those compatible with the user's computer. It is also possible to buy games at far less than over-the-counter prices, and download to your computer. Micronet also allows schools to be connected to other schools to swap ideas and programs written by students and teachers using the system's educational exchange library. Application software is available for business administration including financial planning, accounting and sales analysis. User groups for the major micro manufacturers will maintain news and reference information on Micronet. Users can send messages to their group, or any other Micronet or Prestel users, straight from the user's keyboard. Messages are held on Micronet's "mailbox" service which can only be accessed with the user's personal subscriber number.

In addition, the system has an information service on product comparisons, software reviews, dealership and price details and all the "best buy" information. It has all the features of a magazine, including jobs and classified ads.

As a Micronet subscriber a user can use all new databases as they are added to the system including "shopping" facilities and electronic banking.

The Micronet 800 system is to embrace a business service, which will allow a subscriber to download a business package to assess its suitability for the user's system before deciding to purchase. The program will be "scrambled" to prevent it being "saved" for subsequent reuse when it has not been purchased. If the subscriber decides to purchase the package a second version will be downloaded that will only run on the subscriber's computer. This will probably be accompanied by a "tamper-resistant" module housing a modem and a chip with a unique "encryption/decryption" key. This will also allow data to be "encrypted/decrypted" for security purposes.

The BBC and Acorn have combined to expand the BBC Computer Literacy Project by the introduction of a Ceefax based telesoftware service. By means of the teletext adapter for the BBC micro, the user has free access to any software broadcast over the air and access to all the Ceefax information. This is a non-interactive system as the user cannot indicate his needs to the host computer, whereas Micronet 800 is interactive. This may be overcome by the transmission of the whole database in a continuous stream or loop. The user's computer selects the information/program required as it is received and displayed on the screen. This is a free service but the initial outlay for the adapter is more expensive than the modem for telephone line communications and there are recurring charges for the service provided.

45. Cable games. W.H. Smith intend to introduce a "cable games" service during 1984. Subscribers will initially have a choice from twenty games, but each month new games will be added and others deleted. It is the first service offered by the company's newly formed cable services division, planned to serve cable and satellite television.

MODELLING PACKAGES AND SPREADSHEETS

46. General characteristics of a modelling package. A suite of application programs designed to provide for the needs of business, i.e. financial and corporate planning, including cash flow and balance sheet projections, etc. A package in general consist of a model-building language, model-running language, report generator, What-if? facilities, and a statistical sub-system for data analysis. The language used to describe the model is usually straightforward and easily learned by non-computer specialists, which allows models to be constructed and run on a computer by accountants, corporate planners and managers (*see* **48-50**).

47. Spreadsheets. In addition to the more usual application packages there are business modelling packages available such as Visicalc. It allows the user to create a spreadsheet or electronic worksheet on which to define the problem. A spreadsheet is an alternative technique which allows the computer to be used for what may be called pencil and paper calculations for preparing budgets and profit forecasts, etc. It allows recomputations to be made on all relevant data very speedily in response to changes to specific variables such as selling price, volume or overheads. The "what if" facilities allow budgets to be computed very quickly and amendments made in the simplest possible manner automatically. The underlying principle of the spreadsheet is that the video screen operates as a highly flexible window. The window "rolls" automatically so as to display the area around the current cursor position. The screen can be segregated into smaller windows if necessary. The worksheet is viewed through the window. The window and spreadsheet do not physically exist as they are simulated by controlling the display on the screen. The spreadsheet is divided into a grid of small rectangles known as cells. The cells contain numeric data, text or formulae and each cell can be identified by co-ordinates (*see* Figs. 140 and 141).

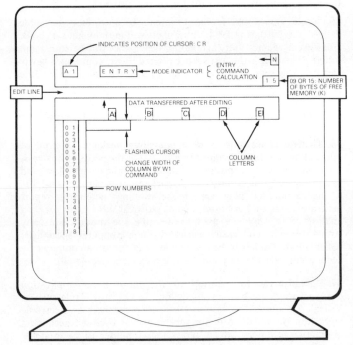

FIG. 140   *Spreadsheet: main features of screen image.*

		QTR 1	QTR2	QTR3	QTR4	TOTAL
PROFIT AND LOSS STATEMENT (£000'S) FOR THE YEAR 1984

		QTR 1	QTR2	QTR3	QTR4	TOTAL
SALES (S)		50	55	60	65	230
DIRECT MTL	COST(V)	5	6.05	7.2	8.45	26.7
DIRECT LBR	COST(D)	10	11.55	13.2	14.95	49.7
VAR O/H(A)		2.5	3.3	4.2	5.2	15.2
TOTAL VAR	COST(A)	17.5	20.9	24.6	28.6	91.6

FIG. 141 *Author's first attempt at running Spreadsheet program on his own Sharp MZ-80K computer.*

MICROMODELLER MODELLING PACKAGE

48. Micromodeller: general characteristics. Micromodeller is a powerful and flexible business modelling package available from Intelligence (UK) PLC. Although designed for use on microcomputers, its power is such that its equal was previously only found on mainframe computers or time-sharing bureaux. It provides the basis for all corporate financial and information systems used in the day to day planning and monitoring of business performance. It can be converted for use on minicomputers and is considered an industry standard.

The facilities of Micromodeller allow a company to carry out the following tasks, functions and activities:

(*a*) produce reports to users' own design;

(*b*) create cash flow forecasts, constantly adjusting the income and expenditure flows;

(*c*) monitor against the budget and produce variance analyses;

(*d*) consolidate any number of expense, reporting or profit centres with differing formats;

(*e*) analyse the effect of changing any number of parameters or ratios within a company;

(*f*) automatic updating of data;

(*g*) automate regular tasks such as monthly consolidations or management reports;

(*h*) integrate planning and reporting systems with other programs on the same or different computers.

49. Applications. The application areas are many and varied but this type of modelling package may be used to advantage for the following:

(*a*) budget preparation;

(*b*) capital budgeting;

(c) strategic planning;
(d) investment analysis and appraisal;
(e) project evaluation;
(f) cost estimating;
(g) cash flow projections;
(h) merger and acquisition analysis;
(i) financial and management reporting.

50. Package composition. Referring to Fig. 142 it will be observed that the Micromodeller package consists of a number of subsystems outlined below to show the elemental nature of such a package.

(a) *Editor*. This is used for the creation of logic files for calculations and relationships. It has a full range of line editing facilities and the ability to interface directly with other systems.

(b) *Logic files*. The logic file describes the relationships the user wishes to apply to the matrix and is defined using row and column numbers. The full range of arithmetic operators is included. It is also possible to look up tables in the logic file which may store a

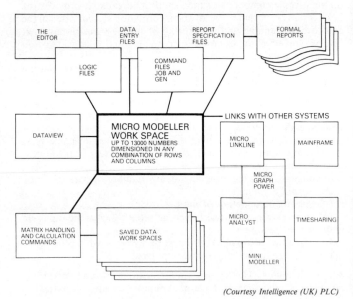

(Courtesy Intelligence (UK) PLC)

FIG. 142   *Micro Modeller consists of a number of major sub-systems, as this overview shows.*

tax table, for instance. A range of powerful financial functions is also available for easy use including Net Present Value, Internal Rate of Return, Depreciation and Sum of Years Digits.

(c) *Data entry*. Data may be entered by keyboard or updated in sequence for each period or column in a given row, or with growth rates specified with the data. Values may be replicated.

(d) *Command files*. These contain a series of instructions which allow jobs to be run with minimal intervention.

(i) Job files. These are essential if any repetitive applications are run. As most companies have the requirement to consolidate large numbers of divisions and report in differing formats, the JOB facility was included to make this possible with a single command.

(ii) GEN files. This facility makes models self-documenting and easier to use. The user is asked relevant questions. GEN then substitutes the answers, checks them for validity and inserts its answers into the correct place in a model.

(e) *Report specification files*. Having created the required results file by using commands for logic, data, matrix handling, etc. the end result must be presented in a form chosen by the user and not by the system. Report specifications are built in the editor, using simple English language commands to give complete control over text, columns and rows to be printed. Row names from the logic file may be used, or different text may be specified and printed with or without row numbers.

(f) *Dataview*. This provides the function that allows the user to watch changes and calculations as they take place. It generates a screen of the precise rows and columns which are considered important. All the manipulation, calculation and matrix handling commands may be used in the Dataview model giving the required visual impact of the changes being made.

(g) **Matrix handling and calculation commands.** A series of commands such as Add file, Shift and Divide file allows the user the flexibility to move between the current workspace in memory and any number of work areas saved on disc. The user may also extract any range of rows and columns from a Calculated Saved Data work area.

(h) *Links to other systems*. Micromodeller systems will read or write a file in a number of formats. This allows them to be integrated with other systems.

(i) Micro linkline. This allows a personal computer to extract data from and return results to another computer.

(ii) Micro graph power. This produces high resolution colour business graphics on a plotter from results produced by Micromodeller.

(*iii*) Micro analyst. This is a company analysis program that enables both planning and analysis to be undertaken on the basis of published company information.

PROGRESS TEST 21

1. What is software? **(1)**
2. What types of software are used in computer operations? **(2 and Table XIII)**
3. Define the nature and function of an operating system. **(3–6)**
4. (*a*) What is the purpose of a job control language (JCL)? (*b*) List FOUR commands in any JCL with which you are familiar and state how and when they are used. **(7,8)** (*C & G*)
5. Explain what is meant by the term UTILITY PROGRAM. Give examples of THREE frequently used utility programs. **(9, 10)** (*C & G*)
6. The ability of computer-using organisations to develop software to exploit the rapidly falling costs of hardware has been seen as a major potential constraint on systems implementation. (*a*) Briefly explain the reasoning behind this statement. (*b*) Describe three ways by which an organisation can attempt to remove the constraints on systems development imposed by software production. **(11–15)** (*ACA*)
7. Indicate the sources of packages, stating the cost factors which must be considered. **(11–13)**
8. Outline the nature of typical accounting and other business packages. **(16–30)**
9. Define the terms: (*a*) electronic card index; (*b*) electronic diary. **(31, 32)**
10. Give the arguments for and against the use of a pre-written computer applications package as the solution to a business problem. Use an example to illustrate your arguments. **(33, 34)** (*C & G*)
11. Specify the nature and purpose of an assembler. **(35–8)**
12. Distinguish between the mode of operation of a compiler and that of an interpreter. **(39–43)** (*C & G*)
13. What is the function of telesoftware? **(44)**
14. Outline the general characteristics of a modelling package. **(46)**
15. Specify the features of spreadsheet packages. **(47)**
16. Summarise the contents of a comprehensive modelling package. **(48–50)**

PART FIVE

PROFILE OF ELECTRONIC TECHNOLOGY

CHAPTER XXII

The Nature of Electronic Technology

OFFICE TECHNOLOGY

1. The office and electronic technology in perspective. The term "information technology" relates to the harnessing of electronic technology, in all its different forms, to office activities. The term "convergence" is used to define the integration of the various aspects of information technology: embracing the use of microcomputers for information processing and storage, including the use of software in the form of electronic spreadsheets and business modelling programs; word processors for preparing standard reports and other correspondence at high speed; electronic mail for the transmission of information from one office or site to another (without the use of paper) by means of data transmission lines linking microcomputers, word processors or workstations (*see* Figs. 143 and 144).

Silicon chips and the advances made in telecommunications have had a profound effect on the nature of office activities, which include all of those administrative activities concerned with the handling of information for the efficient conduct of business operations. Communications is the essential catalyst for integrating all the various office activities and functions. Teletex, the international text communication service, will play an important part in office automation as it will enable text transmissions to take place thirty times faster than telex. It will also provide the necessary standardisation to enable interworking of terminals from any manufacturer on a number of different networks (*see* XXIV, **13**).

Electronic technology enables documents, as well as normal business data relating to business transactions to be stored on magnetic media in binary code generated by electronic signals. Filing cabinets, index cards and "in" and "out" trays may soon be

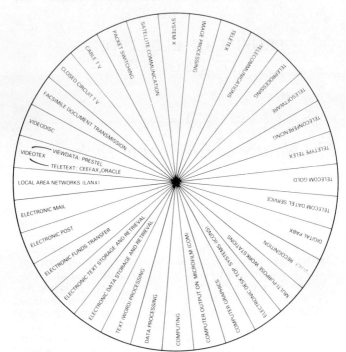

FIG. 143   *Spectrum of information technology.*

redundant, due to advances in electronic storage techniques in the form of text filing and retrieval systems.

Multi-purpose workstations will generally replace those previously performing dedicated tasks because workstations incorporating the latest technology are capable of performing a number of different functions, and this enables them to handle data and information in the form of text, graphics or video displays. They also provide electronic mail facilities (*see* V, **34, 35**).

Digital PABX telephone exchanges are likely to have a great impact on office automation because of their ability to handle both voice and data transmissions and to function as message switching centres for terminals and other devices. They will also control the routeing of data or text from workstations (*see* Fig. 145, **9** and XXIV, **11**).

Information technology embraces the use of interactive

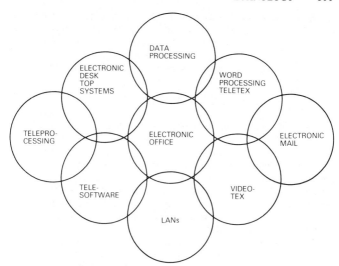

FIG. 144   *Converging technology.*

"viewdata" such as British Telecom's Prestel and private internal viewdata systems such as ICL's Bulletin. These systems support a database for information retrieval requirements and operate in an interactive manner because, after information has been accessed, it is displayed on the screen of a television. The user can then, for example, book hotel accommodation or order goods from a supermarket by means of a keypad which transmits the required information to the relevant computer. This is accomplished by what is known as a "response" page (*see* VIII, **21–7, 28–34**).

Local area networks consisting of combinations of workstations, word processors or microcomputers provide high data transmission speeds between the various devices on the network and allow printing and storage facilities to be shared (*see* XXIII, **1–7**).

Information technology also embraces the technique of COM which allows computer output to be stored on microfilm or microfiche, which can be accessed by a viewer which displays images on a screen. The use of the technique avoids the need to print all the output from a computer, thereby saving in stationery costs and computer printing time. Facsimile document transmission allows detailed images such as drawings and graphs to be transmitted from one place to another at high speed (*see* VI, **13–15**).

2. Historical note. The idea of the electronic office was mooted in 1947 by Lyons, the British catering company, when they assessed the viability of computers for performing office activities. They did in fact build their own computer known as "LEO", an acronym for Lyons Electronic Office, which became operational in 1951.

ELECTRONIC MAIL

3. General features of electronic mail systems. This is the term used to describe the technique of distributing electronically mail which has been created on a word processing or computer system. Once a mail item, message, memo or word processing document is created on the sender's system it is electronically delivered to the receiver's system. The receiver reads the document on a CRT screen exactly as it was mailed, or it may be printed on a local printer in typewriter quality text. The technique enables mail to be available in minutes instead of days.

The mail can be revised, incorporated into other documents, passed to new recipients or filed in the normal manner. Mail may be transmitted to users in local offices in the organisation or to those located in other cities or countries.

4. Dialcom Electronic Mail. This is a service provided by Telecom Gold, an independent company, backed by British Telecom, to promote and develop their services. It is a nationwide communications service which uses the telecommunication network. When a user becomes a subscriber to this service a personal Dialcom electronic mailbox is allotted to him which is opened only by the subscriber's password. The service is "friendly", as it converses in familiar English terms and uses step by step, easy to follow prompts. No paper copy is created except when necessary. Mail is delivered and read at any time from any location using a wide range of terminals linked to the bureau service via the telephone network or PSS—British Telecom's Packet Switching Service.

5. Micromail. An electronic mail system launched by the British computer company ACT, which is based on the electronic mail service Telecom Gold. It is designed for users of microcomputers, particularly the SIRIUS 1 and APRICOT as well as a proposal for the IBM PC. Subscribers will be able to transmit letters at the speed of light with simultaneous copies to up to five hundred people at no extra charge.

The system can also be linked into international services to enable documents to be transmitted to micro users worldwide. A one page A4 size letter of four hundred words can be transmitted to its destination in less than a minute. This can be done at the cost of a first or second class postage stamp, dependent on whether it is peak or off-peak time. The same letter would cost three times as much if sent by telex and take six times as long to transmit.

A recipient makes regular checks by accessing his "mailbox". Messages are then transmitted over the telephone line to his computer. A modem card is required which plugs inside the computer. Micromail software is available on its own for use with other modems/acoustic couplers. Security is accomplished by the use of a password which is registered when the package is purchased.

Information storage costs twenty pence per unit of two thousand characters per month. An optional radio pager can warn of incoming messages. Micromail can produce five hundred automatic copies of each letter and provides an electronic diary as well as a noticeboard for important messages (*see* **3, 4** and XXI, **32**).

WORD PROCESSING

6. Characteristics of word processing. Word processing is primarily concerned with the normal typing requirements of a business as distinct from the reports produced by data processing systems. Whereas data processing is concerned with processing data in the most efficient manner, word processing is concerned with processing words in the most efficient manner.

The term word processing is currently used as a more fashionable or sophisticated name for automatic typing which was first used by IBM. Word processors may be called jet-age typewriters, but that is only part of the story as word processing equipment has electronic intelligence which generally consists of a processing unit supported by a separate memory. It is mainly this intelligence which distinguishes the word processor from the older automatic typewriter.

The technique is meant to provide increased cost effectiveness in respect of the typing requirements of a business. Technological developments are such that it is difficult for the prospective user of word processing equipment to keep pace with the changes taking place. It is this factor which makes the choice of suitable equipment very difficult, especially when this is linked to the need to learn how to use it in the most effective manner. There are many different makes and models on the market which have different characteristics and capabilities.

Word processing equipment should not be implemented without

first conducting a feasibility study as it involves a change of method and necessitates the use of capital intensive equipment instead of typists. The method or technique of word processing is primarily for accomplishing the following office functions:

- (*a*) transcription;
- (*b*) editing;
- (*c*) final typing;
- (*d*) error correction;
- (*e*) copying;
- (*f*) storage and retrieval.

The equipment is designed to speed up such processes by making them more automatic.

7. Personalised letters. Word processors are of significant value where the typing requirements of a business consist of high volume routine correspondence such as personalised standard letters whereby standard paragraphs are stored on magnetic media such as cards, cassettes, diskettes or mini-diskettes. The standard paragraphs and personalised details are indicated on a form by the author. The machine then prints the standard letter, reducing the detail entered by the operator to the personalised details only. It is this factor which achieves the main objectives of economy and efficiency because standard paragraphs are not constantly retyped at the speed of the typist but at the automatic speed of the machine, which can be in the region of 920 words a minute. With conventional typing the speed of a typist is greatly reduced by the need to make corrections and to completely retype text, as well as paper handling, interruptions and fatigue. A possible speed in the region of fifty to seventy words a minute is reduced to ten to fifteen words a minute by these factors. Extensive retyping also increases stationery costs, and produces additional wear on typewriter ribbons and the typewriter.

Lengthy reports or high quality text which usually require extensive editing and revision can be processed to advantage on word processing equipment as the correction of errors is simplified because to erase an error it is only necessary to backspace and retype the character, since characters are stored magnetically in the same way as in a computer system. This feature also enables words to be added to, or inserted on, any line on the magnetic media without having to repeat the remainder of the line. Word processing equipment offers no advantage in respect of short one-off letters or memos.

8. Benefits. The main benefits of word processing systems may be summarised as follows:

    (*a*) increased volume of output;
    (*b*) higher level of quality;
    (*c*) increased speed of output;
    (*d*) higher level of productivity;
    (*e*) reduced level of fatigue;
    (*f*) lower level of costs.

DIGITAL PABX TELEPHONE EXCHANGE

9. General outline of PABX. Digital PABX telephone exchanges are an essential communication catalyst for the electronic office of the present and future. Digital voice and data communication systems provide the foundations for extending office automation.

The digital exchange translates voice analog signals into digital signals, which are the common language of computers and electronic equipment such as workstations, word processors and terminals in general. This technology will widen the horizons for developing automated offices as it makes it possible to access all electronic devices comprising the electronic office. This includes access to local area networks, mainframe computers, terminals, word processors, electronic mail stations, telexes, microcomputers and electronic printing equipment. The devices are connected to the wiring of the digital switchboard at no additional cost. PABX systems can also act as message switching centres for terminals and other devices. They also control the routeing of data or text from workstations (*see* XXIV, **11**).

10. ICL DNX–2000 digital PABX distributed network exchange. The DNX–2000 is a *D*istributed *N*etwork *EX*change which provides the means for integrating office communications as it can talk to and work with computers, word processors, telexes, electronic printing equipment and traditional telephones.

The system has bubble memory (which eliminates tape and disc) as the primary non-volatile storage medium. The exchange can be interlinked or used with other switching systems to provide integrated communications. It can handle 150 to 10 000 lines.

Features include discriminatory barring, automatic route selection, extension metering, automatic number identification and traffic analysis.

The DNX–2000 supports standard dial and MF telephones together with two special terminals—the DNX–50 and DNX–300. The DNX–50 is an electronic telephone providing display capability,

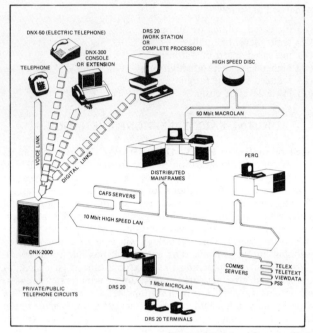

(Courtesy International Computers Limited)

FIG. 145   *ICL DNX-2000 digital PABX distributed network exchange.*

flexible key assignment, hands free operation and an optional data port into the DNX–2000. Features include abbreviated dialling, dial by name, date and time display, numeric keypad for normal telephone operation and alphabetic keys for message generation. The DNX–300 dataphone can function as a console, maintenance position or a secretarial/executive extension. It has DNX–50 features plus electronic mail, diary, directory, full message switching capability and system statistics recovery. Other features include VDU, standard keyboard layout, fixed designation keys including dial keypad and fixed feature keys. It is built on distributed microprocessor architecture (*see* Fig. 145).

PROGRESS TEST 22

1. Define the term "information technology" indicating its effect on the activities of the administrative function of an organisation. **(1,2)**

2. Define the term "electronic mail".   **(3–5)**

3. Specify the nature and benefits of word processing.   **(6–8)**

4. State the difference between the older PABX and the more recent digital PABX system.   **(9,10)**

CHAPTER XXIII

Local Area Networks and Electronic Desktop Display Systems

LOCAL AREA NETWORKS

1. Network defined. A network is a system which links together a number of machines and devices for specific purposes such as electronic mail, information storage and retrieval in respect of a disc based database, and data management systems. The workstations linked together on the network can retrieve data from the database as and when required during processing operations and can utilise high speed printing facilities. Many networks use twisted-pair wires or coaxial cables which allow data transmission speeds in the region of one million bits per second (i.e. one megabit per second) or more. Modems can be used to link networks to the British Telecom telephone system and to provide gateways to other networks (*see* Fig. 146).

2. Corvus Omninet: general description. Omninet has been designed to expand the use of microcomputers by linking them into a network. They share a large database and communicate with other micros on the network, have access to stored data and the use of other peripherals such as a high speed printer. The system eliminates the restricted storage capacity constraint which may be a feature of some micro standalone systems because, for instance, a typical floppy disc can store only five hundred records or so depending upon their size, whereas the smallest Corvus disc can store in the region of 25 000.

The total length of the network can be up to 4,000 ft (1.21 km) which is adequate for a multi-storey office block. The network has twisted-pair cable to which 64 microcomputers or other peripherals are attached. The connection to the main cable is through passive junction boxes. The system uses high capacity Corvus hard discs which have a data transfer rate of 425 kilobytes per second. The capacity according to the size of the disc is 6MB, 10MB or 20MB. Disc capacity can be increased up to 80MB. Each micro on the network can use the database as if it was dedicated to that machine instead of being a shared resource.

Software resident in transporters containing microprocessors controls messages between its own microcomputer and other micros or storage devices on the network. The network operates at 1 million bits per second which is so fast that, even when many users are active on the system simultaneously, delays are not apparent.

Economy and efficiency can be gained in communications and business administration by linking a few micros in a network, but for larger businesses Omninets can be linked together to form a chain of local area networks (LANs) providing benefits to all departments which need access to stored information. The workflow can be streamlined with all information held on-line so that relevant information from different data files can be accessed from the same keyboard to compile reports. The system can provide word processing and message-handling power that could cost over ten times more with stand-alone word processors. The long network permits reports, memos, customer transactions and files to be transmitted throughout the company. Each station has access to the Corvus disc and because each is a microcomputer—not a terminal—text editing, file formatting and so on can be carried out at any point. For the college or school computer room a monitor is available with Apple II and Omninet which allows demonstrations on one micro and facilities for sending the display to all others in the room, for checking progress on any micro from the instructor's computer or for down loading BASIC programs to every micro from the single Corvus disc.

This type of system is also ideal for order processing and stock control because of the facility of having all records on-line, thus

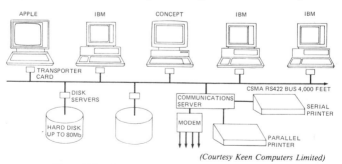

(Courtesy Keen Computers Limited)

FIG. 146 *Corvus omninet local area network.*

enabling credit checking and stock checks to be carried out randomly as events occur. Stock and customer records are also automatically updated to provide the latest information for on-line enquiries.

Transporters receive and check data and immediately confirm to the sender. If the sending transporter does not receive that confirmation, it will despatch the message again as many times as the user has specified for the system. Omninet avoids data collisions by giving a transporter total control of the network for the brief time necessary to send information. The high speed of the network eliminates bottlenecks.

Back-up is provided through the Corvus "MIRROR" which stores data on a cartridge tape system. Mirror capacity is approximately 100 MB per 3-hour tape (*see* Fig. 146).

3. Xerox 8000 Ethernet: general description. Ethernet is the foundation of the Xerox 8000 Network System which is a local area network based on the concept of distributed information processing which allows the sharing of common services, i.e. shared facilities. It enables an increasing variety of workstations to be attached to a single coaxial cable (which is passive), and have access, as required, to shared services. These services include electronic filing, electronic mail, electronic printing and communications "gateways" to remote devices and networks.

Unlike a shared logic system, i.e. a centralised processor shared by various terminals, the processing power of an Ethernet system is distributed to the attached devices, so that files, printers and workstations can be added or removed without constraint in much the same way that conventional organisations, systems and services are expanded or contracted. Devices are attached to the network by means of a simple clamp connector on the coaxial cable to which is attached a transceiver. The transceiver provides the signal connector and recognises information signal conditions on the cable. The transceiver is connected to the attached device, which may be a server or workstation, via an interface cable. There is a controller in the attached device which receives traffic from the Ethernet and places messages on it.

4. Communications server. The communications server, comprising an 8000 series processor and terminal, provides network users with a variety of shared resource communication devices by utilising ordinary telephone line connections. The unit's "gateway service" enables the standalone Xerox 850 Display Typing System and the 860 Information Processing System workstations to access all network resources. Any other word processor, personal computer or typewriter with teletype communications capability can participate as users of the Ethernet services through the communications server. Internet working, which allows Ethernet users to communicate with each other through external tele-communication lines is possible.

5. Print server. The Print Server, comprising an 8000 series processor, terminal and printer, provides local and remote network users with high volume, laser character generated printing at speeds of twelve pages per minute. Everything from simple business letters to lengthy reports can be accommodated by the Server, which prints individualised documents to exact user specifications.

6. File server. The file server, consisting of disc drives, 8000 series processor and terminal, provides shared resource "electronic filing" and optional "electronic mail"services to any number of network users. The file server preserves the local storage capabilities of each workstation for private work files while extending workstation capabilities through shared resource applications. The electronic file server allows storage of documents which can be retrieved and updated as required. The mailboxes are stored in the file server and the user can access his own mailbox from any workstation (*see* Figs. 147 and 148).

7. Symbnet. This is a local area network system from Symbiotic Computer Systems Ltd. It uses fibre optic cable to allow several microcomputers to share a common file. It is said to be the fastest long-range local area network for microcomputers which has a range of seven to nine kilometres. It uses a high intensity semiconductor laser to transmit data, whereas other network systems use flat ribbon or coaxial cable which is sensitive to electrical noise from fluorescent lights and photocopiers, etc.

ELECTRONIC DESKTOP DISPLAY SYSTEMS

8. General features. A revolutionary process is taking place in the use of small computers which allows a complete computer application to be controlled with one hand without recourse to using a keyboard. The main feature of electronic desktop displays is the representation of office functions by displaying on the screen pictures of a desktop containing such items as in- and out-baskets, file folders, file drawers, stationery cupboard, calculator and blank paper (*see* Figs. 149 and 150). The pictures are known as icons (or Ikons) and behave just like the objects they represent so that a document icon can be opened, or placed into a folder icon in the same way as in a normal office operation. Other icons provide

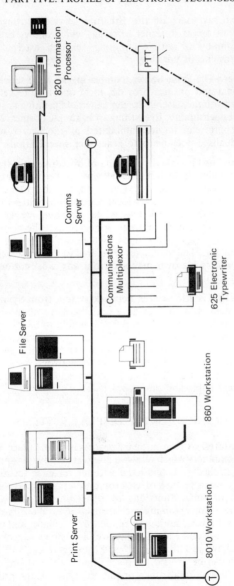

(Courtesy Rank Xerox (UK) Limited)

FIG. 147   *Screen display: Xerox 8000 Ethernet Network System.*

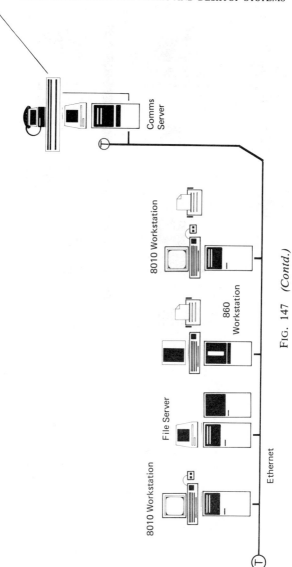

FIG. 147 (Contd.)

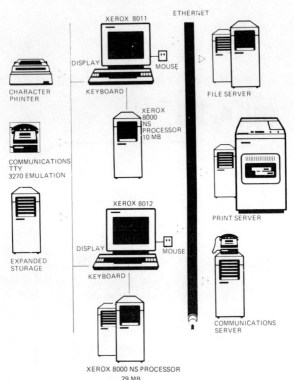

(Courtesy Rank Xerox (UK) Limited)

FIG. 148 *Xerox 8000 Ethernet Network System: Star information system.*

access to the shared resources of the network as shown by the printer, in-basket, out-basket and filing icons. A hand-held cursor control device known as a "mouse" (*see* VI, **20**) is used for pointing to specific icons (*see* Fig. 151) in accordance with the task or function to be performed. This is a means of selecting the required facilities to achieve the desired actions.

Such systems are designed to create and modify, store and retrieve text, graphics and records in an automated way which is a major step forward in the simplification of office tasks and the use of computers. It is possible to create and combine both text and graphics data on the display screen for integration in a single document.

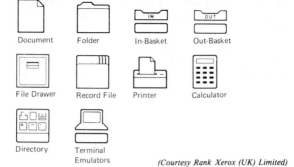

(Courtesy Rank Xerox (UK) Limited)

FIG. 149   *Examples of icons.*

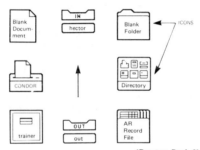

(Courtesy Rank Xerox (UK) Limited)

FIG. 150   *Electronic desktop display indicating the nature of icons.*

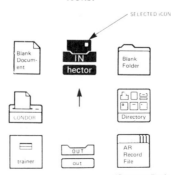

(Courtesy Rank Xerox (UK) Limited)

FIG. 151   *Electronic desktop display showing selection of icon.*

9. Available electronic desktop systems. Currently there are three such systems available, or likely to be available, in the near future, these are:

(a) VisiCorp: VisiON software which is an abbreviation for *V*isi *O*perating e*N*vironment;
(b) Apple, Lisa: which is an abbreviation for *L*ocally *I*ntegrated *S*oftware *A*rchitecture;
(c) Xerox: Star information system.

10. VisiON. This electronic desktop display system consists of four application programs combined with an operating system including word processing, financial spreadsheet, database management and graphics.

Use of the system commences with a selection from the applications list which displays items as separate boxes. A list of commands is displayed across the bottom of the screen: HELP, CLOSE, OPEN, FULL, FRAME, OPTIONS, TRANSFER, STOP, SAVE. Each application is displayed as a "window" on the screen. The window is opened by pointing the "mouse" at the OPEN command. The space allocated to the applications windows is controlled by the mouse. Windows can be interleaved, one on top of the other, in a similar way to stacking a number of papers.

Each new page of a letter is created by pointing the "mouse" (cursor) at the OPEN command and opening a new window. When processing is concluded the windows are CLOSED or SAVED if they need to be retained. A window is simply a portion of the video screen for displaying objects, i.e. icons. TRANSFER moves the contents of different windows around and merges graphical data with text, etc.

The software is designed to run on most 16-bit microcomputers with the relevant storage capacity which is in the region of $\frac{1}{4}$M bytes as the software requires 128K bytes.

11. Lisa. This system is a specific combination of hardware and software. The software was designed to function on the specific hardware and the hardware to be used for processing the defined electronic desktop software.

The computer press implies that Lisa is not a microcomputer in the everyday sense but a reasonably sized mini, verging on a mainframe, as it has a 16-bit processor, three subsidiary processors, 1M byte of RAM, 6.74M bytes of disc capacity and a bit-mapped screen. It has a powerful HELP facility which enables the less experienced user to be guided through the required stages interactively. It does not have any rows of function keys as it uses a mouse for cursor control.

When the machine is switched on the screen has a grey tone, a white menu display across the top and an electronic desktop display of small icons each of which has a small label. The shape of each icon is representative of its use as with the other electronic desktop systems. Pressing the button on the mouse twice either opens the icon (which gets larger) or unrolls a menu.

12. Star. The Star System uses the mouse, windows and icons in a similar way to the other systems outlined. It automates the development and formatting of information and opens the avenues to electronic information processing allowing the distribution of documents by electronic mail to local and remote users of Xerox Ethernet networks. In addition to the electronic desktop facilities outlined above, the Star system allows the choice of a wide range of type styles and sizes from a Property sheet which appears on the screen. Text can be enlarged, reduced, underlined, centred or changed to italic or bold to achieve the right impact. Documents are created by typing them on to the screen, existing documents can be amended and up to six documents can be opened at the same time and parts of one copied to another. When printing is required the document is copied on to one of the printer icons.

PROGRESS TEST 23

1. What are the features and characteristics of local area networks? **(1–6)**

2. What benefits would you expect to achieve from the implementation of local area networks in your organisation? **(1, 2)**

3. What is the nature and purpose of a communications server? **(4)**

4. What is a print server? **(5)**

5. What is the purpose of a file server? **(6)**

6. Define the characteristics and purpose of electronic desktop display systems. **(8–12)**

7. What is the meaning of the following terms: (*a*) icons; (*b*) mouse; (*c*) window? **(8, 10)**

CHAPTER XXIV

Data Transmission

BASIC CONCEPTS

1. General aspects of data transmission. Data transmission is the movement of information in coded form comprising binary digits (bits) over some kind of electrical transmission system (*see* **7** and Table XV, **18–23**). Communication between business units by means of data transmission facilities using either telephone or telegraph lines is increasing. The reason for the increasing use of data transmission rather than voice communication and the normal mail service is due to the expanding use being made of computers in business organisations, especially those with dispersed operating units. This is particularly so with regard to businesses with a centralised computer installation used for processing the data of the various operating units in order to achieve economy in data processing activities and efficient control of business operations.

Instead of despatching data for processing by normal mail services or an internal messenger service, it is much faster to send it by data transmission facilities. The processed data may then be re-transmitted to the originating unit and converted into printed form locally if suitable facilities are available, or, if not, it may be sent through the normal mail service or internal messenger service. Data transmission may be either on-line or off-line, and it is now proposed to outline the characteristics of both communication techniques.

Before proceeding, it is important to appreciate the difference between telephone lines and telegraph lines. The former are referred to as "voice-grade" lines, which allow data to be transmitted at higher speeed than telegraph lines allow (*see* **5**).

2. On-line data transmission. On-line data transmission indicates that the communication lines are connected directly to the computer either by means of a multiplexor or an interface unit (*see* Fig. 152). The interface unit scans the communication lines frequently to detect those ready to send or receive data. When a line is ready to transfer data the scanning ceases and the channel number of the

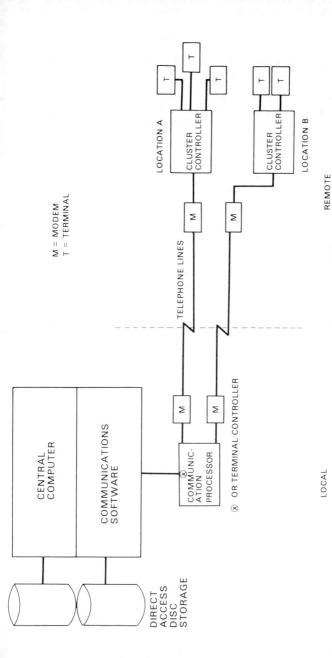

M = MODEM
T = TERMINAL

⊗ OR TERMINAL CONTROLLER

TELEPHONE LINES

LOCATION A

LOCATION B

REMOTE

LOCAL

FIG. 152 *On-line data transmission—clusters of terminals.*

line is signalled to the CPU; if the processor is in a position to accept data, transmission begins.

3. Off-line data transmission. This type of data transmission indicates that the communication lines are not connected directly to the computer. Key-to-disc systems are often used for off-line preparation and transmission of data as remote job-entry systems.

COMMUNICATION EQUIPMENT

4. Multiplexor. A multiplexor is a device which enables a number of data channels to be accommodated on a single communication line, for the purpose of transferring data to and from the computer.

A multiplexor receives data from a number of terminals in the communication system which transmit and receive data at low speed. The multiplexor batches terminal messages and transmits them at high speed to the computer. A number of terminals may share a multiplexor located at a regional office as in time sharing operations. All transmissions are then communicated to the computer by a single communication line via a multiplexor at the central location. This arrangement economises in the number of lines required and reduces the cost of leasing telephone lines.

Multiplexors are used as an alternative to polling which requires dedicated software and more complex terminals (*see* **23** and Fig. 152).

5. Modem. The term "modem" is derived from "modulator" and "demodulator" and is an item of equipment connected to each terminal in a communications complex using telephone lines. As telephone lines use analog signals and data terminals transmit signals in digital form a modem is necessary for converting digital signals to analog signals and vice versa. Telecom modems are designed to a standard interface as recommended by the Consultative Committee International Telephones and Telegraphs (CCITT). Modems are included in the Datel service provided by British Telecom.

6. Front-end communications processors. These are programmable devices which control the functions of communications systems. They support the operations of a mainframe computer by performing functions which it would otherwise be required to perform itself. The functions include code conversions, editing and verification of data, terminal recognition and control of transmission lines. The mainframe computer is then able to devote its time to data processing rather than data transmission (*see* Fig. 152).

TELECOM DATEL SERVICES

7. Definition of Datel. Telecom consider data transmission facilities of such importance to commercial, business and industrial undertakings as to merit the provision of a separate group of communications services known as "Datel Services". Datel is a word derived from (Da)ta (tel)ecommunications and the services available are indicated below. It is important to appreciate that it is necessary to obtain permission from Telecom to connect any communications equipment to Telecom services.

Datel services are summarised in Table XV.

TABLE XV DATEL SERVICES AT A GLANCE

Service	Signal path	Transmission Speed–bits per second	Operating Mode	Remarks
Datel 200	Public Telephone network	300	Asynchronous	300 bit/s may not always be atttainable with older equipment
	Private Circuit	300	Asynchronous	
Datel 600	Public Telephone Network	600	Asynchronous	Speeds of up to 1200 bit/s are also possible.
	Private circuit	1200	Asynchronous	4-wire private circuits are required for duplex working.
Datel 1200 Duplex	Public Telephone Network	1200	Synchronous or Asynchronous	
Datel 2412	Public Telephone Network	2400	Synchronous	Over some connexions it may be necessary to switch to 1200 bit/s.
	Private Circuit	2400	Synchronous	A 4-wire private circuit is required

Table Continued

TABLE XV Continued

Service	Signal path	Transmission Speed—bits per second	Operating Mode	Remarks
Datel 4800	Public Telephone Network	4800/2400	Synchronous	Over some connexions it may be necessary to switch to 2400 bit/s
	Private Circuit	4800/2400	Synchronous	A 4-wire private circuit is required
Datel 4832	Private Circuit	4800/3200	Synchronous	A 4-wire private circuit is required.
	Public Telephone Network (Standby)	4800/3200	Synchronous	PSTN only operation is not available.
Datel 9600	Private Circuit	9600/7200/ 4800	Synchronous	A 4-wire private circuit is required.
	Public Telephone Network	9600/7200/ 4800	Synchronous	
Datel 48K	Wideband Circuit	40.8K 48K 50K	Synchronous	

(*Courtesy British Telecom*)

8. International Datel services. International Datel 200, 600 and 2400 services provide for the transmission of data over the PSTN to most of Europe, the USA and many other countries. The transmission of data internationally can be arranged over privately leased circuits, whether or not the International Datel Service is available to the country concerned.

9. Datel Network Control Systems (DNCS). DNCS are available for use with most Datel Services. Specially equipped racks, housed in an attractive cabinet, provide the termination points for the circuits and hold the modems, control units and other necessary equipment. The systems are modular; as the user's needs increase, more "building bricks" are added to it. Where a customer uses more than one Datel Service, DNCS may contain a mixture of these different services.

10. Multipoint circuits for data transmission. In addition to point to point circuits, data may also be transmitted over a multipoint circuit. This allows from two to twelve terminals to be connected to a central station and allows the transmission of data from the central station to any terminal and from terminals to the central station. Direct communication between terminals is not possible.

OTHER TELECOM SERVICES

11. System X. This is British Telecom's name for their computer controlled telephone exchanges linked by digital transmission and signalling systems. Older exchange equipment is scheduled to be progressively replaced by the new technology system over a number of years. With this system caller voice patterns are represented by on-off digital pulses. The system greatly improves the quality of transmission and calls are connected more quickly. The equipment is also cheaper to buy, install and maintain than older systems and takes up much less space.

Digital exchange systems, like System X, rely on the latest microchip technology. This means that exchanges no longer have moving parts prone to crossed lines, wrong numbers, and line noise as was the case with the older electro-mechanical exchanges and the more modern cross-bar and electronic read relay exchanges.

Eventually there will be integrated links between local and trunk exchanges, referred to as Integrated Digital Access (IDA). In addition to voice services IDA will offer both circuit and packet switched data facilities which can be used for a wide variety of purposes, e.g. facsimile, electronic mail and slow-scan TV. IDA will be a standard feature of System X from 1985 (*see* XXII, **9**).

12. Packet switching. Packet switching is a technique whereby the terminal or computer in a data transmission system collects data into a block which is allocated an address. The block is sent to the local packet switching exchange which transmits it to its destination exchange. The communication lines between exchanges are only engaged when a packet is being transmitted. During lapses in transmission, lines are available to other users. If data is transmitted by the normal telephone network a charge is incurred for the length of time the line is used, even for the time when no data is being transmitted. Packet switching is designed to eliminate this. In the UK this applies where telephone calls or data transmissions on public switched telephone lines are charged on a time used basis.

13. Teletex. At the outset it is important not to confuse "teletex" with "teletext". Teletex is the international text communication service embracing a set of internationally agreed standards, which ensures the interworking of terminals from any manufacturer on a number of different networks. Communication between various equipment cannot be achieved without standardisation. Teletex represents an automatic text transmission system thirty times faster than telex. Business correspondence, documents, data and messages can be transmitted between terminals which may be workstations or word processors in around ten seconds a page. Letters can be typed and sent automatically. Other work can continue while documents are transmitted or received. Copies of documents can be stored electronically or printed for filing in the normal office filing cabinets.

TERMS USED IN DATA TRANSMISSION

14. Serial transmission. With this type of transmission, each bit in a character is sent sequentially to the transmission line; by convention the least significant bit is usually sent first, viz.

$$0100011 \rightarrow$$

Speed of transmission is expressed in bits per second.

15. Parallel transmission. In a parallel transmission system, all the bits in a character are transmitted at the same time, viz.

$$\left. \begin{array}{c} 0 \\ 1 \\ 0 \\ 0 \\ 0 \\ 1 \\ 1 \end{array} \right\} \rightarrow$$

Although it appears that seven signals have to be sent to the transmission lines at the same time, in practice special codes are used in order to limit the number of simultaneous signals which need to be transmitted, thereby reducing the technical problems which are introduced when more than one frequency is transmitted at once. Speed of transmission is expressed in characters per second in a parallel transmission system.

16. Frequency division multiplexing (FDM). With frequency division multiplexing a relatively wide band width (range of frequencies available for signalling) is divided into a number of smaller band widths, to provide more channels of communication.

17. Time division multiplexing (TDM). Time division multiplexing is a process whereby a channel which is capable of a relatively high information transfer rate (bits per second) is divided up into a number of time slots to provide a number of lower speed channels. For example, a line capable of carrying 2400 bits per second could, by the use of TDM, theoretically be divided into four 600 bits per second channels, or a combination of different speed channels up to a maximum of 2400 bits per second.

18. Synchronous transmission. In this type of transmission, the receiver is kept continuously in step with the transmitter by electronic clocking devices. By this means, synchronisation is maintained in the receipt and transmission of signals.

19. Asynchronous transmissions (start/stop). In this type of transmission system, each character is preceded by a start signal which serves to prepare the receiving mechanism for the reception of a character; this is followed by a stop signal which brings the receiving mechanism to rest in preparation for the reception of the next character. Asynchronous transmission may use start and stop elements between blocks of characters rather than between individual characters.

20. Simplex transmission. The transmission of data in one direction only.

21. Duplex transmission. The transmission of data in both directions simultaneously.

22. Half-duplex transmission. The transmission of data in both directions, but not at the same time.

23. Polling. The process of establishing if any terminal in the communication network has a message to transmit. Polling is a continuous process requiring dedicated software and more complex terminals than would be required if using a multiplexor (*see* **4**). The mainframe computer polls each terminal several times each minute to service those with messages to transmit. Messages transmitted by the computer are received by all the terminals in the system but only the terminal to which the message applies displays or prints the message.

PROGRESS TEST 24

1. What do you understand by the term "data transmission"? **(1)**

2. What are the main purposes of using data transmission facilities? **(1)**

3. Define on-line data transmission.   (2)

4. Define off-line data transmission.   (3)

5. (a) Why are data communication (or data transmission) systems in widespread use today? (b) Define the following terms: (i) modulation and demodulation; (ii) acoustic coupler; (iii) simplex; (iv) multiplexor.   (1, 4, 5, 20 and XII, 23) (IDPM)

6. Explain the purpose of the following devices when used as part of a data transmission service: (a) modem; (b) multiplexor; (c) front end processor; (d) intelligent terminal.   (4–6 and V, 26) (IDPM)

7. What do you understand by the term Datel?   (7)

8. Outline the various Datel Services.   (8–10 and Table XV)

9. What is System X?   (11)

10. Explain what is meant by packet switching in data transmission.   (12) (C & G)

11. Define the term "teletex".   (13)

12. Define the terms "FDM" and "TDM".   (16, 17)

13. (a) Describe with the aid of a diagram the main features of a data transmission system. (b) Define the terms: (i) synchronous transmission; (ii) half-duplex transmission; (iii) polling.   (18, 22, 23 and Fig. 152) (ACA)

PART SIX

GENERAL SYSTEMS CONCEPTS AND MANAGEMENT INFORMATION SYSTEMS

CHAPTER XXV

General Systems Theory and its Relationship to Long-Term Planning, Policy Making and the Principles of Management

GENERAL SYSTEMS THEORY (GST)

1. General systems theory. General systems theory provides a spectrum of scientific principles, concepts and philosophy which may be applied to the study of systems of all types. In the context of this book it embraces all types of business systems including control systems relating to quality, production, budgetary control, cost control, financial and cash control, etc. These systems provide the fabric of a management information system (MIS).

GST is based on knowledge obtained from the study of the behaviour of systems in general, including biological, mechanical, electronic and organisational systems. This encompasses the sciences of biology, physics, psychology and control engineering. Knowing the behaviour of systems under varying operating and environmental circumstances enables the behaviour of systems to be predicted to some extent. The behavioural characteristics of systems is obtained from systematic studies over a prolonged period of time, controlled experiments and by simulation. Diverse types of system often have common elements in their composition and the study of such systems generated the science of cybernetics —the science of communication and control in man and machine systems. (*see* XXVII, **8-9**).

2. GST and long-term planning. GST implies scientific analysis of systems to obtain information of their nature, characteristics and behaviour when subjected to random influences. Long-term planning requires in-depth study (analysis) of its environment in order to detect threats and opportunities to its existence. This necessitates an analysis of the various environmental elements:

(*a*) economic;
(*b*) technological;
(*c*) sociological;
(*d*) financial;
(*e*) legislative.

It is then necessary to assess the extent of change in these elements in order to assess its effect on the behaviour of the business, which is essential before long-term plans can be evolved, as events in each of the various elements can create situations which prevent the achievement of objectives.

Long-term planning takes a futuristic view of the business situation, usually five to ten years ahead, for the purpose of obtaining an appreciation of all those factors which can influence the future profitability of the business. It is then possible to determine future strategy to achieve desired objectives. It is necessary to monitor (appraise) the long-term situation continuously by analysing short-term trends as the environment in which the business operates is extremely volatile and dynamic—certainly not static. Continuous appraisal also enables a business to reassess corporate strengths and weaknesses relating to capacity, finance, know-how, manpower, machines and managerial strengths, etc.

3. GST and policy making. Policy making is affected by GST as the relationship of external systems to the business indicate factors which must be considered when formulating the framework of company policy relating to personnel, finance, technology, marketing, production, the policy in relation to outside agencies and the public in general.

The ethical, sociological, technological and economic framework provides guidelines for establishing the internal policies of the business on the basis of which it will conduct its future operations. The corporate policies of the business mould its image as viewed by the various social groups, i.e. employees, customers, suppliers, government departments and the public generally.

The formulation of policy is the responsibility of the Board of Directors but it is established in consultation with managers and relevant personnel in the business. Everyone in an organisation needs to be aware of specific policies as they relate to their sphere of responsibility and authority.

4. GST and the principles of management. The principles of GST may be considered to relate to the principles of management as both are based on scientific analysis. GST is based on scientific analysis of systems to understand their nature and behaviour in varying circumstances and the effect of the environment on its performance. Management principles are based on the scientific analysis of management functions and practice in various environments. It may be said, therefore, that businesses are controlled by management systems which are activated by the various control systems which themselves are based on scientific theories, i.e. GST. GST principles may conflict with the practice of management because *compromise* is often the keynote of success rather than inflexible rulings which appear relevant from previous experience. All management problems have different ingredients, which makes it impossible to preformulate solutions even for similar situations.

Many management problems relate to social conflict between various factions, i.e. employee–employer, customer–supplier, business–government which do not always lend themselves to quantifiable solutions. Standard rules do not apply because they are not always acceptable by all parties to the conflict.

CHARACTERISTICS OF SYSTEMS

5. Definition of a system. A system may be defined as a combination of interrelated elements, or sub-systems, organised in such a way as to ensure the efficient functioning of the system as a whole, necessitating a high degree of coordination between the subsystems, each of which is designed to achieve a specified purpose.

If one considers the human body, it is made up of a number of related sub-systems which are interrelated and interdependent and which, as a whole, form a very powerful system which automatically adjusts its behaviour according to its environment. The human body is an adaptive system which consists of a basic framework in the form of a skeleton, a nervous system, a brain, senses relating to taste, sight, hearing and touch, as well as limbs for walking and holding objects; all coordinated by the central nervous system actuated by the brain.

The human body reacts to its environment in a number of ways, for instance, by shivering to keep warm when it is cold or stopping at a kerb before crossing the road.

6. The business as a system. In the context of a business organisation the production function is a sub-system within the environment of a total system consisting of integrated physical and control systems. The production sub-system itself consists of smaller sub-systems in the form of machines (mechanical sub-systems) which are also inter-related with the machines' operators.

There also exist work-handling sub-systems which may be either human or automatic and the power supply sub-system, all of which interact with each other to form the hub of business operations. Physical sub-systems are governed by control or administrative sub-systems such as production control, quality control, cost control, stock control and budgetary control, etc. Information for control is generated by separately structured data processing sub-systems which are an essential element of management information sub-systems.

7. Business systems. A business system may be defined as a combination of related sub-systems consisting of a series of operations arranged in a logical sequence to achieve a particular purpose as efficiently as possible. Such systems should be standardised whenever possible and should be integrated as far as possible to achieve economy in data processing.

8. System resources. Business systems require resources to enable them to operate in the same way that a factory requires resources and, what is more, the nature of the resources required are similar for both factory and administrative systems. The difference, of course, is in the manner of their use. The major resource is finance because this is an "enabling" resource for obtaining the other resources essential to the effective operation of systems. These resources are personnel, office space, machines and equipment and business forms and documents.

SYSTEMS RELATIONSHIPS

9. Input/output relationships. In many cases systems have a direct relationship because, in many instances, the output from one is the input to another, even though they may be administered as separate systems. This may be due to the way in which the systems were initially developed, but in many instances input/output relationships have been the basis for integrating such systems to take advantage of administrative efficiency which larger systems often achieve (*see* XXIX, **4**).

10. Open systems. Open systems are those which interact with their environment either for the collection of information on which to base strategy, or for conducting business transactions with suppliers, customers, the general public, departments, trade organisations, etc. Such systems adapt to changes in the environment in order to survive, which requires speedy reactions to competitive situations and other threats in the most effective way. Open systems include man, biological, organisational and business systems.

11. Closed systems. These are systems which do not interact with their environment either for the exchange of information or business transactions. Such systems are self-contained and business systems do not conform with this category as they interact with their environment to a great degree as no business exists in a vacuum.

NOTE: The reader should not confuse open and closed systems as indicated above with open-loop and closed-loop systems which are control systems (*see* XXVII, **14-18**).

12. Control relationships. Control systems are often separately structured from the systems which they control; for instance, the production control system controls the production quantity and the quality control system controls the quality of production. In a similar manner, the cost control system controls the cost of production, and so on. These control systems are basically administrative systems for monitoring the results and modifying the state of the physical systems to which they relate.

13. Coupling and decoupling of systems (integration and disintegration). If systems are over integrated they may become too complex to understand and operate and if one part of the system ceases to function correctly this may cause the system as a whole to deteriorate and perhaps cease to function completely. This creates unacceptable delays and disruption to those parts of the system (sub-systems) which are unable to function because of the absence of the necessary inputs from other related sub-systems.

When systems are decoupled it is easier to administer them in some cases as they become less complex and more flexible which enables them to react to random influences as they occur without too much disruption. Decoupling may re-create the former situation whereby systems existed separately on a functional basis but were coordinated by the chief executive for the achievement of overall objectives. Each functional sub-system has more independence even though they are still inter-related in reality, but loosely connected for administrative convenience. Each functional executive must apply initiative to achieve functional objectives but there must also exist a high degree of cooperation between the various sub-systems to avoid sub-optimisation for the business as a whole. The efficiency with which systems are designed and integrated plays a large part in their success or failure.

CLASSIFICATION OF SYSTEMS

14. Planning systems. The purpose of some systems is to plan the operations of other systems. Planning is primarily concerned with the allocation of resources to specific tasks and the setting of performance standards. A plan establishes the guide lines for future action without which a business is likely to drift in the wrong direction. Plans set a course for the business to follow, under the guidance of the navigator, who is usually the chief executive. Plans also provide the basis for preparing budgets.

15. Mechanistic and organic systems. A mechanistic system or organisation structure is rigid in construction and is designed to operate on the basis of standardised rules and regulations which restrict its ability to react to its environment. If non-standard situations arise the system may not be able to deal with them which causes a complete breakdown of the system.

When computer systems are designed, they are usually tested by means of decision tables to ensure that all possible conditions and the relevant actions are included in the computer program. The program is then able to deal with all eventualities on the basis of defined rules. If any condition was overlooked the computer would be unable to deal with the situation until the program was modified.

It is well known that stable conditions do not exist in business for long, as the environment in which the business operates is completely fluid and interacts on the business. A mechanistic system is not sufficiently flexible to deal with such situations and is not able to adapt to the new circumstances easily. On the other hand, an organic system or organisation structure is geared to respond to environmental influences and is able to redefine its objectives according to the prevailing circumstances. It accomplishes this by an efficient re-allocation of resources and retuning of the system to the new circumstances. Mechanistic systems are also referred to as deterministic systems (*see below*).

16. Deterministic systems. Deterministic systems are mechanistic in nature and this type of system has been contrasted with an organic system to define the difference in their behaviour. It is now proposed to consider other characteristics of a deterministic system. In general, this type of system enables the output generated from specific inputs to be predicted without error. This equally applies to a computer program. Business and economic systems do not come into this category however, as they are highly unpredictable. Mechanical systems perform in a pre-defined manner when subjected to specific inputs. As an example, a centre lathe behaves in a predictable manner when a specified gear is engaged (input) as it will process material at a defined speed therefore the rate of output is known. It is important to appreciate that the state of such a system can only be assessed when it is working smoothly without malfunctions and is continually under control. If wear occurs in the machine's parts then it will change its state to a probabilistic system (*see below*).

17. Probabilistic system. Business and economic systems are of a probabilistic nature as they are subjected to random influences from the internal and external environment. It is this factor which prevents their state being predicted precisely; it is only possible to assess their probable behaviour as the effect of random variations or influences cannot be predicted with any great degree of accuracy. Indeed the occurrence of random influences themselves cannot be predicted to any great extent. The state of such systems can therefore only be defined within specified limits even when they are subject to control because stocks of raw materials, parts and finished goods, for instance, are influenced by changes in demand and variations in supply. Stock control systems are implemented to detect and control such variations on a probability basis.

Similarly, production activities are subjected to random variations in respect of manpower availability and level of productivity achieved, machine breakdowns and material supply, etc. Production planning and control systems are implemented to detect and control such variations in order to minimise their effect on the achievement of desired states.

The quality of production also varies randomly due to inconsistency in the quality of raw materials, human error and faulty machine operation. Quality control systems are designed to detect and correct such situations. At a higher level, top management cannot be sure of the outcome of any specific strategy as it is not certain what actions will be taken by competitors, suppliers, customers and the government in the future, as this depends upon the vagaries of the international economic climate at any point in time.

In general, probabilistic systems are of a stochastic nature as it is not certain what outputs will be achieved from specific inputs because it is not possible to ascertain what events will occur outside the direct control of a system which will steer it away from its desired direction or state (*see* XXVII, **23, 26**).

18. Adaptive (self-organising) system. This type of system is dynamic as it responds to changing circumstances by adjusting its behaviour on a self-organising basis. The system alters its inputs as a result of measuring its outputs. It attempts to optimise its performance by monitoring its own behaviour. This class of system includes animal, human and organisational systems. It is of course imperative for a business to adjust its state dynamically otherwise it would not overcome threats to its existence. This also relates to the animal world where it may be said to be the "survival of the fittest" especially in their natural domain. Animals need to use their sensory functions to the full to detect environmental situations either to their advantage or disadvantage. It would be an appeasement of their hunger if they reacted at the right time to the availability of the right type of food in the environment. On the other hand, if the situation was reversed and they did not react to the situation where they were being hunted then the outcome could be a failure to survive.

Computerised systems such as stock control are often adaptive as changes in demand are sensed and responses are speedily implemented to change the state of the system to avoid the following.

(*a*) Overstocking and the related consequences of high average stocks, which increases the investment in stocks over the desired level, increased interest on capital, increased depreciation due to prolonged storage, increased obsolescence due to a complete fall off in demand and the increased costs of storage facilities.

(*b*) Stock shortages, which generate loss of orders or disrupt the flow of production, causing under-utilisation of resources, under-absorbed fixed overheads and loss of profits on units not produced and/or sold.

A computerised stock control system would also adjust the re-order level as a result of changes in demand to avoid re-ordering materials at a previously established re-order level. If this did not occur, then in a situation of reducing demand, a replenishment order may be placed as a result of an automatically produced re-order list which would increase the level of stock to an even higher level than required (*see* (*a*) above).

In the event of increasing demand, a failure to adjust the re-order level would mean that the program would not replenish supplies in accordance with the new circumstances and stock shortages would occur (*see* (*b*) above).

Adaptive systems are often classed as cybernetic systems and these are discussed in XXVII. In respect of functional, total and management information systems in general the reader is referred to XXVIII.

PROGRESS TEST 25

1. Define general systems theory. **(1)**

2. (*a*) Define the term "systems theory", and explain why it is important for the accountant to understand the principal features of "systems theory". (*b*) Briefly explain the meaning of each of the following terms: (*i*) feedback; (*ii*) open-loop system. **(1 and XXVII, 10–12, 14, 15)** (*ACA*)

3. Indicate the ways in which the process of long-term planning and policy making could be considered to be analogous to the application of general systems theory. Your answer should include definitions of "long-term planning and policy making" and "general systems theory". **(1-3)** (*ICMA*)

4. (*a*) Give explanations of the terms POLICY and OBJECTIVES in the context of business management. (*b*) Describe what is meant by business management control. Include in your description some requirements of adequate controls and indicate how and why feedback is obtained. **(2, 12, XXVI, 1–5 and XXVII, 1–12)** (*C & G*)

5. Do you consider that the principles of general systems theory (GST) are related to the principles of management? In what way, if any, do GST principles conflict with the practice of management? **(4)** (*ICMA*)

6. Define the term "system". **(5–7)**

7. Specify the resources required to enable business systems to function. **(8)**

8. Indicate the nature of system input/output relationships. **(9)**

9. Indicate the nature of "open" and "closed" systems. **(10, 11)**

10. What are control relationships? **(12)**

11. Define the term "coupling" and "decoupling" in the context of systems. **(13)**

12. One of the pitfalls a system designer must avoid is that of sub-optimality. (*a*) Define what is meant by sub-optimality and explain how it might be avoided. (*b*) Give a practical example of sub-optimality. **(13, 18)** (*ICMA*)

13. Specify the features of: (*a*) planning systems; (*b*) mechanistic and organic systems; (*c*) deterministic systems; (*d*) probabilistic systems. **(14–17)**

14. Define the nature of adaptive (self-organising) systems. **(18)**

CHAPTER XXVI

Goals and Objectives of Systems

OVERALL OBJECTIVES, UNITY OF DIRECTION AND CORPORATE OBJECTIVES

1. Overall objectives and unity of direction. In order to ensure that systems being developed conform with corporate requirements, it is essential for O & M and systems analysts to have a clear and unambiguous appreciation of the objectives of the business as a whole. If this factor is not taken into account systems will be out of balance with each other and unity of direction will not be achieved. A "total systems approach" is necessary so that the interactive elements of related systems are clearly identified to ensure the achievement of corporate objectives.

Analysts must be aware of the economic purpose of the business, the types of products marketed and the markets aimed at before they can be in a position to assess the relevance of the objectives of individual systems. The objectives of particular systems are not simply assumed by analysts, they are established by discussion with management who must agree them before system development gets under way.

It is also necessary to be aware of constraints which prevent the achievement of defined objectives. Such constraints in a manufacturing type business could include shortages of key materials, shortage of personnel with the relevant training for the technology involved in the manufacture of products, very keen competition and low purchasing power of consumers.

2. Corporate objectives. Whenever possible corporate objectives should be specified in precise meaningful terms. It is then possible to assess the deviation, if any, from the desired achievement by comparing actual results with planned performance. Typical corporate objectives may be defined in the following way:

    (*a*) required rate of return on sales;
    (*b*) required rate of return on assets employed;
    (*c*) required rate of annual growth in respect of sales, earnings per share, market value of shares;

(*d*) maintaining existing capital gearing ratio;

(*e*) reducing cost of products by a stated amount;

(*f*) increase profitability of specified product groups by a defined amount;

(*g*) eliminate products with a contribution less than a defined amount;

(*h*) increase market share of specified products by a defined amount;

(*i*) increase the turnover rate of stocks and WIP;

(*j*) develop new markets—home and export;

(*k*) improve customer satisfaction with respect to price, quality, delivery, credit terms and after-sales service;

(*l*) improve cash flows.

SYSTEM AND SUB-SYSTEM OBJECTIVES

3. System objectives. The objectives of particular systems must be determined within the framework of corporate objectives as indicated above. Production planning systems must ensure that production flows smoothly to achieve a given utilisation of assets so that a higher level of production facilitates a higher level of sales, and a higher level of profit, which achieves a higher rate of return on assets employed in the production process. This factor is also the basis of achieving a specified rate of annual growth in respect of sales—assuming of course that all production is capable of being sold. If production bottlenecks are removed then the turnover rate of WIP is increased and a reduction of product costs is possible because a higher level of production reduces the fixed costs per unit. This assists in attaining increased product profitability.

The objective in respect of customer satisfaction is partly satisfied by efficient production planning as delivery promises will be more likely to be achieved. Customer satisfaction may also be achieved by an effective sales accounting system by ensuring that customers' orders are dealt with efficiently and special orders notified to the product design office without delay. Improved cash flows may also be achieved by speeding up the preparation of invoices and statements of account.

Marketing systems also have an important part to play in developing new markets, improving after-sales service, developing an effective pricing policy and ensuring that orders are received for the most profitable products.

4. Sub-system objectives. A sub-system may be defined as a

TABLE XVI PRODUCTION DEPARTMENT SUB-OBJECTIVES

Sub-objective	Monitored by:
Increase machine utilisation by 5 per cent to 85 per cent	Factory management and production planning and control
Reduce idle time from 2 per cent to 1 per cent of total production time.	Factory management and production planning control
Reduce labour turnover from 15 per cent to 5 per cent	Factory management and personnel department
Increase operator peformance to an average of 120 per cent from present 110 per cent	Factory management and work study department
Reduce scrapped output to 5 per cent of good production from present 8 per cent	Factory management and quality control department

TABLE XVII SALES DEPARTMENT OBJECTIVES AND
SUB-OBJECTIVES

System objective	Sub-objective
Improve customer satisfaction	Reduce delivery time of orders by five days
	Ensure that special orders are notified to the product design office the day they are received
	Ensure that orders are acknowledged and delivery dates quoted within two days
	Improve accuracy of quoting delivery dates—margin or error must not exceed one week
Optimise stock levels	Minimise stock shortages, by more sophisticated stock control and demand forecasting techniques, to 95 per cent confidence level. Reduce average inventory by 10 per cent

departmental activity within the framework of a functional activity. Individual departments are set objectives within the framework of functional objectives and accordingly they may be defined as sub-objectives. The factory objective to reduce production costs may be achieved by a sub-analysis of factors which will achieve this requirement and accordingly sub-objectives may be as shown in Table XVI.

As a further example Table XVII outlines the system objectives and sub-objectives of a sales department processing incoming customers' orders. It may be assumed that the control of finished stock is the responsibility of the sales department.

The objectives indicated above form part of the overall marketing strategy which may include objectives to increase the market share of defined products and their profitability. Product profitability is also dependent upon the factory objectives outlined in Table XVI.

MOTIVATIONAL INFLUENCES AND CONFLICT OF SYSTEM GOALS

5. The influence of the human element on objectives. When management set business objectives they must never ignore the fact that people are involved in their achievement and very often organisational objectives may not correspond with the objectives of the personnel which form the organisation. A great deal depends upon the motivational influences which exist, if any, and their value to the individuals. Incentive schemes are often linked to objectives as a motivating influence but, even so, targets may be set at a level which personnel consider too high, regardless of the monetary inducement which may be available. Other motivating elements may be considered such as a greater participation in decision-making in order to stimulate job interest but even this will have varying reactions from individuals. Some personnel may require a less demanding working environment, increased leisure time, more welfare facilities or, perhaps, higher status. These are socio-technical factors involving consideration of social sciences with respect to the behavioural aspects of people at work.

With automated systems it is possible to predict what outputs will be achieved from specified inputs but such systems require programming and people are not susceptible to being programmed as automatons. Perhaps the answer lies in the area of effective leadership, fair deals, good communications and recognising that people are human beings.

6. Conflict of system goals (sub-optimality). In a manufacturing-and marketing-oriented business, conflict of system goals causing sub-optimality may occur because the two major functions, although interdependent, may have different system goals. In respect of the manufacturing function or system, if standard products are produced the factory manager may wish to produce the longest possible runs to reduce the cost per unit. This would be accomplished by spreading fixed manufacturing costs over a greater volume of production and minimising the setting-up costs which are associated with change-overs to different product lines. The marketing system, however, may wish to obtain orders regardless of minimum quantity considerations on the basis that any order is better than no order. This situation causes conflict of system goals and must be resolved by top management in accordance with company policy.

A further example of conflict of system goals is outlined in the following ICMA examination question.

> The production plan for a company, which was agreed by the board of directors after consideration of all factors, calls for 10 000 units each of product X, Y and Z, to be produced each week. However, to obtain longer production runs and lower production costs per unit, the production manager decided to produce 30 000 units of each product every third week.
>
> Discuss the conflict of system goals inherent in this situation, in the context of the systems approach.

The answer to this question needs careful consideration of the implications outlined in the situation, as the overall production level is the same but it would affect other operational aspects of the business. The production plan calls for a steady pattern of production no doubt to optimise the overall business objectives in respect of stock policy, production costs and sales demand. The production manager's decision is in conflict with the agreed system goals and may have repercussions as follows.

(*a*) The level of demand for each of the products obviously requires a steady, consistent level of production of 10 000 units of each product weekly.

(*b*) The decision to produce 30 000 units of each product every third week may defeat the production manager's goal of reducing the production cost per unit. This would be the situation if the product assembly lines and related machine processes had to be reset every third week. This would not be necessary on the basis of the board's agreement to produce 10 000 units of each product each week as resources would be geared up accordingly. The production manager's decision would probably cause idle facilities to be incurred in the weeks that two of the products were not in production. If idle facilities were not incurred to a great extent there would be a certain level of disruption on changeovers.

(c) The production manager's decision would increase the level of stock as the board's agreement would tend to minimise stock holding requirements. Accordingly, there would be an increase in the level of capital tied up in stocks and increased costs of storage, etc.

(Refer to 1 of this chapter for further details of overall objectives and unity of direction).

Sub-optimality may be further explained by introducing the following ICMA question.

One of the pitfalls a system designer must avoid is that of sub-optimality.

(a) Define what is meant by sub-optimality and explain how it might be avoided.

(b) Give a practical example of sub-optimality.

SOLUTION

Regarding part (a), the meaning of sub-optimality has already been explained above. How sub-optimality might be avoided rests with management which requires them to communicate company policy to all concerned and discuss functional plans within the framework of corporate objectives. It is also necessary to engender cooperation between functional executives, who must realise they are working for a corporate entity and not for themselves, or at least not directly.

In respect of part (b), examples of sub-optimality include under-utilisation of resources, low productivity and non-attainment of corporate objectives. In general, sub-optimality expresses a failure to realise the full potential of the business within the circumstances and environmental conditions which prevail.

PROGRESS TEST 26

1. State the importance of defining over-all objectives in the achievement of "unity of direction". (1)
2. Define the nature of typical corporate objectives. (2)
3. Specify the nature of system objectives. (3)
4. Outline the nature of sub-system objectives. (4)

5. What is the relevance of the human element in the achievement of objectives. **(5)**

6. The major function of a systems analyst is to produce a system which is the best compromise between prescribed objectives and actual constraints. You are required to: (*a*) explain this statement; (*b*) describe how a systems analyst establishes objectives and constraints; (*c*) give examples of typical objectives and constraints that might be found in the investigation of a sales accounting system which is to be computerised. **(1–6)** (*ICMA*)

CHAPTER XXVII

Control Systems Theory

BASIC ELEMENTS OF CONTROL

1. Definition of control system. A control system may be defined as a "control loop" superimposed on another system having a different purpose, e.g. the production system, which is controlled by the production control system (*see* **XXV, 12**). Control is for the purpose of detecting variations in the behaviour of a system so that control signals can be communicated to the appropriate manager. He is then in a position to effect changes to the system he is managing, so that it reverts to the desired state and so achieves its objectives (*see* **26**). Many administrative systems are control-orientated but they do not effect control directly—this is the prerogative of the manager concerned.

2. Basic elements of control. The basis of control in business systems consists of the following elements.

(*a*) *Planning.* The determination of objectives, or parameters: standard time for an operation, level of production activity required, level of sales required, expenditure allowed, performances level required, etc.

(*b*) *Collecting facts.* The collection and recording of data in respect of: actual time taken, level of production achieved, level of sales achieved, expenditure incurred, actual performance level, etc.

(*c*) *Comparison.* The comparison of objectives with actual results for the purpose of indicating variances from planned performance in the various spheres of business operations, and informing the relevant manager of significant deviations (variances).

(*d*) *Corrective action.* Action is taken by the relevant manager (effector) to maintain a state of homeostasis (*see* **26**) or to revise plans.

3. Control and the Pareto Law. An important factor for effective control is the application of the Pareto Law which, in general, states that many business situations have an 80/20 characteristic, for example, 80 per cent of the value of items in stock is represented by 20 per cent of the items. Therefore, the degree of control may be reduced by concentrating control on the 20 per cent high-value items, especially for controlling the total value of items held in stock.

Less rigid control procedures may be applied to the remaining 80 per cent of the items. Similarly, key production materials and parts may consist of 20 per cent of the total range held in stores, therefore tight control must be applied to these items, which should reduce the number of failures to report crucial stock situations, especially if the importance of the 20 per cent is stressed sufficiently and independent checks applied to the stock records, perhaps by the stock controller or auditor.

4. Threshold of control system. The measurement of a systems output by a sensor may be defined as the keystone of control because it is the point at which control begins and is, in fact, the threshold between the physical system and the related control system. For example, the output from the factory is measured and used as a basis of control by the production control system.

5. Control interface. The communication of data from a physical system to its related control system is a means of connecting the two systems and may be defined as "the control interface". This may be accomplished by strategically sited data collection devices forming a factory data collection system. The data is then communicated to a computer for processing. The communication device is in fact the interface in this instance. In a more basic system the provision of source documents, such as progress tickets, to the control system serves the same purpose and may be classified as the control interface.

6. Control based on the exception principle. As can be seen above, control is often based on deviations from planned performance, which is referred to as "management by exception". This concept is extremely important to business control as it allows management to grasp essential facts more speedily and to correct adverse trends much sooner, owing to the fact that only significant factors are reported on. Economy is accomplished in saving on the time required to compile reports either by normal clerical methods or by computer printout. Redundancy of information is eliminated—a feature of detailed schedules in some cases, as, very often, too much information is provided for the control process. Also, detailed schedules often leave the task of filtering essential requirements to management which slows down the process of corrective action and corrective action may not be taken at all as it is very easy for a manager to overlook essential facts in the hurly-burly of daily routine (*see* **32**).

Examples of control techniques using the exception principle are budgetary control and standard costing. Budgetary control compares actual with budgeted results periodically for the purpose of reporting to the relevant manager significant variances for their attention. While budgetary control is used for controlling overall business results, the control of costs relating to products in respect of direct material and direct labour is achieved by standard costing.

7. Requisite variety. Business systems consist of combinations of inter-related variable elements and it is the number of such elements which creates difficulty in designing effective control systems. The number of elements is a measure of a system's inherent variety and the greater the number of elements, the greater the degree of complexity.

A control system needs to be designed with the same degree of variety as the system it is to monitor, in order to allow for all possible conditions likely to arise in the operation of the system. This is a very important feature of control systems, particularly so with regard to computer-based systems, as the range of variety must be fully catered for, so far as it is economically viable to do so, as programs must contain the necessary instructions for processing data according to its classification or significance.

Before coding a computer program for a specific application a program flowchart is normally prepared which itself may be based on a decision table. The decision table is compiled to ensure that all conditions relating to data, and all necessary actions relating to such conditions, are taken fully into account during processing. The flowchart is a means of establishing the logic of computer operations and the establishment of their completeness to achieve a desired result. A decision table is therefore an aid in the preparation of a flowchart which is, in its turn, an aid to program coding.

These factors are particularly relevant to computerised exception reporting applications such as automatic stock re-ordering and credit reporting.

The effectiveness of control is dependent upon the extent to which the variable elements in the system to be controlled have been predicted and, if not included in the computer program (when relevant), are catered for by other control procedures.

CYBERNETIC CONTROL

8. Definition of cybernetics. The subject of cybernetics is important for control systems of all types and the basic concepts apply equally to business control systems and to man and machine systems. Cybernetics may be defined as "the science of communication and control in man and machine systems". The term is derived from the Greek word *kybernētēs*, the derivative of the Latin word *gubernator*, which in English may be translated as governor or controller.

9. Cybernetic control process. The cybernetic control process is identical to the process of control based on exception reporting, i.e. management by exception. The basic elements of the cybernetic control process may be analysed as follows.

(*a*) *Reference input.* The use of resources are planned to achieve a defined objective(s) and appropriate control parameters are established to assist their achievement. The parameters are outlined in 2(*a*) and are referred to as "reference inputs".

(*b*) *Sensor* (*measurement of controlled variable*). Operations are undertaken and data in respect of a system's outputs are measured by a sensor which indicates the actual state of the system, i.e. the magnitude of the output signal. The measured output is referred to as the controlled variable. A sensor may be mechanical, electronic or manual data recorder depending upon the nature of the system being controlled.

(*c*) *Feedback.* The output signal is then communicated by the process of feedback to the control system.

(*d*) *Comparator.* The comparator compares the output signal (the actual state of the system) with the desired state (the reference input). The difference between the two states is a measure of the variance or error. A comparator may be a control clerk (stock control clerk, cost clerk, budgetary control clerk), an automatic device in a machine or a computer program.

(*e*) *Error signal.* The error is signalled (communicated) to the effector.

(*f*) *Effector.* The effector adjusts the controlled variable by modifying the input of resources perhaps to increase or decrease the level of production in accordance with status of the error signal + or − . This action is to modify the behaviour of the system to achieve the reference input and obtain a state of homeostasis (*see* **26**). The effector may be a manager or supervisor in the case of business systems or an automatic device in a process control system.

(*g*) *Modification of reference input.* It may be found that the reference inputs of a system are inaccurately defined, invalid or out of date and require to be modified to conform to the true situation.

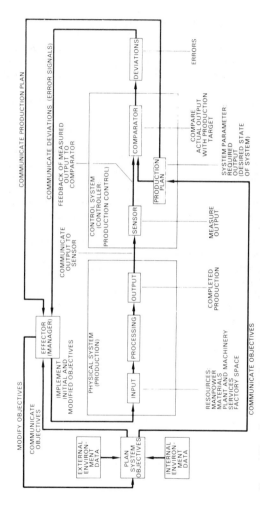

FIG. 153 *A manual closed-loop production control system illustrating cybernetic concepts.*

The elements outlined are illustrated in Fig. 153 which portrays a manual closed-loop production control system.

FEEDBACK AND FEEDFORWARD

10. Features of feedback. An important feature of cybernetics is feedback, which is the communication of a systems-measured output to a comparator for the detection of deviations (errors) (*see* Fig. 153).

The *Watt governor* is usually regarded as the first man-made feedback mechanism for controlling the speed of an engine.

The governor has weighted arms mounted on pivots, so that they are free to rise by centrifugal force as they revolve.

The arms turn at an increasing speed as the engine speed increases. The arms operate a valve which admits energy to the engine. The arms rise higher as the engine speed increases and the valve is closed proportionately thereby reducing the amount of energy supplied to the engine which tends to limit its speed.

If the engine fails to attain a given speed the arms are so positioned that the valve is opened more, admitting more energy until the required speed is reached. The required output (defined engine speed) is achieved by self-regulation as the input to the engine is adjusted by its own output on the feedback principle.

Self-regulation is not usually possible with business systems as the deviations from a required performance must be observed by a human being in the control system or by a computer program. Action to achieve the desired state of homeostasis (*see* **26**) must be taken by a manager after being notified of the deviations from the required state of the system. If the controller of the system fails to observe the deviations, then no effector action can take place. Even when deviations are noted and communicated to an effector he may fail to take the appropriate action.

Feedback is essentially an output signal causing error signals to be generated as the basis for adjusting the input to a system which, in respect of an automatic control system such as the Watt governor, is achieved by an inbuilt control mechanism.

11. Negative feedback. Most business control systems are "negative" error-actuated systems as the actual behaviour of the system is compared with the desired behaviour and the differences are detected as positive deviations (errors) and action is effected in the opposite direction to counteract them. For example, if the actual output from a production system is lower than the planned output, the difference between them would be detected as an error below standard. Corrective action would then be taken to increase output to the desired level which would necessitate an adjustment in the opposite direction to the error—an increase in production. The signal(s) which modify the behaviour of a system is not feedback but the result of feedback (*see* **10**).

12. Positive feedback. The characteristics of some types of system are such that the detected deviations need to be amplified. The process of amplification in telecommunications is defined as "a unidirectional device which creates an enlargement of a waveform".

Amplification applies to servo-mechanisms whereby a small manual force is detected and amplified to achieve a defined purpose. For example, a small manual force applied to aircraft controls is detected and amplified to the force necessary to adjust the control surfaces.

If unfavourable deviations detected in business systems were amplified, corrective action would not be achieved as the errors would be amplified and cause the systems to deteriorate until they went completely out of control.

In situations causing favourable deviations in business systems there is a case for their amplification or an adjustment to the control parameters. For example, if a lower-priced material was used in production instead of the standard material at a higher price, then the material cost of production would be lower. This situation assumes that the alternative material is suitable for its purpose and may be considered for further use thereby amplifying the deviations. For policy reasons it may be considered prudent to maintain the original standard for a while. Alternatively, the parameter (standard) may be amended immediately, in which case the deviation will disappear completely and will not be subjected to amplification as the desired state of the system has been modified.

13. Feedforward. The error signals generated by a system are usually used to adjust the current input to a system to utilise resources more fully and to achieve system objectives. The error signals may be noted over a period of time by a monitoring process and used as a basis for planning future system resources. This approach ensures that the historical trend or inherent behaviour of a system is allowed for when establishing control parameters for future operations.

OPEN-LOOP SYSTEM

14. Basic characteristics of open-loop systems. The basic characteristic of an open-loop system is that it does not contain the element of feedback. Without feedback, a system does not provide for the sensing of measured outputs for comparison with the desired outputs. Such a system does not therefore contain the element of control at all.

15. Example of open-loop-system. A basic type of open-loop system could be a domestic hot-water system without a thermostat, in which case there would be no automatic regulation of the water temperature. In such a case the heater would have to be switched off manually when the desired temperature was attained.

If the heater was switched off prematurely then the desired temperature would not have been reached or, if the heater was switched off a little late, the temperature of the water would be too high. Such a system is not effective.

Within a business, control of stocks by a stock control system would not be in existence, in which case storekeepers would have to report stock shortages as they occurred which, of course, is a little late in the day to obviate the consequences of such circumstances. In addition, excessive stocks may not be noted until the year-end stocktaking by which time it is too late to take effective action to minimise losses when the excess stocks are written off or disposed of below cost.

CLOSED-LOOP SYSTEM

16. Basic characteristics of closed-loop systems. An essential element of a closed-loop system is the communication of measured outputs to the control system—feedback. Such a system is defined as a closed-loop, which is a basic requirement of cybernetic systems.

Many closed-loop systems are self-regulating as they contain a built-in control mechanism, for example, the Watt governor and the thermostat in a domestic water-heating system.

Business systems containing integrated control systems performing continuous monitoring activities are also closed-loop systems as they contain the essential element of feedback (*see* Fig. 153 and Fig. 154).

17. Automatic closed-loop business systems. Computers are widely used for business data processing applications and the computer programs often contain in-built control functions. For example, a stock control application includes the processing of a transaction file and the updating of the stock master file for the purpose of calculating the new stock balance for each item in stock.

The program may also provide for the comparison of the actual

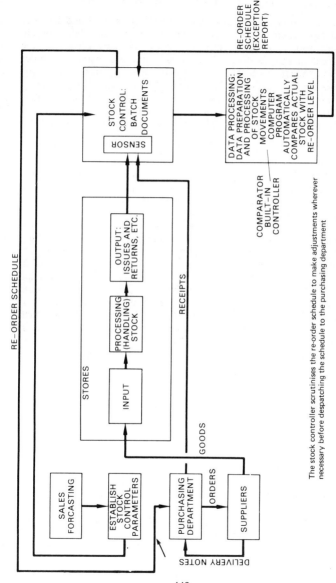

The stock controller scrutinises the re-order schedule to make adjustments wherever necessary before despatching the schedule to the purchasing department

FIG. 154 *An automatic computerised closed-loop stock control system (outline only).*

quantity in stock with the maximum permissible stock and print out an "excess stock" report for management control. The program may also incorporate automatic stock re-ordering whereby the actual quantity in stock of each item is compared with the re-order level. When the balance in stock is equal to, or less than, the re-order level a re-order list may be printed which is despatched to the purchasing department for the placing of purchase orders. Alternatively, a purchase order may be printed by the computer line printer which would reduce the lead time for the replenishment of supplies.

If, however, the balance in stock is greater than the re-order level no action is effected and the computer continues with the basic routine. The program may be defined as a built-in controller and the computer system a closed-loop system, as the actual state of the system is compared with the desired state and exception reports automatically printed (error signals).

It is essential to incorporate safeguards in this type of system which can take the form of a manual override to the action indicated by the computer program. In this way abnormal random situations not built into the computer program can be dealt with. If, for instance, there is a sudden increase or decrease in demand or supply, managerial intervention is necessary to avoid the consequences of excessive stocks on the one hand and shortages on the other. It is also necessary to modify the parameters of each item held in stock to provide for changing trends so that stock re-ordering is effected on the basis of current and not historic circumstances—only in this way can stock shortages and excessive stocks be avoided.

18. Manual closed-loop business system. Manual control systems are widely used in business and providing they contain feedback, may be classed as closed-loop systems. Indeed, to be classed as a control system at all feedback must be incorporated (*see* Fig. 153 above).

With regard to a manual stock control system, a stock control clerk is required to observe the stock status of each item, usually when updating the master record with current transactions, and trigger off the re-ordering procedure as necessary. However, through lack of concentration or interruptions, the clerk may fail to observe items which require to be re-ordered and no action will be effected to replenish supplies for stock requirements. This is the danger of a manual control system, as human beings are not infallible.

Failure to take action either to reduce excessive stocks or re-order supplies may have drastic consequences. In the first instance, excessive stocks lock up capital unnecessarily, increase interest charges, stock handling costs and the cost of storage facilities. On the other hand, failure to obtain supplies may create stock shortages and production delays, creating excessive idle time, under-absorbed fixed overheads, loss of profit on products not produced and possible loss of future orders (*see* XXV, **18**).

The solution to such a problem may be the employment of conscientious clerks who fully understand the consequences of their failure to report on situations requiring action. The incorporation of checking facilities such as random or spot checks may also provide the means of detecting previously unobserved situations.

DELAY FACTOR

19. Time-lag between physical event and information flows. If as a result of feedback unfavourable deviations are detected and action taken to eliminate them, the ultimate result will depend upon when the action was effected. Careful consideration must be given to the time-lag between a physical event and the information flows informing the effector of the event. For instance, if an unfavourable production output is detected and action is taken too late to alter the situation, then it is out of phase because the state of the system has probably changed in the meantime and action is taken to remedy a situation which no longer exists. This is referred to as the "delay factor" and such circumstances cause systems to hunt or oscillate around the desired state (*see* **23**).

In the circumstances outlined, if production failed to meet the desired target, action would be taken to increase production but if the necessary adjustment was delayed it is possible that, in the meantime, production has taken an upward swing. The result of the delayed action to increase production would tend to increase production even more, perhaps to a greater level than is warranted by the previous shortfall.

An adjustment may then be effected to reduce production but by this time production may have taken a downward swing and the delayed action would decrease production below the desired level thereby amplifying the situation.

20. Amplification and damping. The principles outlined show that if action to remedy a situation is delayed then the result achieved is of a positive feedback nature, whereby deviations are amplified instead of being damped down. What was meant to be negative feedback becomes positive feedback.

21. Practical example. In order to demonstrate the above principles and concepts Table XVIII outlines the actual production output in five different weeks, the delayed information flow in respect of each week's output the "corrective" action taken, and

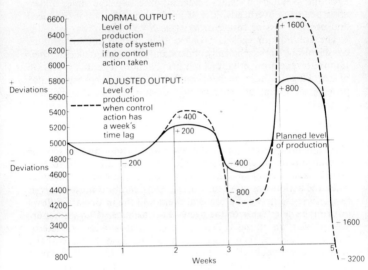

FIG. 155 *Effect of time-lag in an oscillating system.*

TABLE XVIII RESULT OF THE TIME LAG BETWEEN PHYSICAL EVENT
AND INFORMATION FLOW

Week 1	Week 2	Week 3	Week 4	Week 5
Normal output − 200	Normal output + 200	Normal output − 400	Normal output + 800	Normal output − 1600
	Information received for week 1	Information received for week 2	Information received for week 3	Information received for week 4
	Corrective action + 200	Corrective action − 400	Corrective action + 800	Corrective action − 1600
	Adjusted output + 400	Adjusted output − 800	Adjusted output + 1600	Adjusted output − 3200

the resulting output. The table should be studied in conjunction with Fig. 155.

22. Timeliness of information. Other aspects of the timing of information flows and the resulting action may be related to the preparation of annual accounts and the Balance Sheet of a company at the end of the financial year. These are, of course, historical and, although delay in their preparation should be minimised, no action can be taken to remedy the situation disclosed even if the facts are available within one day of the year-end. The operations for the year are complete and what is done is done as it were. Recognition of this situation has led to the development of periodical short-term accounting reports, statements and statistics. This involves reporting on events as soon after the conclusion of an operating control period as is feasible, so as to effect adjustments to the situations being controlled, either to eliminate adverse variances or to take advantage of favourable conditions.

It is important to appreciate that the best possible type of information will not affect control without a human or automated controller to effect adjustments to the systems being controlled, based on the information provided. The time factor must be considered with regard to its importance in achieving the degree of control required. For example, if information in respect of scrapped production is not reported early enough, no remedial action can be taken to stop production and to remove the cause of the scrap. It becomes necessary to introduce quality controllers to monitor the quality of production at strategic locations in the production processes. By this means, production may be stopped when it is discovered that the acceptable level of quality is not being achieved. Quality control charts are normally employed for monitoring the quality of production. By this means, corrective action may be taken to remove the cause of the scrap and so ensure that production achieves the desired level of quality (the desired state of the system).

23. Hunting or oscillating. Business activities hardly ever achieve a steady state as they are subjected to random influences from both the internal and the external environments. This causes results, or the level of performance, to fluctuate above and below the average or normal state. For example, stocks of materials attain an overall average level, but vary on a day-to-day basis, which is a normal state of affairs. It is extreme variations which must be controlled, as these cause a system to "hunt" or "oscillate" around its standard or normal state, corrective action being effected as a result of feed-

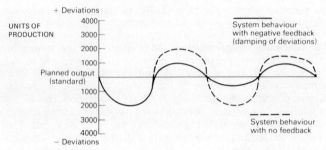

FIG. 156   *Effect of negative feedback in an oscillating system.*

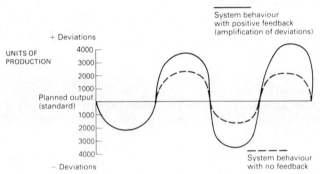

FIG. 157   *Effect of positive feedback in an oscillating system.*

back. The effect of negative and positive feedback in an oscillating system is shown in Figs. 156 and 157.

24. Buffeting. Unusual disturbances to a system's behaviour are caused by "buffeting" and this results in fluctuating system states, i.e. a tendency to "hunt" or "oscillate" and deviate from the desired course. For example, a strong cross wind on a motorway will buffet a motor vehicle, causing it to deviate sharply from the desired direction. The driver of the vehicle must apply corrective action to remedy the effect of the cross wind, usually by the application of negative feedback, i.e. steering in the opposite direction to the wind. *See also* **23** and **26**.

25. System tuning. When a car engine is out of tune it does not run smoothly and is said to be out of tune. To improve its performance it must be retuned, and the same considerations apply to business systems as they also require retuning from time to time to accord with current circumstances. This is the reason systems studies take place, to modify the operations performed in a system or the method employed.

26. Homeostasis. Systems, to be effective, must maintain a state of balance, which requires the elimination of unnecessary "hunting" or "oscillating". The term "homeostasis" may be defined as the process of holding steady or "balancing" the output of a system, i.e. the "controlled variable", despite disturbances and "buffeting". It is the process of restoring a system to its desired state when subjected to changing environmental conditions (*see* **23** and **24**).

In a stock control system, unusual variations in demand and supply may be interpreted as disturbances to normal behaviour. Safety stocks are integrated into the system to overcome this situation, but in the case of extreme variations the stock control parameters (reference input) may require modification to allow for changing trends.

With regard to a heating system, a thermostat situated in a water tank holds the temperature of the water steady—in a state of balance—because when the heater is switched on the temperature rises to the desired level and the thermostat then switches off the heater. After a while the water temperature begins to fall and when it is below the desired level the thermostat switches the heater back on. This action maintains the system in a steady state.

A further example of homeostasis is outlined in **10** in respect of the Watt governor.

27. Response time. This term is usually used in the context of computing systems and is a measure of the time elapsed from making a request for information to the time it takes for the computer to respond. A clerical information system may react too slowly to requests for information which is one of the reasons why MIS are often computer-orientated. In real time systems a computer must respond to changing circumstances as they occur in order that the system may be effectively controlled.

COMMUNICATION THEORY

Before defining specific aspects of communication and noise in the narrow sense of everyday business activities, it is important to appreciate the wider concepts involved in communication.

All systems contain the element of communication, especially closed-loop systems providing the basis of feedback. Communication may therefore be defined as the provision of information on which to base a decision to control the state of a system (*see* Fig. 153).

28. Elements of communication. The elements of communication may be described by an example from telecommunications: a wireless operator using a morse key transmits messages to a distant location where they are received by another wireless operator who records the messages.

The elements of such activities are as follows.

(*a*) *Information source.* Originator of message wishing to convey information to another person.

(*b*) *Message.* Details of situation on message pad.

(*c*) *Transmitter.* Wireless operator transmitting message by means of morse key connected to transmitting set.

(*d*) *Signal.* The signal produced by the transmitting set when the morse key is depressed.   ·

(*e*) *Receiver.* Wireless operator receiving message by means of a receiving set and earphones and writing message on a message pad.

(*f*) *Information destination.* Receipt of message by addressee. (*see* Fig. 157).

29. Elements of communication in cost control system. In order to relate the elements of communication outlined above to a business environment, a cost control system is used as an example: it is desired to communicate the incidence of scrap production to the cost control system.

(*a*) *Information source.* Inspector responsible for informing cost office of scrap production.

(*b*) *Message.* Details of scrap recorded on scrap notes (source documents).

(*c*) *Transmitter.* Distribution of scrap notes by messenger service.

(*d*) *Signal.* Delivery of scrap notes to cost office.

(*e*) *Receiver.* Cost clerk receiving scrap notes.

(*f*) *Information destination.* This may be the cost clerk receiving the scrap notes, or the cost controller after the cost clerk has processed the scrap notes.

30. The noise element in communications. Noise is a telecommunications term which indicates the presence of unwanted signals in electrical and electronic devices. In the context of data communication, noise is any disturbance to the transmission of the required signal which causes the signal being received to differ from the signal transmitted. In the business context, this implies that as the effective control of business is dependent upon accurate information, the incidence of noise is likely to distort the information being received by either the controller or the effector. Consequently the state of a system may be misinterpreted as a result of the distorted information, and incorrect action to remedy the situation may be applied.

In general terms, noise alters the content of a message received from that which is meant to be conveyed. This situation can arise simply by misinterpretation of the context of a message, the use of terms not understood by the recipient (jargon), the presence of static on the line during a telephone conversation, too much padding in a report which tends to hide the essential facts, and inadequately worded communications, etc.

31. Redundancy and the noise factor. The element of redundancy is often incorporated into communications to overcome the problem of noise. Redundancy refers to the addition of bits, characters or digits to ensure that messages are received correctly or that the correct record is being processed. Examples of redundancy are as follows.

(*a*) The spelling-out of a value in addition to presenting it in the normal way, i.e. £20 (twenty pounds).

(*b*) The inclusion of a parity bit (binary digit) in addition to the bit combination of a character in coded form. The parity bit is an additional 1 bit which is included in character codes punched into paper tape or encoded on magnetic tape for either data transmission or data transfer in computer operations. The parity bit is inserted automatically by the data preparation equipment, and is for the purpose of checking that data is being transferred or transmitted free of corruption. A 1 bit is added to ensure that the 1 bits accord either to an even number count or to an odd number count, depending on the mode in use (*see* IX, **7, 8**).

(*c*) Quite frequently in computer data processing applications, check digits are used to ensure the accuracy of stock numbers and account numbers prior to processing. A check digit is a number which is added to such numbers for the purpose of producing a "self-checking" number. A check digit has a unique mathematical relationship to the number to which it is added. The editing routine of a computer program performs check digit verification and data is rejected as invalid when the check digit derived is any number other than the correct one (*see* X, **24-8**).

32. Redundancy and management reports. Redundancy incorporated in management reports tends to overshadow the essential facts. For example, a complete listing of cost-centre budgeted and actual expenditure, although conveying all the facts, does not in fact convey a clear appreciation of the situation directly. The manager concerned is required to establish the significance of each of the items listed by going through the list item by item comparing each budgeted and actual expenditure amount to determine those which require his immediate attention.

If reporting is restricted to items with significant variations of actual expenditure from budgeted expenditure, then a greater impact is made and the recipient of the report can speedily respond to the situation disclosed. In the complete listing indicated above, the significant details were not highlighted and in fact the essential requirement, the disclosure of variances, was not included. In such a case, the control system is inefficient, as a complete listing in such a case is an obstacle to the clear understanding of the situation.

PROGRESS TEST 27

1. As the management accountant and member of a design team investigating the possibility of computerising your organisation's well-established variance accounting system, you have been asked to prepare a report to senior management explaining the following. (a) The principles of control systems theory which the proposed scheme will incorporate. (b) The advantages that specifications and operation of the proposed scheme will bring. (c) The requirements for effective involvement of line management in the operational system. (1–32) (ICMA)

2. Define the nature of a control system. (1)

3. The concept of control occupies an important place in systems theory and is a major part of the function of the management accountant. (a) List the basic elements of control and discuss how these are implemented in an effective control system. (b) Describe the safeguards which must be incorporated in systems design to ensure the continued effectiveness of a control system. (2, 8) (ICMA)

4. What is the significance of the Pareto Law to the effective control of systems? (3)

5. State your understanding of the following terms: (a) threshold of control system; (b) control interface. (4, 5)

6. "Control is often based on deviations from planned performance which is the basis of 'management by exception'—a very important management concept." Discuss this statement. (6)

7. Define the term "cybernetics" and indicate its incidence to exception reporting. (8, 9)

8. Outline the elements of the cybernetic control process. (9)

9. A company operates a stock control procedure which has the essential features of a closed-loop system, comprising: (*a*) stores, dealing with the physical receipt, holding and issue of materials; (*b*) a stock control office which: (*i*) is supplied with copies of goods received notes, requisitions and return to store notes; (*ii*) maintains stock records; (*iii*) establishes parameters for stock and re-order levels, incorporating future usage data from the production control department; (*iv*) originates purchase requisition as required; (*c*) a purchasing department.

You are required to draw an outline flow chart of the system described, showing the necessary major information flows and linkages. Identify on your chart the three points in the system which function as sensor, comparator and effector. (Fig. 154 may be used as the basis for the solution.) (ICMA)

10. Define the nature of feedback. **(10)**

11. Define and discuss the characteristics of negative and positive feedback in relation to information systems. Give an example of each. **(11, 12)** **(ICMA)**

12. Define the term "feedforward". **(13)**

13. Define the nature of "open-loop" and "closed-loop" systems. **(14–18)**

14. Using a computerised inventory control system as background: (*a*) explain what is meant by "automatic decision making"; (*b*) state the factors which should be taken into account when a systems designer is considering whether or not to incorporate this feature; (*c*) state the safeguards which should be included in the system if automatic decision making is incorporated. **(16, 17)** **(ICMA)**

15. The quality of management information is directly related to its timing. (*a*) Discuss this statement, with particular reference to: (*i*) the different purposes for which the information may be required; and (*ii*) the relative merits of speed versus accuracy in each case. (*b*) Explain in what ways the timing of information flows should be taken into account when designing information systems. **(19–22, 27)** **(ICMA)**

16. Explain the following system terms: (*a*) hunting or oscillating; (*b*) buffeting; (*c*) system tuning; (*d*) homeostasis; (*e*) response time. **(23–7)**

17. Indicate the basic elements of communication both in telecommunications and the normal business environment. **(28, 29)**

18. Define what is meant by "noise" in communications. **(30)**

19. "Redundancy is very often incorporated into business communications to overcome the problem of noise but can on occasions create noise." Discuss this statement. **(31, 32)**

CHAPTER XXVIII

Concepts of Management Information Systems

BASIC REQUIREMENTS OF MANAGEMENT INFORMATION SYSTEMS (MIS)

1. Management information system. Very often MIS is based on routine data processing systems for the purpose of generating business administrative documents such as payroll and payslips, invoices and statements of account, stock schedules, lists of debtors and creditors, etc. Such systems may be extended to produce various analyses for managerial control and for decision making, particularly on the basis of reports produced on the exception principle, i.e. exception reports which notify management of essential facts. A computerised system is ideal for an MIS in many instances as it is capable of an extremely fast response time when geared up for on-line interrogation or enquiry systems or even real-time control systems. The objectives of MIS includes the provision of information to all levels of management, at the most relevant time, at an acceptable level of accuracy and at an economical cost. An essential requirement of an MIS is the provision of feedback which is the process of communicating a system's measured outputs to the control system for the purpose of modifying the input to the system in order to attain a state of homeostasis. Information systems must be future orientated for strategic planning needs and current and past orientated for decision making and control of current situations (*see* Fig. 158).

2. Functional information systems. Most business organisations are structured on a functional basis whereby each function is controlled by a functional specialist to obtain the benefits of specialisation. When a business first comes into existence it is often a one-man concern and most of the information relating to business transactions is stored mentally by the proprietor. The proprietor may of course supplement his memory by maintaining simple records of items ordered and sold, how much he owes and how much he is owed, etc.

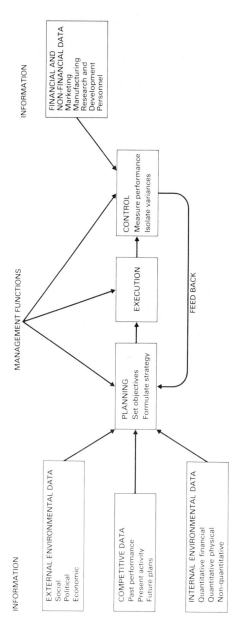

FIG. 158 *Structure of a management information system.*

When a business expands the proprietor delegates responsibility for the control of specific functions to his assistants who eventually become managers in their own right as the business grows. Delegation is necessary since it is not possible for the proprietor to effect direct control over all the functional activities as he did previously. In these circumstances each manager develops his own functional systems and information files, often in isolation from other functional systems also developed in isolation. It is this situation which causes the objectives of the various functions to conflict with each other creating sub-optimisation of the business activities as a whole. *See* **XXIX, 5**, for further considerations of developing functional systems.

3. Total information systems. A total information system is by definition a single all-embracing system, i.e. a completely integrated system, covering all business activities (*see* **XXIX, 4**). Such a system is, in most instances, more idealistic than a practical reality due to the inherent complexity of business organisations necessitating a detailed knowledge of system relationships and their interdependence.

It is also necessary to establish the information requirements of functions and the information flows between functions. Partial integration of systems is possible and desirable and the structure of business systems may consist of groupings of integrated systems each consisting of a number of related sub-systems, e.g. order processing, credit control, invoicing, sales ledger updating, stock ledger updating and stock replenishment, etc.

The objective of integrated or total systems is increased administrative efficiency which is largely achieved by eliminating the shortcomings of functional information systems. The expected benefits of integration include:

(*a*) data input once only, thereby avoiding duplication of data recording and processing;

(*b*) elimination of copying errors, which arise when copying common data onto several documents for various functional requirements;

(*c*) elimination of duplicated files, in each of the functions requiring access to common information;

(*d*) elimination of out-of-phase information files, which arise when systems are functionalised.

Integrated systems are often developed on the basis of output/input relationships whereby the output from one system provides the input to another related system.

Such systems need to be computer orientated because of the

highly complex inter-relationship of data flows that must be processed in an acceptable time-scale and stored for ease of retrieval for effective decision making.

RETRIEVAL AND PRIVACY OF INFORMATION

4. On-line interrogation facilities. Most computer-orientated management information systems have on-line facilities which allow managers to gain access to information by means of interrogation (direct access) terminals. The terminals are connected to a central processor by means of communication lines. Requests for information are activated by keying in messages on the terminal keyboard and the computer responds interactively by retrieving the information required from backing storage (information files) and printing or displaying the results on the terminal screen depending which type of terminal is used. This facility enables managers to obtain information on demand when they need it rather than when it is possible to supply it from batch processing operations.

5. Privacy and confidentiality of information. It is important to ensure that the confidentiality of information relating to individuals is respected and that such information is not used to their disadvantage in any way. Privacy is the right of individuals to data protection and is the subject of a government White Paper. This will be followed by further consultation and a parliamentary bill. The Government is being approached to consider the abuse of confidential information held in computerised databanks as a civil law offence.

The Law Commission wants the person who originally supplied information under an express or implied pledge of confidentiality to be able to sue for breach of contract if that occurs, or to seek an injunction to prevent an anticipated breach. The duty to keep information supplied confidential also applies to government departments where a promise of confidentiality was given. The Home Office is one of the largest collectors of data relating to UK citizens and is also the guardian of data protection legislation.

6. Methods of ensuring privacy and confidentiality. The need for privacy and confidentiality applies to everyday data processing situations whether relating to time sharing systems, database applications or the processing of routine applications such as payroll. Each of these factors will now be discussed.

(*a*) *Timesharing systems.* As part of the logging-in procedure on a time sharing system, each user is allocated a password. The password is requested by the computer system and it is entered via the terminal keyboard but is not printed or displayed to ensure privacy. This prevents anyone obtaining the password and accessing confidential files. The password ensures that only authorised personnel can use the system and gain access to specific programs and files.

(b) *Database*. The ICL Bulletin Viewdata system requires each information owner to explicitly list those user names allowed to access his data. The list may include other information owners who can look at (access), but not amend, his part of the database. Individual pages can also be restricted to giving them a list of user names. The system checks the name of a user when entered against the parts of the database the user wishes to access. In addition, a password is required when information is confidential or of a restricted nature. Access to some parts of the database may be restricted to specific terminals.

(c) *Package programs*. A payroll package program used on PET microcomputers requires the entry of a password before the program can be run. In addition, a number on the screen counts down with time and if it reaches zero the system will time out. This means that if the computer is left unattended for more than two minutes it will be necessary to re-enter the password. This is to protect the information stored should the user be called away from the computer. If the system times out the screen is cleared and a TIMED OUT message is printed on the PET computer.

DATA RELATING TO BUSINESS OPERATIONS

7. Data is not information. It is important to appreciate that "data" is not an alternative term to "information". Data is the term used to define facts relating to business operations which do not serve any useful purpose until they have been converted into a more meaningful form by means of data processing operations.

8. Input element. Data is the input element of a data processing system and as such is the means of generating information after it has been subjected to validation checks, sorting, calculations and comparison with other related data. Such comparisons may include actual cost data compared with standard cost data or actual expenditure compared with budgeted expenditure. From this type of comparison, variances are calculated, i.e. differences, from standards or budgets. This is the basis of exception reporting (*see* XXVII, **6**).

9. Collection of facts. In its original form data is merely a collection of facts recorded on source documents in readiness for data conversion, prior to batch processing operations. It is perhaps interesting to note that the smallest unit of data is a binary digit or "bit", which is a 0 or 1, the basis of coding characters in binary code for processing by computer, i.e. machine code.

INFORMATION RELATING TO BUSINESS OPERATIONS

10. Purpose of information. Information is essential for planning and controlling business operations both at the strategic and tactical level of management. Information is playing an ever increasing part in the day-to-day management of business as it provides the means for assessing the results of specific courses of action. It also supplies the facts with which to steer business operations along the correct glidepath by making tactical adjustments to control surfaces in order to achieve a safe landing, i.e. achieve its desired objectives. It also enables management to assess uncertainty and reduce the element of risk in decision-making.

To serve a useful purpose, information must be meaningful and understood by the recipient who must appreciate its significance and the action to be taken as a consequence of receiving it. If it does not serve a useful purpose there is a good case for not producing it and deploying the resources used to other more productive purposes. To be useful, information must inform the recipient of a situation with which he is concerned to enable corrective action to be taken, if appropriate, to modify the system to attain its desired state. Even if no action is taken this is quite in order providing the information indicates that no action is necessary as the manager is fully aware that the situation is satisfactory—he does not have to ponder if he needs to take any action, a state which the absence of information would engender.

11. Output element. Information is the output element of a data processing system which may be displayed visually on a screen by means of a VDU or printed out as a report on a computer systems printer.

12. Information from time sharing systems. By means of time sharing systems users are linked to a central computer by terminal which enables managers, accountants and corporate planners to develop information for themselves by means of modelling systems. This facility enables the user to access a computer on an on-line basis to develop business models relating to capital investments requiring a DCF approach for their evaluation, and models regarding projected profit and loss statements and balance sheets which may be subjected to "what if" facilities to establish the outcome of changing specific variables and constraints in respect of levels of activity and cost factors, etc.

13. Incomplete information. It may not be economical to produce all the information needs of management but it is essential that managers are aware of the extent and importance of any information not provided. The manager is then in a position to assess the inherent risk in making decisions without the information, and can act accordingly. Managers should be aware that it is not possible to make precise decisions on the basis of incomplete facts and this is where their managerial intuition comes to the fore.

14. Importance of information. Information is the lifeblood of business and is playing an ever increasing part in the day-to-day management of business—it is becoming a highly valuable business resource both for planning and control. Business managers are increasingly becoming confronted with complexity because of growth, and in this instance, complexity arises due to the size of the business unit and the interactions between various factors, increasing volumes of transactions and diversity of operations. Competition is also becoming much more critical in many instances, particularly from overseas manufacturers—one only needs to consider cars, motor cycles, cameras, calculators and hi-fi equipment—which requires management to develop alternative strategies based on market intelligence, i.e. information.

Technological developmens requires management to become responsive to change because it is imperative to adopt the latest technology in many cases, in order to maintain operational efficiency as a means of warding off competitive threats. There is also the need to comply with changing government policies and legislation. All of these situations require the provision of vital information so that management can react at the right time with the most suitable strategy for the prevailing circumstances.

15. Desirable properties of management information. These properties are summarised below:

(*a*) must serve a useful purpose;

(*b*) must be relevant to the responsibilities of specific managers to enable them to control operations effectively;

(*c*) must contain an appropriate level of detail for the level of management;

(*d*) must relate to current circumstances as outdated information is not only useless but dangerous as wrong decisions may be made; dynamic information systems rather than static systems are essential;

(*e*) must have an acceptable level of accuracy—not necessarily complete accuracy;

(*f*) must be available at the right time to comply with the response time needs of the system being controlled;

(*g*) must be based on the exception principle when appropriate;

(*h*) must be produced at an acceptable level of cost;

(*i*) must be easily understood;

(*j*) must avoid unnecessary redundancy.

PLANNING INFORMATION

16. Futuristic information. Information for planning purposes is futuristic, predictive or forward looking and attempts to assess the future situation on the basis of trends and forecasts derived from the use of forecasting techniques.

This type of information is produced by planning systems and is required at two basic organisational levels—the strategic level and the tactical level. Information for planning is generally obtained from the external environment but internal environmental data is also essential and it is used for responding to change at the right moment of time in order to remain profitable on the one hand and to survive on the other (*see* Fig. 158).

17. Information for responding to change. Responding to change at the right moment requires information which is obtained by adopting an analytical approach in an attempt to foresee events which will necessitate change to particular business systems. Managers need to adopt an outwards-looking, rather than a narrow, inwards-looking stance, so that they may have a panoramic view—instead of a mere foreground snapshot—of the business environment. Only by this means will they see the wood for the trees, and only in this way will business systems be tuned to changing circumstances. Indeed, only in this way will the purpose and objectives of systems be redefined.

18. External environmental information. This source of information is for the purpose of identifying threats and opportunities which may arise and to which management must respond either to maintain the business on a steady keel or to navigate new waters according to circumstances. This source of information provides information in respect of the following factors:

(*a*) main competitors' share of market;

(*b*) new market opportunities, the third world countries, for instance;

(*c*) national economic growth rate compared with internal growth rate;

(*d*) state of labour market (manpower resources);

(*e*) possible threats to continuity of supplies in respect of crop failures or political issues in respect of pay awards, etc.;

(*f*) technological developments and their likely effect on the business: microtechnology, for instance;

(*g*) trends in the rate of inflation;

(*h*) world economic climate;

(*i*) trends in demand and consumer preference;

(*j*) likely level of interest rates—the cost of funds for investment in capital projects;

(*k*) impending government legislation (*see* Fig. 158).

19. Internal environmental information. This source of information outlines the profile of the internal environment which may affect future courses of action in accordance with company policy and constraints which may limit desired courses of action, e.g. because of a low liquidity position and manpower problems. These factors would be particularly relevant in respect of capital investment projects for expansion. Information from this source provides the following factors in respect of the state of the company:

(*a*) type of product manufactured and sold or merely distributed as in the case of a wholesale food warehouse;

(*b*) type of market—home/export/wholesale/retail/consumsumable/capital;

(*c*) share of market obtained;

(*d*) state of labour relations;

(*e*) quality/cost effectiveness of products;

(*f*) profitability of company compared with other companies in same industry;

(*g*) liquidity of company;

(*h*) turnover rate of assets in relation to sales;

(*i*) sales turnover;

(*j*) discount policy;

(*k*) credit policy;

(*l*) types of process;

(*m*) main functions;

(*n*) stock policy;

(*o*) investment level in research and development;

(*p*) organisation structure—grouping of activities/centralised or decentralised operations (*see* Fig. 158).

20. Strategic planning information. Information for strategic planning is provided by top level systems (*see* XXIX, **8**), which aim at assisting management in exploiting a company's major strengths and overcoming weaknesses, while continuously searching for new opportunities either to ensure the survival of the business in the critical environment which exists, or to achieve a desired rate of growth and profitability.

Business strategy is concerned with how a company means to achieve its objectives which must include an assessment of risk and uncertainty as well as constraints on any proposed course of action as indicated above. The degree of risk involved in various courses of action must be evaluated by such techniques as risk analysis.

The determination of a suitable strategy to achieve the long range objectives of the business is dependent upon obtaining sufficiently accurate information on the company's specific strengths and inherent weaknesses in addition to general environmental information as outlined above (*see* **18** and **19**).

It should be appreciated that the longer the planning period the more information becomes a matter for conjecture and judgement—but even this is better than no assessment of the future at all. It is much better to have some idea of the direction in which the company can steer, or desires to steer, and be aware of the obstacles to be overcome in the process.

Strategic decisions often have long range consequences, especially when concerned with the development of new products, the building of new factories and warehouses or the extending of existing premises to provide additional capacity for manufacturing. It is also important to obtain market intelligence information for assessing the extent of future competition to enable products to be redesigned or methods of production to be improved so as to reduce costs and selling prices, thus warding off the effects of such competiton.

Long range planning requires long range forecasting which is a systematic information gathering activity of a continuous nature embracing the company as a whole. By this means changes in the economic, technological, financial, sociological and legislative environment in which the business operates are continuously under review. This enables a business to react dynamically in order to contend with threats which endanger the achievement of its objectives, or to take advantages of of new opportunities (*see* Fig. 158).

21. Tactical and operational planning information. Information for tactical planning is obtained by expanding the quantified strategic objectives in respect of production, sales, expenditure and stocks, etc. into detailed plans for the achievement of the strategic plan. Such plans normally take the form of budgets and production and sales programmes, based on information derived mainly from forecasts or from judgment.

The factors to consider include the planning of an effective organisation structure, product-market development planning, resource development planning, capital planning and operational planning. Such plans are concerned with the tactics to be employed to facilitate the attainment of strategic objectives and are prepared by functional managers responsible for the achievement of specified objectives in respect of sales, production, finance and purchasing, etc. The managing director is responsible for ensuring that all the detailed plans are coordinated within the framework of company policy and the overall strategic plan.

CONTROL INFORMATION

22. Programmable information. Information of a control nature is more programmable, as control systems are designed to produce information in respect of operational achievements. A great deal of information in this category is obtained from budgetary control and standard costing systems, whereby comparisons are made with budgeted or standard data and actual achievements. The differences or variances are the basis of exception reporting (*see* XXVII, **6**). These requirements may be built into computer programs as they are structured on the basis of standardised rules. Routine decision making may also be computerised in a similar manner (*see* XXX, **2**).

23. Tactical control information. Examples of this type of information may be summarised as follows (*see* Fig. 158).

(*a*) Gross profit to sales—analysed by product or product group.

(*b*) Net profit or contribution to sales—analysed by product or product group.

(*c*) Net profit to capital employed.

(*d*) The extent of deviations from budgeted sales, analysed as follows:

      (*i*) price variance;

      (*ii*) mix variance;   } volume variance

      (*iii*) quantity variance; }

(*e*) Material price and usage variances.

(*f*) Labour-rate and efficiency variances.

(*g*) Stock turnover ratios.

(*h*) Average investment in stocks compared with budget.

(*i*) Value of slow-moving and obsolete stocks.

(*j*) Departmental activity ratios.

(*k*) Departmental usage of capacity ratios.

(*l*) Departmental analysis of cost of scrapped production.

(*m*) Departmental analysis of ratio of cost of scrapped production to cost of good production.

(*n*) Departmental analysis of labour turnover.

(*o*) Cash flow statements.

(*p*) Overhead expenditure variances.

PROGRESS TEST 28

1. Indicate the characteristics of a management information system. **(1)**

2. (*a*) Briefly explain the meaning of the term "Management Information System". (*b*) Outline a general approach by which an organisation could develop a computer-based Management Information System. **(1, 4** and **XXIX, 3–10)** (*ACA*)

3. Define the nature of: (*a*) functional information systems; (*b*) total information systems. **(2, 3)**

4. A large manufacturing company is contemplating the installation of a computer based interrogation system for use by top management and some functional specialists, notably the financial and management accountants.

(*a*) Explain the general features of interrogation systems and how they would be of service to users. (*b*) What are the major hardware and system design features necessary for an interrogation system to operate effectively? **(4–6)** (ICMA)

5. The output of a management information system is, by definition, information. Define information and discuss ways in which a company might assess the value of information to be produced by a new management information system. **(10–23)** (ICMA)

6. (*a*) Explain the difference between "data" and "information". (*b*) List with brief comments, five of the desirable properties of information produced for management. **(7–15)** (Part of ACA)

7. Indicate the purpose and importance of information. **(6, 10)**.

8. A medium-sized manufacturer of domestic equipment has a well-established management information system (MIS) which is computer based. Although the computer equipment has been

updated recently and has been found to be entirely satisfactory, the design of the MIS has remained virtually unchanged for eight years.

As a systems consultant you have been requested to carry out a review of the effectiveness of the MIS with the object of recommending changes where appropriate.

How would you carry out such a review and to what matters would you direct your attention? **(1–3, 15) (ICMA)**

9. Indicate the nature of: (*a*) futuristic information; (*b*) information for responding to change; (*c*) external environmental information; (*d*) internal environment information; (*e*) strategic planning information; (*f*) tactical and operational planning information: (*g*) programmable information; (*h*) tactical control information. **(16–23)**

10. Although the overall objective in the design of management information systems is the optimisation of the system as a whole, other factors are also of considerable importance. Discuss these other factors. **(3)**

CHAPTER XXIX

Development of Management Information Systems

ESTABLISHING THE INFORMATION NEEDS OF MANAGEMENT

1. Discussion. When information systems are being developed analysts must be aware that some managers do not appreciate what their information needs are, or even what information is available. In such circumstances, it is the duty of systems analysts to discuss with each manager the specific problems encountered within his area of responsibility, the decisions which have to be made, the information provided to assist him in making decisions, any information required but not provided, the interpretation of reports and how to use them effectively.

To illustrate this point, a businessman was concerned about his company making losses so he decided to implement a computer to analyse business transactions to provide management information. The businessman was quite pleased with the information provided, even though the business continued to make losses, because he knew precisely where the losses were being made—rather a negative situation but at least the businessman was better informed than previously.

2. Informal information. Managers often receive information informally, rather than from formal documentation. If these factors are overlooked when developing a computerised MIS they will not be provided for in the system specification and consequently the system will be doomed to failure at the outset.

THE APPROACH TO THE DEVELOPMENT OF MIS

3. Management information approach. Systems are often developed for routine administrative requirements rather than for management information purposes. This situation may require a reappraisal of priorities in some circumstances to decide which should come first—routine business documents, or information for decision making and control.

The routine administrative activities of a business must of necessity be provided for as no organisation can operate without records of transactions and basic documents in the form of payslips, orders and invoices, etc. On the other hand, effective management of a business relies on efficient control of operations and making the right decisions at the right time. Information is, of course, required to accomplish these requirements.

4. Total systems approach. Some systems are developed on the basis of a "total systems" approach or philosophy. The approach recognises that all business systems are related to each other to a greater, or lesser, extent. This must be so because the business as a whole is a complete system, a corporate entity, comprising all the functional systems.

The "total systems" philosophy recognises the relationships and interdependence of systems, particularly as the flow of information throughout a business transcends arbitrary functional demarcation lines which are structured for administrative convenience. This approach enables a number of related sub-systems to be integrated to form a larger system. This offers a number of advantages, e.g. with regard to an integrated computer system, data are entered as input to a system only once and all relevant records are updated automatically. By this means data can be retrieved according to functional information needs, especially if the integrated system is supported by an integrated file structure—a database.

Fundamental changes may be required for administering integrated systems as they become inter-functional systems, rather than loosely connected functional systems. This factor must be recognised, since a greater degree of coordination and cooperation between managers is essential to ensure smooth operation, free of inter-functional conflict. It must not be overlooked, however, that the coordination of functional activities is one of the prime responsibilities of a managing director or general manager.

A computer will probably be necessary to process the data of integrated systems to facilitate their response-time needs in respect of information for effective control and the need to process large volumes of data speedily and accurately (*see* XXVII, **27**).

This implies that it may only be the larger type of business which can afford a high degree of systems integration owing to the cost of the computer configuration needed to support this data processing commitment. Looking at this point in a different way, it may also mean that it is only the larger business which needs a high degree of integration of systems for reasons of efficiency, because size often generates systems complexity due to the many inter-relationships which exist between functions and systems. Large firms tend to be structured in a very detailed functional manner with a high degree of specialisation; it is this factor which may cause problems of integration, particularly as a compromise may be necessary with regard to individual functional objectives so that the objectives of the business as a whole are optimised rather than those of individual functions (sub-systems). Once integration has been developed, however, the benefits may be enormous.

A smaller business may not require a high degree of systems integration due to less complexity in its operations but, on the other hand, the systems may be much more simply combined than is possible for the larger business.

The "total systems" approach requires a detailed analysis of all business systems in order to define the relationships between inputs, files and outputs as well as types of information and the frequency with which it is required by specific managers for control and decision making. The business must be looked upon as a complex communications network, which indeed it is, as one only has to consider the most elementary data or information interchanges which occur even in the smallest business. The very task of collecting facts and defining their relationships is formidable in itself, but the design of integrated systems, providing for all functional needs, is even more formidable.

Systems can only operate effectively if they are fully understood by managers and staff and integration can detract from this due to the greater complexity of such systems. Of course, Rome was not built in a day and this implies that systems integration should be developed on an evolutionary basis rather than a revolutionary basis.

A further important factor is the need to integrate systems in such a way that they operate smoothly and achieve the desired objectives as effectively as possible. This also implies their development on a modular basis for full integration at a later date (*see* XXVIII, 3).

5. Functional (piecemeal) systems approach. The development of systems on an unplanned, uncoordinated basis is known as the piecemeal approach. Such an approach is for the purpose of developing individual functional systems, or systems to deal with specific types of problems. Although this may achieve functional optimisation the business as a whole will perform at less than full effectiveness as there will be a clash of objectives of the various functions (*see* XXVIII, 2).

Various functional systems may require information of a

common nature which is often stored in separately structured functional files. Apart from duplication of files the danger is that files of some functions may be updated regularly, and others less regularly, causing conflict when the information from the various sources is compared either for control or for decision-making.

This approach does not consider the interdependence of systems and views each system as if it existed in a vacuum which, indeed, it does not. The overall result will achieve a whole galaxy of systems which are connected to each other in reality, but this fact is not recognised when they are being developed. It is a matter of not letting the right hand know what the left hand is doing to some extent. Such systems must be steered in a common direction by the chief executive exercising one of the elements of management, that of coordination.

6. Input to output approach. This approach considers a system from the input stage together with the processing operations and file references necessary to produce defined outputs. This may appear to be quite logical on the face of it as data must first of all be input to a system before it can be processed to produce a desired output in the form of a document or report.

The disadvantage of this approach is that output can only be produced on the basis of the data available, rather than the data that should be available, for processing. The data currently captured in the system may not relate to the true output requirements in respect of particular elements of information, whether on a basic document, such as an invoice, or a profitability report, for instance.

7. Output to input approach. From the foregoing comments it would seem more appropriate to develop systems from back to front, which on the face of it seems to be the wrong way round. It must be appreciated, however, that to obtain a defined output it is necessary to assess the "ingredients" that must be used to produce it. Only in this way will the "plum pudding" be of the correct "recipe", i.e. specification. The data to be input for processing can only be defined after establishing the specific output required.

8. Top-down approach. This approach is the development of top-level systems initially, for the purpose of supplying management with information relating to the strategic aspects of business. This is in distinction to information for the tactical control of operations. The top-level systems are then supported by operational systems at the departmental level, hence the term "top-down".

Operational systems are developed subsequently to top-level systems, which is the opposite to the normal approach of developing the lower-level systems initially and then building upwards.

9. Bottom-up approach. This approach develops systems from the operating level upwards, which is the reverse direction to that indicated above. In fact, as stated, this is the normal approach, most systems being implemented at this level because it is less difficult to define data flows and relationships. The information needs of management are then provided for by enhancing the departmental or functional systems by the addition of processing routines for analysing data as a basis for producing reports. The reports are then used by management for strategic planning, decision-making and control.

This approach puts more emphasis on the provision of detailed information in respect of activities to the operating management level so that they are in a position to make tactical decisions. Only in this way can they be provided with the means of achieving the objectives for which they are responsible.

10. The database approach. The development of database philosophy provides the means for providing all the information requirements of a business and of the various levels of management within the business. The development of a database must, of necessity, specify the information needs of all levels of management.

An essential requirement of a database is not merely to store data but also to provide an effective means of retrieval by all personnel authorised to access the database. The objective of a database is to provide reliable, up-to-date, unambiguous data on demand (*see* VIII).

CORPORATE INFORMATION ADVISER

11. Responsibilities of information adviser. Particularly in the larger type of organisation the post of corporate information adviser may well be considered a necessary requirement. He would be a specialist in respect of managing the information resources and requirements of the business in the same way that other managers control the use of resources connected with their activities.

The responsibilities of the post are envisaged as far-ranging, embracing all aspects of information ranging from that required for initial planning and policy formulation to the provision of information for the tactical control of operations embracing all functions: sales, production, purchasing, stock control, finance and accounting, research and development, personnel, etc. If a business is developing a database the information adviser may have the title of database administrator (*see* VIII, **19, 20**).

12. Coordinating element. An information adviser would act as a catalyst for generating all the information needs of the business and collecting information to produce cohesive reports, fully intelligible by their recipients. He should act in a consultative capacity and should conduct discussions with managers throughout the organisation for defining their specific information needs.

After the discussions have been concluded, meetings should be arranged with the data processing manager and organisation and methods manager to outline current and future information requirements. The outcome would be the establishment of priorities for the development of specific systems to produce particular information. Such systems may be computer-oriented or clerical-oriented or a combination of both depending upon volumes of data to be processed, response time needs for control and other relevant factors.

When systems are developed and ultimately implemented they should be monitored by the information adviser to ensure they are achieving their defined purpose and operating smoothly and efficiently.

INFORMATION AND THE LEVEL OF MANAGEMENT

13. Top management. As a general guide, the higher the level of management to whom information is provided, the more it must relate to strategic aspects for future planning and policy determination. This type of information is derived from the use of forecasting techniques and the assessment of uncertainty and risk to provide a basis for effective decision-making.

14. Functional management. Functional management need to be informed of results currently being achieved in their areas of responsibility for the purpose of applying corrective action on the one hand and to use information relating to trends for tactical planning on the other. Information for control purposes normally takes the form of exception reports, and information for planning purposes is often in the form of schedules relating to operating expenses, distribution of manpower, plant capacity and capital expenditure, etc.

15. Operating or departmental management. The operating level of management require more detailed information in respect of their area of responsibility for day-to-day control of operations and operational decisions. In this respect a department or section manager would require to know the efficiency of performance of each operator under their control or the number of units scrapped analysed by operation, cause and cost. Similarly, a credit controller would require to know each customer who had exceeded credit limit so that appropriate action can be taken to remedy the situation. In a similar manner, a stock controller requires to know the status of each item in stock so that he is aware of stock shortages, excessive stock and stock which require to be replenished.

INFORMATION RELATED TO THE TYPE OF BUSINESS

16. General information. Most businesses will require similar types of information particularly that which relates to the internal environment. Such information relates to employee details regarding type of job, salary, qualifications, positions held, etc. Most manufacturing-type organisations require information on stock status, the progress of orders through the factory, production costs and variances from budgets, etc. Sales organisations require information in respect of product profitability, performance of sales representatives, sales by area and other market intelligence.

17. Specific information. According to the type of business, specific types of information are required to assist in the effective control of the particular class of operation undertaken in order to achieve defined objectives. Specific examples are provided below.

    (*a*) Car manufacturer:
        (*i*) Extent of competition from overseas manufacturers;
        (*ii*) technological developments;
        (*iii*) current styling techniques;
        (*iv*) success of productivity deals;
        (*v*) share of market obtained compared with that required.
    (*b*) Tour operators:
        (*i*) status of hotels in various countries and resorts;
        (*ii*) medical facilities and health hazards in various countries;
        (*iii*) political unrest in specific countries detrimental to particular holiday centres;
        (*iv*) expected level of future costs of package holidays, i.e. accommodation and aircraft charter;

(*v*) availability of holiday accommodation at all times.
(*c*) Stock brokers:
    (*i*) movement of share prices (share index);
    (*ii*) state of money market;
    (*iii*) economic climate;
    (*iv*) climate in particular industries.
(*d*) Building societies:
    (*i*) clients overdue with mortgage repayments;
    (*ii*) balances on customer investment, share and mortgage accounts;
    (*iii*) likely trend in interest rates and its effect on investment building society funds;
    (*iv*) likely future level of house prices;
    (*v*) Government policy in respect of housing programmes and restrictions on mortgages.

PROGRESS TEST 29

1. Specify the factors to be considered when establishing the information needs of management. **(1–10)**

2. Outline the various approaches to the development of management information systems including: (*a*) management information approach; (*b*) total systems approach; (*c*) functional (piecemeal) systems approach; (*d*) input to output approach; (*e*) output to input approach; (*f*) top-down approach; (*g*) bottom-up approach; (*h*) database approach. **(3–10)**

3. Although the overall objective in the design of management information systems is the optimisation of the system as a whole, other factors are also of considerable importance. Discuss these other factors. **(4)**

4. Outline the nature of the responsibilities of an information adviser. **(11, 12)**

5. Discuss important aspects in respect of: (*a*) information and the level of management; (*b*) information related to the type of business. **(13–17)**

6. Typically information within an organisation can be classified into three levels.

Using a typical manufacturing company as background define the three levels and give examples of the information which would be provided at each level. In what ways does the destination level influence the presentation of the information? **(13–15 and XXVIII, 20, 21)** (*ICMA*)

CHAPTER XXX

Use of Computers in Management Information Systems

MANAGEMENT PLANNING AND DECISIONS

1. Management decisions. Certain classes of decision can be computerised or automated, and are known as routine or "structured" decisions because they are made on the basis of standardised rules. This class of decision is usually made by the operating level of management, therefore, if managers have fewer routine decisions to make they are able to spend more time on problems of an "unstructured" type which do not conform to standardised rules for their solution. The computer when used in this way is a very valuable tool of management but does not in any way change the real functions of management.

A notable example is that of stock control—for instance, where items held in stock have reached a pre-defined re-order level a list may be printed out in order that supplies may be replenished. It is also possible to design a system which would print a purchase order (from data held in backing files) thus eliminating a clerical operation at the same time. This technique eliminates the need to scan files by a human being, thereby reducing the risk of overlooking any item of stock due to be replenished. If items to be reordered were overlooked, then production delays might be encountered or supplies might have to be purchased in an emergency at increased cost.

A further example relates to the issue of works orders. It is possible to issue works orders automatically (under computer control) in a pre-determined sequence after the completion of each previous order in the queue. This system requires the installation of data recorders in the works for the purpose of transmitting data, relating to each order completed, to the central computer in order that files may be updated and new orders issued.

2. Management planning and problem solving. It is sometimes found that a misconception arises in the use of a computer, in as much as it is considered necessary to have high-volume routine processing needs as a pre-requisite for its installation. However, the more sophisticated applications must not be overlooked, especially in the area of planning and problem-solving. In this respect, the computer becomes a real tool of management if used for complex situations such as the following.

(*a*) *Capital budgeting*. This technique involves using the computer to assist management in making decisions with regard to the alternative courses of action which are possible when seeking to maximise the return from investments of a capital nature (e.g. choosing a particular machine from a range of similar machines, each having different capital and operating costs). It is necessary to make assumptions with regard to future cash flows, therefore this element of uncertainty must be provided for on a probability basis. It is also necessary to "discount" future cash flows (by means of an appropriate interest rate) to "present" values in order to allow for the difference in timing of cash flows of the possible alternative investments. Discounting is necessary, as the returns to be received in the future are not worth so much as returns currently obtained, because of the interest which could be earned on re-investment. Cash flows must take into account tax allowances and tax on profits earned (or expected) in respect of each alternative. When using the "present value" concept for investment appraisal, the choice is usually made on the basis of the investment which provides the highest "net present value". It is in performing this type of calculation that the computer is eminently suitable, because of its speed of operation. From the information printed out by the line printer, management can select the investment which seems most suitable. The information is presented much more quickly by the computer than is possible by other means because of the laborious nature of the calculations.

(*b*) *Demand forecasting*. By means of demand forecasting it is possible to assess the changing pattern of demand for goods and, by feeding appropriate data to the computer, it is possible to adjust the stock control parameters, e.g. the quantity to re-order at a predetermined re-order level to allow for the changing circumstances.

This technique enables working capital locked up in stocks to be reduced because, through the increased level of control, it is possible to reduce stock levels, especially if re-ordering is automatic.

An additional advantage is that storage space and costs may be reduced as a result of the improvement in control.

(*c*) *Budget preparation*. The preparation of budgets can be a difficult task because of the large number of variables which must be coordinated to form the master budget. The master budget is very rarely accepted by management in the first instance, consequently budget amendments are necessary for the establishment of corporate objectives. Budget amendments may require changes being made to sales quantities which generate a host of other amendments to sales costs and margins, production quantities, stocks and manpower requirements, etc. Changes to these variable factors can be processed very speedily by the computer and provide an amended master budget much more quickly than by other methods, especially those of a purely clerical nature. The computer can also process varying quantities of particular budget elements e.g. sales or production quantities and the related income, costs and profits in order to develop a series of alternative budgets for use in corporate planning.

(*d*) *Production scheduling*. The computer may be used to prepare production plans, in the form of schedules, much more speedily than by clerical methods. Also when amendments are necessary it is possible to make them very quickly by means of the computer. Amendments to one part of the production plan may have a chain effect on the remainder and it is this aspect which makes the task so laborious when using clerical methods.

It is also possible to prepare a series of alternative plans very quickly by means of the computer, thus enabling management to select the most suitable plan for implementation.

Production plans prepared by a computer are usually more reliable and as a result delivery dates are more realistic, resources are utilised more effectively, the number of planning staff is reduced and the throughput of jobs is speeded up.

The scheduling technique used depends to a great extent upon the type of production undertaken, i.e. whether one-off projects such as a bridge, a power station, a ship or a motorway are predominant, which requires the application of a network planning technique. The network plan may be printed out by the computer either in the form of a printed schedule or in graphical form. If batch or mass production techniques are used then linear programming or queuing theory may be applied.

BUSINESS MODELS AND SIMULATION

3. Business models. One approach to solving specific problems inherent in particular business systems is to construct a model of the system. Variables and constraints in business systems are represented in models symbolically in the form of algorithms or algebraic equations. By this means they may be subjected to statistical or mathematical analysis in order to observe their behaviour when subjected to changing variables. This then enables optimum solutions to particular problems to be obtained. This is actually experimenting with models as an aid to studying real life situations and is less costly and speedier than experimenting with the real life system itself. Different combinations of variables may be fitted into the model and the results obtained.

As an example, a model of a stock control system may be prepared for experimentation purposes, perhaps to optimise the investment in stocks. Variations in lead time and usage rates may be established from historical information and applied to the model, progressively changing the variables one at a time. It will then be possible to observe:

(*a*) the number of occasions when items would be out of stock;

(*b*) the number of occasions the maximum stock level may be exceeded;

(*c*) the average investment of working capital in stocks for varying stock levels;

(*d*) the effect on stock levels through changes in safety stock levels, re-order levels, order quantities, lead times and usage rates.

When a computer is used to process the data several years' operations may be obtained within a matter of hours.

One problem associated with the construction of models for complex systems is the need to ensure that variables and constraints are representative of the real life situation. Only in this way will a model react in a similar way to the real situation.

Models are often over-simplified because of the difficulties encountered in identifying all variables and their relationships.

PROFIT AND LOSS STATEMENT
FOR THE YEAR 198—
(£000s)

LINE	1ST QTR	2ND QTR	3RD QTR	4TH QTR	YEARLY TOTAL
1 SALES (S)	50	55	60	65	230
2 DIRECT MATERIAL COST (V)	% OF SALES (INPUT MATL. FACTOR)				
3 DIRECT LABOUR COSTS (D)	% OF SALES (INPUT LABOUR FACTOR)				
4 VARIABLE OVERHEAD (X)	% OF SALES (INPUT VARIABLE O/H FACTOR)				
5 TOTAL VARIABLE COST (A)	V + D + X		(LINE 2 + 3 + 4)		
6 CONTRIBUTION (G)	S – A		(LINE 1-5)		
7 FIXED OVERHEADS (F)	10	11	12	13	
8 NET PROFIT (BEFORE TAX) (P)	G – F		(LINE 6-7)		
9 CONTRIBUTION TO SALES RATIO (R)	G/S		(LINE 6/1)		

FIG. 160 *Business model: identifying the nature of a problem.*

Models are dynamic in the sense that they can be used repeatedly to predict the results of different situations when different values are assigned to variables. It is possible to construct models very accurately but assign inaccurate values to variables which prevents accurate results from being obtained in respect of a systems behaviour. Fig. 160 outlines a profit and loss model for running on a microcomputer.

4. Simulation. When experimenting with a model the behaviour of the real life system is being simulated. In some instances, however, a system cannot be specified in precise algorithms because the system behaves in a non-predictable manner, i.e. it is a stochastic or probabilistic system. In such instances, historical data or estimated values have to be collected regarding the frequency with which events occur and Monte Carlo techniques are used to simulate the random behaviour of the system.

The situation applies during the development of a computer-based communications system, as it is necessary for the system designer to simulate the behaviour of the proposed system. This is undertaken in order to assess the traffic density in respect of terminals in order to evaluate system performance as it is necessary to know the average time it takes to handle messages, the number of messages handled in various time periods, the number of messages waiting for service in a queue, etc.

The results of the simulation will assist in determining the number of telephone lines required to avoid bottlenecks on the one hand and the possibility of terminals sharing lines on the other without impairing the level of service required.

This type of simulation is facilitated by simulation models in the form of computer programs which are designed to behave in a similar manner to the real-life system. It is not always necessary to write simulation programs as packages are available for the purpose.

5. Modelling package. A modelling package is a suite of application programs designed to cover a wide range of business needs with regard to financial and corporate planning and forecasting, etc. (*See* XXI, **46–50**).

PROGRESS TEST 30

1. Much publicity has been given to the impact of computers in business, yet "it is still true that management's real functions remain unchanged". Discuss. **(1, 2)** (*ICMA*)

2. Simulation is often employed in the design of computerised

inventory control systems. Explain in detail what is meant by the above statement. What other areas of systems design employ simulation? (3, 4) (*ICMA*)

3. An increasing number of companies are using models to simulate corporate activities and a number of computer packages have been developed to provide assistance in this area. (*a*) Explain what is meant by "models" in this context; and (*b*) give details of the facilities you would expect a comprehensive modelling package to provide. (3–5) (*ICMA*)

4. A group consists of three different-sized factories, each of which produces varying quantities of a mix of five products and uses the same raw material which is in short supply. In order to optimise its own production facilities, each factory prepares a production plan, using a Linear Programming model, in order to utilise its allocation of raw material from group headquarters.

As an exercise, a young systems analyst at group headquarters entered the various production constraints of all the factories into a single LP model and found that an overall production plan emerged which differed from the earlier three individual plans and produced a higher total contribution. You are required to discuss: (*a*) the systems problems inherent in the above situation; and (*b*) ways in which the problems can be avoided in the future. (3-5) (*ICMA*)

APPENDIX

Examination Technique

Examination questions in respect of data processing and management information systems are often descriptive and aim to test the candidates' knowledge of how well-defined principles are applied to business situations or problems.

The subject is very wide and practical, candidates should always take care to demonstrate fully the wider implications of what may appear to be very narrow questions.

The examination candidate is recommended to observe the following points.

1. Read each question thoroughly before attempting an answer, in order to avoid any initial misunderstanding of the requirements of the question. A good answer to the wrong question does not score marks.

2. Allocate sufficient time to answering each question. It is fatal to omit an answer to a question through spending too much time on other questions. It is much better to have a fairly complete answer on all the questions rather than no answer at all on some of them.

3. Having determined the requirements of each question, the first one to be attempted should be selected. It is good practice before committing yourself to the answer paper to jot down main headings or topics to be covered on a scrap pad. By this means, initial thoughts may be clarified and the full scope of the question appreciated.

4. The answer may then be written on the answer paper, observing the following points.

(*a*) Write legibly to enable the examiner to interpret your answer easily.

(*b*) Show a good command of English, sentence structure and grammar.

(*c*) Outline the answer on the basis of topic or subject headings sub-analysed as appropriate as follows:

(*a*)
    (*i*)
    (*ii*)
(*b*)
(*c*)
    (*i*)
    (*ii*)
    (*iii*)

By this means the examiner can easily assess the points being made and can more readily appreciate their relevance and award marks accordingly.

(*d*) Keep to the subject and be as concise as possible without unnecessary padding—you either know the subject or you do not. Make sure you do before sitting the examination, even if only to save examination fees.

5. Allow sufficient time to read the answers before handing in the paper so that corrections can be effected.

6. Answer questions from your own experience whenever possible, as this shows the examiner that you are conversant with the subject in question.

7. Some answers require the presentation of a flowchart or other recording technique, and it is important to use drawing aids in their construction, i.e. charting symbol templates, coins (for circles), and a rule (for straight lines). Neatness of presentation is very important if maximum marks are to be gained. It is also essential to determine the type of flowchart required, e.g. procedure chart, system flowchart (runchart) or program flowchart.

Index

accounting package, 73, 380–6
accumulator, 40
accuracy,
  computers, 49
  information, 19
acoustic coupler, 107
ACT Apricot, 68, 132
adaptive systems, 432
add-on
  keyboards, 63
  units, 52
addition, 40
address
  bus, 59, 62
  generation, 148
  register, 40
  translation chip, 35, 37
administrative
  controls, 201
  efficiency 10
advantages
  computer, 49
  database, 169
  direct access storage, 197
  high-level language, 344
  low-level language, 344
  magnetic tape, 188
Algol, 12, 335
allophones—*see* speech synthesis
alpha mosaic graphics, 65
alphabetic characters, 46
alphanumeric layout, 70
ALU—*see* arithmetic logic unit
amendments, 224
amplification, 451
amplitude envelope, 64
amplitude parameter, 64
analog (analogue), 107, 119

analytical tools, 181
AND gate, 41, 44
AND/OR searching, 172
ANSI Standard Subset G, 339
Applesoft, 132
application
  packages, 378–80
  processing, 8, 229
applications, microcomputer, 56
Apricot—*see* ACT Apricot
architecture, 35
archiving, 154
areas of control, 200
arithmetic logic unit (ALU), 40
arithmetic operations, 40
article numbering, 111
ASCII, 26, 133
ASCII keyboard, 62, 65
assembler, 11, 387
assembly code, 11, 334
asynchronous transmission, 423
Atari, 133
attribute, 163
audio cassette unit, 56
audit trail, 209
auditing, 208
auto answer modem, 69
auto dial, 69
auto teller terminal, 112
automatic
  checking, 19
  decision making, 41
  operation, 49
  repeat, 63

backing storage, 60, 183–98
balance sheet, 73, 250
bank transactions, 87

banking terminals, 58
bar
  charts, 125
  code, 111
  coded labels, 112
BASIC, 11, 71, 337
  interpreter, 113
batch
  control, 207
  processing, 13, 32, 128, 221–8
BEEP command, 64
benchmark tests, 298
benefits
  computer, 279
  on-line systems, 232
bi-directional printer, 73
billionth of a second, 30
binary
  chop, 151
  code, 25, 67
  coded characters, 25
  digits—see bits
  number system, 46
bit slice microprocessor, 60
bits, 26, 46, 67
  per inch, 185
block
  coding, 302
  diagram, 294
  graphics, 133
  number, 153
  size, 148
blocking of records, 148
blocks of characters, 109, 115
Boolean algebra, 41
bootstrap loader, 374
BOS system, 71
bottom-up approach, 477
BREAK key, 63
break-even models, 56
breakpoint, 333
British Telecom, 107, 175
Brother EP22, 123
bubble memory, 48
budgetary control, 41
buffered, 108
buffeting, 454
Bulletin, 178–80

bus, 54, 62
business
  models, 483–5
  systems, 428
byte, 46, 67
bytes per inch, 186

cable games, 391
cache memory, 49
CAD—see computer aided design
calculator key, 70
calender, built-in, 113
capacity, storage, 46
capital budgeting, 482
card reader, 110
cassette
  tape, 189
  unit, 14
cathode ray tube (CRT), 108
Ceefax, 65, 175
central processing unit, 25, 38
central processing chip, 35, 37
centralised processing, 256
Centronics, 70
ceramic cover, 57
chaining, 147
channels, 59
character
  images, 127
  set, 65, 125
  CMC 7, 99
  magnetic ink, 98
  optical, 100
  repertoire, 67
characteristics, D.P. system, 6
characteristics of systems, 427
characters, 46
check digit, 138, 212
  verification 212–14
checkout scanning, 111
checks and controls, 200–18
chief
  programmer, 80
  systems analyst, 79
chip slice microprocessor, 60
circuit board, 16, 35, 52
CIS COBOL, 338

classification
  computers, 12
  systems, 430
clerical work, 10
clock, 64
closed-loop system, 448
closed shop programming, 346
closed subroutine, 346
closed systems, 429
CMC 7, 99
COBOL, 31, 71, 337
codasyl committee, 171
code, magnetic tape, 184
coding systems, 299
collecting facts, 283
colour display, 67
colour number key, 68
COM—*see* computer output on microfilm
  recorder 129
  formatted magnetic tape, 129
commands, 67
commodore, 64
common carrier, 175
communication, elements of, 456
communications
  server, 408
  software, 231
  subsystem, 37
comparative, 444
comparative balance sheet, 250
comparing, 40
compatibility, 38
compile time errors, 345
compiler, 12, 388
complement, 40, 213
composing music, 64
Compsoft, 171
computations, 5
computer
  accuracy, 49
  advantages, 49
  aided design (CAD), 130, 135
  benefits, 16
  bureaux, 19, 265–70
  definition, 25
  development, 29
  disadvantages, 49

flexibility, 49
games, 52, 133
graphics, 129–35
input, 86–119
instructions, 331
language, 11
literacy, 10
logic, 41
operation, 12
output, 121–36
  CAD, 135
  COM, 128
  graphical, 128, 129–35
  magnetic, 127
  on microfilm (COM), 128
  printed, 121–7
  punched, 127
  visual display, 128
purpose, 9
reliability, 49
social aspects, 22
speak, 11
system elements, 8
Computer Users' Year Book, The, 22
computing
  concepts, 11
  services 271
concurrent CP/M, 71
conditional transfer (branch), 41
confidentiality, 118, 206, 463
configuration, 31, 32, 34, 38
conflict of system goals, 437, 438
connector pins, 53, 57
consultancy, 271
CONT command, 63
control
  bus, 62
  information, 470
  interface, 442
  of processes, 58
  subsystem, 127
  system
    definition, 441
    elements, 441
    theory, 441–58
    threshold, 442
  unit, 26, 39

converging technology, 379
conversational mode, 12
conversing with a computer, 12
Coral, 339
core
  planes, 46
  storage, 46
corporate
  database, 116
  information adviser, 477
  objectives, 434
Corvus Omninet, 406
cost effectiveness, 17
counter, 332
coupling, 429
CPU—*see* central processing unit
CP/M, 32, 58, 373
CP/M, adaptor, 58
CP/M 80, 73
CP/M 86, 71, 73
criteria, economic viability of a
    computer, 17
critical path, 217
CRT—*see* cathode ray tube
CTRL key, 68
cursor, 68
cursor control, 63, 70, 133
customer
  file, 155
  sales history file, 155
cut-sheet, 125
cybernetics, 443–7
cycle of operations, 40
cylinder, 152
cylinder index, 147, 153
cylindrical magnets—*see* bubble
    memory

damping, 451
data, 67, 464
  capture, 88, 113, 115
    terminal, 113, 116
  collection, 88, 110–16
  elements, 169
  entry terminal, 115
  independence, 174
  description language (DDL),
    171
  management systems, 170–3

manipulation, 181
  language (DML), 171
module, 192
processing, 1, 6, 82
  manager, 77
  standards, 217, 218
transfer channels, 39
transmission, 106, 416–23
validation, 210
database, 13, 31, 165, 168, 170,
    173, 174, 177, 180
  administrator, 174
  approach, 477
  software, 170, 179
data-driven design, 342
Datakey, 202, 214
DataStream International Ltd, 180
Datel, 419–21
DCF—*see* discounted cash flow
decimal number system, 46
decision tables, 358–67
decisions, 26, 481
decoder, 39
decoupling, 429
dedicated machines, 56
definition
  computer, 25
  microcomputer, 52
delay factor, 451
demand printer, 129
designing a form, 291
desirable properties of informa-
    tion, 466
detachable keyboard, 70, 74
deterministic system, 430
development of computer
    technology, 29
device controller, 14
dial-in, 180
dialogue, 12, 233
digital
  calendar, 69
  input, 125
  PABX, 107, 398, 403
  signals, 107, 119, 131
Digital Research Personal BASIC,
    71
digitiser, 119
digitising tablet, 131

diodes, 30, 57
direct input, 87
directory, 154
disadvantages
  computer, 49
  magnetic tape, 188
  direct access storage, 197
  high-level language, 344
  low-level language, 344
disc drives, 14
disc operating system (DOS), 154, 373
discounted cash flow, 56
discrete, 119, 153
disintegration—*see* decoupling
diskettes, 193
display, 14
display address, 133
display code, 65, 133
display screen, 67
distributed, 13, 35, 112
  electronic printer, 124
  office systems, 260–4
  processing 258–60
division, 40
document
  analysis form, 286–9
  handling, 21
  processing, 118
documentation, 209
domains—*see* bubble memory
DOS—*see* disc operating system
double height characters, 65
double-sided, double density discs, 193
DRAW command, 130
DRS 20 workstations, 260
dual 8/16 bit processor, 73
dump/restart, 345
dumping, 206
duplex transmission 423
dynamic
  labelling, 70
  RAM, 47

EAN, 111
EBCDIC, 26
EBM—*see* end of block marker

EDS—*see* exchangeable disc storage
effector, 444
EFM—*see* end of field marker
electrical flows, 25
electricity bill computations, 5
electronic
  card index, 386
  desk-top displays, 131, 409–15
  filing, 116, 161
  key click, 70
  ledger card accounting machine, 20
  mail, 31, 71, 116, 400
  mailbox, 177
  printer, 123
  printing system, 125
  retrieval, 161, 162
  work study, 113
elements
  of a computer system, 8
  of a data processing system, 6
emulation, 32, 35
encapsulated, 57
end
  of block marker, 150
  of field marker, 150
  of record marker, 150
envelope command, 64
environmental controls, 202
EPROM, 48
ergonomically designed, 70
error signal, 444
ESCAPE key, 63
European Article Number (EAN)—*see* EAN
exception principle, 40, 442
exception reporting, 41
exchangeable disc storage (EDS), 189
execution cycle, 40
execution time errors, 345
expansion slots, 70
EXPLODE command, 64
ERM—*see* end of record marker
external
  environment, 467
  storage, 183
eyestrain, 118

E13B, 99

faceted code, 300
facilities management, 271
factory terminals, 92, 110
family, computer, 38
father tape, 204
feasibility study, 273, 277–80
feedback, 444, 446, 447
feedforward, 447
ferromagnetic, 46
FET—*see* field effect transistor
    technology
fiche reader, 129
file
    access, 151
    activity, 142
    amendments, 142
    analysis form, 289
    conversion, 139
    copying, 206
    creation, 139
    management system, 161
    organisation, 146–51
    record specification, 297
    security, 140, 204
    server, 132, 409
    structure, 171
    updating, 140
filestore, 118
financial
    information system, 180
    modelling, 56
    reports, 250
    terminals, 35
first generation computers, 29
fixed
    assets, 381
    data, 92
    discs, 193
    length records, 150
flashing character, 65
flexibility of computers, 49
floppy discs—*see* diskettes
flowchart, 349
    symbols, 304, 305, 349, 350
flowcharting, 304, 349, 350–6
flowcharts, 308, 310, 311, 313–15
    319–21, 323–6, 361, 363–7

font
    cartridge, 125
    memory, 127
form design, 291
formatting, 154
formatted page, 127
Forth, 12, 339
Fortran, 11, 71, 339
four-byte words, 37
fourth generation computers, 31,
    68
frame, 94
free text
    documents, 161
    searching, 172
frequency division multiplexing,
    422
front-end processor, 418
function keys, 63, 70
functional
    decomposition, 342
    information systems, 460
futuristic information, 467

gateway, 177
general
    accounting package, 73
    files, 118
    ledger, 246
    purpose terminal—*see* VDU
    systems theory, 425–7
generation technique, 204
gigabytes, 193
grandfather tape, 204
graph plotter, 128
graphic
    characters, 68
    keys, 63
graphical designs, 135
graphics—*see* computer graphics
    tablet, 131

half-duplex transmission, 423
handpoint data entry terminal,
    115
hard
    copy, 122, 128
    discs, 189–93
    sectoring—*see* formatting

hardware controls, 203
HELP, 70, 118
high level language, 12, 335
high resolution graphics, 70, 132
highlighting, 68
hit rate, 142
hobbyist machines, 56
hologram, 48
holographic memory, 48
homeostasis, 455
host
   computer, 32, 127
   processor, 129
hunting, 453
Husky computer, 112

IBM PC—*see* IBM Personal
      Computer
IBM Personal Computer, 59, 72
IBM 360 series, 59
ICL PERQ, 132
icons (ikons), 69, 131, 409, 412
identification number—*see* record
      key
IDMS—*see* integrated data
      management system
IF-THEN ELSE, 341
image, 108, 129–32
   generator, 127
   processing, 116
imaging subsystem, 127
impact printer, 121
implementing a computer,
      273–302
inaccurate control data, 19
incomplete information, 466
incorrect decisions, 19
indexed sequential, 147
indirect input, 87
industrial terminals, 35
information, 9, 10, 465
   and the level of management,
      478
   database, 177
   management processor (IMP),
      116
   providers, 175
   related to the type of business,
      479

initial cost, 50
input, 86–119, 464
   controls 203
   specification, 296
   subsystem, 125
   to output approach, 476
input/output, 14, 35, 37, 47, 428
instant responses, 10
instruction counter, 39
   cycle, 40
   register, 39
   storage unit, 35
Insurance broker software, 385
integral line display, 115
integrated
   circuits, 30, 57
   components 30
   data management system
      (IDMS), 171
   data processing, 39
   discs, 14
   file structure, 168
   handset, 117
   keyboard, 62
   nominal ledger, 307, 308
integration, 70, 429,—*see also*
      coupling
Intel 8080, 59
Intel 8086, 69
Intel 8087, 69
Intel 8089, 69
intelligent terminals—*see* terminals
interactive processing, 12, 245–55
interface, 16, 35, 54, 62, 124
internal
   check, 202
   environment, 468
   memory, 20, 25, 60
   storage—*see* internal memory
internally stored program, 26
interpreter, 389
interviewing, 283
inventory control, 380
inverted files, 162
inverter, 43
invoice computations 5, 146

JCL—*see* job control language

job
  control language, 12, 375, 376
  interest, 20
  titles, 221
joy sticks, 16
jump, 332

K, 46
key, 118
  field, 138, 162
keyboard, 14, 16, 20, 54, 62, 64, 70
  encoding, magnetic tape, 95
  printer terminal, 107
key-to cassette, 98
key-to-disc, 95
key-to-diskette, 96
kilobytes per second, 193
Kimball tags, 93

language, computer, 11
laser
  beam, 127, 195
  light, 48
  printer, 122
latent image, 129
LCD—see liquid crystal display
LED—see light emitting diode
ledger cards, 20, 22
leisure time, 23
Level 11 COBOL, 338
light emitting diodes (LED), 67
light pen, 16, 130, 135
limited-function microprocessor,
  60
line printer, 121
link editing, 347
liquid crystal display (LCD), 67,
  71, 113
Lisa, 414
Lisp, 339
list processing, 118
loading program, 52
local area network (LAN), 70,
  399, 406–9
log in/out, 241
logic
  circuit, 41
  gate, 41
  operations, 40

logical
  files, 173
  functions, 40
  records, 146
Logo, 134, 339
loop, 332
Lotus 1-2-3, 73
loudspeakers, 64
low-level language, 333, 334

machine
  code, 12, 333
  sensible, 111
magnetic
  drum, 29
  ink characters, 98
  tape, 184–9
  tape, COM formatted, 129
magnetically encoded, 127
mailbox, 132
main memory, 49
mainframe computer, 9, 10, 13,
  21
management
  information, 49
    system, 460
    system development, 473–7
  services manager, 82
masking, 162
master file, 138–61
  activity, 142
  amendments, 142, 224
  conversion, 139
  customer, 155
  definition, 138
  off-line storage, 227
  orders, 158
  organisation, 146
  payroll, 154
  plant register, 158
  problems, 159
  product, 155
  relationship, 148
  sales history, 155
  security, 140
  stock, 158
  structured, 154
  updating, 140

matrix printer, 121
ME29, 171
mechanistic systems, 430
megabyte, 37, 48
megabytes per second, 186, 193
megahertz—see MHz
memory
  array chip, 35
  capacity, 14, 59
  chip, 16
  interface, 35
menu, 70, 118, 171, 247, 248
menu-driven package, 381
merging, 40
metal-oxide semiconductor (MOS)
    technology, 47
metal-oxide semiconductor field
    effect transistor technology
    (MOSFET), 47
meter readings, 87
methods, collecting data, 88
MHz (megahertz), 59
microcassette, 20
microcomputer
  applications, 56
  backing storage, 60
microcomputers, 9, 10, 13, 14, 19
    21, 52–75
microdrive, 60, 195
microfiche, 128
microfilm, 128
microfilm/fiche viewer, 129
micro-floppy disc drive, 60
micromail, 400
microminiaturisation, 30
micromodeller, 393
microns, 48
microprocessor, 37, 57
  applications, 58
micro-programmable, 35
microprograms, 47
microscreen, 69, 70
microsecond, 30
Microsoft BASIC, 71
microtechnology, 31
millisecond, 29
minicomputer, 10, 13, 14, 19
mnemonic code, 11

modelling package, 73, 391, 393,
    485
modem, 418
modular programming, 340
modulated light, 127
modulus, 213
monitor, 54, 67, 70
monitoring, 14, 58, 298
monochrome display, 67
monolithic programming, 340
MOS—see metal oxide semicon-
    ductor (MOS) technology
MOS technology 6502, 58
MOSFET—see metal oxide
    semiconductor field effect
    transistor technology
motivational influences, 437
Motorola 68000, 71
mouse, 16, 69, 131, 412
mousetrap, 70
MS-DOS, 73
multi-font, 125
multi-function keyboard, 70
multi-functional workstation—see
    information management
    processor
multi-platter disc, 192
multi-processors, 263
multi-task, 71
multi-user, 71
multiple split-platen, 21
multiplexor, 14, 416, 418
multiplication, 40
multiprogramming, 30, 35, 237
MVS/SP operating syatem, 374

NAND (Not AND), 43
nanosecond, 30
NCR 9300, 35
NCR Decision Mate V, 73
NCR Tower 1632, 71
negative
  feedback, 446
  polarity, 46
network structure, 406
networks, 56
NMOS silicide process, 35
noise, 456

nominal ledger, 307, 308, 380
non-moving keys, 62
non-volatile, 47
NOR, 43
NOT, 43, 44
number crunching, 14, 110
numeric
  characters, 46
  key pads, 63

objectives, 43
OCR, 101, 103
OCR-A, 101
OCR-B, 101
octaves, 64
off-line storage, 227
off-lining, 239
office
  automation, 116
  information systems, 31
  productivity, 116
  technology 397–400
OMR, 103
on-line, 10, 26, 32, 229–36
  interrogation facilities, 463
  order-entry system, 10
open
  subroutine, 346
  systems, 428
open-loop system, 447
open shop programming 346
operands, 40
operating systems, 12, 71, 72,
    236, 237, 373–8
operation, computer, 12, 25
operational
  controls—see procedure controls
  planning information—see tac-
    tical information
operations
  manager, 80
  research, 82
optical
  characters, 100
  disc, 195
  marks 102
  memory—see holographic
    memory

OR (inclusive OR), 43, 44
Oracle, 65, 175
Order processing, 321–9, 381
orders file, 158
organic systems—see mechanistic
    systems
organisation and methods, 82
organisation
  D.P. department, 77
  management services depart-
    ment, 82
organisational controls, 200
ORIC-1, 132
oscillating—see hunting
output, 121–36
  analysis chart, 289
  to input approach, 476
  specification, 296
  subsystem, 127
overflow, 147
  address, 147
overlay technique, 147

package—see package programs
  compatibility, 379
  programs, 20
packet switching, 421
paddles, 16
page printing, 122
pages, 148
paper tape, 94, 127
  code, 94
parallel
  interface, 125
  operation, 18
  transmission, 422
parameter, 129, 172
Pareto law, 441
parity bit, 185, 187
partitioned file, 148
Pascal 12, 71, 338
password 118, 202
payroll
  application, 8, 224–7, 268, 381
  file, 154
PEEK command, 65
peripheral bus, 62

personal
  files, 118
  microcomputers, 54
  number, 112
personality module, 60, 194
personnel records, 118
phosphor dots, 134
photo-diode, 130
  array, 48
photo engraving, 58
photolithographic, 57
photoreceptor, 127
photo-sensitive plate, 48
physical
  files, 174
  needs, 118
  records, 146
  variables, 119
picture elements—*see* pixel
  graphics
piecemeal systems approach—*see*
  functional systems approach
PING command, 64
pixel, 132, 133
  graphics, 132
planning
  information, 467–70
  systems, 430
plant register, 158
plastic
  badge (card), 110
  card—*see* plastic badge
player missile graphics, 133
PLOT command, 130
plotter, 16
plotting vectors, 132
PL/1, 339
point-of-sale terminals, 58
POKE command, 65
polling, 423
portability, 70, 335
portable
  computer, 57, 112–4
  data capture, 112
  printing terminal, 123
positive
  feedback, 447
  polarity, 46

power failure, 47
power, processors, 39
pre-punched card, 91
pressure sensitive, 115
PRESTEL, 175
print
  hammers, 121
  server, 409
  wires, 121
printed
  circuit, 30
    board, 35, 57
  output, 121–7
printer, 14, 122
printer/plotter, 123
privacy, 118, 463
private database—*see* Travicom
  and Bulletin
probabilistic systems, 431
problem solving, 481
procedural controls, 203–15
procedure
  chart, 283, 295
    symbols, 284
  narrative, 295
process control, 14
processing
  costs, 20
  operations, 4
  routine, 306
processor
  elements, 8
  memory bus, 35, 37
  subsystem, 35
product
  article number, 111
  file, 155
production
  control system, 317–21
  scheduling, 483
productivity, 23
profit and loss accounts, 73
program
  documentation, 330
  dump, 344
  flowchart (procedure flowchart),
    295
  portability, 39

program—*continued*
    specification, 330
programmable read only memory
    (PROM)—*see* PROM
programming, 12, 330–47
    standards, 331
PROM, 47
    programming, 48
pseudo real-time system, 10
psychological needs, 118
public database—*see* PRESTEL
pulse generator, 54, 59, 64
punched card, 91, 127
purchase
    accounting, 269, 309–17
    ledger, 380
purpose of computers, 9

Q-sign option, 115
questionnaire, 283
QWERTY keyboard, 62

RAM, 16, 47
    chips, 47
random access memory—*see*
    RAM
random
    enquiries, 106
    file organisation, 148
range searching, 172
Rank Xerox 2700 printer, 124
RAPID, 171
read-only memory—*see* ROM
real-time, 10, 34, 39, 106, 234–6
record
    key, 138, 147
    type, 170
recording techniques, 283–90
recruitment, 275
reduction ratio, 129
redundancy, 48, 457
reference
    file, 146
    input, 144
    key—*see* record key
refreshing, 47
relational
    database, 71
    structure, 170

reliability, computers, 49
remote batch, 73, 231
    terminals, 112
remote job entry—*see* remote
    batch
remote locations, 112
REPEAT-UNTIL statement, 341
requisite variety, 443
RESET command, 133
resolution, 132
response pages, 177
retail
    shoe shops, 91
    terminal, 31, 35
reverse video, 68
robot—*see* turtle
robotics, 23
roll film, 129
ROM, 16, 47
Root search, 162
RS 232, 70

sales
    accounting, 270
    appliances, 8
    invoices, 269, 380
    ledger, 380
scanning, 111
schema, 174
screen
    display, 21, 108
    planes, 133
search parameters, 172
second generation computers, 29
security, 112
seek area, 153
selecting, 40
selection, computer, 21
self-checking number, 138
self-organising systems—*see* adap-
    tive systems
semiconductor, 35
    memory, 46
sensor, 444
sequential
    access, 151
    file, 148
    list structure, 170

serial
  access, 151
  code, 151
  organisation, 147
  port, 62
  transmission, 422
SET command, 133
sets, 170
shape
  definition, 133
  table, 133
shared resources, 56, 117
shift, 40
  keys, 56
SHOOT command, 64
silicon
  chip, 12, 16, 47, 57
  crystal, 57
  disc, 54
  technology, 30
  wafer, 57
simplex transmission, 423
simulated movement, 133
simulation, 56, 485
single-address computer, 39
single dot resolution, 132
single key keyword keyboards, 63
single-sided, double density discs, 166
sixteen-bit processor, 14, 35, 59, 68
social aspects of computers, 22
social unrest, 24
sociological controls, 176
Softbox, 58
Softcard, 58
soft discs—see diskettes
soft sectoring—see formatting
software, 12, 61, 369–96
  portability, 71
  suite, 71
solid state, 30
son tape, 204
SORD M5 computer, 133
sorting, 40
sound
  effects, 64
  generation, 63

synthesising circuits, 64
special characters, 46
speech
  pattern, 118
  synthesis, 118
  synthesisers, 119
speed of processing, 18, 49
split screen, 108
speadsheets, 56, 391
Sprite, 133
Sprite graphics, 133
stand-alone machines, 56
stand-by facilities, 50
standards, 217, 218
Star system, 415
static RAM, 47
steering committee, 275
stock
  control
    application, 8, 41
    computations, 5
  file, 158
storage capacity, 39
Storage of unstructured
  documents—see unstructured
  documents
store cycle time, 39
strategic planning information, 469
structural data relationships, 169, 170
structure, microcomputer, 52
structured master files—see master files
structured programming, 340
stylus, 131
sub-optimality, 438
sub-schema, 174
sub-set, 171
sub-system objectives, 435–7
subroutine library, 347
subtraction, 40
supermarket check out, 86
Supersoft HR-40, 132
switching device, 39
Symbnet, 409
synchronisation pulses, 131
synchronous transmission, 423

synonyms, 162
syntax, 12
  errors, 67
system
  controller, 127
  definition, 427
  development controls, 215
  interface chip, 35, 37
  maintenance, 298
  messages, 67
  monitoring, 14
  network architecture (SNA), 35
  objectives, 435
  resources, 428
  specification, 292
  tuning, 454
System X, 421
systems
  analysis, 280–90
  analysis team, 281
  design, 290–302
  flowchart, 295
  implementation, 298

tactical information, 469
tactile keyboard, 113
tax software, 382–5
technological
  change, 23
  controls, 202
  obsolescence, 50
Telecom—see British Telecom
telecommunications, 35
telegraph line, 107
TEL-time data collection terminal, 113
telephone bill computations, 5
telesoftware, 389
Teletex, 422
Teletex character set, 125
Teletext, 65
teletype—see terminals
telex—see terminals
telex network—see terminals
terminals
  portable printing, 123
  purpose of, 106, 239
  teletype, 107, 121

VDU, 107, 128
  intelligent, 109
  teleprinter/telex, 107
Texas Instruments, 133
text
  and voice handling, 116
  editing, 70
  filing, 161
  processing, 71
third generation computers, 30
thirty-two bit processor, 14, 35, 54, 58
time division multiplexing, 423
timeliness of information, 453
T199/04A, 133
top management support, 273
top-down approach, 341, 476
total information systems, 462
total systems approach, 474
track, index, 147
tracks, 94
transaction file, 145
transfer of data, 39
transistors, 30, 57
transmission of data, 106
transparent, 32
transposed digits, 138
Travicom, 177
tree structure, 170
trial balance, 250
truth table, 41
turnaround documents, 104
turnkey services, 271
Turtle, 134
  graphics, 134
types of backing storage, 183

UCSD p System operating system, 71, 373
ultraviolet light, 48
unconditional branch, 332
undetected errors, 19
units of storage, 46
unity of direction, 434
UNIX operating system, 71
unpackaged semiconductor, 57
unstructured documents, 161
updating, 26, 92

uppercase, 65
upwards compatible, 31
use of computers in management,
    481–5
user
    definable keys, 63
    defined
        forms, 118
        graphics, 234
utility programs, 376

variable, 12
    character sizes, 123
    data, 110
    length records, 150
    pitch, 64
variance reports, 41
VAT returns, 73
VDU—*see* terminals
vector graphics, 130
very large scale integration
    (VLSI), 35, 37, 57
video
    screen, 14
    unit, 107
Viewdata, 175, 399
virtual
    machine, 32
    memory, 37
    storage, 148
visible record computer, 22
VisiOn, 414
visual display unit (VDU)—*see*
    terminals
visual video RAM, 68
VM/SP operating system, 375
vocabulary—*see* speech synthesis
voice
    communications, 107
    grade telephone lines, 107, 416,
        handling, 116

messages, 116
volatile, 47
volume (storage), 153
volume of data, 18, 21
VRC—*see* visible record computer

wages computations, 5
wand, 112
wastebin, 118
weights, 213
WHILE-WEND statement, 341
white noise, 64
Winchester discs, 56, 192
windows, 68, 70, 108
winking cursor, 108
word processing, 31, 116, 401–3
words 46
work
    measurement terminal, 113
    study—*see* electronic work
        study
workstations, 10, 14, 32, 39,
    116–18
working
    registers, 40
    storage, 47

X chart, 286
X-OR (exclusive OR), 43
xerographic subsystem, 127
Xerox
    2700 printer, 124
    8000 Ethernet, 408
    9700 printing system, 125

Z-80A, 73
ZAP command, 64
Zilog Z 80, 58
Zilog Z800, 59
zone bits, 185